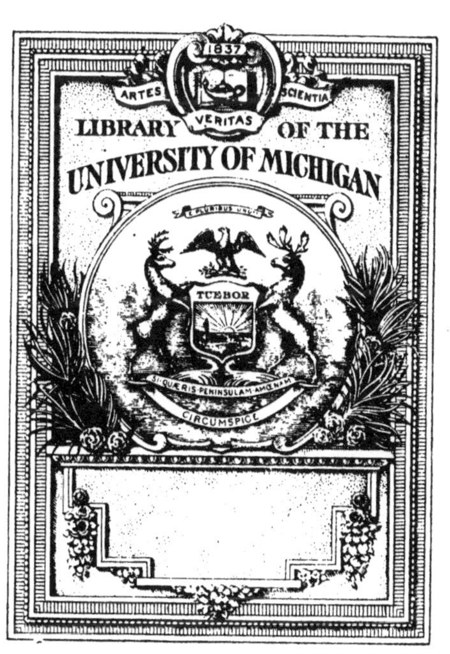
1837
ARTES
SCIENTIA
VERITAS
LIBRARY OF THE
UNIVERSITY OF MICHIGAN
TUEBOR
SI QUAERIS PENINSULAM AMOENAM
CIRCUMSPICE

I0754276

STANDARD SPECIFICATIONS
FOR
PERSONAL SERVICE

PREPARED BY THE

Bureau of Personal Service

FOR THE

Board of Estimate and Apportionment of the City of New York

April, 1917

TABLE OF CONTENTS

This revised edition of the standard specifications now in use covering duties, titles, compensation and qualifications of employes, published by the Committee on Salaries and Grades, embodies such changes as have been indicated by two years of current application, including the preparation and adjustment of personal service schedules for the annual tax budgets for 1915, 1916 and 1917.

WILLIAM A. PRENDERGAST, Chairman,
Comptroller.

JOHN PURROY MITCHEL,
Mayor.

LEWIS POUNDS,
President, Borough of Brooklyn.

INTRODUCTORY STATEMENT

The standard specifications for personal service aim to furnish a simple and logical classification of all employments in the city government, with general descriptions of duties, appropriate titles and rates of compensation, and conditions governing initial appointment, advancement and promotion as a basis for appropriation and current fiscal and civil service control and for information to present and prospective employes and the public.

1. BASIS OF CLASSIFICATION—

The general classification is in the form of grand divisions called Services, divisions of Services called Groups and Grades within Groups. The following are the definitions of these terms:

Service—

The term " Service " is used to designate the broadest convenient division of related offices and employments determined irrespective of the legal class to which they belong, such as Professional Service, Inspectional Service, Clerical Service.

All employments have been divided into the following services:

Executive
Legislative
Judicial
Professional
Sub-Professional
Investigational
Educational
Clerical
Inspectional
Custodial
Institutional
Police
Fire
Street Cleaning
Skilled Trades
Unskilled

Group—

The term " Group " is used to designate a subdivision of a service established for the purpose of distinguishing the work or duties generally performed in the same profession, vocation, trade or calling, such as:

Physician Group
Bookkeeper Group
Prison Keeper Group

Grade—

The term "Grade" is used to designate a subdivision of a group distinguishing the specific quality of work or duties to be performed by individual officers or employes and an appropriate range of salary, the distinctions between grades being based upon clearly discernible differences in the importance, difficulty, responsibility and value of the work.

Discussion and Explanation of Services—

The services which have been adopted do not represent the only possible divisions of employments, but they seem to be those which are best suited to the needs of New York City. It will be seen that although the theory of standardization is that the divisions are along functional rather than departmental lines, it was not possible to maintain this distinction in all cases.

The Executive Service includes only the functions of the executive heads of departments, in all cases elective or appointive officers. It is, however, recommended that the secretaries of departments who are at present exempt officers should in future be classified as competitive in order to provide for a high permanent officer in each department, who will not be affected by change of administration.

The Legislative Service includes the functions of the board of aldermen, and the Judicial Service those of the judges and magistrates. Up to the present time no recommendation as to salary has been made for these services. They are included more for the purpose of providing a complete classification of all employments than with any immediate prospect of adjusting the present salaries. These services may be completed at any time in the future.

The Professional Service includes only the recognized professional employments requiring such high qualifications of professional training and experience as clearly differentiate them from employments in the sub-professional service. The Sub-Professional Service includes positions as assistants to members of the professions, such as draftsmen, laboratory assistants, law clerks, etc., who should have an opportunity to graduate into the professional ranks, but should not be classified or paid on a professional basis.

The Investigational Service includes the higher type of examining and investigational work in central staff agencies and in public charitable and social work.

The Educational Service as presented includes only positions as industrial instructors, recreation instructors and other miscellaneous instructors. The main body of teachers is at present under the control of the Board of Education and their salaries are fixed by law. At some time in the future it may be thought advisable to bring the salaries of these teachers under the control of the Board of Estimate and Apportionment.

The reasons for creating the Clerical Service are obvious. The word "clerical" is a very comprehensive term and under it are included all kinds of office work not requiring particular training and skill of the kinds set forth in the other services.

The INSPECTIONAL SERVICE includes health, trade, building, public works, safety and other inspections involving observation and inquiry of a more routine and stereotyped nature than that included in the investigational service.

The CUSTODIAL SERVICE includes work or the supervision of work closely related to laboring work, but of a character involving the custody of public property, such as the work of caretakers, janitors, watchmen, storekeepers, bridgetenders, animal keepers, etc., and of their supervisors.

The INSTITUTIONAL SERVICE is another service which is not entirely functional and does not include all employes in the city performing a certain kind of work. It includes in general all positions in institutions other than those involving professional work, from helpers and artisans up to and including lay administrators. A helper in an institution who receives maintenance may be doing work very similar to that of a laborer or skilled laborer in other departments, but the conditions of employment and salary are so different from those of employes in other departments as to constitute for purposes of classification a separate and distinct kind of employment.

The POLICE, FIRE and STREET CLEANING SERVICES consist of the largest specialized uniformed forces of the city. It is true that the duties of the rank and file of the street cleaning department are very similar to those of laborers and that the duties of the police are similar to those of inspectors, investigators and watchmen, but these forces have peculiar identities and duties of their own, and no purpose could be served by classifying them otherwise than separately. The police and fire services are not included in this volume. The police service has been printed in tentative form. The fire service is not yet ready for initial printing. Both of these services involve legislative action. They will be presented to the Board of Estimate and Apportionment in the near future.

The SKILLED TRADES SERVICE includes the recognized skilled trades, mostly unionized trades, and, in addition, helpers in the skilled trades, the supervisors of skilled workers and a few classes of technical employes, such as fire telegraph dispatchers and employes on city boats, who have been placed in this service because the work is more closely related to the skilled trades than to any other class of employment in the city service. There is a great advantage in keeping the skilled trades, particularly the unionized trades, together, since the problem of determining prevailing rates for these employes should be dealt with as a whole.

The UNSKILLED SERVICE includes positions as laborers, park workers, drivers, hostlers, stablemen, cleaners and supervisors of laborers, in general, employments requiring physical strength or the ability to supervise physical workers.

Provision was originally made for a managerial service to include administrative offices other than those of the highest executives, such as superintendents of bureaus of public buildings and offices, ferries and parks, the chief of the fire prevention bureau, etc., with the idea that these positions, although associated with particular groups in other services (for example, the heads of the bureaus of buildings with the inspectors of buildings in the inspectional service, the chief of the fire prevention bureau with the inspectors of fire prevention, the head of the bureau of public buildings and offices with the caretakers and janitors of these buildings) are not in the line of promotion in these other services, but are positions for which general administrative ability and experience constitute the primary qualifications, rather than experience along any particular specialized lines. However, after considerable discussion it was decided to abandon this service because it was found impossible to limit the number of positions included in it and because it complicated the classification. It was also found that a considerable number of these administrative positions, although now appointive, might at some time in the future be filled by promotion from positions of lower but corresponding character. Moreover, in fixing salaries these positions could not be considered as isolated administrative positions, but had to be considered in relation to the groups of employes under supervision. It was, therefore, finally decided to place these positions at the head of the groups with which they are most closely associated. For example, the caretaker group in the custodial service includes positions all the way from that of caretaker or janitor to that of superintendent of public buildings and offices, even though the superintendent of public buildings and offices is at present an exempt officer, appointed not because he has had experience in the lower grades, but because in the opinion of the appointing officer he has sufficient administrative ability to take charge of the maintenance of public buildings.

2. BASIS OF DESCRIPTIONS OF DUTIES—

The descriptions of duties have been drafted as the result of exhaustive studies of work performed and required in existing positions throughout the various departments and offices of the city government. These studies have been supplemented by conferences with department heads and other employes.

An attempt has been made to make the descriptions of duties as clear and concise as possible. It was not thought wise to introduce too much detail because the details of duties attached to a particular position are necessarily variable, because only a general description is required in order to identify and appraise a position and because space and time are saved by cutting down all descriptions to absolute essentials. However, in order that no differences of opinion may arise in appraising positions, specific examples of work performed have been given, where necessary, to amplify and illustrate the duties definitions. In addition, the footnotes to certain grades include references to the titles and location of existing positions appraised in these grades.

3. BASIS OF DETERMINATION OF TITLES—

The standard titles have been determined in accordance with the following principles and are approved by the Municipal Civil Service Commission:

(*a*) Titles have been made descriptive of duties. Long titles have been avoided. Such qualifying words as "expert" have not been used.

(*b*) Titles have been made generic wherever possible, such as Chief Clerk, Senior Clerk, Clerk, Assistant Clerk, Junior Clerk, or Chief Engineer, Engineer, Senior Assistant Engineer, Assistant Engineer, Junior Engineer.

Where specialized titles are required, they have been created by adding descriptive words after the generic title. For example, if a specialized position requiring the services of an assistant engineer conversant with the installation, operation and maintenance of power plants is to be created, the title should be Assistant Engineer (Power Plant Supervision) and *not* Power Plant Expert or Fuel Engineer. In this way, in all but a few cases, the title will immediately identify the rank and grade of an employe and the specialized field in which he is qualified will be indicated by a word or words in brackets.

4. BASIS OF RATES OF COMPENSATION—

The rates of compensation which the Bureau of Personal Service recommends are based upon the following factors:

(a) The Market Value of the Particular Kind of Work Performed.

In determining this, inquiries were made of leading corporations, such as the insurance companies and public utility corporations, department stores, large contractors, charitable organizations, business and banking houses in the city of New York and in other places where work and living conditions were thought to be comparable. Inquiries were also made to determine the rates of compensation in the national government and in the larger American city and state governments, especially where scientific methods have been employed to determine salaries. It has been found unwise to use rates paid in other government units without careful consideration of differences in local conditions and methods adopted in fixing rates. The rates paid in private corporations in the city of New York have been of greater value. Studies have also been made of rates and conditions governing advancement in European cities.[1]

Since the first edition of this volume appeared, abnormal industrial conditions have led to a rise in salaries and wages in a large number of private employments. These conditions have also been reflected in the city government. The question of just what influence such market conditions should have on standard rates of compensation is extremely complex. In general, it may be said that although the city must in the long run pay somewhat higher rates than private employers, sudden, abnormal and presumably temporary rises in rates in private employment, excepting in the skilled trades and unskilled services, may not be recognized by the city. Permanence of service and the prospect of regular increases in salary in the city service, are considerations which in the majority of cases more than offset high salaries in temporary positions in private employment. It is not, however, to be supposed that the proposed standard rates of compensation are immutable even for a few years. There must always be changes in the rates to meet

[1] For Salary Schedules in Frankfort-on-the-Main, Germany, see Appendix F of Report on Cost of Living for an Unskilled Laborer's Family in New York City, published by the Bureau of Personal Service, 1915. Copies of this pamphlet are available for distribution.

market and industrial conditions, as well as to meet changes in organization and in other local conditions within the city service. Two methods of changing compensation rates are recommended, one to meet temporary conditions and the other to meet conditions which are likely to continue. In the former case, it is recommended that the Board of Estimate and Apportionment pass a resolution temporarily suspending one or more of the initial rates in a grade.[1] This involves no permanent change in the specifications. In the latter case, it is recommended that the Board of Estimate and Apportionment, upon report of its Committee on Salaries and Grades, pass a resolution changing the specifications, that is, substituting a new regulation for the existing one.[2]

(b) Conditions Peculiar to Government Service in General.

Excepting a relatively small number of positions, the city service is not yet attractive to the best talent in professional life, business, universities and schools. Advancement and promotion are slow, and it is still believed by many that they are not based solely upon merit. In the case of many positions private employers do not regard experience in the city government as a good recommendation. Many persons, particularly ambitious young men, do not think that as good experience can be gained in the city service under existing conditions of leadership and working standards as in private employment in which proper leadership and severe working standards are an economic necessity. It is the prevailing opinion outside of the city government itself that the business of the city is not transacted as efficiently as the business of large private employers. Many persons refuse to enter the city service because they do not wish to submit to civil service examinations for initial appointment or promotion. In many branches private business offers far greater opportunities for conspicuous material success than government employment. Great improvements have undoubtedly been made in the city government in these respects, but the fact still remains that it is necessary to pay higher rates than those paid in the most progressive private employments if it is hoped to attract and retain equally competent employes.

(c) Special Conditions Surrounding Certain Employments in the City Service.

There are numerous positions in the city service not found in private employment, or differing from positions with the same or related titles in private employment in so many essentials that comparisons in salary are often of apparent rather than real value. For example, although Fire Telegraph Despatchers are performing work similar in some respects to the work of regular telegraph despatchers and train despatchers, a large part of their duties is peculiar to a city fire alarm system. The fixation of their compensation by comparison with private employment without regard to

[1] See page 343.

[2] See page 342.

their peculiar duties would be unfair and inaccurate. The difference is even more marked in the supervisory positions in the city fire alarm system.

There are other positions in the city service which have no exact parallel in private employment, but for which the salary rates cannot be fixed without reference to the salaries of related positions in private employments; for example, the rates for inspectors in the city service must be fixed with due regard to the rates for the laborers, journeymen or foremen whose work they examine and from whose ranks they are generally recruited. It does not, however, follow that an Inspector of Public Works must receive as much as a Foreman of Asphalt Workers or that an Elevator Inspector must receive as much as an Elevator Constructor. In the original editions of the specifications the minimum rate for inspectors was fixed at $1,140 and the maximum in a number of cases at $1,380. As the result of experience in the application of existing rates, it has been thought wise to raise the minimum slightly to a uniform figure of $100 per month and to recommend a single maximum rate of $1,500 for the different kinds of inspection work which are of approximately equal value. It must be admitted that ideal inspectors cannot be obtained even at these rates. The solution of the inspectional problem lies in the extension wherever possible of the employment of professional men under titles and salaries in the professional service; for example, a wide use should be made of Engineering Assistants and Junior Engineers in buildings, public works and electrical inspections and of Physicians, Veterinarians and Pharmacists for food and sanitary inspection.

There are, in connection with certain positions, conditions of location, housing, long hours and surroundings which have had a direct bearing upon the rates of compensation finally recommended. This is especially true in the case of institutional employes. The remote location of institutions, the unpleasant character of inmates and patients, poorly prepared food, bad physical conditions, overcrowding, undesirable associates in dormitories and rooms have been some of the causes which in the past have contributed to the refusal of properly qualified and respectable persons to enter and remain in the institutional service.[1]

While some of these conditions have been greatly improved since the first edition of the specifications became effective, and will no doubt continue to improve, there are others, such as remote location and the character of inmates and patients, which will remain. As a result, the rates for some of the domestics and helpers in city institutions must be higher than those in private hospitals and institutions. On the other hand, there are employes in institutions, such as male helpers and artisans, who will render satisfactory service at rates considerably lower than those received by persons performing similar work in private employment and even in other branches of the city service. For example, there are persons who have some

---

[1] See a Brief Report on the Institutional Helper Problem, published with the original tentative edition of the specifications for the Institutional Service by the Bureau of Personal Service. Copies of this pamphlet are available for distribution.

skill and experience in carpentry, plumbing and other skilled trades, but who, on account of age, lack of ambition and other causes, are willing to accept employment at low salaries in institutions where they will receive maintenance. These persons in many cases render satisfactory service in the current upkeep and repair of the physical plant.

In fixing the salaries for almost all the lower class of help in institutions, provision has been made for an additional allowance of $240 annually, in lieu of maintenance, so that as many employes as possible may live outside the institutions. Some progress has been made during the past two years in reducing the number of persons receiving maintenance. In practically all cases it has been found that a more desirable class of help can be secured where residence is not required and a satisfactory allowance is made in lieu of maintenance. The reduction of the number of employes maintained in institutions lessens overcrowding, lightens the administrative burden of the heads of institutions, and effects considerable economy for the city. It may possibly be desirable when the next edition of the specifications appears to raise the allowance in lieu of maintenance from $240 to $300.

(d) Peculiarly Favorable Conditions Surrounding Certain Employments in the City Service.

In a large number of employments in the city service, hours of work, physical surroundings and provisions for vacations and sick leave are more favorable than those found in private employment. There are certain employments, particularly in the skilled trades, in which the city is an exceedingly generous employer if such factors as continuity of employment, vacation and the possibility of a pension are taken into consideration. The city is employing a large number of skilled workmen from 278 to 365 days a year and paying them the prevailing rate for each day, including a liberal vacation period. Some of these employes are kept at work of minor importance when there is not a full day's work in their particular trade. A number of employes who nominally work every day in the year, such as Stationary Engineers and Firemen, are, in fact, relieved three or four days a month.

The rate which the city pays is based upon Section 3 of Article 2 of the New York State Labor Law, commonly called the prevailing rates of wages law. In the absence of any recognized definite procedure governing the determination of the prevailing rate and in the absence of regular investigations by city examiners, the city has in many cases paid a rate which is not the prevailing rate but the union rate. It is obvious that the prevailing rate in the skilled trades is high, largely because the work is seasonal, resulting in long periods of idleness and unemployment. In the case of city employment, however, a great many skilled laborers are not subject to any trade fluctuations, but are employed constantly. The Bureau of Personal Service has made a detailed study of this wage and salary problem in the skilled trades. The following are the conclusions reached by the Bureau of Personal Service as to the fixation of rates for the Skilled Trades and Unskilled Services:

(1) The prevailing rate is the rate paid to the majority. If no one rate is received by a majority, the prevailing rate is the rate received by the largest number, provided that this number is considerably larger than the number receiving any other rate. However, in the case of several different rates with almost equal numbers receiving each rate, the most reasonable solution would appear to be to take the average of all the rates. The State Labor Law requires that the wages paid by the city government be based upon a daily rate.

(2) The union rate is a rate set up by the union, which may or may not be a prevailing rate. In a number of cases it is not a prevailing rate, but a rate which the union tries to enforce. The fact that the union establishes a certain rate is not in itself proof that this is the prevailing rate. In some instances the facts disclosed by investigation have indicated the contrary. On the other hand, there is a considerable number of cases in which the union rate appears to be the prevailing rate.

(3) Although it is argued by many employers that laborers, workmen and mechanics may legally be employed at a fixed annual salary, it is not recommended at this time that annual rates be paid except where this practice is already established in the city government and prevails in private employment.

(4) The city should make inquiry at least once every year to discover what is the prevailing rate. This information can be obtained most readily by co-operating with the State Industrial Commission in sending questionnaires to employers. Co-operation with the state department will insure from employers compliance with this request for information. No municipal body, however, is authorized to make the final and conclusive determination as to the rates of wages. An employe may at any time question the correctness of the rate as provisionally fixed and may take the matter to the courts for decision. However, an employe who accepts the rate as provisionally fixed without protest waives his right to any greater sum. Whenever a claim is made, supported by evidence that there has been a considerable change in the rate, the city should revise this provisional rate in conformity with the facts developed by a special investigation.

(e) The Assumption That New York City Wishes, as Far as It Is Financially Able, to Be a Model Employer.

In those employments in which private corporations generally pay inadequate salaries or take advantage of unemployment and other market conditions, the Bureau of Personal Service has recommended salaries considerably higher than private corporations pay under normal industrial conditions. For example, the almost uniform rate of $2.50 a day which has been paid by the city of New York to its unskilled laborers for some years was never based upon the rate prevailing in private employment in and in the neighborhood of the city. At the time of the first publication of these specifications private employers and contractors were paying as little as $1.70 a day to unskilled labor. Now they are paying as much as $3 a day. The prevailing rate in private employment has been invariably determined by market conditions, that is, by the lowest rate for which satisfactory labor service can be purchased at any given time. It has not been based in any way upon minimum wage principles or upon studies of the cost of living, although these elements have entered indirectly into the willingness of the laborer to accept the prevailing rate. Upon the assumption that the city of New York wishes to pay its employes salaries or wages which bear a proper relation to the salaries or wages prevailing among representative private employers, and at the same time wishes itself to be a model employer, the Bureau of Personal Service, at the suggestion of the Bureau of Municipal Research, decided that it was essential to make a study of the cost of living for unskilled laborers in the city of New York. A separate report on this subject was made in 1915 by the Bureau of Personal Service with the assistance of the Bureau of Municipal Research.[1] This report has gone into a second edition and has been in considerable demand in all parts of the country.

The conclusions drawn in this report were that below $840 a year or $2.70 a day an unskilled laborer's family of five persons could not maintain a standard of living consistent with American ideas. As a practical application of this conclusion no maximum rate below $840 was recommended for the rank and file of the Street Cleaning Department and the Bureaus of Street Cleaning in Queens and Richmond, for unskilled laborers, stablemen, hostlers, drivers, cleaners, deckhands and other unskilled manual workers. A minimum of $720 was established for positions in these groups, but the corresponding per diem rate of $2.30 was never made effective in the case of laborers, who have continued to receive $2.50 a day.

Since the appearance of this report the cost of the necessities of life has materially increased. A second study of the cost of living was therefore made during February, 1917, by the Bureau of Personal Service with the co-operation of the Bureau of Municipal Research, which indicates that the minimum wage for the family above-mentioned has risen from $840 to about $980.[2] It is not to be presumed that this is a permanent condition requiring complete revision of rates, but it is at least fair to assume that some change in rates is required. The lowest maximum for the unskilled groups, excepting cleaners, has, therefore, been placed at $888 per annum, or $2.80 per diem, and the minimum at $792 per annum, or $2.50 per diem.

It will be desirable from time to time to make further studies of the cost of living in New York City. It may be desirable to extend these studies to classes of employes above unskilled laborers. For example, there is obviously such a thing as a minimum wage for a clerk, policeman or fireman with a family of five persons.

---

[1] See Report on The Cost of Living for an Unskilled Laborer's Family in New York City, 1915. Copies of this pamphlet are available for distribution.

[2] See Report on Increased Cost of Living for an Unskilled Laborer's Family in New York City, Bureau of Personal Service, 1917. Copies of this pamphlet may be obtained through the Municipal Reference Library. A brief summary is included in this volume. (See page 344 of the appendix.)

(f) The Theory That a Range of Salary Rather Than a Fixed Rate Should Be Established for Most Grades in the City Service.

The experience of the most progressive private corporations and governments in this and other countries indicates that even if it is possible to determine exactly the value of a particular position, it is nevertheless preferable to establish a range of salary with a minimum compensation somewhat below and a maximum somewhat above that exact value. This range of salary reflects the fact that in many cases an employe enters a position with relatively little experience and that through application and experience over a considerable period of time his usefulness increases to its maximum value. Advancement within this range of salary from the minimum to the maximum is held out as an incentive to efficient service. In the case of a classification of city employments in which a number of positions of similar but not identical value must necessarily be placed in the same grade, it is absolutely essential that there should be a range of salary fixed for the grade, the minimum of which should be a proper minimum for the least important position in the grade and the maximum of which should be a proper maximum for the most important position in the grade. In the lower grades, all positions are usually worth from the minimum to the maximum compensation, assuming that the quality and quantity of service rendered by the incumbents are up to standard. However, in the higher grades, where positions within the same grade frequently differ in importance and value irrespective of the efficiency of the incumbents, the maximum rate and, in some cases, the initial rate must be determined upon the basis of a specific appraisal of the value of the position in question. The principle involved has long been recognized by implication in the grades established by the Municipal Civil Service Commission. Under the rules of the Commission persons who are successful in passing the qualifying tests become eligible for salaries between a minimum and a maximum. It should be added that the ranges of salary proposed as compensation rates by the Bureau of Personal Service have been set up on lines parallel to the qualification requirements recognized by the Municipal Civil Service Commission. In certain cases an exception to the general rule of a range of salary has been made and flat rates have been established, notably in positions as foreman in the various skilled trades. This exception is necessary because of the relation which must be preserved between the rates paid these foremen and the prevailing daily rates paid the skilled workmen whom they supervise.

(g) The Establishment of a Proper Pension System.

There are at the present time separate pension funds for several groups of employes and a general pension provision under the so-called Grady law covering all employes other than those provided for under the special funds. The Grady law provides for retirement on account of disability at the end of thirty years of service. A number of the separate pension funds are bankrupt or actuarially unsound. The Pension Division of the Bureau of Personal Service, formerly the Commission on Pensions, will ultimately prepare a plan which will undoubtedly confer greater benefits than now accrue to the average employe through the provisions of the Grady law. The present pension conditions and future pension plans of the city have been as far as possible borne in mind in connection with the fixation of rates and conditions governing advancement throughout the service. The fact that since January 1, 1917, the pension agency has become associated with the former Bureau of Standards in a single Bureau of Personal Service should insure harmonious development of all personal service work. The proposed new pension system or systems will, undoubtedly, be a contributory system. The influence on salaries of a contribution of about 4 per cent., especially in the lower grades, must soon be considered. The new pension plans have not as yet progressed far enough toward adoption to warrant thorough reconsideration of salaries in the lower grades from the point of view of pension contributions.

(h) The Simplification of Accounting and Payroll Audit.

For this purpose all rates are exact multiples of twelve. This will simplify accounting and payroll methods in almost all cases. Where the accounting and payroll system is based on an hourly rate, as in the Street Cleaning Department, the proposed rates are not ideal. In this case, however, it was decided that the adoption of a system of rates divisible by 313 days and 8 hours a day would involve difficulties and expenditures out of proportion to the accounting and payroll advantages.

5. BASIS OF CONDITIONS GOVERNING INITIAL APPOINTMENT AND PROMOTION—

The qualifications required for original appointment and promotion have been discussed at numerous conferences with heads of departments and employes, and have been agreed to by the Municipal Civil Service Commission. The qualifications for initial appointment as originally proposed by the Bureau of Personal Service were more definite and stringent than those which now appear in the third edition of the specifications. The change is due to the fact that the Municipal Civil Service Commission has objected to those qualifications which were too specific and inelastic. For example, the Municipal Civil Service Commission has objected to qualifications for entrance which prescribe exactly the kind and length of study and experience required for positions not of a distinctly professional or highly technical character on the ground that many desirable persons might be excluded through such qualifications. The intention of the Commission is not that entrance requirements should be lowered, but that sufficiently flexible rules should be established governing these requirements to allow a final decision to be made as to minimum qualifications before each examination is advertised.

At least one of the objections to higher experience requirements in civil service examinations has been removed by the establishment of proper salary rates. Up to the present time the Municipal Civil Service Commission has been greatly handicapped in holding examinations for some positions by the low salaries offered. The proposed new salary rates should in almost all cases attract a very desirable class of candidates to examinations. It now rests with the Municipal Civil Service Commission to establish such experience requirements and examination and rating standards for entrance and promotion, and to hold examinations at such intervals as will insure the appointment and promotion of persons qualified to receive the standard salary rates which the Board of Estimate and Apportionment is willing to pay.

The history of the 1st Grade Clerk list which expired recently affords an example of the necessity of higher standards in Civil Service examinations. In the examination held in May, 1913, the subjects and requirements were inadequate. The rating standards were low; the age requirements were from 14 to 18. The result was that of 3731 who took the mental examination, 3121 candidates passed. The list was promulgated in December, 1913, and was, therefore, in existence almost three years. Candidates as low on the list as No. 2191 were certified for appointment. Some of these candidates who took the examination at the age of 17 were over 21 years old when they were certified. The salary range of $300 to $540 originally recommended by the Bureau of Personal Service should under normal business conditions attract a very satisfactory type of office boy. This range was not, however, established for an incumbent 21 years old who during the three years which elapsed since he took the examination had made so little progress that he was willing to accept a position as office boy at a salary of $300. In the last examination for 1st Grade Clerk, which was held by the present Civil Service Commissioners, higher age, educational and examination requirements and rating standards were set up. 1480 candidates filed applications for this examination. The decrease in number was in a large part due to abnormal industrial conditions and to the objections of Public School and High School teachers to having their pupils leave school, but it was also due to the rise in requirements. Of 1228 who took the mental examination only 331 passed. Only 263 finally passed the examination. If this examination is held once every year, with an even lower maximum age limit and higher standards, and the minimum rate conforms to market conditions, the city will be sure of getting the proper recruits in its large clerical service and in the other services which are fed by the clerical service.

Under present pension conditions, age requirements should receive much greater emphasis than they have received in the past. Up to the present time, excepting positions for which there is a statutory limit of age at entrance into the service, age requirements have been set up with the sole idea of immediate fitness to perform the duties of the position. In the absence of provision for compulsory retirement, a large number of employes who enter the service late in life remain in the service after their mental and physical powers have become impaired. Pending the adoption by the Board of Estimate and Apportionment of a sound pension plan for the whole city, the question of proper age requirements for entrance into the city service should be discussed by representatives of the Board of Estimate and Apportionment, the Bureau of Personal Service and the Municipal Civil Service Commission.

6. BASIS OF CONDITIONS GOVERNING ADVANCEMENT, I. E., OF SALARY INCREASES WITHIN GRADE—

The amount of increase, that is, the difference between one salary rate and the next salary rate, is based upon a table which has been applied, with some exceptions, to all groups.[1] This amount represents about 10 per cent. of the average of the salary range in question.

There are several possible methods of granting increases in salary:

(a) They may be entirely subject each year, as regards the individuals benefited and the amount of increase, to the recommendation of the head of each department based on whatever principle or method he and his advisers or superiors may choose to apply and to agreement with these recommendations by the appropriating bodies. This is the old method of granting increases which was in use in the majority of the departments up to this year and which is still in use in the higher grades.

(b) They may be mandatory as in the case of uniformed firemen whose salary increases are provided for by law.

(c) They may be automatic as in the case of patrolmen in the police department. In this case the amount of increase and minimum time of service are fixed in the Charter. Recently it has been the policy of the Police Commissioner and the appropriating bodies to give everyone who is eligible an increase.

(d) They may be based upon service records, the amount of money available for increases being determined at least in part by accruals, the increases in the lower grades being more nearly automatic than in the higher grades and increases in the higher grades depending upon exceptional service and positive achievement rather than upon length of merely satisfactory service.

The last method is undoubtedly the only sound and scientific one and is the method recommended by the Bureau of Personal Service and put into partial effect respecting the lower grade of employes in the 1917 budget. After the budget estimates for 1917 had been received, the Comptroller called for supplementary requests for increases for the lower grade employes on the basis of efficiency and length of service.[2] Supplementary increases affecting over 3000 people and aggregating somewhat less than $200,000 were made on this basis. The new service record system is now being extended by the Municipal Civil Service Commission to all departments and before the work on the 1918 budget is commenced, it will be possible to formulate a plan for the making of all increases below $1500 and a considerable number above this amount on the basis of service records. Below $1500 it is recommended that increases be made as follows: The Service Record Bureau of the Municipal Civil Service Commission will prepare statistics for the service record year ending May 1st indicating how many employes are rated, for example, Above Standard, Conspicuously Above Standard, and Far

[1]See page 27.

[2]See page 338 for copy of the Comptroller's letter to heads of departments.

Above Standard, and how long each employe has served since his last increase in salary. It will then be possible for the tax budget committee to fix such standards of merit and length of service as a basis for increases, as are compatible with the amount of money available for this purpose. This will do away in large measure with the prolonged consideration of individual cases by the sub-committee on tax budget. Department heads will retain the right to present exceptional cases for consideration. This or some similar plan will place the increasing of employes within grade upon the same basis which now determines promotions from grade to grade under the existing civil service law. This would greatly reduce the work of the budget committee and sub-committee in reviewing the budget and would put the whole question of granting increases in the lower grades on a practical and sound basis. Under this plan the increases are not mandatory or automatic, that is, they do not depend merely upon length of service. They are in all cases predicated upon a workable system of service records, such as the one which is now being developed by the Municipal Civil Service Commission, together with control by the Board of Estimate and Apportionment, which will render ineffective any attempts to insure increases by unduly high ratings.

It is recommended that increases be made only in the preparation of the annual tax budget to take effect on January 1st, excepting the lower grades in the Institutional Service in which provision is made for increases to take effect on July 1st as well as January 1st. Unless otherwise indicated, the length of service required at one rate before advancement to the next rate is one year. In certain of the lower grades the length of service required before advancement has been fixed at two years instead of one year. These requirements are indicated at the foot of the page in each of these grades under the heading "Special Condition Governing Advancement." The fact that the city under present financial conditions cannot possibly grant increases every year, even to deserving employes, has necessitated this two years' requirement. Service for two years or more is required before advancement in positions where little previous training is required or where there are small opportunities for promotion and where employes become valuable mainly through long experience in the city service. On account of the important part which individual capacity must play in determining advancement from rate to rate in the higher grades, no attempt has been made to fix the length of service required for advancement in these grades, excepting that these increases are also governed by the general rule requiring at least one year of service.

It should be distinctly understood that it is not recommended that every employe shall receive an increase in salary at the end of the periods established, but only those giving evidence of *meritorious* service for the period required, the standard of meritorious service being progressively higher in each succeeding grade.

Because of the financial limitations which must control the appropriations recommended by the Board of Estimate and Apportionment, the standard of service entitling an employe to an increase must be determined annually for each department in the preparation of the tax budget. Conversely, employes who render exceptional service are not prevented from getting increases in less time than that established in the grade or to a rate higher than the one immediately above. Such cases are covered by a special provision governing increases to higher rates than the one immediately above and within a shorter time than that stipulated for ordinary cases.[1]

In a large number of cases a minimum of one year of service is required at the lower rates within a grade and of two years of service at the higher rates. This is done because it is desirable to afford encouragement to employes just entering the service and because spreading the increases over a number of years provides an additional stimulus to maintain a proper standard of satisfactory service. Moreover, since the intermediate rates within a grade correspond most closely to the rates paid in private employment, it is at those rates that employes may properly be expected to serve the longest time.

When all increases in salaries are made to depend upon service ratings, employes will make every effort to be rated fairly, and administrative officers will ultimately give much closer thought to their administrative and judicial functions as rating officers than they now give.

The adoption of the principle of basing salary increases as far as possible upon "slack," *i. e.*, upon accruals arising through not filling vacant positions or eliminating unnecessary positions and through filling vacancies at the lowest rate in each grade, will serve to encourage department heads to economize. It will also ultimately provide an adequate amount for increases in all excepting the smallest departments in which few positions can be eliminated and in which there is little change in personnel. In the case of these departments, special provision must be made for increases, so that there may be no discrimination against their employes. It must, however, be borne in mind that until the system of increases within the new grades has been under way for some time, accruals alone will not suffice to sustain the system. In the meantime the question of the number and amount of increases to be granted to bureaus within departments and to groups of employes within bureaus must be carefully worked out in co-operation with the service record bureau of the Municipal Civil Service Commission, with due reference to the necessity of providing reasonably regular increases for a reasonably large proportion of employes in the lower grades.

7. USE OF SPECIFICATIONS AS A BASIS FOR APPROPRIATION AND CURRENT FISCAL CONTROL—

The proposed standard specifications and salary rates have been in practical operation in the City of New York since February 1, 1915. The immediate result of the policy adopted by the Board of Estimate and Apportionment at that time, in regard to filling positions becoming vacant, was to place a complete embargo upon the inflation of existing salaries and the fixation of salaries at unfairly high rates.

---

[1]See exceptions under General Rules Governing Advancement, page 30.

The tax budget committee, in preparing the budget for the year 1916, decided that it would make use of the standard specifications and salary rates in measuring all existing employment. Appraisals were made and submitted by the Bureau of Personal Service showing the minimum and maximum values of the work being done in all positions. Upon these appraisals the Board of Estimate and Apportionment based its official action regarding salaries. It was the feeling of the majority of the Board that a rigid application of standard rates to all salaries would bring too great hardship upon employes. Under the operation of this policy, approximately 5500 increases in salary were granted besides the mandatory or automatic increases for policemen, firemen and teachers. There were approximately 1100 decreases in salary, 2100 new positions added and 2800 unnecessary positions eliminated. The net saving in personal service, excepting the salaries of policemen, firemen and teachers, was approximately $625,000.

During 1915, the application of standard rates of compensation to the filling of vacant positions had been made by the Board of Estimate and Apportionment without regard to the necessity for filling these positions. In other words, if a position became vacant and the head of the department wished to fill it, the Board of Estimate and Apportionment concerned itself only to the extent that it should be filed under the proper title and at the proper rate. In the budget for 1916 the Board took a further step in applying standards to vacancies, by requiring a certificate from the Committee on Salaries and Grades that the position was necessary. This rule has been in successful operation since January 1, 1916. A large proportion of positions which became vacant after January 1, 1916, were eliminated entirely, combined with other positions or filled at the minimum rate within the grade. The result of this control of personal service was that in preparing estimates for the 1917 budget, it was found that a large amount of "slack" was available out of which to make increases in salary within grade. Increases were made in this way, *i. e.*, without increasing the personal service appropriations of the preceding year, affecting 2375 persons and amounting to $310,696.60

Experience gained both in the current application of standards during the year 1915 and in the preparation of the budget for 1916 made it clear to the Board of Estimate and Apportionment that the greater part of the economies possible in its effort to place city employment on a proper business basis lay in the elimination of unnecessary positions rather than in the reduction of salaries, therefore no further reduction in the salaries of the present incumbents of positions was made in the 1917 budget by the Board of Estimate and Apportionment.

The old plan of preparing budgets upon the basis of existing methods and salaries and of making only annual surface changes in these methods and salaries at budget time is being rapidly replaced by a synthetic plan based upon the actual work to be done. With an accurate knowledge of proposed work in each department, it has proved by no means difficult to determine the number and kinds of employes needed to accomplish it. The organization arrived at by this process furnishes theoretically correct schedules of personal service upon which the administrative authorities of the departments are gradually modelling their operating schedules.

8. USE OF SPECIFICATIONS AS A BASIS FOR CIVIL SERVICE CONTROL—

The present civil service classification of positions is in need of careful revision and simplification. New and undescriptive titles have found their way into the classification during the last few years. There are positions in the exempt class which should be classified as competitive. In the absence of accepted general definitions of duties to be performed under the various titles, of a current file of duties being performed by employes and of a system of inspection and control by examiners, employes have in many cases been assigned to duties for which they never qualified by examination. The regulations and procedure involved in the present civil service classification have become so complicated that only a few persons understand them. A new civil service classification based upon the proposed standard services, groups, grades, titles, definitions of duties, qualifications and salary limits has been agreed to by the Municipal Civil Service Commission, which is now urging upon the heads of all departments the desirability of adopting the new standard titles in place of the present obsolete ones. The Commission is also prepared to use the standard specifications as the basis for establishing examination standards, advertising examinations, checking payrolls and investigating the performance of work under proper title.

9. USE OF SPECIFICATIONS AS A BASIS FOR INFORMATION TO PRESENT AND PROSPECTIVE EMPLOYES AND TO THE PUBLIC—

Up to the present time there have been no definite printed regulations indicating to present and prospective employes duties, conditions of compensation and lines of advancement in the various classes of employment in the city service. The standard specifications clearly indicate duties, conditions of compensation and lines of advancement in every group in the city service, and also indicate the lines of advancement from the less important to the more important groups. For example, the lines of advancement are indicated within the Bookkeeper Group of the Clerical Service and from the Bookkeeper Group of the Clerical Service to the Accountant Group of the Professional Service. Similarly, lines of advancement are indicated within the Draftsman, Instrumentman and Law Clerk Groups of the Sub-Professional Service, and from these groups to the Engineer and Lawyer Groups of the Professional Service. This information, which is now being published separately by the Board of Estimate and Apportionment, should be revised currently and republished annually as a joint publication of the Bureau of Personal Service and the Municipal Civil Service Commission.

CONCLUSION—

It cannot be claimed that all the rates of compensation proposed are satisfactory to all present city employes. In the numerous original conferences held by the Bureau of Personal Service, many employes expressed what appeared to the Bureau to be exaggerated estimates of the relative importance and value of the work they were doing. In most instances, however, both employes and superior officers, after reviewing the data upon which the proposed rates were predicated and after experience in filling positions at the proposed rates, have agreed that these rates are reasonable and judging by the public hearings held in September, 1916, on the standard specifications for personal service, the majority of employes are now satisfied with the proposed ranges and rates of compensation.

In presenting this revised edition of the standard specifications for personal service it is proper that acknowledgment should again be made of the continuous and invaluable co-operation of the Bureau of Municipal Research, notably of Mr. Robert Moses, who is in charge of the division of personal service in that Bureau, and of Mrs. Harrison Thomas.

GEORGE L. TIRRELL,
Director, Bureau of Personal Service.

PRINCIPLES GOVERNING COMPENSATION

I. Regulations Governing Amount of Increases—

The regulations governing amount of increases are embodied in the following table:

Salaries up to $1,200............Advances of $24, $30, $36, $48 or $60
Salaries from $1,200 to $1,800....................Advances of $120
Salaries from $1,800 to $2,400....................Advances of $180
Salaries from $2,400 to $3,600....................Advances of $240
Salaries from $3,600 to $4,800....................Advances of $300
Salaries from $4,800 to $6,120....................Advances of $420
Salary rates above $6,120........$6,600, $7,200, $7,800, $8,400, $9,000, $9,600, $10,200

No recommendation is made above $10,200, excepting in the Commissioner Group.[1]

The following general principles determine the amount of increase, whether $24, $30, $36, $48 or $60, in salaries up to $1,200:

1. $24 increases per annum (or $0.10 increases per diem) are applied in the case of positions involving manual labor of the simplest character in the lowest grades of the Unskilled, Skilled Trades, Institutional and Street Cleaning Services, such as Laborer, Cleaner, Deckhand, Hospital Helper and Sweeper.

2. $30 increases are applied in the majority of positions in the Institutional Service involving domestic or handicraft work in institutions of a more difficult or supervisory character, such as Senior Hospital Helper, Cook and Hospital Attendant.

3. $36 increases are applied in the case of positions in the lowest grades of the Custodial Service involving work requiring ability and responsibility

[1]See exception on page 32.

somewhat above that required in ordinary manual labor, but not ranking with the skilled trades in these respects, such as Bridgetender, Caretaker, Elevator Operator, etc.

4. $48 increases are applied in the case of positions as Assistant Foreman in the Street Cleaning Service.

5. $60 increases are applied in the case of the following positions:

a. Positions in the lower grades of the Professional, Sub-Professional, Investigational, Educational, Clerical and Inspectional Services.

b. Positions in the Skilled Trades Service to which annual salaries are attached, involving work in recognized skilled trades and similar employments, such as Fire Telegraph Despatcher, Motor Driver, Photographer, etc.

c. Positions as Foreman in the Unskilled and Street Cleaning Services. (A per diem increase of $0.20 is also provided for Foremen.)

d. Positions in the Institutional Service involving the more difficult forms of non-professional work in connection with institutions, such as Coffee Roaster, Laundryman, etc.

II. Exceptions to Regulations Governing Amount of Increases—

1. It has been found necessary to make special regulations governing increases from certain rates. Where there is a rate of $1,140, $1,740, $2,340, $3,480, $3,540, $4,620, $4,680, $4,740, the increase appropriate to the range immediately above has been applied. Therefore, the next rate after $1,140 is $1,260, after $1,740 is $1,920, after $2,340 is $2,580, after $3,480 is $3,780, after $3,540 is $3,840, after $4,620 is $5,040, after $4,680 is $5,100, after $4,740 is $5,160. The next rate after $2,280 is $2,460, unless the increase involves promotion to a higher grade, in which case the next rate is $2,520.

2. In the case of a higher grade involving initially much greater responsibilities and much more important duties than any in the grade below, the minimum salary rate for the higher grade has been placed above the amount fixed by the general rule. For example, the maximum salary for a Head Dietitian in Grade 2 is $1,380, while the minimum salary for a Departmental Dietitian in Grade 3 is $1,800.

3. Below $1,200, $120 increases are applied in some cases, for example, where the city is employing professional men who can not be expected to remain long within a grade at a low salary rate. The first grade in the Engineer Group is an example of this kind of exception.

Increases of $120 are also applied to rates below $1,200 in the Laboratory Assistant Group. This exception is made because of the fact that persons with almost professional qualifications are attracted into the city service as Laboratory Assistants. They could not be expected to remain long enough to reach the maximum in a grade whose range is so wide, with an increase of only $60. Moreover, the Laboratory Assistant Group constitutes in the case of bacteriology and pathology the only avenue through which persons may be promoted into the responsible professional laboratory positions, because of the absence of an apprentice grade in the laboratory groups of the Professional Service.

$120 increases are also applied in some cases where a considerable period of apprenticeship is required before entrance into the grade; where, therefore, mature persons for whom a $60 increase would not be adequate, enter at a comparatively low salary rate, and the maximum rate represents the proper salary at the end of two or three years' experience in the city service, as in Grade 1 of the Bookkeeper Group and Grade 2 B of the Clerk Group.

4. Above $1,200, $60 increases are applied in some cases, for example, where it is expected that employes will remain within a grade for a long time and an increase of $120 is thought to be too large. The salary rates for Supervising Field Nurse in Grade 2 of the Nurse Group are examples of this kind of exception. $60 increases are maintained in the first grade of all inspectional groups up to $1,500.

5. It is recommended that Internes in the city service be paid rates ranging from $120 to $240, and Pupil Nurses rates ranging from $96 to $180, according to the desirability of the training afforded in the institution in which they are serving. This is not in the nature of a salary; it is a stipend to provide for personal needs beyond the bare maintenance which the majority receive at present.

6. In the Deputy Commissioner Group, the rates recommended are as follows: $3,600, $3,900, $4,200, $4,500, $4,800, $5,100, $5,400, $6,000, $6,600, $7,500.

In the Commissioner Group the rates recommended are as follows in Grade 1: $3,600, $4,500, $5,100, $6,000; in Grade 2, $7,500, $9,000, $10,500, $12,000, $13,500, $15,000.

III. Service Every Day in the Year—

Provision is made in only a very limited number of cases for a special range of annual salary for regular service every day in the year, as it is not desirable that any employe should work so constantly. It is recommended that wherever possible employes be relieved from work not less than one day in seven. In almost all cases where Sunday employment is necessary, relief can be provided for another rest day in the same way in which it is provided for holidays. Pending a complete adjustment of this problem it is recommended that per diem rates be set up in the budget for the seventh day's work separate from the regular annual salaries. These per diem rates may be paid to regular employes who work an extra day or to temporary employes who relieve them.

GENERAL RULES GOVERNING ADVANCEMENT, I. E., INCREASES IN SALARY WITHIN GRADE—

Beginning with the lowest rate advancement from rate to rate within each grade shall be made in the preparation of the annual tax budget upon the completion of the required term of meritorious service.[1] The length of this required term of service shall be not less than one year. In certain of the lower grades a term of service of more than one year is required for advancement from rate to rate. Such requirements are indicated in these grades under the heading "Special Condition Governing Advancement."

Proof of meritorious service shall be established in the case of exempt, non-competitive and labor positions by the recommendation of the head of the department made in accordance with the service record regulations of the Municipal Civil Service Commission, and in the case of competitive positions by the service records of the Municipal Civil Service Commission, in either case supplemented by investigation under the rules of the Board of Estimate and Apportionment. The standard of meritorious service which shall entitle an employe to an increase shall be determined annually for each department in the preparation of the tax budget and shall be progressively higher in each succeeding grade.

Exceptions:

1. In cases of conspicuous service or achievement recognized by the Board of Estimate and Apportionment, advancement may be made after fewer years than the number prescribed or after the prescribed number of years to a rate higher than the one immediately above. In no case, however, excepting certain positions in the institutional service, shall advancement be made before the lapse of one year.

2. In those grades specifically designated, advancement shall be made only after an appraisal of the value of the work to be performed. In other grades specifically designated, the initial rate also shall be determined after an appraisal. These appraisals shall be made under the rules of the Board of Estimate and Apportionment.

3. Appointments to vacant positions made prior to March 1 of each year will be regarded as dating from January 1, when considering length of service in connection with salary increases.

4. In the case of certain positions in the lower grades of the Institutional Service, increases shall be provided to take effect at the end of three months from date of appointment, subsequent increases to take effect on the anniversary of appointment.

---

[1]The term "advancement" is used only in connection with increases within grade as distinguished from "promotion" from grade to grade. These rules do not apply to promotions, *i. e.*, increases to a higher grade. Such promotional increases may be made at any time to the minimum of the grade in which a vacant position is appraised, or to a rate higher than the minimum in the case of specifically designated grades.

EXECUTIVE SERVICE.

SYMBOL (X).

The term Executive Service is applied to those offices or employments the duties of whose incumbents are to assume primary responsibility for the planning, direction, control and result of every action taken within their jurisdiction.

EXECUTIVE COUNCIL GROUP

SYMBOL (X C)

The term Executive Council Group is applied to those elective offices of the Executive Service in which incumbents are required to discharge the functions of members of the Board of Estimate and Apportionment, and such additional duties as Mayor, Comptroller, President of the Board of Aldermen and President of Borough as are outlined in the Charter of the City of New York.

No specific recommendations are made as to the proper salary for members of the Executive Council of the city.

COMMISSIONER GROUP

SYMBOL (X K)

The term Commissioner Group is applied to those appointive offices of the Executive Service in which incumbents are required to be responsible for the administration of entire city departments or commissions, and of independent executive bureaus or boards ranking in importance with departments and commissions.

GRADE 1 (X K 1)

TITLES OF POSITIONS—

ASSESSOR
COMMISSIONER

DUTIES—

The duties of incumbents of these positions are to act as heads of the smaller executive city departments or commissions, or of those executive city departments presenting the less complex administrative problems.

QUALIFICATIONS—

1. Such qualifications as are outlined in the Charter of the City of New York.
2. Ability to discharge the duties of the position satisfactory to the appointing officer.

COMPENSATION—

Range of annual compensation—$3600 to $6000 inclusive.
Salary rates—$3600, $4500, $5100, $6000.

SPECIAL REGULATION GOVERNING COMPENSATION—

Persons entering this grade need not necessarily be paid the lowest rate. Fixation of the rate to be paid is conditional upon appraisal under the rules of the Board of Estimate and Apportionment.

GRADE 2 (X K 2)

TITLES OF POSITIONS—

CHAMBERLAIN
COMMISSIONER
CORPORATION COUNSEL
EXECUTIVE MANAGER (EDUCATION)

DUTIES—

The duties of incumbents of these positions are to act as heads of the largest executive city departments or commissions, or of those executive city departments presenting the most complex administrative problems involving reorganization and planning of the most difficult order, or to act as executive manager under the Board of Education in charge of the business administration of the public schools.

QUALIFICATIONS—

1. Such qualifications as are outlined in the Charter of the City of New York.
2. Ability to discharge the duties of the position satisfactory to the appointing officer.

COMPENSATION—

Range of annual compensation—$7500 to $15000 inclusive.
Salary rates—$7500, $9000, $10500, $12000, $13500, $15000.

SPECIAL REGULATION GOVERNING COMPENSATION—

Persons entering this grade need not necessarily be paid the lowest rate. Fixation of the rate to be paid is conditional upon appraisal under the rules of the Board of Estimate and Apportionment.

DEPUTY COMMISSIONER GROUP

SYMBOL (X D)

The term Deputy Commissioner Group is applied to those appointive offices of the Executive Service in which incumbents are required to act as deputies to heads of city departments or commissions.

GRADE 1 (X D 1)

TITLES OF POSITIONS—

DEPUTY COMMISSIONER
DEPUTY COMPTROLLER

DUTIES—

The duties of incumbents of these positions are to act as deputies to heads of city departments or commissions.

QUALIFICATIONS—

1. Such qualifications as are outlined in the Charter of the City of New York.
2. Ability to discharge the duties of the position satisfactory to the appointing officer.

COMPENSATION—

Range of annual compensation—$3600 to $7500 inclusive.
Salary rates—$3600, $3900, $4200, $4500, $4800, $5100, $5400, $6000, $6600, $7500.

SPECIAL REGULATION GOVERNING COMPENSATION—

Persons entering this grade need not necessarily be paid the lowest rate. Fixation of the rate to be paid is conditional upon appraisal under the rules of the Board of Estimate and Apportionment.

EXECUTIVE SECRETARY GROUP

SYMBOL (X S)

The term Executive Secretary Group is applied to those offices or employments of the Executive Service in which incumbents are required to perform such duties as secretaries of city departments or commissions as involve not merely departmental correspondence and central clerical work, but responsibility for detailed administrative work, for knowledge of administrative work in all units, and for making effective the orders and policies outlined by executives.

Note 1.—It is recommended that the position of executive secretary of a department or board be placed in the competitive class. Positions as secretaries of departments are at present exempted under the state civil service law. The position of secretary should be that of the highest permanent official of a department who is not affected by a change in administration, whose duties are not policy determining, but administrative and interpretative. The secretary of a department should be thoroughly familiar with the functions, activities and personnel of the department. He should be prepared to inform the heads of departments on all matters of detail and should be able to carry out the details of such policies as are outlined by these executives. It is of great importance that in a department such as the Department of Public Charities there should be a permanent secretary, able to coordinate the various activities of the bureaus of the department and to inform a new commissioner and his deputies on all details of departmental administration. A complete change in the executive personnel of the department, including the department secretary, would place upon a new administration the burden of becoming acquainted with the departmental machinery through a number of independent subordinate officials. The establishment of the principle of a permanent secretary or under secretary between the changing executives and the permanent rank and file has been successfully established in Great Britain, Germany, France and other continental nations, and has often been recommended in American state governments and in the national government. It is not to be expected that in all departments the position of secretary can be established at once on the plan above suggested. The functions of executive secretaries at the present time extend all the way from merely clerical work to administrative and executive work.

Note 2.—No provision is made in these specifications for a position as assistant executive secretary. It is recommended that the existing positions be abolished or filled by employes in the Clerk Group as vacancies occur. The existing assistant secretaryships of departments are either unnecessary, or else the duties performed by incumbents are those of Assistant Clerks B, Clerks or Senior Clerks in grades 2 B, 3 and 4 of the Clerk Group of the Clerical Service. The present positions as secretaries of boards, where the functions are clerical and involve no administration of departments, are also properly included in the fourth and fifth grades of the Clerk Group.

GRADE 1 (X S 1)

TITLES OF POSITIONS—

EXECUTIVE SECRETARY

DUTIES—

The duties of incumbents of these positions are to be responsible for departmental correspondence, for issuing orders and notices from heads of departments to employes, for the preparation of calendars and reports of executive meetings and for special investigations and plans, to notify all employes of appointment, promotion or transfer, to make requisitions on and notify the Municipal Civil Service Commission in civil service matters and to perform such other general executive or administrative work as may be assigned bv the head of the department.

QUALIFICATIONS—

1. Such qualifications as are outlined in the Charter of the City of New York.
2. Ability to discharge the duties of the position satisfactory to the appointing officer.
3. Such qualifications as may be required by the Municipal Civil Service Commission.

If the position is classified as exempt, the minimum qualifications shall consist of 1 and 2. If the position is classified as competitive in accordance with the recommendations of the Bureau of Personal Service, the minimum qualifications shall consist of 1 and 3.

COMPENSATION—

Range of annual compensation—$3000 to $5100 inclusive.

Salary rates—$3000, $3240, $3480, $3780, $4080, $4380, $4680, $5100.

SPECIAL REGULATION GOVERNING COMPENSATION—

Persons entering this grade need not necessarily be paid the lowest rate. Fixation of the rate to be paid is conditional upon appraisal under the rules of the Board of Estimate and Apportionment.

EXECUTIVE COUNTY OFFICER GROUP

SYMBOL (X O)

The term Executive County Officer Group is applied to those elective or appointive offices of the Executive Service in which incumbents are required to perform the functions of heads of county offices.

No specific recommendations are made as to the proper grading or salary for these offices.[1]

---

[1]For recommendations regarding the merger of county governments with the city government, or a consolidation of several county establishments, see "Study of County Government within the City of New York and a Plan for Its Reorganization, Prepared by the Commissioner of Accounts and the City Chamberlain," 1915.

LEGISLATIVE SERVICE

SYMBOL (L)

The term Legislative Service is applied to those offices or employments the duties of whose incumbents are to exercise the legislative powers vested by the Charter of the City of New York and by statute in the members of the Board of Aldermen.[1]

[1]See page 10 of the introductory statement.

JUDICIAL SERVICE

SYMBOL (J)

The term Judicial Service is applied to those offices or employments the duties of whose incumbents are to exercise the judicial powers vested by the Charter of the City of New York and by statute in City Magistrates and in Justices of the City Court, the Municipal Court and the Court of Special Sessions.[1]

[1]See page 10 of the introductory statement.

PROFESSIONAL SERVICE.

SYMBOL (O).

The term PROFESSIONAL SERVICE is applied to those offices or employments the duties of whose incumbents are to perform apprentice, routine, advisory, administrative or research work, which is based upon the established principles of and which requires training or experience in a recognized profession.

ACCOUNTANT GROUP

SYMBOL (O A)

The term Accountant Group is applied to those offices or employments of the Professional Service in which incumbents are required to analyze and interpret evidence of financial transactions, to report on the accuracy and significance of records and accounts and the justice of claims, to devise, install and supervise business procedure, financial and auditing methods, records and documents, and to collect and interpret physical and operating data.

GRADE 1 (O A 1)

TITLES OF POSITIONS[1]—

JUNIOR ACCOUNTANT

DUTIES—

The duties of incumbents of these positions, which may or may not involve supervision, are to execute according to general instructions the detail work connected with audits and investigations and reports thereon, and to carry on independently audits and investigations of minor scope.

Examples:

Analyzing and reconciling simple accounts.
Verifying registers and postings to controlling accounts.
Devising forms of incidental records.

QUALIFICATIONS—

1. A certificate granted on the completion of a standard course of instruction in accountancy in an accounting school of recognized standing, or proof of other training or experience in accountancy recognized by the Municipal Civil Service Commission as the equivalent.
2. Such additional qualifications as may be required by the Municipal Civil Service Commission.
3. Not less than two years of experience in Grade 1 of the Bookkeeper Group or in Grade 2 B of the Clerk Group of the Clerical Service or experience in Grade 2 of the Bookkeeper Group or in Grade 3 of the Clerk Group of the Clerical Service.

The minimum qualifications shall consist of 1 and 2 or 2 and 3.

COMPENSATION—

Range of annual compensation—$1260 to $1920 inclusive.

Salary rates—$1260, $1380, $1500, $1620, $1740, $1920.

Persons promoted from Grade 2 of the Bookkeeper Group or Grade 3 of the Clerk Group of the Clerical Service to Grade 1 of the Accountant Group of the Professional Service shall receive the salary rate nearest to that received before promotion and involving no decrease.

---

[1]The following positions are among those appraised by the Bureau of Personal Service in this grade on the basis of duties performed by present incumbents:

Junior Accountant assisting in the audit of stores accounts in the Department of Water Supply, Gas and Electricity.

SPECIAL REGULATION GOVERNING COMPENSATION—

Beginning with the lowest rate, advancement within this grade is conditional upon appraisal under the rules of the Board of Estimate and Apportionment, indicating that the rate requested does not exceed the value of the work to be performed.

GRADE 2 (O A 2)

TITLES OF POSITIONS[1]—

ACCOUNTANT
AUDITOR

DUTIES—

The duties of incumbents of these positions are to carry on independently and to prepare reports on audits, examinations and investigations of wide scope, to devise and install new methods of accounting for large activities or departments, or to supervise and be responsible for the entire work of a large bookkeeping division in a department maintaining a complex accounting system.

Examples:

Analyzing and reconciling intricate accounts.

QUALIFICATIONS—

1. The minimum qualifications prescribed for Grade 1.
2. If appointed by promotion, not less than two years of appropriate experience in Grade 1, or if appointed as the result of an open competitive examination, experience in work of the character and standard of Grade 1.
3. Such additional qualifications as may be required by the Municipal Civil Service Commission.
4. Not less than one year of experience in Grade 3 of the Bookkeeper Group of the Clerical Service.

The minimum qualifications shall consist of 1, 2 and 3, or 3 and 4.

COMPENSATION—

Range of annual compensation--$2100 to $3180 inclusive.

Salary rates—$2100, $2280, $2460, $2700, $2940, $3180.

Persons promoted from Grade 3 of the Bookkeeper Group of the Clerical Service to Grade 2 of the Accountant Group of the Professional Service shall receive the salary rate nearest to that received before promotion and involving no decrease.

SPECIAL REGULATION GOVERNING COMPENSATION—

Persons entering this grade need not necessarily begin at the lowest rate. Fixation of the initial salary rate and advancement within this grade are conditional upon appraisal under the rules of the Board of Estimate and Apportionment, indicating that the rate requested does not exceed the value of the work to be performed.

---

[1]The following positions are among those appraised by the Bureau of Personal Service in this grade on the basis of duties performed by present incumbents:

Accountant in charge of the Division of Audit and Accounts in the office of the President of the Borough of Manhattan.

Accountant in charge of the installation of the general ledger in the Department of Finance.

GRADE 3 (O A 3)

TITLES OF POSITIONS[1]—

SENIOR ACCOUNTANT
SENIOR AUDITOR

DUTIES—

The duties of incumbents of these positions are to supervise and be responsible for audits, investigations and constructive accounting work of the widest scope, excepting those mentioned in Grade 4, to lay out programs for the carrying on of work of this character and to prepare general plans and broad policies relating to methods of accounting and auditing.

QUALIFICATIONS—

1. The minimum qualifications prescribed for Grade 2.
2. If appointed by promotion, not less than three years of appropriate experience in Grade 2, or if appointed as the result of an open competitive examination, experience in work of the character and standard of Grade 2.
3. Such additional qualifications as may be required by the Municipal Civil Service Commission.

COMPENSATION—

Range of annual compensation—$3420 to $4560 inclusive.
Salary rates—$3420, $3660, $3960, $4260, $4560.

SPECIAL REGULATION GOVERNING COMPENSATION—

Persons entering this grade need not necessarily begin at the lowest rate. Fixation of the initial salary rate and advancement within this grade are conditional upon appraisal under the rules of the Board of Estimate and Apportionment, indicating that the rate requested does not exceed the value of the work to be performed.

GRADE 4 (O A 4)

TITLES OF POSITIONS[2]—

CHIEF ACCOUNTANT
CHIEF AUDITOR

DUTIES—

The duties of incumbents of these positions are to act as responsible heads of the bureaus which are charged with devising and installing accounting systems throughout the departments and offices of the city and county governments or with the auditing and reconcilement of the accounts of these offices.

---

[1]The following positions are among those appraised by the Bureau of Personal Service in this grade on the basis of duties performed by present incumbents:

Senior Auditor in charge of the Division of Disbursements of the Auditing Bureau in the Department of Finance.

Senior Auditor of receipts in the Division of Receipts of the Auditing Bureau in the Department of Finance.

[2]The following positions are among those appraised by the Bureau of Personal Service in this grade on the basis of duties performed by present incumbents:

Chief Accountant of the Bureau of Accounts of the Finance Department.

Chief Auditor of accounts of the Bureau of Audit of the Finance Department.

QUALIFICATIONS—

1. The minimum qualifications prescribed for Grade 3.

2. If appointed by promotion, not less than two years of appropriate experience in Grade 3, or if appointed as the result of an open competitive examination, experience in work of the character and standard of Grade 3.

3. Such additional qualifications as may be required by the Municipal Civil Service Commission.

COMPENSATION—

Range of annual compensation—$4860 and up.
Salary rates—$4860, $5280, $5700, $6120.[1]

ARCHITECT GROUP

SYMBOL (O R)

The term Architect Group is applied to those offices or employments of the Professional Service in which incumbents are required to make architectural surveys, studies, designs, plans and specifications for municipal buildings, parks or other municipal projects, and to inspect or to supervise the construction, repair or alteration of such projects.

GRADE 1 (O R 1)

TITLES OF POSITIONS—

ARCHITECTURAL ASSISTANT

DUTIES—

The duties of incumbents of these positions are to perform under supervision architectural apprentice work in field or office.[2]

Examples:

Laying out simple architectural drawings.
Assisting employes in Grades 2 and 3 on assigned details of their work.

QUALIFICATIONS[3]—

1. A degree granted on the completion of a standard course of instruction in an architectural school of recognized standing, or proof of other training recognized by the Municipal Civil Service Commission as the equivalent, but not necessarily any experience in the practice of architecture other than that which is incident to the attainment of these qualifications.

2. Such additional qualifications as may be required by the Municipal Civil Service Commission.

COMPENSATION—

Range of annual compensation—$1020 to $1380 inclusive.
Salary rates—$1020, $1140, $1260, $1380.

---

[1]No recommendation is made above $6120.

[2]See also Grades 1 and 2 of the Inspector of Buildings Group of the Inspectional Service.

[3]It is recommended that the examination for this grade be held in June or July, when the professional schools and universities have closed. Examinations should be such as would attract the best students who have just graduated from professional schools. This grade is not a promotional grade from the Sub-Professional Service. Provision is made for promotion from Grade 1 of the Draftsman Group of the Sub-Professional Service to Grade 2 of this Group. Employes in Grade 1 will compete with employes in Grade 2 of the Draftsman Group for promotion to Grade 2.

GRADE 2 (O R 2)

TITLES OF POSITIONS—

JUNIOR ARCHITECT
JUNIOR ARCHITECT (LANDSCAPE)

DUTIES—

Junior Architect:

The duties of Junior Architects, which may or may not involve supervision, are to execute definite instructions in minor architectural work in field or office.[1]

Examples:

Supervising a group of junior draftsmen, draftsmen or architectural assistants.
Preparing important working drawings, details or sketches.
Inspecting or investigating architectural work.
Solving the easier problems of construction.
Making final inspections on buildings.

Junior Architect (Landscape):

The duties of Junior Architects (Landscape), which may or may not involve supervision, are to execute definite instructions in minor architectural landscape work in field or office.

QUALIFICATIONS—

Junior Architect:

1. The minimum qualifications prescribed for Grade 1.
2. If appointed by promotion, not less than one year of appropriate experience in Grade 1, or if appointed as the result of an open competitive examination, experience in work of the character and standard of Grade 1.
3. Such additional qualifications as may be required by the Municipal Civil Service Commission.
4. Not less than one year of experience in Grade 2 of the Draftsman Group of the Sub-Professional Service.

The minimum qualifications shall consist of 1, 2 and 3, or 3 and 4.

Junior Architect (Landscape):

1. Evidence of the completion of a standard course in landscape architecture in a university or technical school of recognized standing, or proof of other training or experience recognized by the Municipal Civil Service Commission as the equivalent.
2. Experience in design in a landscape architect's office of recognized standing.
3. Such additional qualifications as may be required by the Municipal Civil Service Commission.

COMPENSATION—

Range of annual compensation—$1500 to $2100 inclusive.

Salary rates—$1500, $1620, $1740, $1920, $2100.

Persons promoted from Grade 2 of the Draftsman Group of the Sub-Professional Service to Grade 2 of the Architect Group of the Professional Service shall receive the salary rate nearest to that received before promotion and involving no decrease.

SPECIAL REGULATION GOVERNING COMPENSATION—

Beginning with the lowest rate, advancement within this grade is conditional upon appraisal under the rules of the Board of Estimate and Apportionment, indicating that the rate requested does not exceed the value of the work to be performed.

[1]See also Grade 2 of the Inspector of Buildings Group of the Inspectional Service.

GRADE 3 (O R 3)

TITLES OF POSITIONS[1]—

ASSISTANT ARCHITECT
ASSISTANT ARCHITECT (LANDSCAPE)

DUTIES—

Assistant Architect:

The duties of Assistant Architects, which involve supervision of employes in Grades 1 and 2, are to exercise architectural judgment and skill in and to be responsible for designing, planning, inspecting, constructing and preparing specifications for small building projects or minor divisions of large building projects; or to give critical architectural advice for executive action incident to the designing, planning or construction of such projects.[2]

Assistant Architect (Landscape):

The duties of Assistant Architects (Landscape) are to exercise a high degree of architectural judgment and skill in and to be responsible for designing, planning, inspecting, constructing and preparing specifications for architectural landscape work in parks or other similar projects; or to give critical architectural advice for executive action incident to the designing, planning or construction of such projects.

QUALIFICATIONS—

1. The minimum qualifications prescribed for Grade 2.
2. If appointed by promotion, not less than two years of appropriate experience in Grade 2, or if appointed as the result of an open competitive examination, experience in work of the character and standard of Grade 2.
3. Such additional qualifications as may be required by the Municipal Civil Service Commission.

COMPENSATION—

Range of annual compensation—$2280 to $2940 inclusive.
Salary rates—$2280, $2460, $2700, $2940.

SPECIAL REGULATION GOVERNING COMPENSATION—

Beginning with the lowest rate, advancement within this grade is conditional upon appraisal under the rules of the Board of Estimate and Apportionment, indicating that the rate requested does not exceed the value of the work to be performed.

---

[1]The following positions are among those appraised by the Bureau of Personal Service in this grade on the basis of duties performed by present incumbents:

- Assistant Architect for the Department of Parks, Manhattan.
- Assistant Architect in charge of a group of employes engaged in the preparation of plans for structural steel work.
- Assistant Architect acting as assistant to the Deputy Superintendent of School Buildings in charge of the preparation of plans for new buildings.
- Assistant Architect in charge of writing specifications.
- Assistant Architect responsible for designing.

[2]See also Grade 3 of the Inspector of Buildings Group of the Inspectional Service.

GRADE 4 (O R 4)

TITLES OF POSITIONS[1]—

ARCHITECT
ARCHITECT AND DEPUTY SUPERINTENDENT OF SCHOOL BUILDINGS
ARCHITECT (LANDSCAPE)

DUTIES—

Architect, Architect and Deputy Superintendent of School Buildings:

The duties of incumbents of these positions are to perform executive or supervisory work entailing entire responsibility for a major division of a large architectural department, bureau or project; or to give independent expert or critical architectural advice of a high order for executive action relative to work of this scope.[2]

Architect (Landscape):

The duties of Architects (Landscape) are to perform the highest order of executive or supervisory work entailing entire responsibility for an important department, bureau, division or project of architectural landscape work; or to give independent expert or critical architectural advice of the highest order for executive action.

QUALIFICATIONS—

1. The minimum qualifications prescribed for Grade 3.
2. If appointed by promotion, not less than two years of appropriate experience in Grade 3, or if appointed as the result of an open competitive examination, experience in work of the character and standard of Grade 3.
3. Such additional qualifications as may be required by the Municipal Civil Service Commission.

COMPENSATION—

Range of annual compensation—$3180 to $4560 inclusive.
Salary rates—$3180, $3420, $3660, $3960, $4260, $4560.
Per diem compensation—$25 and up for each full day of service.

SPECIAL REGULATION GOVERNING COMPENSATION—

Persons entering this grade need not necessarily begin at the lowest rate Fixation of the initial salary rate and advancement within this grade are conditional upon appraisal under the rules of the Board of Estimate and Apportionment, indicating that the rate requested does not exceed the value of the work tc be performed.

GRADE 5 (O R 5)

TITLES OF POSITIONS—

SENIOR ARCHITECT
SENIOR ARCHITECT AND DEPUTY SUPERINTENDENT OF SCHOOL BUILDINGS

At the present time there are no positions in this grade.

---

[1]The following positions are among those appraised by the Bureau of Personal Service in this grade on the basis of duties performed by present incumbents:

Architect (Landscape) for the Park Board.
Architect and Deputy Superintendent of School Buildings in charge of the preparation of plans for new buildings in all boroughs.
Architect and Deputy Superintendent of School Buildings in each borough in charge of construction, inspection and the preparation of plans for alterations to buildings.

[2]See also Grade 4 of the Inspector of Buildings Group of the Inspectional Service.

GRADE 6 (O R 6)

TITLES OF POSITIONS[1]—

CHIEF ARCHITECT
CHIEF ARCHITECT AND SUPERINTENDENT OF SCHOOL BUILDINGS
CONSULTING ARCHITECT

DUTIES—

The duties of incumbents of these positions are to perform the highest order of executive or supervisory work, entailing entire responsibility for all architectural work in the largest and most important architectural departments, bureaus or projects, involving the most complex problems of design, construction or maintenance and administration, or to give independent expert or critical architectural advice of the highest order for executive action relative to work of this scope.

QUALIFICATIONS—

1. The minimum qualifications prescribed for Grade 4.
2. If appointed by promotion, not less than four years of appropriate experience in Grade 4 or ten years of appropriate experience in Grade 5, or if appointed as the result of an open competitive examination, experience in work of the character and standard of Grade 4 or Grade 5.
3. Such additional qualifications as may be required by the Municipal Civil Service Commission.

COMPENSATION—

Range of annual compensation $6120 and up.

Salary rates—$6120, $6600, $7200, $7800, $8400, $9000, $9600, $10200.[2]

SPECIAL REGULATION GOVERNING COMPENSATION—

Persons entering this grade need not necessarily begin at the lowest rate. Fixation of the initial salary rate and advancement within this grade are conditional upon appraisal under the rules of the Board of Estimate and Apportionment, indicating that the rate requested does not exceed the value of the work to be performed.

BACTERIOLOGIST GROUP

SYMBOL (O B)

The term Bacteriologist Group is applied to those offices or employments of the Professional Service in which incumbents are required to procure, prepare and mount bacteriological specimens, to examine them microscopically or otherwise, and to diagnose disease on the basis of such examinations; to make and prepare media for the growth of bacteria; to make, prepare for use and administer antitoxins, serums and vaccines in the prevention or cure of disease, and to perform such other services as may be required in the procuring, preparation, examination and diagnosis of bacteriological specimens.

GRADE 1 (O B 1)

TITLES OF POSITIONS—

ASSISTANT BACTERIOLOGIST

DUTIES—

The duties of incumbents of these positions are to exercise independent judgment in and to be responsible for bacteriological examinations and to perform research work under supervision.

---

[1]The following positions are among those appraised by the Bureau of Personal Service in this grade on the basis of duties performed by present incumbents:

Chief Architect and Superintendent of School Buildings in the Department of Education.

[2]No recommendation is made above $10200.

Examples:

Making bacteriological examinations of milk, water, etc.
Examining specimens of sputum, diphtheria culture.
Producing toxins, antitoxins, vaccines.
Making disinfection tests.
Conducting research studies in animal experimentation to discover causes of disease.

QUALIFICATIONS—

1. A medical degree granted on the completion of a standard course of instruction in a medical school of recognized standing.
2. Evidence of the completion of a standard course in bacteriology, not less than two years in length, in a college or university of recognized standing.
3. Experience as either interne or assistant in a bacteriological or biological laboratory of recognized standing.
4. Such additional qualifications as may be required by the Municipal Civil Service Commission.

The minimum qualifications shall consist of either 1, 3 and 4, or 2, 3 and 4.

COMPENSATION—

Range of annual compensation for full-time service—$1500 to $2100 inclusive.

Salary rates—$1500, $1620, $1740, $1920, $2100.

Range of annual compensation for part-time service, averaging not less than 28 hours a week—$1200 to $1800 inclusive.

Salary rates—$1200, $1320, $1440, $1560, $1680, $1800.

SPECIAL REGULATION GOVERNING COMPENSATION—

Beginning with the lowest rate, advancement within this grade is conditional upon appraisal under the rules of the Board of Estimate and Apportionment, indicating that the rate reauested does not exceed the value of the work to be performed.

GRADE 2 (O B 2)

TITLES OF POSITIONS[1]—

BACTERIOLOGIST

DUTIES—

The duties of incumbents of these positions, which may or may not involve supervision of employes in Grade 1, are to supervise and be responsible for special laboratory work in a division of the bacteriological service or to perform independent experiments and to conduct original research of wide scope and importance.

Examples:

Directing rabies treatment and experimentation.
Directing original investigation and animal experimentation to discover causes and means of prevention of disease.

QUALIFICATIONS—

1. The minimum qualifications prescribed for Grade 1, including a medical degree granted on the completion of a standard course of instruction in a medical school of recognized standing.

---

[1]The following positions are among those appraised by the Bureau of Personal Service in this grade on the basis of duties performed by present incumbents:

Bacteriologist in charge of the smallpox vaccine laboratories of the Department of Health.

2. If appointed by promotion, not less than two years of appropriate experience in Grade 1, or if appointed as the result of an open competitive examination, experience in work of the character and standard of Grade 1.

3. Such additional qualifications as may be required by the Municipal Civil Service Commission.

COMPENSATION—

Range of annual compensation for full-time service—$2280 to $3180 inclusive.

Salary rates—$2280, $2460, $2700, $2940, $3180.

Range of annual compensation for part-time service, averaging not less than 28 hours a week—$1980 to $2820 inclusive.

Salary rates—$1980, $2160, $2340, $2580, $2820.

SPECIAL REGULATION GOVERNING COMPENSATION—

Beginning with the lowest rate, advancement within this grade is conditional upon appraisal under the rules of the Board of Estimate and Apportionment, indicating that the rate requested does not exceed the value of the work to be performed.

GRADE 3 (O B 3)

TITLES OF POSITIONS—

SENIOR BACTERIOLOGIST

At the present time there are no positions in this grade.

GRADE 4 (O B 4)

TITLES OF POSITIONS—

DIRECTOR OF HEALTH LABORATORIES

DUTIES—

The duties of incumbents of these positions, which require the highest order of specialized knowledge, are to supervise and be responsible for the entire work of a large bacteriological laboratory, or a group of a bacteriological and other laboratories, and to furnish expert and critical advice of the highest order in the practice of bacteriology.

QUALIFICATIONS—

1. Experience in an administrative capacity in a large bacteriological and chemical laboratory, together with extended experience and notable achievement in independent bacteriological and chemical research.

2. Such additional qualifications as may be required by the Municipal Civil Service Commission.

COMPENSATION—

Range of annual compensation for full-time service—$5100 and up.

Salary rates—$5100, $5520, $5940.[1]

SPECIAL REGULATION GOVERNING COMPENSATION—

Persons entering this grade need not necessarily begin at the lowest rate. Fixation of the initial salary rate and advancement within this grade are conditional upon appraisal under the rules of the Board of Estimate and Apportionment, indicating that the rate requested does not exceed the value of the work to be performed.

---

[1]No recommendation is made above $5940.

CHAPLAIN GROUP.

SYMBOL (O C)

The term Chaplain Group is applied to those offices or employments of the Professional Service in which incumbents are required to minister to the religious needs and comfort of persons in the employ, care or custody of the city.

GRADE 1 (O C 1)

TITLES OF POSITIONS[1]—

CHAPLAIN

DUTIES—

The duties of incumbents of these positions are to minister to the religious needs and comfort of persons in the employ, care or custody of the city.

COMPENSATION—

Salary rate for persons giving full-time service or on call at all times—$900 with or without maintenance.

Salary rate for part-time service, averaging not less than one day a week—$480 without maintenance.

If more than one chaplain of one denomination is employed in an institution or group of institutions, the senior chaplain shall receive $900 and his assistant $600.

CHEMIST AND PHYSICIST GROUP

SYMBOL (O K)

The term Chemist and Physicist Group is applied to those offices or employments of the Professional Service in which incumbents are required to perform routine or research work in chemistry or physics involving the making and recording of chemical or physical tests or analyses, to diagnose the contents of substances, to testify in court regarding their analyses and to perform such other services as may be required in the analysis and testing of substances.

GRADE 1 (O K 1)

TITLES OF POSITIONS—

JUNIOR CHEMIST
JUNIOR PHYSICIST

DUTIES—

The duties of incumbents of these positions are to perform under supervision definite details of work in a chemical or physical laboratory.

Examples:

Analyzing asphalt, milk, rubber, paints, ink, cement, rope, paper, drugs, water, foods, etc.

QUALIFICATIONS—

1. A degree in science granted on the completion of a standard course of instruction with chemistry or physics as the major subject in a college or technical school of recognized standing, or proof of other training recognized by the Municipal Civil Service Commission as the equivalent.
2. Such additional qualifications as may be required by the Municipal Civil Service Commission.

---

[1]The following positions are among those appraised by the Bureau of Personal Service in this grade on the basis of duties performed by present incumbents:

Chaplain for the Fire Department.
Chaplain at the Workhouse on Blackwells Island.

COMPENSATION—

Range of annual compensation for full-time service[1]—$1020 to $1380 inclusive.
Salary rates—$1020, $1140, $1260, $1380.
Monthly rate[2]—$100.

GRADE 2 (O K 2)

TITLES OF POSITIONS[3]—

ASSISTANT CHEMIST
ASSISTANT CHEMIST (FOOD AND DRUGS)
ASSISTANT PHYSICIST

DUTIES—

Assistant Chemist, Assistant Physicist:

The duties of Assistant Chemists and Assistant Physicists, which may or may not involve supervision of laboratory assistants, are to take charge of and be responible for a division of chemical or physical work in a large laboratory or for all the chemical or physical work in a minor laboratory, or to do research work under supervision.

Examples:

Taking charge of the analysis of asphalt, milk, rubber, paints, ink, cement, rope, paper, drugs, water, foods, etc.
Inspecting the manufacture and composition of paving materials.

Assistant Chemist (Food and Drugs):

The duties of Assistant Chemists (Food and Drugs), which may or may not involve supervision of laboratory assistants, are to take charge of and be responsible for the chemical analysis of food and drugs in a large laboratory and to do research work in the analysis of food and drugs under supervision.

QUALIFICATIONS—

Assistant Chemist, Assistant Physicist:

1. The minimum qualifications prescribed for Grade 1.
2. If appointed by promotion, not less than one year of appropriate experience in Grade 1, or if appointed as the result of an open competitive examination, experience in work of the character and standard of Grade 1.
3. Such additional qualifications as may be required by the Municipal Civil Service Commission.

Assistant Chemist (Food and Drugs):

1. The minimum qualifications prescribed for Grade 1.
2. Experience in the chemical analysis of food and drugs.
3. Such additional qualifications as may be required by the Municipal Civil Service Commission.

COMPENSATION—

Range of annual compensation for full-time service—$1500 to $2100 inclusive.
Salary rates—$1500, $1620, $1740, $1920, $2100.

Range of annual compensation for part-time service, averaging not less than 18 hours a week—$1020 to $1380 inclusive.
Salary rates—$1020, $1140, $1260, $1380.

---

[1]Where work will last continuously throughout the year, the annual rate shall be paid.

[2]Where work is temporary and will not last continuously throughout the year, but is measurable by months, the monthly rate shall be paid.

[3]The following positions are among those appraised by the Bureau of Personal Service in this grade on the basis of duties performed by present incumbents:

Assistant Chemist in charge of the testing of supplies for the Board of Education.

SPECIAL REGULATION GOVERNING COMPENSATION—

Beginning with the lowest rate, advancement within this grade is conditional upon appraisal under the rules of the Board of Estimate and Apportionment, indicating that the rate requested does not exceed the value of the work to be performed.

GRADE 3 (O K 3)

TITLES OF POSITIONS[1]—

CHEMIST
CHEMIST (MICROANALYST)
CHEMIST (PHARMACEUTICAL)
PHYSICIST

DUTIES—

Chemist, Physicist:

The duties of Chemists and Physicists, which may or may not involve supervision of employes in Grades 1 and 2 and of other assistants, and which require a high degree of skill and judgment in the practice of chemistry or physics, are to be responsible for all the chemical or physical work in important laboratories and to initiate and carry out difficult chemical or physical research work.

Chemist (Microanalyst):

The duties of Chemists (Microanalyst), which may or may not involve supervision of employes in Grades 1 and 2 and of laboratory assistants, are to take charge of and be responsible for microanalysis of food and drugs and to initiate and carry out difficult research work in microanalysis.

Chemist (Pharmaceutical):

The duties of Chemists (Pharmaceutical), which may or may not involve supervision of employes in Grades 1 and 2 and of laboratory assistants, are to take charge of and be responsible for chemical analysis of drugs, patent and proprietary medicines and other medicines and to initiate and carry out difficult pharmaceutical research work.

QUALIFICATIONS—

Chemist, Physicist:

1. The minimum qualifications prescribed for Grade 2.
2. If appointed by promotion, not less than two years of appropriate experience in Grade 2, or if appointed as the result of an open competitive examination, experience in work of the character and standard of Grade 2.
3. Such additional qualifications as may be required by the Municipal Civil Service Commission.

---

[1]The following positions are among those appraised by the Bureau of Personal Service in this grade on the basis of duties performed by present incumbents:

Chemist or Physicist in charge of all analytical work of the Central Testing Laboratory or of the laboratories of the Bureau of Highways in the Borough of Manhattan or Brooklyn.

Chemist in charge of the drug laboratories of the Department of Public Charities.

Chemist or Physicist in charge of all routine analysis in the Department of Water Supply, Gas and Electricity.

Chemist (Microanalyst) in the Bureau of Food and Drugs in the Department of Health.

Chemist (Microanalyst):

1. The minimum qualifications prescribed for Grade 2.
2. Experience in microanalysis of food and drugs.
3. Such additional qualifications as may be required by the Municipal Civil Service Commission.

Chemist (Pharmaceutical):

1. The minimum qualifications prescribed for Grade 2.
2. Experience in the practise of pharmaceutical chemistry.
3. Such additional qualifications as may be required by the Municipal Civil Service Commission.

COMPENSATION—

Range of annual compensation for full-time service—$2280 to $3180 inclusive.
Salary rates—$2280, $2460, $2700, $2940, $3180.

SPECIAL REGULATION GOVERNING COMPENSATION—

Persons entering this grade need not necessarily begin at the lowest rate. Fixation of the initial salary rate and advancement within this grade are conditional upon appraisal under the rules of the Board of Estimate and Apportionment, indicating that the rate requested does not exceed the value of the work to be performed.

GRADE 4 (O K 4)

TITLES OF POSITIONS—

SENIOR CHEMIST
SENIOR PHYSICIST

At the present time there are no positions in this grade.

GRADE 5 (O K 5)

TITLES OF POSITIONS—

DIRECTOR (CENTRAL TESTING LABORATORY)

DUTIES—

The duties of incumbents of these positions, which require the highest degree of specialized knowledge of chemistry and physics, and which involve the application of the most advanced scientific methods, are to direct and to be entirely responsible for an entire chemical and physical department or bureau, and to perform or direct the most difficult chemical and physical research work.

QUALIFICATIONS—

1. Experience in an administrative capacity in a large chemical and physical laboratory, together with extended experience and notable achievement in independent chemical or physical research.
2. Such additional qualifications as may be required by the Municipal Civil Service Commission.

COMPENSATION—

Range of annual compensation—$5100 and up.
Salary rates—$5100, $5520, $5940.[1]

SPECIAL REGULATION GOVERNING COMPENSATION—

Persons entering this grade need not necessarily begin at the lowest rate. Fixation of the initial salary rate and advancement within this grade are conditional upon appraisal under the rules of the Board of Estimate and Apportionment, indicating that the rate requested does not exceed the value of the work to be performed.

---

[1]No recommendation is made above $5940.

DENTIST GROUP

SYMBOL (O D)

The term Dentist Group is applied to those offices or employments of the Professional Service in which incumbents are required to perform such services in the investigation, reporting, prevention, care and treatment of diseases or abnormal conditions of the teeth and adjoining structures as may lawfully be performed by dentists.

GRADE 1 (O D 1)

TITLES OF POSITIONS—

DENTAL INTERNE

DUTIES—

The duties of incumbents of these positions are to execute under supervision dental work commonly required of a dental interne in the care and treatment of hospital patients or institutional inmates.

QUALIFICATIONS—

1. Either a professional degree granted on the completion of a standard course of instruction in a dental college of recognized standing, or a license to practice dentistry issued by the Board of Regents of the University of the State of New York, but not necessarily any experience in the practice of dentistry other than that which is incident to the attainment of these qualifications.
2. Such additional qualifications as may be required by the Municipal Civil Service Commission.

COMPENSATION—

Range of annual compensation—$120 to $240 inclusive, with maintenance.
Salary rates—$120, $240.

GRADE 2 (O D 2)

TITLES OF POSITIONS[1]—

DENTIST

DUTIES—

The duties of incumbents of these positions, which require a high degree of dental skill, are to perform all operations common to general dental practice either independently in a small unit or under supervision in large hospitals or groups of clinics.

Examples:

Filling and cleansing teeth.
Correcting dental deformities.

QUALIFICATIONS—

1. The minimum qualifications prescribed for Grade 1, including a license to practice dentistry issued by the Board of Regents of the University of the State of New York.
2. If appointed by promotion, not less than one year of appropriate experience in Grade 1, or if appointed as the result of an open competitive examination, experience in work of the character and standard of Grade 1.
3. Such additional qualifications as may be required by the Municipal Civil Service Commission.

---

[1]The following positions are among those appraised by the Bureau of Personal Service in this grade on the basis of duties performed by present incumbents:

Dentist employed in the dental clinics of the Bureau of Child Hygiene or the Bureau of Preventable Diseases of the Department of Health.

COMPENSATION—

Range of annual compensation for full-time service in hospitals or institutions—$900 to $1380 inclusive, with maintenance.

Salary rates—$900, $1020, $1140, $1260, $1380.

Range of annual compensation for part-time service, averaging not less than 18 hours a week—$1020 to $1380 inclusive.

Salary rates—$1020, $1140, $1260, $1380.

Range of annual compensation for part-time service, averaging not less than 24 hours a week—$1140 to $1500 inclusive.

Salary rates—$1140, $1260, $1380, $1500.

GRADE 3 (O D 3)

TITLES OF POSITIONS[1]—

SUPERVISING DENTIST

DUTIES—

The duties of incumbents of these positions, which involve supervision of employes in Grades 1 and 2, are to supervise and be entirely responsible for the dental work of a large hospital or institution, a group of hospitals or institutions, or the dental clinics of a department, and in addition to execute dental work requiring the highest degree of dental skill and judgment.

QUALIFICATIONS—

1. The minimum qualifications prescribed for Grade 2.
2. If appointed by promotion, not less than two years of appropriate experience in Grade 2, or if appointed as the result of an open competitive examination, experience in work of the character and standard of Grade 2.
3. Such additional qualifications as may be required by the Municipal Civil Service Commission.

COMPENSATION—

Range of annual compensation for full-time service in hospitals or institutions—$1500 to $1740 inclusive, with maintenance.

Salary rates—$1500, $1620, $1740.

Range of compensation for part-time service, averaging not less than 18 hours a week—$1500 to $1740 inclusive.

Salary rates—$1500, $1620, $1740.

SPECIAL REGULATION GOVERNING COMPENSATION—

Beginning with the lowest rate, advancement within this grade is conditional upon appraisal under the rules of the Board of Estimate and Apportionment, indicating that the rate requested does not exceed the value of the work to be performed.

ENGINEER GROUP

SYMBOL (O E)

The term Engineer Group is applied to those offices or employments of the Professional Service in which incumbents are required to conduct surveys, to prepare, supervise or investigate designs, plans, estimates, specifications and contracts or to construct, operate, maintain and inspect such projects and works as highways, bridges, transportation, harbor and terminal facilities, buildings, and such projects and works as are incidental to the production, distribution and utilization of light, heat and power, the collection, purification and distribution of water, and the collection and disposal of sewage, garbage, snow and other municipal waste, or to perform services in organizing and reorganizing administrative units for which training and experience in engineering are conspicuous qualifications.

---

[1]The following positions are among those appraised by the Bureau of Personal Service in this grade on the basis of duties performed by present incumbents:

Supervising Dentist in the dental clinics in the Department of Health.

GRADE 1 (O E 1)

TITLES OF POSITIONS—

ENGINEERING ASSISTANT

DUTIES—

The duties of incumbents of these positions are to perform under supervision elementary or apprentice work in field, works or office in one or more of the specialized engineering branches.[1]

Examples:

Using surveying, measuring and drafting instruments, engineering tables and diagrams.

Inspecting or investigating minor details of engineering work and materials.

Computing.

Assisting employes in Grades 2 and 3 on assigned details of their work.

QUALIFICATIONS[2]—

1. Such training in civil, mechanical, electrical, sanitary or other engineering branches as is evidenced by a professional degree granted on the completion of a standard course of instruction in an engineering school of recognized standing, or proof of other training in engineering recognized by the Municipal Civil Service Commission as the equivalent, but not necessarily any experience in the practice of engineering other than that which is incident to the attainment of such qualifications.

2. Such additional qualifications as may be required by the Municipal Civil Service Commission.

COMPENSATION—

Range of annual compensation—$1020 to $1380 inclusive.
Salary rates—$1020, $1140, $1260, $1380.

GRADE 2 (O E 2)

TITLES OF POSITIONS—

JUNIOR ENGINEER
JUNIOR ENGINEER (CIVIL)
JUNIOR ENGINEER (ELECTRICAL)
JUNIOR ENGINEER (MECHANICAL)
JUNIOR ENGINEER (SANITARY)

DUTIES—

The duties of incumbents of these positions, which may or may not be supervisory in character, are to execute definite instructions in a minor division of engineering work in field, works, or office.[3]

---

[1]See also Grades 1 and 2 of the Inspector of Public Works, Inspector of Buildings and Inspector of Electricity and Lighting Groups of the Inspectional Service.

[2]It is recommended that the examination for this grade be held in June or July, when the professional schools and universities have closed. Examinations should be such as would attract the best students who have just graduated from professional schools. This grade is not a promotional grade from the Sub-Professional Service. Provision is made for promotion from Grade 2 of the Draftsman and Instrumentman Groups of the Sub-Professional Service to Grade 2 of this group. Employes in Grade 1 will compete with employes in Grade 2 of the Draftsman and Instrumentman Groups for promotion to Grade 2.

[3]See also Grade 2 of the Inspector of Public Works, Inspector of Buildings and Inspector of Electricity and Lighting Groups of the Inspectional Service.

DUTIES—

Assistant Engineer, Assistant Engineer (Civil), Assistant Engineer (Electrical), Assistant Engineer (Mechanical), Assistant Engineer (Sanitary):

The duties of incumbents of these positions are to exercise engineering judgment and to assume responsibility in making studies and computations necessary to the preparation of plans, designs, specifications and contracts for or in supervising or inspecting construction work on a minor section of a large engineering project, or a major section of a small engineering project; or in the operation of a completed section of a project of either kind; or to make under supervision engineering investigations for executive action, incident to the criticism of the design, plan, construction or operation of the above projects.[1]

Examples:

Independently designing and preparing plans for more important work.

Supervising:

A large squad or division or small bureau in designing and preparing plans, preparing estimates, assessment lists, specifications.

Engineering examinations of plans and specifications for new buildings and alterations.

Inspections of new buildings and alterations.

Assuming responsible charge of:

The construction, installation or operation of structures, plants or appurtenances for a division under the distribution, pumping, watershed, power production, purification or disposal plant functions or a combination of these functions; installation of a heating, lighting or electrical plant.

The construction, maintenance or repair of a system of sewers, conduits, or highways, of bridges, viaducts, tunnels, piers, bulkheads, retaining walls, or of public buildings, etc.

Topographical or sub-surface surveys.

Preparation of street layout and grades.

Making independent engineering investigations and reports relating to:

Encroachments, pavement conditions and valuations.

Sewer construction, garbage, snow and sewage disposal.

Traffic studies and statistics for local improvements.

Map changes, drainage plans and street opening proceedings.

Unauthorized structures, applications for franchises.

Operation of refrigeration plants.

Making:

Engineering inspections, investigations, estimates and reports for municipal improvements, including requests for appropriations of public funds, approval of contracts, plans and specifications for modifications of contemplated improvements for work under construction or completed, or for adjustment of claims or audit.

Engineering investigations incident to the preparation of standard specifications for work, supplies, material, equipment and methods.

Assistant Engineer (Power Plant Supervision):

The duties of Assistant Engineers (Power Plant Supervision) are to be in responsible charge of all mechanical equipment and of the plant and works employed in the production, distribution and utilization of heat, light and power for the various institutions or buildings of a department, including responsibility for organization and equipment, for economy in operation, and for new installations where required.

---

[1]See also Grade 3 of the Inspector of Public Works, Inspector of Buildings and Inspector of Electricity and Lighting Groups of the Inspectional Service.

QUALIFICATIONS—

1. The minimum qualifications prescribed for Grade 2.
2. If appointed by promotion, not less than two years of appropriate experience in Grade 2, or if appointed as the result of an open competitive examination, experience in work of the character and standard of Grade 2.
3. Such additional qualifications as may be required by the Municipal Civil Service Commission.

COMPENSATION[1]—

Range of annual compensation—$2280 to $3180 inclusive.
Salary rates—$2280, $2460, $2700, $2940, $3180.

SPECIAL REGULATIONS GOVERNING COMPENSATION—

Assistant Engineer, Assistant Engineer (Civil), Assistant Engineer (Electrical), Assistant Engineer (Mechanical), Assistant Engineer (Sanitary):

Beginning with the lowest rate, advancement within this grade is conditional upon appraisal under the rules of the Board of Estimate and Apportionment, indicating that the rate requested does not exceed the value of the work to be performed.

Assistant Engineer (Power Plant Supervision):

Persons entering this grade need not necessarily begin at the lowest rate. Fixation of the initial salary rate and advancement within this grade are conditional upon appraisal under the rules of the Board of Estimate and Apportionment, indicating that the rate requested does not exceed the value of the work to be performed.

GRADE 4 (O E 4)

TITLES OF POSITIONS[2]—

SENIOR ASSISTANT ENGINEER
SENIOR ASSISTANT ENGINEER (CIVIL)
SENIOR ASSISTANT ENGINEER (ELECTRICAL)
SENIOR ASSISTANT ENGINEER (MECHANICAL)
SENIOR ASSISTANT ENGINEER (SANITARY)

---

[1] Appropriate deductions from salary will be made in case of Assistant Engineers receiving part or full maintenance.

[2] The following positions are among those appraised by the Bureau of Personal Service in this grade on the basis of duties performed by present incumbents:

Senior Assistant Engineer (Civil) acting as surveyor in the Department of Taxes and Assessments.
Senior Assistant Engineer in charge of the maintenance and reconstruction of a large bridge, such as the Brooklyn, Williamsburg, Queensboro or Manhattan Bridge.
Senior Assistant Engineer in charge of the Division of Interior Electrical Inspection in the Department of Water Supply, Gas and Electricity.
Senior Assistant Engineer in the Bureau of Highways, Brooklyn.
Senior Assistant Engineer in the Bureau of Sewers, Manhattan.
Senior Assistant Engineer of the Department of Public Charities.
Senior Assistant Engineer in charge of the Bureau of Design and Survey, The Bronx.

DUTIES—

The duties of incumbents of these positions are to assume responsibility for a major division of work on a large engineering project, including its plan, design, construction, inspection or operation; or to assume responsibility for the whole of a small engineering project, including its plan, design, construction, inspection or operation; or to give independent critical engineering advice for executive action incident to the plan, design, construction or operation of such projects.

Examples:

Supervising a major bureau of design.

Supervising the operation of a combination of the distribution, pumping or water shed functions for an entire borough.

Supervising the installation or operation of a major heating, lighting or electrical plant.

Supervising the construction, maintenance or repair of a major division of sewers, conduits, highways, bridges, water mains, aqueducts, reservoirs, viaducts, tunnels, public buildings, piers, bulkheads, retaining walls, etc.

Supervising or making independently the most important engineering investigations, inspections, estimates and reports for municipal improvements, including requests for appropriations of public funds, approval of contracts, plans, specifications or modifications, adjustment of claims or audits on work contemplated, under construction, or completed.

Supervising engineering investigations in the preparation of standard specifications for work, salaries, supplies, equipment, materials or methods.

Supervising engineering investigations of local improvements, map changes, drainage plans, street opening proceedings, applications for franchises, etc.

QUALIFICATIONS—

1. The minimum qualifications prescribed for Grade 3.

2. If appointed by promotion, not less than two years of appropriate experience in Grade 3, or if appointed as the result of an open competitive examination, experience in work of the character and standard of Grade 3.

3. Such additional qualifications as may be required by the Municipal Civil Service Commission.

COMPENSATION[1]—

Range of annual compensation—$3420 to $4560 inclusive.

Salary rates—$3420, $3660, $3960, $4260, $4560.

SPECIAL REGULATION GOVERNING COMPENSATION—

Beginning with the lowest rate, advancement within this grade is conditional upon appraisal under the rules of the Board of Estimate and Apportionment, indicating that the rate requested does not exceed the value of the work to be performed.

---

[1]Appropriate deductions from salary will be made in the case of Senior Assistant Engineers receiving part or full maintenance.

GRADE 5 (O E 5)[1]

TITLES OF POSITIONS[2]—

ENGINEER
ENGINEER (CIVIL)
ENGINEER (ELECTRICAL)
ENGINEER (MECHANICAL)
ENGINEER (SANITARY)

DUTIES—

The duties of incumbents of these positions, which require a high order of executive ability and specialized knowledge, are to assume responsibility for a large and important engineering department, bureau, division or project involving complex problems of construction or maintenance and administration, or to give independent expert or critical engineering advice of a high order for executive action relative to work of this scope.

QUALIFICATIONS—

1. The minimum qualifications prescribed for Grade 4.
2. If appointed by promotion, not less than two years of appropriate experience in Grade 4, or if appointed as the result of an open competitive examination, experience in work of the character and standard of Grade 4.
3. Such additional qualifications as may be required by the Municipal Civil Service Commission.

COMPENSATION—

Range of annual compensation—$4860 to $5700 inclusive.
Salary rates—$4860, $5280, $5700.

SPECIAL REGULATION GOVERNING COMPENSATION—

Beginning with the lowest rate, advancement within this grade is conditional upon appraisal under the rules of the Board of Estimate and Apportionment, indicating that the rate requested does not exceed the value of the work to be performed.

---

[1]For purposes of civil service classification and grading, Grades 5 and 6 constitute one grade.

[2]The following positions are among those appraised by the Bureau of Personal Service in this grade on the basis of duties performed by present incumbents:

Engineers in the Bureau of Contract Supervision under the Board of Estimate and Apportionment.
Engineer in charge of the Topographical Bureau, Brooklyn.
Engineer in charge of sewer work in the Bureau of Sewers and Highways, The Bronx.
Engineer of the Topographical Bureau, Queens.

GRADE 6 (O E 6)[1]

TITLES OF POSITIONS[2]—

CHIEF ENGINEER
CONSULTING ENGINEER

DUTIES—

The duties of incumbents of these positions, which require the highest order of executive or advisory ability, are to assume entire responsibility for all engineering work in the largest and most important engineering departments, bureaus or projects, involving the most complex problems of construction or maintenance and administration, or to give independent expert or critical engineering advice of the highest order for executive action relative to work of this scope.

QUALIFICATIONS—

1. The minimum qualifications prescribed for Grade 5.
2. If appointed by promotion, not less than two years of appropriate experience in Grade 5, or if appointed as the result of an open competitive examination, experience in work of the character and standard of Grade 5.
3. Such additional qualifications as may be required by the Municipal Civil Service Commission.

COMPENSATION—

Range of annual compensation—$6120 and up.
Salary rates—$6120, $6600, $7200, $7800, $8400, $9000, $9600, $10200.[3]
Per diem compensation—$25 and up for each full day of service.

---

[1] For purposes of civil service classification and grading, Grades 5 and 6 constitute one grade.

[2] The following positions are appraised at the present time in this grade:

Consulting Engineers in all boroughs.
2 Consulting Engineers in the Board of Estimate and Apportionment, now known as Chief and Deputy Chief Engineers in the Bureau of Public Improvements.
1 Chief Engineer of the Bureau of Franchises of the Board of Estimate and Apportionment.
1 Chief Engineer of the Bureau of Contract Supervision of the Board of Estimate and Apportionment.
1 Consulting Engineer in the Department of Water Supply, Gas and Electricity, now known as the Chief Engineer of that Department.
1 Chief Engineer of the Department of Water Supply, Gas and Electricity, now known as the Deputy Chief Engineer of that department.
1 Chief Engineer in the Department of Plant and Structures.
1 Consulting Engineer in the Department of Docks and Ferries, now known as Chief Engineer of the Department of Docks and Ferries.
1 Chief Engineer in the Bureau of Sewers, Manhattan.
1 Chief Engineer in the Bureau of Highways, Manhattan.
1 Chief Engineer in the Bureau of Sewers, Brooklyn.
1 Chief Engineer in the Bureau of Highways, Brooklyn.
1 Chief Engineer in the Bureau of Sewers and Highways, The Bronx.
1 Chief Engineer in the Bureau of Sewers and Highways, Queens.
1 Chief Engineer of Light and Power in the Department of Water Supply, Gas and Electricity.
1 Chief Electrical Engineer in charge of the installation of the new fire alarm telegraph system of the Fire Department. This is a temporary position.

The Board of Estimate and Apportionment will list specifically by departments such additional positions as it considers properly appraised in this grade.

[3] No recommendation is made above $10200.

SPECIAL REGULATION GOVERNING COMPENSATION—

Persons entering this grade need not necessarily begin at the lowest rate. Fixation of the initial salary rate and advancement within this grade are conditional upon appraisal under the rules of the Board of Estimate and Apportionment, indicating that the rate requested does not exceed the value of the work to be performed.

FORESTER GROUP

SYMBOL (O O)

The term Forester Group is applied to those offices or employments of the Professional Service in which incumbents are required to supervise the work of planting, cultivating, conserving and protecting from destructive insect life, fungus and other diseases, trees, shrubs and plants in public parks or streets.

GRADE 1 (O O 1)

TITLES OF POSITIONS—

FORESTER

DUTIES—

The duties of incumbents of these positions are to make studies, inspections and specifications relating to the conservation of trees, shrubs and plants and their protection from insects, fungus, or other parasites and diseases; to plan, supervise and inspect the work of all the forces employed in spraying, pruning, trimming, planting and otherwise caring for trees, shrubs and plants in the public parks, streets or nurseries of one or more boroughs; to supervise the issuance of permits for removing or planting trees, erecting poles, stringing ropes or wires, moving houses, or for other acts which may involve injury to trees or shrubs.

QUALIFICATIONS—

1. Such training in forestry as is evidenced by a degree granted on the completion of a standard course of instruction in a forestry school of recognized standing, or proof of other training recognized by the Municipal Civil Service Commission as the equivalent.
2. Experience in the practice of forestry.
3. Such additional qualifications as may be required by the Municipal Civil Service Commission.

COMPENSATION—

Range of annual compensation—$2100 and up.
Salary rates—$2100, $2280, $2460, $2700.[1]

SPECIAL REGULATION GOVERNING COMPENSATION—

Beginning with the lowest rate, advancement within this grade is conditional upon appraisal under the rules of the Board of Estimate and Apportionment, indicating that the rate requested does not exceed the value of the work to be performed.

LAWYER GROUP

SYMBOL (O L)

The term Lawyer Group is applied to those offices or employments of the Professional Service in which incumbents are required to conduct actions and proceedings in which the city, or a county or borough contained therein, a department, or an officer thereof, is a party or is interested, or to render legal advice or assistance to public officers.

---

[1]No recommendation is made above $2700.

GRADE 1 (O L 1)

TITLES OF POSITIONS—

JUNIOR LAW ASSISTANT

DUTIES—

The duties of incumbents of these positions are to perform under supervision definite details of legal work.

Examples:

Collecting legal authorities for briefs or opinions.
Assembling facts and exhibits for trials.
Answering calendar.
Preparing papers in actions and proceedings.
Taxing bills of costs.
Entering orders and judgments.

QUALIFICATIONS[1]—

1. Either a degree granted on the completion of a standard course of instruction in a law school of recognized standing, or a certificate or record of admission to the bar in the State of New York, but not necessarily any experience in legal work other than that which is incident to the attainment of these qualifications.

2. Such additional qualifications as may be required by the Municipal Civil Service Commission.

COMPENSATION—

Range of annual compensation—$1020 to $1380 inclusive.
Salary rates—$1020, $1140, $1260, $1380.

GRADE 2 (O L 2)

TITLES OF POSITIONS[2]—

JUNIOR ASSISTANT CORPORATION COUNSEL
JUNIOR LEGAL EXAMINER

DUTIES—

The duties of incumbents of these positions are to conduct less important cases, to assist in more important cases and to perform other legal work not involving great responsibility under advice or direction of other counsel.

Examples:

Preparing memoranda of law.
Arguing incidental motions.
Assisting in the preparation and trial of cases.
Conducting the trial of routine or less difficult cases.

---

[1]It is recommended that the examination for this grade be held in June or July, when the professional schools and universities have closed. Examinations should be such as would attract the best students who have just graduated from professional schools. This grade is not a promotional grade from the Sub-Professional Service. Provision is made for promotion from Grade 2 of the Law Clerk Group of the Sub-Professional Service to Grade 2 of this Group. Employes in Grade 1 will compete with employes in Grade 2 of the Law Clerk Group for promotion to Grade 2.

[2]The following positions are among those appraised by the Bureau of Personal Service in this grade on the basis of duties performed by present incumbents:

Junior Assistant Corporation Counsel engaged in helping Assistants to prepare for trial actions on contract.

Junior Assistant Corporation Counsel engaged in trying short weight cases in the lower courts.

QUALIFICATIONS—

1. A certificate or record of admission to the bar in the State of New York.

2. If appointed by promotion, not less than one year of appropriate experience in Grade 1, or if appointed as the result of an open competitive examination, experience in work of the character and standard of Grade 1.

3. Such additional qualifications as may be required by the Municipal Civil Service Commission.

4. Not less than one year of experience in Grade 2 of the Law Clerk Group of the Sub-Professional Service.

The minimum qualifications shall consist of 1, 2 and 3, or 1, 3 and 4.

COMPENSATION—

Range of annual compensation—$1500 to $2280 inclusive.

Salary rates—$1500, $1620, $1740, $1920, $2100, $2280.

Persons promoted from Grade 2 of the Law Clerk Group of the Sub-Professional Service to Grade 2 of the Lawyer Group of the Professional Service shall receive the salary rate nearest to that received before promotion and involving no decrease.

SPECIAL REGULATION GOVERNING COMPENSATION—

Beginning with the lowest rate, advancement within this grade is conditional upon appraisal under the rules of the Board of Estimate and Apportionment, indicating that the rate requested does not exceed the value of the work to be performed.

GRADE 3 (O L 3)

TITLES OF POSITIONS[1]—

DEPUTY ASSISTANT CORPORATION COUNSEL
LEGAL EXAMINER

DUTIES—

The duties of incumbents of these positions are to supervise or perform important legal work requiring professional experience, skill and judgment.

Examples:

Preparing opinions, briefs, instruments and pleadings.
Arguing important motions, demurrers or appeals.
Trying actions and proceedings.

QUALIFICATIONS—

1. The minimum qualifications prescribed for Grade 2.

2. If appointed by promotion, not less than two years of appropriate experience in Grade 2, or if appointed as the result of an open competitive examination, experience in work of the character and standard of Grade 2.

3. Such additional qualifications as may be required by the Municipal Civil Service Commission.

COMPENSATION—

Range of annual compensation—$2520 to $4680 inclusive.

Salary rates—$2520, $2760, $3000, $3240, $3480, $3780, $4080, $4380, $4680.

---

[1] The following positions are among those appraised by the Bureau of Personal Service in this grade on the basis of duties performed by present incumbents:

Legal Examiner for the Commissioner of Health. The present title of this position is Law Clerk.

Deputy Assistant Corporation Counsel engaged in preparing drafts of opinions on franchise matters.

Deputy Assistant Corporation Counsel engaged in trial of accident cases.

SPECIAL REGULATION GOVERNING COMPENSATION—

Persons entering this grade need not necessarily begin at the lowest rate. Fixation of the initial salary rate and advancement within this grade are conditional upon appraisal under the rules of the Board of Estimate and Apportionment, indicating that the rate requested does not exceed the value of the work to be performed.

GRADE 4 (O L 4)

TITLES OF POSITIONS[1]—

ASSISTANT CORPORATION COUNSEL
CHIEF LEGAL EXAMINER
SENIOR LEGAL EXAMINER

DUTIES—

The duties of incumbents of these positions are to direct and be responsible for the most important work of legal branches, bureaus or divisions, or to perform independently the highest order of legal work.

Examples:

Acting as consulting counsel on the most important legal matters.
Conducting the most important litigation.

QUALIFICATIONS—

1. The minimum qualifications prescribed for Grade 3.
2. If appointed by promotion, not less than four years of appropriate experience in Grade 3, or if appointed as the result of an open competitive examination, experience in work of the character and standard of Grade 3.
3. Such additional qualifications as may be required by the Municipal Civil Service Commission.

COMPENSATION—

Range of annual compensation—$5100 and up.
Salary rates—$5100, $5520, $5940, $6600, $7200, $7800, $8400, $9000, $9600, $10200.[2]

SPECIAL REGULATION GOVERNING COMPENSATION—

Persons entering this grade need not necessarily begin at the lowest rate. Fixation of the initial salary rate and advancement within this grade are conditional upon appraisal under the rules of the Board of Estimate and Apportionment, indicating that the rate requested does not exceed the value of the work to be performed.

---

[1] The following positions are among those appraised by the Bureau of Personal Service in this grade on the basis of duties performed by present incumbents:

Assistant Corporation Counsel in charge of the Brooklyn office of the Law Department, or of the Bureau of Street Opening Proceedings.
Assistant Corporation Counsel acting as legal adviser to the Mayor.
Assistant Corporation Counsel acting as representative of the Corporation Counsel at the State Capitol.
Chief Legal Examiner in charge of the Division of Law and Adjustment in the Department of Finance.

[2] No recommendation is made above $10200.

NURSE GROUP

SYMBOL (O N)

The term Nurse Group is applied to those offices or employments of the Professional Service in which incumbents are required to perform such services in the nursing, care and treatment of the sick, and in the investigation, reporting, prevention and correction of conditions unfavorable to the health of individuals or communities as may lawfully be performed by nurses.

GRADE 1 (O N 1)

TITLES OF POSITIONS[1]—

NURSE
FIELD NURSE

DUTIES—

Nurse:

The duties of Nurses are to perform under supervision routine nursing in hospitals and other institutions in which such routine nursing is not performed by pupil nurses, or to supervise and be responsible for the nursing work performed in a hospital ward by pupil nurses or other helpers.

Field Nurse:

The duties of Field Nurses are to perform under supervision such definite details of field nursing or social service work as may be required in the investigation, reporting, prevention and correction of diseases or conditions unfavorable to the health or welfare of individuals or communities, or to supervise small units of field nursing work.

Examples:

Supervising the health of school children and visiting the homes of parents to secure treatment for children requiring treatment or care.
Investigating and reporting cases of communicable diseases.
Visiting the homes of the sick to provide nursing care or to assist in their social betterment.
Investigating conditions or circumstances attending the birth of children.
Visiting midwives to examine their equipment and methods.

QUALIFICATIONS—

1. A certificate or license to practice as registered nurse issued by the Board of Regents of the University of the State of New York.
2. Such additional qualifications as may be required by the Municipal Civil Service Commission.

COMPENSATION—

Nurse:

Range of annual compensation[2]—$600 to $720 inclusive, with maintenance.
Salary rates—$600, $660, $720.
Per diem compensation[3]—$3.50.

---

[1]The following positions are among those appraised by the Bureau of Personal Service in this grade on the basis of duties performed by present incumbents:

Field Nurse in charge of a branch office or clinic of the Bureau of Preventable Diseases of the Department of Health.

[2]Where work will last continuously throughout the year, the annual rate shall be paid.

[3]Where work is temporary and will not last continuously for a period measurable by years, the daily rate shall be paid.

Nurse employed continuously in tuberculosis, psychopathic or alcoholic hospitals or wards:

Range of annual compensation[1]—$660 to $720 inclusive, with maintenance.

Salary rates—$660, $720.

Per diem compensation[2]—$4.00.

An additional allowance of $240 may be made when a nurse is not provided with lodging.

Field Nurse:

Range of annual compensation—$960 to $1140 inclusive.

Salary rates—$960, $1020, $1080, $1140.

GRADE 2 (O N 2)

TITLES OF POSITIONS[3]—

CHIEF NURSE
SENIOR FIELD NURSE

DUTIES—

Chief Nurse:

The duties of Chief Nurses are to supervise and be responsible for the nursing work of a small division or group of wards in a hospital, or to direct the training of a group of pupil nurses in a training school.

Examples:

In charge of nurses in a group of medical or surgical wards.

In charge of nurses in an operating room or rooms.

Supervising the routine nursing work in a psychopathic or alcoholic service.

Acting as special instructor of probationers and pupil nurses in practical and theoretical nursing and related subjects.

Senior Field Nurse:[4]

The duties of Senior Field Nurses are to supervise the field nursing or social service work of a group of nurses, or to make special field investigations requiring a high degree of technical nursing ability or experience in the treatment of the sick or prevention of disease.

Examples:

Making special investigation of the work of other nurses as a special investigator or inspector for the head of a bureau or department.

QUALIFICATIONS—

1. The minimum qualifications prescribed for Grade 1.
2. If appointed by promotion, not less than one year of appropriate experience in Grade 1, or if appointed as the result of an open competitive examination, experience in work of the character and standard of Grade 1.
3. Such additional qualifications as may be required by the Municipal Civil Service Commission.

---

[1]Where work will last continuously throughout the year, the annual rate shall be paid.

[2]Where work is temporary and will not last continuously for a period measurable by years, the daily rate shall be paid.

[3]The following positions are among those appraised by the Bureau of Personal Service in this grade on the basis of duties performed by present incumbents:

Senior Field Nurse in the Bureau of Preventable Diseases or the Bureau of Child Hygiene in the Department of Health.

[4]In the case of supervisory positions, only heads of large district units are included in this grade. In the case of small units, it is expected that several will be grouped together under one supervisor.

COMPENSATION—

Chief Nurse:

Range of annual compensation—$780 to $1200 inclusive, with maintenance.
Salary rates—$780, $840, $900, $960, $1020, $1080, $1140, $1200.

Chief Nurse employed continuously in tuberculosis, psychopathic or alcoholic hospitals or wards, or in night supervision of nurses:

Range of annual compensation—$840 to $1200 inclusive, with maintenance.
Salary rates—$840, $900, $960, $1020, $1080, $1140, $1200.

Chief Nurse engaged in instruction of pupil nurses or in charge of nurses in operating room:

Range of annual compensation[1]—$900 to $1200 inclusive, with maintenance.
Salary rates—$900, $960, $1020, $1080, $1140, $1200.

Senior Field Nurse:

Range of annual compensation—$1200 to $1440 inclusive.
Salary rates—$1200, $1260, $1320, $1380, $1440.

GRADE 3 (O N 3)

TITLES OF POSITIONS[1]—

ASSISTANT SUPERINTENDENT OF NURSES
ASSISTANT DIRECTOR OF FIELD NURSES

DUTIES—

Assistant Superintendent of Nurses:

The duties of Assistant Superintendents of Nurses are to act as assistant to the Superintendent of Nurses of a large hospital, or to superintend the entire nursing staff in a small hospital with or without a training school for nurses.

Assistant Director of Field Nurses

The duties of Assistant Directors of Field Nurses are to act as assistant to the Director of Field Nurses and to be responsible for the performance of assigned duties in an entire bureau composed of several large units, or to direct and be responsible for the work of the field nurses of a small and independent bureau.

QUALIFICATIONS—

1. The minimum qualifications prescribed for Grade 2.
2. If appointed by promotion, not less than two years of appropriate experience in Grade 2, or if appointed as the result of an open competitive examination, experience in work of the character and standard of Grade 2.
3. Such additional qualifications as may be required by the Municipal Civil Service Commission.

COMPENSATION—

Assistant Superintendent of Nurses:

Range of annual compensation—$1320 to $1560 inclusive, with maintenance.
Salary rates—$1320, $1440, $1560.

---

[1]The following positions are among those appraised by the Bureau of Personal Service in this grade on the basis of duties performed by present incumbents:

Assistant Superintendent of Nurses in Bellevue or Metropolitan Hospital.
Assistant Superintendent of Nurses superintending the nursing force in Fordham or Harlem Hospital.
Assistant Director of Field Nurses in the Bureau of Preventable Diseases.
Assistant Director of Field Nurses at Bellevue Hospital.

Assistant Director of Field Nurses:

Range of annual compensation—$1560 to $1680 inclusive.
Salary rates—$1560, $1680.

SPECIAL REGULATION GOVERNING COMPENSATION—

Beginning with the lowest rate, advancement within this grade is conditional upon appraisal under the rules of the Board of Estimate and Apportionment, indicating that the rate requested does not exceed the value of the work to be performed.

GRADE 4 (O N 4)

TITLES OF POSITIONS[1]—

SUPERINTENDENT OF NURSES
DIRECTOR OF FIELD NURSES

DUTIES—

Superintendent of Nurses:

The duties of Superintendents of Nurses, which require a high degree of nursing and executive ability, are to direct the entire nursing staff in a large hospital with or without a training school for nurses, or to act as superintendent of nurses and lay superintendent in a small hospital, or to be responsible for the entire administration of a small hospital where knowledge of nursing and hospital work is required, but not necessarily professional training in medicine.[2]

Director of Field Nurses:

The duties of Directors of Field Nurses, which require a high degree of executive ability and experience in field nursing, are to direct and be responsible for the nursing work of the field nurses of an entire bureau composed of several large units.

QUALIFICATIONS—

1. The minimum qualifications prescribed for Grade 3.
2. If appointed by promotion, not less than two years of appropriate experience in Grade 3, or if appointed as the result of an open competitive examination, experience in work of the character and standard of Grade 3.
3. Such additional qualifications as may be required by the Municipal Civil Service Commission.

COMPENSATION—

Superintendent of Nurses:

Range of annual compensation—$1680 to $1980 inclusive, with maintenance.
Salary rates—$1680, $1800, $1980.

Director of Field Nurses:

Range of annual compensation—$1800 to $2160 inclusive.
Salary rates—$1800, $1980, $2160.

---

[1]The following positions are among those appraised by the Bureau of Personal Service in this grade on the basis of duties performed by present incumbents:

Superintendent of Nurses in Metropolitan, Bellevue, City or Kings County Hospital.

Superintendent of Nurses in charge of Gouverneur, Fordham or Sea Breeze Hospital.

Director of Field Nurses in the Bureau of Preventable Diseases of the Department of Health.

[2]It is intended to provide for the assignment of a Superintendent of Nurses to work as administrative head of a small hospital where training in medicine is not required. Such an assignment should not involve a change of title. An office title could be given indicating the specific institution of which the Superintendent of Nurses is in charge.

SPECIAL REGULATION GOVERNING COMPENSATION—

Persons entering this grade need not necessarily begin at the lowest rate. Fixation of the initial salary rate and advancement within this grade are conditional upon appraisal under the rules of the Board of Estimate and Apportionment, indicating that the rate requested does not exceed the value of the work to be performed.

GRADE 5 (O N 5)

TITLES OF POSITIONS[1]—

GENERAL SUPERINTENDENT OF NURSES

DUTIES—

The duties of incumbents of these positions, which require the highest degree of nursing and executive ability, are to direct the entire nursing staff in a group or department of hospitals, with or without training schools for nurses.

QUALIFICATIONS—

1. The minimum qualifications prescribed for Grade 4.
2. If appointed by promotion, not less than two years of appropriate experience in Grade 4, or if appointed as the result of an open competitive examination, experience in work of the character and standard of Grade 4.
3. Such additional qualifications as may be required by the Municipal Civil Service Commission.

COMPENSATION—

Range of annual compensation—$2160 to $3060 inclusive, with maintenance.

Salary rates—$2160, $2340, $2580, $2820, $3060.

SPECIAL REGULATION GOVERNING COMPENSATION—

Persons entering this grade need not necessarily begin at the lowest rate. Fixation of the initial salary rate and advancement within this grade are conditional upon appraisal under the rules of the Board of Estimate and Apportionment, indicating that the rate requested does not exceed the value of the work to be performed.

PATHOLOGIST GROUP

SYMBOL (O G)

The term Pathologist Group is applied to those offices or employments of the Professional Service in which incumbents are required to perform autopsies or post mortem examinations, to recognize and report pathological conditions discovered by microscopic or other examinations, to prepare and mount specimens of tissue for examination or exposition, and to perform such other services as may be required in the procuring, preparation, examination, or analysis of specimens of human tissue.

GRADE 1 (O G 1)

TITLES OF POSITIONS—

ASSISTANT PATHOLOGIST

DUTIES—

The duties of incumbents of these positions are to exercise independent judgment in and to be responsible for pathological examinations and to perform research work under supervision.

---

[1]The following positions are among those appraised by the Bureau of Personal Service in this grade on the basis of duties performed by present incumbents:

General Superintendent of Nurses in Bellevue and Allied Hospitals.

Examples:

Examining pathological and surgical specimens.
Performing autopsies.

QUALIFICATIONS—

1. A medical degree granted on the completion of a standard course of instruction in a medical school of recognized standing.

2. Experience as either interne or assistant in a pathological laboratory of recognized standing.

3. Such additional qualifications as may be required by the Municipal Civil Service Commission.

COMPENSATION—

Range of annual compensation for full-time service—$1740 to $2100 inclusive.
Salary rates—$1740, $1920, $2100.

SPECIAL REGULATION GOVERNING COMPENSATION—

Beginning with the lowest rate, advancement within this grade is conditional upon appraisal under the rules of the Board of Estimate and Apportionment, indicating that the rate requested does not exceed the value of the work to be performed.

GRADE 2 (O G 2)

TITLES OF POSITIONS[1]—

PATHOLOGIST

DUTIES—

The duties of incumbents of these positions, which may or may not involve supervision of employes in Grade 1, are to supervise and be responsible for special laboratory work in a division of the pathological service, or to perform independent experiments and to conduct original research of wide scope and importance.

Examples:

Directing the performance of autopsies, the examination of body tissues and fluids, the preparation of culture media and serums, the performance of dissection, microscopical examinations and diagnoses.

QUALIFICATIONS—

1. The minimum qualifications prescribed for Grade 1.

2. If appointed by promotion, not less than two years of appropriate experience in Grade 1, or if appointed as the result of an open competitive examination, experience in work of the character and standard of Grade 1.

3. Such additional qualifications as may be required by the Municipal Civil Service Commission.

COMPENSATION—

Range of annual compensation for full-time service—$2280 to $3180 inclusive.
Salary rates—$2280, $2460, $2700, $2940, $3180.

Range of annual compensation for part-time service, averaging not less than 18 hours a week—$1500 to $1920 inclusive.
Salary rates—$1500, $1620, $1740, $1920.

SPECIAL REGULATION GOVERNING COMPENSATION—

Beginning with the lowest rate, advancement within this grade is conditional upon appraisal under the rules of the Board of Estimate and Apportionment, indicating that the rate requested does not exceed the value of the work to be performed.

---

[1]The following positions are among those appraised by the Bureau of Personal Service in this grade on the basis of duties performed by present incumbents:

Pathologist in Bellevue and Allied Hospitals.

GRADE 3 (O G 3)

TITLES OF POSITIONS[1]—

SENIOR PATHOLOGIST

DUTIES—

The duties of incumbents of these positions, which require a high order of specialized knowledge, are to perform independent experiments and to conduct original research in pathology of the widest scope and importance.

QUALIFICATIONS—

1. The minimum qualifications prescribed for Grade 2.
2. If appointed by promotion, not less than two years of appropriate experience in Grade 2, or if appointed as the result of an open competitive examination, experience in work of the character and standard of Grade 2.
3. Such additional qualifications as may be required by the Municipal Civil Service Commission.

COMPENSATION—

Range of annual compensation for full-time service—$3420 to $4560 inclusive.
Salary rates—$3420, $3660, $3960, $4260, $4560.

SPECIAL REGULATION GOVERNING COMPENSATION—

Beginning with the lowest rate, advancement within this grade is conditional upon appraisal under the rules of the Board of Estimate and Apportionment, indicating that the rate requested does not exceed the value of the work to be performed.

GRADE 4 (O G 4)

TITLES OF POSITIONS[2]—

DIRECTOR OF PATHOLOGICAL LABORATORIES

DUTIES—

The duties of incumbents of these positions, which require the highest order of specialized knowledge, are to supervise and be responsible for the entire work of a pathological laboratory, or of a group of pathological and other laboratories, and to furnish expert and critical advice of the highest order in the practice of pathology.

QUALIFICATIONS—

1. The minimum qualifications prescribed for Grade 3.
2. If appointed by promotion, not less than two years of appropriate experience in Grade 3, or if appointed as the result of an open competitive examination, experience in work of the character and standard of Grade 3.
3. Such additional qualifications as may be required by the Municipal Civil Service Commission.

COMPENSATION—

Range of annual compensation for full-time service—$5100 and up.
Salary rates—$5100, $5520, $5940.[3]

---

[1]The following positions are among those appraised by the Bureau of Personal Service in this grade on the basis of duties performed by present incumbents:

Senior Pathologist in the Central Testing Laboratory.

[2]The following positions are among those appraised by the Bureau of Personal Service in this grade on the basis of duties performed by present incumbents:

Director of the Pathological Laboratories of Bellevue and Allied Hospitals.

[3]No recommendation is made above $5940.

SPECIAL REGULATION GOVERNING COMPENSATION—

Persons entering this grade need not necessarily begin at the lowest rate. Fixation of the initial salary rate and advancement within this grade are conditional upon appraisal under the rules of the Board of Estimate and Apportionment, indicating that the rate requested does not exceed the value of the work to be performed.

PHARMACIST GROUP

SYMBOL (O F)

The term Pharmacist Group is applied to those offices or employments of the Professional Service in which incumbents are required to compound, preserve and dispense drugs according to prescriptions of medical practitioners or standard formulae, or to perform such services in the investigation, reporting, prevention and correction of conditions involved in the manufacture, handling and sale of drugs and other medicines as may properly be performed by pharmacists.

GRADE 1 (O F 1)

TITLES OF POSITIONS[1]—

ASSISTANT PHARMACIST

DUTIES—

The duties of incumbents of these positions, which are performed under supervision of a Pharmacist in Grade 2, are to compound, preserve and dispense drugs and medicines, to manufacture standard preparations and to keep records of prescriptions filled.

QUALIFICATIONS—

1. A certificate or license to practice pharmacy issued by the Board of Regents of the University of the State of New York, but not necessarily any experience in the practice of pharmacy other than that which is incident to the attainment of these qualifications.
2. Such additional qualifications as may be required by the Municipal Civil Service Commission.

COMPENSATION—

Range of annual compensation with maintenance—$600 to $840 inclusive.
Salary rates—$600, $720, $840.
Range of annual compensation without maintenance—$900 to $1140 inclusive.
Salary rates—$900, $1020, $1140.

GRADE 2 (O F 2)

TITLES OF POSITIONS[2]—

PHARMACIST

DUTIES—

The duties of incumbents of these positions, which are performed independently in an institution, or in the field, and which may involve supervision of employes in Grade 1 and of other helpers, are to compound, preserve, and dispense drugs and medicines, to manufacture standard preparations, and to keep records of prescriptions filled, or to perform such services in the investigation, reporting, prevention and correction of conditions involved in the manufacture, handling and sale of drugs and other medicines as may properly be performed by pharmacists.

---

[1]The following positions are among those appraised by the Bureau of Personal Service in this grade on the basis of duties performed by present incumbents:

Assistant Pharmacist at Kings County Hospital.

[2]The following positions are among those appraised by the Bureau of Personal Service in this grade on the basis of duties performed by present incumbents:

Pharmacist at Kings County, Metropolitan, Harlem and City Hospitals.

QUALIFICATIONS—

1. The minimum qualifications prescribed for Grade 1.
2. If appointed by promotion, not less than one year of appropriate experience in Grade 1, or if appointed as the result of an open competitive examination, experience in work of the character and standard of Grade 1.
3. Such additional qualifications as may be required by the Municipal Civil Service Commission.

COMPENSATION—

Range of annual compensation with maintenance—$960 to $1200 inclusive.
Salary rates—$960, $1080, $1200.
Range of annual compensation without maintenance—$1260 to $1500 inclusive.
Salary rates—$1260, $1380, $1500.

GRADE 3 (O F 3)

TITLES OF POSITIONS[1]—

HEAD PHARMACIST

DUTIES—

The duties of incumbents of these positions, which involve supervision of the compounding, preserving and dispensing of drugs and medicines, the bottling and delivery of supplies, the preparation of special reports and requisitions, and of various drug dispensing branches, are to act as chief pharmacist in a manufacturing interdepartmental laboratory under the direction of a chemist, or to take charge of the largest institutional drug laboratories.

QUALIFICATIONS—

1. The minimum qualifications prescribed for Grade 2.
2. If appointed by promotion, not less than two years of appropriate experience in Grade 2, or if appointed as the result of an open competitive examination, experience in work of the character and standard of Grade 2.
3. Such additional qualifications as may be required by the Municipal Civil Service Commission.

COMPENSATION—

Range of annual compensation—$1620 to $2460 inclusive.
Salary rates—$1620, $1740, $1920, $2100, $2280, $2460.

SPECIAL REGULATION GOVERNING COMPENSATION—

Beginning with the lowest rate, advancement within this grade is conditional upon appraisal under the rules of the Board of Estimate and Apportionment, indicating that the rate requested does not exceed the value of the work to be performed.

PHYSICIAN GROUP

SYMBOL (O P)

The term Physician Group is applied to those offices or employments of the Professional Service in which incumbents are required to perform such services in the care and treatment of the sick, and in the investigation, reporting, prevention and correction of conditions unfavorable to the health of individuals or communities as may lawfully be performed by physicians.

---

[1]The following positions are among those appraised by the Bureau of Personal Service in this grade on the basis of duties performed by present incumbents:

Head Pharmacist in the general drug laboratory of the Department of Public Charities.
Head Pharmacist in Bellevue Hospital.

GRADE 1 (O P 1)

TITLES OF POSITIONS—

MEDICAL INTERNE

DUTIES—

The duties of incumbents of these positions are to perform under supervision such medical work in the care and treatment of hospital patients or institutional inmates as is commonly required of a medical interne.

Examples:

Making physical examinations of hospital patients or institutional inmates and keeping records of the same.
Diagnosing and treating medical or surgical cases and keeping clinical records of the same.
Making bacteriological or pathological examinations.
Acting as ambulance surgeon.
Assisting at operations.

QUALIFICATIONS—

1. Either a medical degree granted on the completion of a standard course of instruction in a medical school of recognized standing, or a certificate or license to practice medicine issued by the Board of Regents of the University of the State of New York, but not necessarily any experience in the practice of medicine other than that which is incident to the attainment of these qualifications.

2. Such additional qualifications as may be required by the Municipal Civil Service Commission.

COMPENSATION—

Range of annual compensation—$120 to $240 inclusive, with maintenance.
Salary rates—$120, $240.

An additional compensation of $10 per month may be paid to Medical Internes employed exclusively in tuberculosis work or in the hospitals of the Department of Health.

GRADE 2 (O P 2)

TITLES OF POSITIONS[1]—

ASSISTANT PHYSICIAN (HOSPITAL)
ASSISTANT PHYSICIAN (MEDICAL CLERK)

DUTIES—

Assistant Physician (Hospital):

The duties of Assistant Physicians (Hospital) are to perform under supervision such services as may be required in the medical examination of applicants for admission to hospitals or other institutions or in the routine medical or surgical care and treatment of hospital patients or institutional inmates, or to supervise internes in Grade 1 in this work.

Examples:

Acting as resident physician in a hospital or other institution.

---

[1]The following positions are among those appraised by the Bureau of Personal Service in this grade on the basis of duties performed by present incumbents:
Assistant Physician (Hospital) in Bellevue Hospital.
Assistant Physician (Medical Clerk) in the Department of Health.

Assistant Physician (Medical Clerk):

The duties of Assistant Physicians (Medical Clerk) are to issue permits for the removal, transfer, or burial of dead bodies, and to receive and examine certificates of births and deaths, as a safeguard against violation of the provisions of the sanitary code relating to the filing and recording of vital statistics.

QUALIFICATIONS—

1. A certificate or license to practice medicine issued by the Board of Regents of the University of the State of New York, unless in accordance with the rules of the Board of Health this provision is waived by the Municipal Civil Service Commission in the case of medical officers working under supervision in institutions.[1]

2. Not less than one year of experience as hospital interne or as assistant to an established practitioner or in independent practice.

3. Such additional qualifications as may be required by the Municipal Civil Service Commission.

COMPENSATION—

Assistant Physician (Hospital):

Range of annual compensation—$900 to $1380 inclusive, with maintenance.
Salary rates—$900, $1020, $1140, $1260, $1380.

Assistant Physician (Hospital) employed exclusively in tuberculosis or contagious disease work or in the institutions of the Department of Correction:[2]

Range of annual compensation—$1260 to $1380 inclusive, with maintenace.
Salary rates—$1260, $1380.

Assistant Physician (Medical Clerk):

Range of annual compensation—$1140 to $1500 inclusive.
Salary rates—$1140, $1260, $1380, $1500.

GRADE 3 (O P 3)

TITLES OF POSITIONS[3]—

---

[1]Medical officers working in institutions under the supervision of medical superintendents or medical boards are not required by the rules of the Board of Health to have a license to practice in the State of New York. At present it is not possible to require a license locally in the case of Assistant Physicians since there is not available for these positions a sufficient number of internes who have received a license to practice in the State of New York. In future internes who desire to advance to positions as Assistant Physician may be required to pass the New York State examinations for license to practice.

[2]It is suggested that the medical service in the correctional institutions on Blackwell's Island should be supplied by the Department of Public Charities.

[3]The following positions are among those appraised by the Bureau of Personal Service in this grade on the basis of duties performed by present incumbents:

Physician (Hospital) at the Municipal Lodging House.
Physician (Hospital) for an investigation bureau of the Department of Public Charities.
Physician (Clinic) in charge of a Wassermann or anti-rabic clinic.
Physician (Field) inspecting for communicable and other diseases in the Department of Health.
Physician (Anaesthetist) in Bellevue Hospital.
Physician (Oculist) in the Bureau of Child Hygiene of the Department of Health.
Physician (Hospital) at the Penitentiary, Blackwell's Island.
Physician (Clinic) to the tuberculosis or other clinics of the Department of Health.
Physician (Clinic) to out-patient clinics of Bellevue and Allied Hosptals.
Physcian (Clinic) to out-patient clinics at the hospitals of the Department of Public Charities.

PHYSICIAN (ALIENIST)
PHYSICIAN (ANAESTHETIST)
PHYSICIAN (CLINIC)
PHYSICIAN (DIAGNOSTICIAN)
PHYSICIAN (FIELD)
PHYSICIAN (HOSPITAL)
PHYSICIAN (LARYNGOLOGIST)
PHYSICIAN (OCULIST)
PHYSICIAN (ROENTGENOLOGIST)
PHYSICIAN (SUPERVISING DISTRICT)

DUTIES—

Physician (Alienist):

The duties of Physicians (Alienist) are to assist the Senior Physician (Alienist) of a hospital or other institution in the examination, care and treatment of the insane or mentally abnormal.

Physician (Anaesthetist):

The duties of Physicians (Anaesthetist) are to supervise and be responsible for the administration of anaesthetics or the instruction of medical internes in the administration of anaesthetics in city hospitals.

Physician (Clinic):

The duties of Physicians (Clinic) are to attend the clinics maintained by the city for the treatment of out-patients and to examine and give medical and surgical treatment to such patients.

Physician (Diagnostician):

The duties of Physicians (Diagnostician) are to exercise independent judgment in and to be responsible for the diagnosis of communicable diseases in the Department of Health.

Physician (Field):

The duties of Physicians (Field) are to be responsible for the medical examination and treatment of school children or of applicants for admission to city institutions, or to investigate, recognize, report, prevent or correct diseases or conditions unfavorable to the health of individuals or communities.

Physician (Hospital):

The duties of Physicians (Hospital) are to supervise and be responsible for the care and treatment of hospital patients or institutional inmates.

Examples:

Acting as resident physician in a hospital or other institution in which the duties of the resident require a high degree of supervisory or executive ability, or as resident physician in charge of a group of wards in a large hospital.

Physician (Laryngologist):

The duties of Physicians (Laryngologist) are to be responsible for the diagnosis and treatment of diseases and other pathological conditions of the throat and adjacent structures in city hospitals, clinics or other institutions.

Physician (Oculist):

The duties of Physicians (Oculist) are to be responsible for the diagnosis and treatment of diseases and other pathological conditions of the eyes in city hospitals, clinics or other institutions.

Physician (Roentgenologist):

The duties of Physicians (Roentgenologist) are to supervise and be responsible for the taking, preparation and interpretation of X-ray photographs in city hospitals.

Physician (Supervising District):

The duties of Physicians (Supervising District) are to direct and supervise the medical work of a district of the Bureau of Preventable Diseases, including examination and treatment of patients attending a clinic, field work, and the general management of the branch office.

QUALIFICATIONS—

Physician (Anaesthetic) Physician (Clinic), Physician (Diagnostician), Physician (Field), Physician (Hospital), Physician (Laryngologist), Physician (Oculist), Physician (Roentgenologist), Physician (Supervising District):

1. The minimum qualifications prescribed for Grade 2.
2. If appointed by promotion, not less than two years of appropriate experience in Grade 2, or if appointed as the result of an open competitive examination, experience in work recognized by the Municipal Civil Service Commission as qualifying for the specialized field in question.
3. Such additional qualifications as may be required by the Municipal Civil Service Commission.

Physician (Alienist):

1. A certificate issued by a judge of a court of record to act as examiner in lunacy as prescribed by the laws of the State of New York.
2. Such additional qualifications as may be required by the Municipal Civil Service Commission.

COMPENSATION—

Physician (Anaesthetist), Physician (Field), Physician (Hospital), Physician (Laryngologist), Physician (Oculist), Physician (Roentgenologist):

Range of annual compensation for full-time service with maintenance—$1500 to $2280 inclusive.

Salary rates—$1500, $1620, $1740, $1920, $2100, $2280.

Range of annual compensation for full-time service without maintenance—$2100 to $2760 inclusive.

Salary rates—$2100, $2280, $2520, $2760.

Range of annual compensation for part-time service, averaging not less than 24 hours a week—$1380 to $1500 inclusive.

Salary rates—$1380, $1500.

Range of annual compensation for part-time service, averaging not less than 18 hours a week—$1140 to $1380 inclusive.

Salary rates—$1140, $1260, $1380.

Physician (Alienist):

Range of annual compensation for full-time service with maintenance—$1920 to $2280 inclusive.

Salary rates—$1920, $2100, $2280.

Range of annual compensation for full-time service without maintenance—$2520 to $2760 inclusive.

Salary rates—$2520, $2760.

Physician (Clinic):

Range of annual compensation for part-time service, averaging not less than 8 hours a week—$300 to $660 inclusive.

Salary rates—$300, $420, $540, $660.

Physician (Diagnostician), Physician (Supervising District):

Range of annual compensation for full-time service without maintenance—$2280 to $2760 inclusive.

Salary rates—$2280, $2520, $2760.

Range of annual compensation for part-time service, averaging not less than 18 hours a week—$1260 to $1500 inclusive.

Salary rates—$1260, $1380, $1500.

Physician (Field) in the Department of Education:

Range of annual compensation for part-time service, averaging not less than 6 nor more than 12 hours a week—$480 to $720 inclusive.

Salary rates—$480, $600, $720.

Physician (Hospital) acting as first assistant to the resident physician in charge of a hospital in the Department of Health:

Range of annual compensation for full-time service with maintenance—$1740 to $2280 inclusive.

Salary rates—$1740, $1920, $2100, $2280.

SPECIAL REGULATION GOVERNING COMPENSATION—

Physician (Clinic),[1] Physician (Field) in Department of Education:

Persons entering this grade need not necessarily begin at the lowest rate. Fixation of the initial salary rate and advancement within this grade are conditional upon appraisal under the rules of the Board of Estimate and Apportionment, indicating that the rate requested does not exceed the value of the work to be performed.

GRADE 4 (O P 4)

TITLES OF POSITIONS[2]—

SENIOR PHYSICIAN (ALIENIST)
SENIOR PHYSICIAN (ASSISTANT REGISTRAR)
SENIOR PHYSICIAN (FIELD)[3]
SENIOR PHYSICIAN (ORTHOPEDIST)
ASSISTANT MEDICAL SUPERINTENDENT

DUTIES—

Senior Physician (Alienist):

The duties of Senior Physicians (Alienist) are to exercise a high degree of technical skill and ability in the examination, care and treatment of the insane or mentally abnormal in a hospital or other institution.

---

[1]Physicians (Clinic) on the 8-hour schedule shall not receive an initial rate of more than $300, except in the case of those supervising a clinic, who shall receive $540.

[2]The following positions are among those appraised by the Bureau of Personal Service in this grade on the basis of duties performed by present incumbents:

Senior Physician (Field) acting as Assistant Director of the Bureau of Preventable Diseases in the Department of Health.

Assistant Medical Superintendent in charge of Greenpoint Hospital, Department of Public Charities.

Assistant Medical Superintendent of Bellevue or Metropolitan Hospital.

[3]This title and the accompanying salary range is intended to apply to positions as medical officers and surgeons in the Police, Fire and Street Cleaning Departments, and as physicians to coroners.

Senior Physician (Assistant Registrar):

The duties of Senior Physicians (Assistant Registrar) are to supervise and be responsible in a small unit for the gathering of vital and other related statistics, including tabulation of births, marriages, deaths and the causes of deaths.

Senior Physician (Field):

The duties of Senior Physicians (Field) are to supervise and be responsible for important work calling for the exercise of a high degree of professional skill, judgment and executive ability in the examination, diagnosis and treatment of individual cases as well as in the detection, prevention and correction of conditions adverse to public health, and to make special investigations or research relative to the control of disease.

Examples:

Supervising groups of field medical inspectors as field supervisor of the Department of Health.

Making special investigations or research in the causation and methods of prevention of disease.

Senior Physician (Orthopedist):

The duties of Senior Physicians (Orthopedist) are to exercise a high degree of technical skill and ability in the diagnosis and treatment of physical deformities in city hospitals, clinics or other institutions.

Assistant Medical Superintendent:

The duties of Assistant Medical Superintendents are to perform such details of supervisory work in the management and control of a large hospital or group of hospitals as may be assigned by the Medical Superintendent, or to act as superintendent of a small hospital.

QUALIFICATIONS—

1. The minimum qualifications prescribed for Grade 3.

2. If appointed by promotion, not less than two years of appropriate experience in Grade 3, or if appointed as the result of an open competitive examination, experience in work of the character and standard of Grade 3.

3. Such additional qualifications as may be required by the Municipal Civil Service Commission.

COMPENSATION—

Senior Physician (Alienist), Senior Physician (Field), Senior Physician (Orthopedist), Assistant Medical Superintendent:

Range of annual compensation for full-time service with maintenance—$2520 to $3480 inclusive.

Salary rates—$2520, $2760, $3000, $3240, $3480.

Range of annual compensation for full-time service without maintenance—$3000 to $3480 inclusive.

Salary rates—$3000, $3240, $3480.

Range of annual compensation for part-time service, averaging not less than 18 hours a week—$1620 to $2100 inclusive.

Salary rates—$1620, $1740, $1920, $2100.

Senior Physician (Assistant Registrar):

Range of annual compensation—$2520 to $3000 inclusive.

Salary rates—$2520, $2760, $3000.

SPECIAL REGULATION GOVERNING COMPENSATION—

Beginning with the lowest rate, advancement within this grade is conditional upon appraisal under the rules of the Board of Estimate and Apportionment, indicating that the rate requested does not exceed the value of the work to be performed.

GRADE 5 (O P 5)

TITLES OF POSITIONS[1]—

CHIEF PHYSICIAN (ALIENIST)
CHIEF PHYSICIAN (DIAGNOSTICIAN)
CHIEF PHYSICIAN (FIELD)
MEDICAL CONSULTANT (LAW DEPARTMENT)
MEDICAL SUPERINTENDENT

DUTIES—

Chief Physician (Alienist):

The duties of Chief Physicians (Alienist) are to direct and supervise the examination, care and treatment of the insane or mentally abnormal in a large hospital.

Chief Physician (Diagnostician):

The duties of Chief Physicians (Diagnostician) are to exercise the highest degree of technical skill in and to be entirely responsible for the diagnosis of communicable diseases in the Department of Health.

Chief Physician (Field):

The duties of Chief Physicians (Field) are to perform such services as assistants or advisers to the directors of bureaus within the Department of Health, as require an exceptionally high degree of administrative and technical ability, special training and expertness in the supervision of specialized health work.

Medical Consultant (Law Department):

The duties of the Medical Consultant (Law Department), which are performed for the Board of Estimate and Apportionment, the Department of Finance and the Law Department, are to examine and to determine the condition of city employes who are temporarily absent from duty because of illness or who may be physically or mentally incapacitated for further performance of duty and eligible for pensions; to act as medical examiner in accident cases and other litigations where a medical witness is needed by the city; and to make such reports and to give such court testimony as may be required.

Medical Superintendent:

The duties of Medical Superintendents are to be responsible for the entire administration of large hospitals or other institutions.

QUALIFICATIONS—

1. The minimum qualifications prescribed for Grade 4.
2. If appointed by promotion, not less than two years of appropriate experience in Grade 4, or if appointed as the result of an open competitive examination, experience in work of the character and standard of Grade 4.
3. Such additional qualifications as may be required by the Municipal Civil Service Commission.

COMPENSATION—

Range of annual compensation for full-time service—$3780 to $4680 inclusive, with maintenance for physicians in hospital or institutional service.

Salary rates—$3780, $4080, $4380, $4680.

Range of annual compensation for part-time service, averaging not less than 18 hours a week—$2280 to $2700 inclusive.

Salary rates—$2280, $2460, $2700.

---

[1] The following positions are among those appraised by the Bureau of Personal Service in this grade on the basis of duties performed by present incumbents:

Chief Physician (Alienist) in charge of the psychopathic service at Kings County Hospital.

SPECIAL REGULATION GOVERNING COMPENSATION—

Beginning with the lowest rate, advancement within this grade is conditional upon appraisal under the rules of the Board of Estimate and Apportionment, indicating that the rate requested does not exceed the value of the work to be performed.

GRADE 6 (O P 6)

TITLES OF POSITIONS[1]—

CHIEF MEDICAL EXAMINER
DIRECTOR OF PSYCHOPATHIC SERVICE
GENERAL MEDICAL SUPERINTENDENT
HEALTH DIRECTOR[2]

DUTIES—

Director of Psychopathic Service:

The duties of the Director of Psychopathic Service, which require the highest order of specialized knowledge, are to direct and be responsible for the psychopathic and alcoholic service of Bellevue and Allied Hospitals.

General Medical Superintendent:

The duties of General Medical Superintendents are to direct, control and supervise the administration of a group or department of hospitals.

Health Director:

The duties of Health Directors are to direct, control and supervise one of the major bureaus of the Department of Health, or to act as chief consultant and staff adviser of the department in one of the most important specialized fields.

QUALIFICATIONS—

Director of Psychopathic Service:

1. The minimum qualifications prescribed for Grade 5.
2. Experience in hospital administration together with extended experience and notable achievement in the study and treatment of psychopathic conditions.
3. Such additional qualifications as may be required by the Municipal Civil Service Commission.

General Medical Superintendent, Health Director:

1. The minimum qualifications prescribed for Grade 5.
2. If appointed by promotion, not less than two years of appropriate experience in Grade 5, or if appointed as the result of an open competitive examination, experience in work of the character and standard of Grade 5.
3. Such additional qualifications as may be required by the Municipal Civil Service Commission.

COMPENSATION—

Range of annual compensation for full-time service—$5100 and up, with maintenance for physicians in hospital or institutional service.

Salary rates—$5100, $5520, $5940.[3]

---

[1] The following positions are among those appraised by the Bureau of Personal Service in this grade on the basis of duties performed by present incumbents:

General Medical Superintendent of Bellevue and Allied Hospitals.

Health Director, Bureau of Child Hygiene or Bureau of Hospitals of the Department of Health.

Director of Psychopathic Service at Bellevue Hospital.

The new position of Chief Medical Examiner, which is to replace the existing position of Coroner, should later be defined in this grade.

[2] The specific specialized directorship should be indicated in brackets, as Health Director (Child Hygiene), Health Director (Hospitals), Health Director (Sanitary Superintendent).

[3] No recommendation is made above $5940.

SPECIAL REGULATION GOVERNING COMPENSATION—

Persons entering this grade need not necessarily begin at the lowest rate. Fixation of the initial salary rate and advancement within this grade are conditional upon appraisal under the rules of the Board of Estimate and Apportionment, indicating that the rate requested does not exceed the value of the work to be performed.

VETERINARIAN GROUP

SYMBOL (O V)

The term Veterinarian Group is applied to those offices or employments of the Professional Service in which incumbents are required to perform such services in the investigation, reporting, prevention and treatment of diseases of animals and in the preparation of animal serums, antitoxins and vaccines as may lawfully be performed by veterinarians.

GRADE 1 (O V 1)

TITLES OF POSITIONS[1]—

VETERINARIAN

DUTIES—

The duties of incumbents of these positions are to prevent and treat the diseases of and to perform operations on animals, to investigate and report ante mortem and post mortem physiological and pathological conditions in domestic animals, and to inspect and report upon sanitary conditions affecting the public health.

Examples:

Diagnosing glanders and rabies.
Inspecting animals slaughtered for food.
Inspecting dairies.
Inoculating and bleeding animals.
Preparing blood specimens for laboratory use.

QUALIFICATIONS—

1. A certificate or license to practice veterinary science issued by the Board of Regents of the University of the State of New York.
2. Experience in the practice of veterinary science.
3. Such additional qualifications as may be required by the Municipal Civil Service Commission.

COMPENSATION—

Range of annual compensation for full-time service—$1800 to $2340 inclusive.

Salary rates—$1800, $1980, $2160, $2340.

Range of annual compensation for part-time service, averaging not less than 28 hours a week—$1500 to $1740 inclusive.

Salary rates—$1500, $1620, $1740.

Range of annual compensation for part-time service, averaging not less than 18 hours a week—$1200 to $1440 inclusive.

Salary rates—$1200, $1320, $1440.

---

[1] The following positions are among those appraised by the Bureau of Personal Service in this grade on the basis of duties performed by present incumbents:

Veterinarian in the Department of Street Cleaning.
Veterinarian in the Bureau of Food and Drugs in the Department of Health.

GRADE 2 (O V 2)

TITLES OF POSITIONS[1]—

SUPERVISING VETERINARIAN

DUTIES—

The duties of incumbents of these positions are to supervise and be responsible for the work of veterinarians and to exercise in consultation and practice the highest degree of veterinary skill and judgment.

QUALIFICATIONS—

1. The minimum qualifications prescribed for Grade 2.
2. If appointed by promotion, not less than three years of appropriate experience in Grade 1, or if appointed as the result of an open competitive examination, experience in work of the character and standard of Grade 1.
3. Such additional qualifications as may be required by the Municipal Civil Service Commission.

COMPENSATION—

Range of annual compensation for full-time service—$2580 to $3300 inclusive.

Salary rates—$2580, $2820, $3060, $3300.

Range of annual compensation for part-time service, averaging not less than 21 hours a week—$1800 to $2340 inclusive.

Salary rates—$1800, $1980, $2160, $2340.

SPECIAL REGULATION GOVERNING COMPENSATION—

Persons entering this grade need not necessarily begin at the lowest rate. Fixation of the initial salary rate and advancement within this grade are conditional upon appraisal under the rules of the Board of Estimate and Apportionment, indicating that the rate requested does not exceed the value of the work to be performed.

---

[1] The following positions are among those appraised by the Bureau of Personal Service in this grade on the basis of duties performed by present incumbents:

Supervising Veterinarian in the Department of Street Cleaning.

SUB-PROFESSIONAL SERVICE

SYMBOL (B)

The term Sub-professional Service is applied to those offices or employments the duties of whose incumbents are to perform technical work subordinate or preparatory to work outlined in the various groups of the Professional Service.

APPRENTICE PHARMACIST GROUP

SYMBOL (B F)

The term Apprentice Pharmacist Group is applied to those offices or employments of the Sub-professional Service in which incumbents are required to receive such instruction and to perform under supervision such practical apprentice work in the handling, compounding, and dispensing of drugs and medicines as constitute preparation for the examination for a certificate or license to practice pharmacy issued by the Board of Regents of the University of the State of New York.

GRADE 1 (B F 1)

TITLES OF POSITIONS—

APPRENTICE PHARMACIST

DUTIES—

The duties of incumbents of these positions, which are performed under the supervision of licensed pharmacists, are to receive such instruction and to perform such practical apprentice work in the handling, compounding, and dispensing of drugs and medicines and in the manufacture of standard preparations as constitute preparation for the examination for a certificate or license to practice pharmacy issued by the Board of Regents of the University of the State of New York.

QUALIFICATIONS—

1. An apprentice license issued by the State Board of Pharmacy according to provision 233, chapter 422 of the Laws of 1910 of the State of New York.
2. Such additional qualifications as may be required by the Municipal Civil Service Commission.

COMPENSATION—

Range of annual compensation with maintenance—$360 to $480 inclusive.
Salary rates—$360, $420, $480.
Range of annual compensation without maintenance—$600 to $720 inclusive.
Salary rates—$600, $660, $720.

DENTAL ASSISTANT GROUP

SYMBOL (B S)

The term Dental Assistant Group is applied to those offices or employments of the Sub-professional Service in which incumbents are required to remove deposits, accretions and stains from the teeth and to give instruction in oral hygiene.

GRADE 1 (B S 1)

TITLES OF POSITIONS—

DENTAL ASSISTANT

DUTIES—

The duties of incumbents of these positions are to remove deposits, accretions and stains from the teeth and to give instruction in oral hygiene.

QUALIFICATIONS—

1. A certificate to practice as dental hygienist issued by the Regents of the University of the State of New York.
2. Such additional qualifications as may be required by the Municipal Civil Service Commission.

COMPENSATION—

Range of annual compensation—$720 to $900 inclusive.
Salary rates—$720, $780, $840, $900.

DRAFTSMAN GROUP

SYMBOL (B D)

The term Draftsman Group is applied to those offices or employments of the Sub-professional Service in which incumbents are required to perform drafting work incident or subordinate to the practice of engineering or architecture but not requiring professional training or experience.

GRADE 1 (B D 1)

TITLES OF POSITIONS[1]—

JUNIOR DRAFTSMAN

DUTIES—

The duties of incumbents of these positions are to perform under supervision ordinary drafting work requiring training or experience in general drafting but not requiring professional training or experience in engineering or architecture.

Examples:

- Tracing plans, sketches, charts and maps.
- Making pencil and ink drawings from sketches.
- Comparing tracings and drawings.
- Lettering plans, charts and drawings.
- Plotting rough surveys.
- Copying street layouts into book of record from inspectors' reports.
- Enlarging or reducing water distribution maps showing street boundaries and location of mains, gates, etc.
- Preparing project maps showing limits of streets and proposed location of water mains from engineer's sketch.

QUALIFICATIONS—

1. Such qualifications as may be required by the Municipal Civil Service Commission.

COMPENSATION—

Range of annual compensation—$900 to $1200 inclusive.
Salary rates—$900, $960, $1020, $1080, $1140, $1200.

---

[1]It is recommended that no specialized titles be created in this grade, and that the Municipal Civil Service Commission maintain a single general list for Junior Draftsman.

GRADE 2 (B D 2)

TITLES OF POSITIONS—

DRAFTSMAN
PLAN EXAMINER

DUTIES[1]—

Draftsman:

The duties of Draftsmen, which require ability to lay out work and to direct subordinates, or a high degree of technical skill, are to supervise and be responsible for a group of employes in Grade 1, or to perform the most difficult specialized drafting work not requiring professional training or experience in engineering or architecture.

Examples:

Preparing general working drawings or maps.
Making computations and compiling data.
Making assembly drawings from details.

Plan Examiner:

The duties of Plan Examiners, which require a knowledge of the building, tenement house, plumbing and sanitary codes and laws and of building construction, but which do not require professional training and experience in engineering or architecture, are to examine and check building plans and surveys for the purpose of discovering violations of laws, rules, regulations and city ordinances.

QUALIFICATIONS—

Draftsman:

1. The minimum qualifications prescribed for Grade 1.
2. If appointed by promotion, not less than two years of appropriate experience in Grade 1, or if appointed as the result of an open competitive examination, experience in work of the character and standard of Grade 1.
3. Such additional qualifications as may be required by the Municipal Civil Service Commission.

Plan Examiner:

1. The minimum qualifications prescribed for Grade 1.
2. If appointed by promotion, not less than two years of appropriate experience as Junior Draftsman in Grade 1 of the Draftsman Group, or as Building Inspector in Grade 1 of the Inspector of Buildings Group, or in other work of corresponding standard and character, or if appointed as the result of an open competitive examination, such experience as may be required by the Municipal Civil Service Commission.
3. Such additional qualifications as may be required by the Municipal Civil Service Commission.

COMPENSATION—

Range of annual compensation—$1320 to $1800 inclusive.
Salary rates—$1320, $1440, $1560, $1680, $1800.

---

[1]No provision is made in this group for a position as head of a plan examining, drafting or surveying bureau or division. The chief of such a unit should be an engineer in Grade 2, 3 or 4 of the Engineer Group or an architect in Grade 2, 3 or 4 of the Architect Group of the Professional Service. Draftsmen and Plan Examiners who have served a year in this grade are eligible for promotion to Grade 2 of the Engineer and Architect Groups of the Professional Service.

SPECIAL REGULATION GOVERNING COMPENSATION—

Beginning with the lowest rate, advancement within this grade is conditional upon appraisal under the rules of the Board of Estimate and Apportionment, indicating that the rate requested does not exceed the value of the work to be performed.

SPECIAL CONDITION GOVERNING ADVANCEMENT—

The following table indicates the minimum number of years of meritorious service required at each rate before advancement to the next rate. See also page 30.

$1320	1 year
1440	1 "
1560	2 years
1680	2 "

INSTRUMENTMAN GROUP

SYMBOL (B I)

The term Instrumentman Group is applied to those offices or employments of the Subprofessional Service in which incumbents are required to perform work incident or subordinate to the practice of engineering which involves the use of surveying and other engineering instruments and of mathematical tables but which does not require professional training or experience in engineering.

GRADE 1 (B I 1)

TITLES OF POSITIONS—

JUNIOR INSTRUMENTMAN

DUTIES—

The duties of incumbents of these positions are to perform routine work requiring the use of surveying and other engineering instruments and of mathematical tables, but not requiring professional training and experience in engineering.

Examples:

Running levelling rod.
Running tape.
Checking readings on transit.
Caring for instruments, tapes, etc.
Operating or assisting in operating other engineering instruments.
Checking field notes.
Performing minor inspectional work.
Making miscellaneous computations.
Preparing data in connection with engineering work.

QUALIFICATIONS—

1. Such qualifications as may be required by the Municipal Civil Service Commission.

COMPENSATION—

Range of annual compensation—$900 to $1200 inclusive.
Salary rates—$900, $960, $1020, $1080, $1140, $1200.

GRADE 2 (B I 2)

TITLES OF POSITIONS—

INSTRUMENTMAN

DUTIES—

The duties of incumbents of these positions, which may or may not involve supervision of employes in Grade 1, are to perform the most important and difficult routine work involving the use and adjustment of surveying and other engineering instruments and the use of logarithmic and mathematical tables but not requiring professional training and experience in engineering.

Examples:

Taking charge of a field party on survey, construction or repair work.
Preparing sketches.
Making computations and compiling data for reports and cost records.
Adjusting surveying instruments.
Keeping and checking survey notes.
Inspecting on construction or repair work.
Supervising plotting of survey notes.

QUALIFICATIONS—

1. The minimum qualifications prescribed for Grade 1.

2. If appointed by promotion, not less than two years of appropriate experience in Grade 1, or if appointed as the result of an open competitive examination, experience in work of the character and standard of Grade 1.

3. Such additional qualifications as may be required by the Municipal Civil Service Commission.

COMPENSATION—

Range of annual compensation—$1320 to $1800 inclusive.
Salary rates—$1320, $1440, $1560, $1680, $1800.

SPECIAL REGULATION GOVERNING COMPENSATION—

Beginning with the lowest rate, advancement within this grade is conditional upon appraisal under the rules of the Board of Estimate and Apportionment, indicating that the rate requested does not exceed the value of the work to be performed.

SPECIAL CONDITION GOVERNING ADVANCEMENT—

The following table indicates the minimum number of years of meritorious service required at each rate before advancement to the next rate. See also page 30.

$1320	1 year
1440	1 "
1560	2 years
1680	2 "

LABORATORY ASSISTANT GROUP

SYMBOL (B B)

The term Laboratory Assistant Group is applied to those offices or employments of the Sub-professional Service in which incumbents are required to assist professional laboratory workers in the collection and examination of specimens, the preparation of media, toxins and anti-toxins, in physical tests, or other laboratory work.

GRADE 1 (B B 1)

TITLES OF POSITIONS—

LABORATORY APPRENTICE[1]

DUTIES—

The duties of incumbents of these positions are to perform such general apprentice work about laboratories as may be of assistance to professional laboratory workers and laboratory assistants.

QUALIFICATIONS—

1. Evidence of ability to perform the duties of the position satisfactory to the appointing officer.
2. Such additional qualifications as may be required by the Municipal Civil Service Commission.

COMPENSATION—

Range of annual compensation—$360 to $600 inclusive.

Salary rates—$360, $480, $600.

SPECIAL REGULATION GOVERNING COMPENSATION—

Persons entering this grade need not necessarily begin at the lowest rate. Fixation of the initial salary rate and advancement within this grade are conditional upon appraisal under the rules of the Board of Estimate and Apportionment, indicating that the rate requested does not exceed the value of the work to be performed.

GRADE 2 (B B 2)

TITLES OF POSITIONS—

LABORATORY ASSISTANT (BACTERIOLOGY)
LABORATORY ASSISTANT (CHEMISTRY)
LABORATORY ASSISTANT (PATHOLOGY)
LABORATORY ASSISTANT (PHYSICS)

DUTIES—

The duties of incumbents of these positions are to assist professional laboratory workers in the collection and examination of specimens, the preparation of media, toxins and anti-toxins, in physical tests, or other laboratory work.

Examples:

Cutting and staining sections.
Mixing solutions.
Preparing culture media.
Performing routine work in the preparation of media, toxins and anti-toxins.
Taking specimens for tests.
Caring for slides, plates and specimens.
Collecting and plating samples of water.
Counting bacteria.
Recording findings.
Making reports.

---

[1]These positions are classified as non-competitive. Persons holding these positions may compete in open competitive examinations for positions as Laboratory Assistant.

QUALIFICATIONS—

1. Not less than two years of study of elementary bacteriology, chemistry, pathology, physics or related sciences, including experience in laboratory work, in a secondary school or higher institution of recognized standing, or other experience recognized by the Municipal Civil Service Commission as the equivalent.

2. Such additional qualifications as may be required by the Municipal Civil Service Commission.

COMPENSATION—

Range of annual compensation—$720 to $1200 inclusive.
Salary rates—$720, $840, $960, $1080, $1200.

LAW CLERK GROUP

SYMBOL (B L)

The term Law Clerk Group is applied to those offices or employments of the Sub-professional Service in which incumbents are required to perform specialized clerical work not essentially professional in character but involving a knowledge of legal procedure and in some cases requiring admission to the bar.

GRADE 1 (B L 1)

TITLES OF POSITIONS—

JUNIOR LAW CLERK

DUTIES—

The duties of incumbents of these positions are to perform clerical work requiring some knowledge of legal procedure.

Examples:

Entering orders and judgments.
Filing papers in public offices.
Obtaining transcripts.
Taxing costs.
Issuing executions.

QUALIFICATIONS—

1. Experience in clerical work in a law office, or other training or education recognized by the Municipal Civil Service Commission as qualifying.

2. Such additional qualifications as may be required by the Municipal Civil Service Commission.

COMPENSATION—

Range of annual compensation—$900 to $1200 inclusive.
Salary rates—$900, $960, $1020, $1080, $1140, $1200.

GRADE 2 (B L 2)

TITLES OF POSITIONS[1]—

LAW CLERK

[1] The following positions are among those appraised by the Bureau of Personal Service in this grade on the basis of duties performed by present incumbents:

Law Clerk in the Bureau of Penalties of the Law Department in charge of the initiation of penalty proceedings.

Law Clerk in the Personal Tax Bureau of the Law Department in charge of bankruptcy proceedings.

DUTIES—

The duties of incumbents of these positions are to exercise continuing judgment in and to be responsible for the performance of important clerical work requiring a knowledge of legal procedure.

Examples:

Preparing papers in actions and proceedings.
Drawing complaints in routine actions.
Grouping violation reports.
Initiating penalty proceedings.
Examining witnesses and investigating the facts in litigations.

QUALIFICATIONS—

1. The minimum qualifications prescribed for Grade 1.
2. If appointed by promotion, not less than two years of appropriate experience in Grade 1, or if appointed as the result of an open competitive examination, experience in work of the character and standard of Grade 1.
3. Such additional qualifications as may be required by the Municipal Civil Service Commission.

COMPENSATION—

Range of annual compensation—$1320 to $1800 inclusive.
Salary rates—$1320, $1440, $1560, $1680, $1800.

SPECIAL REGULATION GOVERNING COMPENSATION—

Beginning with the lowest rate, advancement within this grade is conditional upon appraisal under the rules of the Board of Estimate and Apportionment, indicating that the rate requested does not exceed the value of the work to be performed.

SPECIAL CONDITION GOVERNING ADVANCEMENT—

The following table indicates the minimum number of years of meritorious service required at each rate before advancement to the next rate. See also page 30.

$1320	1 year
1440	1 "
1560	2 years
1680	2 "

GRADE 3 (B L 3)

TITLES OF POSITIONS[1]—

SENIOR LAW CLERK

DUTIES—

The duties of incumbents of these positions, which may or may not involve supervision of other employes, are to perform independently or to be responsible for important work of a legal nature which is not essentially professional in character.

---

[1]The following positions are among those appraised by the Bureau of Personal Service in this grade on the basis of duties performed by present incumbents:

Senior Law Clerk in charge of the collection of judgments in the Law Department.
Senior Law Clerk preparing all cases for trial in the Brooklyn branch of the Law Department, involving supervision of examiners and law clerks.
Senior Law Clerk acting as diary clerk in the main office of the Law Department.
Senior Law Clerk acting as taxing officer for bills of costs in the office of the Clerk of Kings County.

QUALIFICATIONS—

1. The minimum qualifications prescribed for Grade 2.

2. If appointed by promotion, not less than three years of appropriate experience in Grade 2, or if appointed as the result of an open competitive examination, experience in work of the character and standard of Grade 2.

3. Such additional qualifications as may be required by the Municipal Civil Service Commisssion.

COMPENSATION—

Range of annual compensation—$1980 to $2820 inclusive.
Salary rates—$1980, $2160, $2340, $2580, $2820.

SPECIAL REGULATION GOVERNING COMPENSATION—

Beginning with the lowest rate, advancement within this grade is conditional upon appraisal under the rules of the Board of Estimate and Apportionment, indicating that the rate requested does not exceed the value of the work to be performed.

SPECIAL CONDITION GOVERNING ADVANCEMENT—

The following table indicates the minimum number of years of meritorious service required at each rate before advancement to the next rate. See also page 30.

$1980	1 year
2160	1 "
2340	2 years
2580	2 "

GRADE 4 (B L 4)

TITLES OF POSITIONS[1]—

ASSISTANT CHIEF LAW CLERK
ASSISTANT MANAGING CLERK (LAW DEPARTMENT)

DUTIES—

The duties of incumbents of these positions, which may or may not involve supervision of large groups of employes, are to take charge of the non-professional service in the largest divisions of legal offices, or to perform individual work of the most difficult technical character requiring highly specialized knowledge of legal procedure, but not work essentially professional in character.

QUALIFICATIONS—

1. The minimum qualifications prescribed for Grade 3.

2. If appointed by promotion, not less than three years of appropriate experience in Grade 3, or if appointed as the result of an open competitive examination, experience in work of the character and standard of Grade 3.

3. A certificate or record of admission to the bar in the State of New York.

4. Such additional qualifications as may be required by the Municipal Civil Service Commission.

---

[1]The following positions are among those appraised by the Bureau of Personal Service in this grade on the basis of duties performed by present incumbents:

Assistant Chief Law Clerk of the Brooklyn office of the Law Department.

Assistant Managing Clerk acting as assistant to the executive secretary or managing clerk of the Law Department.

Assistant Chief Law Clerk acting as taxing officer upon bills of costs in the office of the Clerk of New York County.

COMPENSATION—

Range of annual compensation—$3060 to $4140 inclusive.
Salary rates—$3060, $3300, $3540, $3840, $4140.

SPECIAL REGULATION GOVERNING COMPENSATION—

Beginning with the lowest rate, advancement within this grade is conditional upon appraisal under the rules of the Board of Estimate and Apportionment, indicating that the rate requested does not exceed the value of the work to be performed.

GRADE 5 (B L 5)

TITLES OF POSITIONS—

MANAGING CLERK (LAW DEPARTMENT)[1]

DUTIES—

The duties of the incumbent of this position, which require a high degree of executive ability and knowledge of legal practice and procedure, are to take charge of the entire non-professional service of the Law Department.

QUALIFICATIONS—

1. The minimum qualifications prescribed for Grade 4.
2. If appointed by promotion, not less than one year of appropriate experience in Grade 4, or if appointed as the result of an open competitive examination, experience in work of the character and standard of Grade 4.
3. A certificate or record of admission to the bar in the State of New York.
4. Such additional qualifications as may be required by the Municipal Civil Service Commission.

COMPENSATION—

Range of annual compensation—$4440 to $5160 inclusive.
Salary rates—$4440, $4740, $5160.

PUPIL NURSE GROUP

SYMBOL (B N)

The term Pupil Nurse Group is applied to those offices or employments of the Sub-professional Service in which incumbents are required to receive such instruction and to perform under supervision such general apprentice work in the care and treatment of hospital patients as are part of the regular course of training qualifying for the position of graduate nurse.

GRADE 1 (B N 1)

TITLES OF POSITIONS—

PUPIL NURSE

DUTIES—

The duties of incumbents of these positions are to receive such instruction and to perform under supervision such general apprentice work in the care and treatment of hospital patients as are part of the regular course of training qualifying for the position of graduate nurse.[2]

---

[1]This position is more properly regarded as that of Executive Secretary of the Law Department (see the Executive Secretary Group of the Executive Service). If a position of Executive Secretary should be established in the competitive class, the position of Managing Clerk should be abolished.

[2]See also Grade 1 of the Hospital Attendant Group of the Institutional Service.

Examples:

Waiting on patients.
Giving prescribed medicines.
Serving special diets.
Assisting physicians in preparing patients for examinations and operations.
Performing other similar duties under the direction of the nurse in charge.

QUALIFICATIONS—

1. Evidence of ability to perform the duties of the position satisfactory to the appointing officer.
2. Such additional qualifications as may be required by the Municipal Civil Service Commission.

COMPENSATION—

Bellevue and Allied Hospitals:

Annual compensation—$96 with maintenance.

Department of Public Charities:

Range of annual compensation—$120 to $180 inclusive, with maintenance.
Salary rates—$120, $144, $180.

TITLE EXAMINER GROUP

SYMBOL (B X)

The term Title Examiner Group is applied to those offices or employments of the Subprofessional Service in which incumbents are required to perform technical or supervisory work requiring a knowledge of conveyancing in examining, searching, abstracting, block indexing and in recording or certifying the actual evidence of titles to real property.

GRADE 1 (B X 1)

TITLES OF POSITIONS—

JUNIOR TITLE EXAMINER

DUTIES—

The duties of incumbents of these positions are to perform routine technical work in the searching, abstracting, block indexing and reindexing of titles, and other work dealing with the actual evidence of titles which requires a considerable knowledge of conveyancing and cannot be properly performed by Assistant Clerks in Grade 2 A of the Clerk Group.

Examples:

Searching indexes and locating premises.
Posting instruments in proper block and section of the land map and in proper indexes.
Preparing diagram descriptions of property.

QUALIFICATIONS—

1. Experience in clerical work in a law office or conveyancing office, or other training or education recognized by the Municipal Civil Service Commission as qualifying.
2. Such additional qualifications as may be required by the Municipal Civil Service Commission.

COMPENSATION—

Range of annual compensation—$960 to $1320 inclusive.
Salary rates—$960, $1080, $1200, $1320.

GRADE 2 (B X 2)

TITLES OF POSITIONS[1]—

TITLE EXAMINER

DUTIES—

The duties of incumbents of these positions, which may or may not involve supervision of employes in Grade 1 and other employes, are to perform independently responsible work in searching records for instruments and proceedings affecting real property, examining titles, preparing abstracts and certifying to the status of titles.

QUALIFICATIONS—

1. The minimum qualifications prescribed for Grade 1.
2. If appointed by promotion, not less than two years of appropriate experience in Grade 1, or if appointed as the result of an open competitive examination, experience in work of the character and standard of Grade 1.
3. Such additional qualifications as may be required by the Municipal Civil Service Commission.

COMPENSATION—

Range of annual compensation—$1440 to $1980 inclusive.
Salary rates—$1440, $1560, $1680, $1800, $1980.

SPECIAL CONDITION GOVERNING ADVANCEMENT—

The following table indicates the minimum number of years of meritorious service required at each rate before advancement to the next rate. See also page 30.

$1440	1 year
1560	1 "
1680	2 years
1800	2 "

GRADE 3 (B X 3)

TITLES OF POSITIONS[2]—

SENIOR TITLE EXAMINER

---

[1]The following positions are among those appraised by the Bureau of Personal Service in this grade on the basis of duties performed by present incumbents:

- Title Examiner examining titles to real property ceded to the city.
- Title Examiner examining titles preliminary to foreclosure of mortgages for tax liens.
- Title Examiner certifying to the status of titles in the Register's office on special request.
- Title Examiner in charge of a group in the preparation of a block or locality index system in the office of the Register in New York County.
- Title Examiner in charge of the record room in the office of the Register in New York County.

[2]The following positions are among those appraised by the Bureau of Personal Service in this grade on the basis of duties performed by present incumbents:

- Senior Title Examiner acting as head of the Mortgage Satisfaction Bureau in the office of the Register of New York County. This position is at present in the exempt class.
- Senior Title Examiner acting as head of a consolidated alphabetical and block index system in the office of the Register of New York County, should such a consolidation be effected.

DUTIES—

The duties of incumbents of these positions are to take charge of large and important bureaus engaged in title work or to perform independently the most difficult and responsible work in the examination of titles requiring long experience and great expertness in conveyancing.

QUALIFICATIONS—

1. The minimum qualifications prescribed for Grade 2.

2. If appointed by promotion, not less than three years of appropriate experience in Grade 2, or if appointed as the result of an open competitive examination, experience in work of the character and standard of Grade 2.

3. Such additional qualifications as may be required by the Municipal Civil Service Commission.

COMPENSATION—

Range of annual compensation—$2160 to $3060 inclusive.

Salary rates—$2160, $2340, $2580, $2820, $3060.

SPECIAL CONDITION GOVERNING ADVANCEMENT—

The following table indicates the minimum number of years of meritorious service required at each rate before advancement to the next rate. See also page 30.

$2160	1 year
2340	1 "
2580	2 years
2820	2 "

MISCELLANEOUS SUB-PROFESSIONAL WORKER GROUP

SYMBOL (B Z)

The term Miscellaneous Sub-professional Worker Group is applied to those offices or employments of the Sub-professional Service in which incumbents are required to perform routine or specialized sub-professional work of an exceptional nature not included in the other groups of the Sub-professional Service.

GRADE 1 (B Z 1)

TITLES OF POSITIONS[1]—

PSYCHOLOGIST

DUTIES—

Psychologist:

The duties of Psychologists are to give the Binet and other psychological tests to persons thought to be mentally abnormal, to interpret and compile the results of these tests, and to assist in conducting psychological research.

QUALIFICATIONS—

1. Not less than two years of training in experimental psychology at a college, university or psychological laboratory of recognized standing, or other training recognized by the Municipal Civil Service Commission as qualifying.

2. Such additional qualifications as may be required by the Municipal Civil Service Commission.

---

[1]The following positions are among those appraised by the Bureau of Personal Service in this grade on the basis of duties performed by present incumbents:

Psychologist at the clinic for atypical children, Department of Public Charities.

COMPENSATION—

Range of annual compensation for full-time service—$1500 to $1920 inclusive.

Salary rates—$1500, $1620, $1740, $1920.

Range of annual compensation for part-time service averaging not less than 21 hours a week—$900 to $1260 inclusive.

Salary rates—$900, $1020, $1140, $1260.

SPECIAL REGULATION GOVERNING COMPENSATION—

Persons entering this grade need not necessarily begin at the lowest rate. Fixation of the initial salary rate and advancement within this grade are conditional upon appraisal under the rules of the Board of Estimate and Apportionment, indicating that the rate requested does not exceed the value of the work to be performed.

INVESTIGATIONAL SERVICE

SYMBOL (V)

The term Investigational Service is applied to those offices or employments the duties of whose incumbents are to collect, examine into, classify and interpret facts pertaining to subjects, persons or things under investigation for the purpose of securing an independent basis for official action, to draw general conclusions or to make constructive suggestions and recommendations, where required, and to take such official action based upon the results of these investigations as may properly be delegated by responsible executives.

ATTENDANCE OFFICER GROUP

SYMBOL (V A)

The term Attendance Officer Group is applied to those offices or employments of the Investigational Service in which incumbents are required to perform such duties in connection with the enforcement of the compulsory education law, the taking of the school census and the employment of children in violation of the labor law as may be required by the by-laws, rules and regulations of the Board of Education.

GRADE 1 (V A 1)

TITLES OF POSITIONS—

ATTENDANCE OFFICER

DUTIES—

The duties of incumbents of these positions are to warn parents of the requirements of the compulsory education law and to prosecute them for violation of this law, to investigate cases of absence from school and to return truants to school, to enforce provisions of the labor law in regard to employment of children, to assist in taking the school census and to perform such other related duties as may properly be assigned.

QUALIFICATIONS—

1. A certificate of graduation from a public high school of the State of New York or proof of other training recognized by the Municipal Civil Service Commission as the equivalent.
2. Experience in probation work, teaching in the public schools, related settlement work, visiting for an organized charity or other charitable society, or in other charitable, social or investigational work recognized by the Municipal Civil Service Commission as qualifying or experience as Assistant Clerk B in the Bureau of Attendance.
3. Such additional qualifications as may be required by the Municipal Civil Service Commission.

COMPENSATION—

Range of annual compensation—$1200 to $1560 inclusive.
Salary rates—$1200, $1260, $1320, $1380, $1440, $1500, $1560.

GRADE 2 (V A 2)

TITLES OF POSITIONS—

SENIOR ATTENDANCE OFFICER

DUTIES—

The duties of incumbents of these positions are to be responsible for all attendance and census work in a district, to assign and supervise the work of large groups of Attendance Officers in Grade 1 and to perform investigations in special cases of a difficult character.

QUALIFICATIONS—

1. The minimum qualifications prescribed for Grade 1.
2. If appointed by promotion, not less than two years of appropriate experience in Grade 1, or if appointed as the result of an open competitive examination, experience in work of the character and standard of Grade 1.
3. Such additional qualifications as may be required by the Municipal Civil Service Commission.

COMPENSATION—

Range of annual compensation—$1680 to $2160 inclusive.
Salary rates—$1680, $1800, $1980, $2160.

SPECIAL REGULATION GOVERNING COMPENSATION—

Beginning with the lowest rate, advancement within this grade is conditional upon appraisal under the rules of the Board of Estimate and Apportionment, indicating that the rate requested does not exceed the value of the work to be performed.

SPECIAL CONDITION GOVERNING ADVANCEMENT—

The following table indicates the minimum number of years of meritorious service required at each rate before advancement to the next rate. See also page 30.

$1680	1 year
1800	2 years
1980	2 "

GRADE 3 (V A 3)

TITLES OF POSITIONS—

ASSISTANT CHIEF ATTENDANCE OFFICER

DUTIES—

The duties of incumbents of these positions are to conduct hearings for commitment and to supervise and direct the presentation of court cases in the boroughs of Manhattan and The Bronx or Brooklyn and Queens.

QUALIFICATIONS—

1. The minimum qualifications prescribed for Grade 2.
2. If appointed by promotion, not less than two years of appropriate experience in Grade 2, or if appointed as the result of an open competitive examination, experience in work of the character and standard of Grade 2.
3. Such additional qualifications as may be required by the Municipal Civil Service Commission.

COMPENSATION—

Range of annual compensation—$2340 to $2820 inclusive.
Salary rates—$2340, $2580, $2820.

SPECIAL REGULATION GOVERNING COMPENSATION—

Beginning with the lowest rate, advancement within this grade is conditional upon appraisal under the rules of the Board of Estimate and Apportionment, indicating that the rate requested does not exceed the value of the work to be performed.

GRADE 4 (V A 4)

TITLES OF POSITIONS—

CHIEF ATTENDANCE OFFICER

DUTIES—

The duties of the incumbent of this position are to supervise and be responsible for the work of employes in Grades 1, 2 and 3; to review commitment papers and monthly reports on children on parole or probation; to supervise the work of the newsboy squad and the child welfare division; to interview parents and children on parole or probation; to act as Secretary to the Board of Parole and to perform such other supervisory and administrative duties as may be required by the Director of the Bureau of Attendance.

QUALIFICATIONS—

1. The minimum qualifications prescribed for Grade 3.
2. If appointed by promotion, not less than two years of appropriate experience in Grade 3, or if appointed as the result of an open competitive examination, experience in work of the character and standard of Grade 3.
3. Such additional qualifications as may be required by the Municipal Civil Service Commission.

COMPENSATION—

Range of annual compensation—$3060 to $3540 inclusive.
Salary rates—$3060, $3300, $3540.

SPECIAL REGULATION GOVERNING COMPENSATION—

Beginning with the lowest rate, advancement within this grade is conditional upon appraisal under the rules of the Board of Estimate and Apportionment, indicating that the rate requested does not exceed the value of the work to be performed.

GRADE 5 (V A 5)

TITLES OF POSITIONS—

ASSISTANT DIRECTOR OF SCHOOL ATTENDANCE

DUTIES—

The duties of the incumbent of this position are to assist the Director of School Attendance in the enforcement of the compulsory education law, the taking of the school census and the investigation of the employment of children in violation of the labor law, and to perform such other related duties as may properly be assigned.[1]

QUALIFICATIONS—

1. The minimum qualifications prescribed for Grade 4.
2. If appointed by promotion, not less than two years of appropriate experience in Grade 4, or if appointed as the result of an open competitive examination, experience in work of the character and standard of Grade 4.
3. Such additional qualifications as may be required by the Municipal Civil Service Commission.

---

[1]It is probable that the position of Assistant Director of School Attendance could be eliminated under a proper organization. At the present time the positions of Director and Assistant Director are both statutory. If the position of Assistant Director were eliminated, a higher range of salary should be provided for the Director.

COMPENSATION—

Range of annual compensation—$3840 to $4140 inclusive.

Salary rates—$3840, $4140.

SPECIAL REGULATION GOVERNING COMPENSATION—

Beginning with the lowest rate, advancement within this grade is conditional upon appraisal under the rules of the Board of Estimate and Apportionment, indicating that the rate requested does not exceed the value of the work to be performed.

GRADE 6 (V A 6)

TITLES OF POSITIONS—

DIRECTOR OF SCHOOL ATTENDANCE

DUTIES—

The duties of the incumbent of this position, which involve supervision of employes in Grades 1, 2, 3, 4 and 5, are to enforce the compulsory education law, to commit and parole truant and delinquent children, to institute proceedings against persons in parental relation, to supervise the taking of the school census and to perform such other related duties as may be required by the by-laws, rules and regulations of the Board of Education.

QUALIFICATIONS—

1. The minimum qualifications prescribed for Grade 5.
2. If appointed by promotion, not less than one year of appropriate experience in Grade 5, or if appointed as the result of an open competitive examination, experience in work of the character and standard of Grade 5.
3. Such additional qualifications as may be required by the Municipal Civil Service Commission.

COMPENSATION—

Range of annual compensation—$4440 to $5160 inclusive.

Salary rates—$4440, $4740, $5160.

SPECIAL REGULATION GOVERNING COMPENSATION—

Persons entering this grade need not necessarily begin at the lowest rate. Fixation of the initial salary rate and advancement within this grade are conditional upon appraisal under the rules of the Board of Estimate and Apportionment, indicating that the rate requested does not exceed the value of the work to be performed.

CIVIL SERVICE EXAMINER GROUP

SYMBOL (V E)

The term Civil Service Examiner Group is applied to those offices or employments of the Investigational Service in which incumbents are required to gather information and to formulate questions for civil service examinations, to rate examination papers, to conduct physical, medical, practical and oral examinations, and to perform other assigned examining, investigating, publicity or supervisory work incident to filling positions in the civil service, to the installation and operation of a service record system, and to carrying out the provisions of the State Civil Service Law and the rules and regulations of the Municipal Civil Service Commission.

GRADE 1 (V E 1)

TITLES OF POSITIONS—

CIVIL SERVICE EXAMINER
PHYSICAL EXAMINER (CIVIL SERVICE)

DUTIES—

Civil Service Examiner:

The duties of Civil Service Examiners, which require familiarity with the organization and current work of city departments, and with the duties of assigned groups of city employes, are to formulate questions for civil service examinations, to rate examination papers, to conduct practical and oral examinations, to make under supervision special investigations of the work of departments or individuals, to assist in enforcing the rules and regulations of the Municipal Civil Service Commission regarding service records and the proper assignment of employes, to supervise the preparation and review of service records and to make recommendations governing their revision or acceptance.

Physical Examiner (Civil Service):

The duties of the Physical Examiner (Civil Service) are to conduct physical examinations under the supervision of the Supervising Civil Service Examiner (Medical) in accordance with the standards prescribed by the Municipal Civil Service Commission and to perform incidental clerical work.

QUALIFICATIONS—

Civil Service Examiner:

1. Such education as is evidenced by a degree, diploma or certificate granted on completion of a course in a university, college, technical school or normal school of recognized standing, or proof of other education or training recognized by the Municipal Civil Service Commission as the equivalent.
2. Experience in the city service, teaching, graduate work or other work recognized by the Municipal Civil Service Commission as qualifying.
3. Such additional qualifications as may be required by the Municipal Civil Service Commission.

Physical Examiner (Civil Service):

1. Experience as athletic instructor, instructor in recreation or gymnasium work, or trainer or coach of athletic teams.
2. Such additional qualifications as may be required by the Municipal Civil Service Commission.

COMPENSATION[1]—

Civil Service Examiner:

Range of annual compensation—$2100 to $2700 inclusive.
Salary rates—$2100, $2280, $2460, $2700.
Compensation per diem—$5 or $7.

Physical Examiner (Civil Service):

Range of annual compensation—$1680 to $2160 inclusive.
Salary rates—$1680, $1800, $1980, $2160.

---

[1]So far as possible, all the minor rating work, such as the rating of papers in examinations for 1st Grade Clerk, Caretaker, Bridge Tender and Court Attendant, should be performed by the per diem examiners at a rate of $5 a day. The minimum full-time rate at $2100 has been established on the assumption that the full-time examiners will be employed on the more important work of the Commission and not on the rating of elementary papers. The $7 per diem rate is established for the more important rating work in this grade which would ordinarily be done by full-time examiners, but which may be assigned to per diem examiners on account of pressure of work.

SPECIAL CONDITION GOVERNING ADVANCEMENT—

The following table indicates the minimum number of years of meritorious service required at each rate before advancement to the next rate. See also page 30.

Physical Examiner (Civil Service):

$1680	1 year
1800	2 years
1980	2 "

GRADE 2 (V E 2)

TITLES OF POSITIONS—

SENIOR CIVIL SERVICE EXAMINER
SENIOR CIVIL SERVICE EXAMINER (ENGINEERING)
SENIOR CIVIL SERVICE EXAMINER (MEDICAL)

DUTIES—

Senior Civil Service Examiner, Senior Civil Service Examiner (Engineering):

The duties of Senior Civil Service Examiners and Senior Civil Service Examiners (Engineering) are to perform work incident to highly technical examinations requiring an intimate knowledge of a recognized science or profession and of its place in and relation to the city government, or other work requiring the highest degree of efficiency and dependability in general examining and investigating work, or to direct and be responsible for the installation and keeping of service records in city departments and for investigation of the performance of work inappropriate to titles.

Examples:

Performing the duties of civil engineering examiner, or of examiner in charge of accounting, bookkeeping and business methods examinations.

Senior Civil Service Examiner (Medical):

The duties of Senior Civil Service Examiners (Medical) are to conduct original and promotional physical examinations under the supervision of the Supervising Civil Service Examiner (Medical) in accordance with the standards prescribed by the Municipal Civil Service Commission, and to assist, when called upon, in the preparation and rating of examinations for positions in or closely related to the medical field.

QUALIFICATIONS—

Senior Civil Service Examiner, Senior Civil Service Examiner (Engineering).

1. The minimum qualifications prescribed for Civil Service Examiner in Grade 1.

2. If appointed by promotion, not less than two years of appropriate experience as Civil Service Examiner in Grade 1, or if appointed as the result of an open competitive examination, experience in work of the character and standard of Grade 1.

3. In the case of examiners doing technical work, evidence of the completion of a standard course in a university, college or technical school of recognized standing, appropriate to the work contemplated, as in engineering, accounting, etc., and experience in the practice of that profession, or proof of other education or training recognized by the Municipal Civil Service Commission as qualifying.

4. Such additional qualifications as may be required by the Municipal Civil Service Commission.

The minimum qualifications shall consist of 1, 2, and 4, or 3 and 4.

Senior Civil Service Examiner (Medical):

1. A certificate or license to practice medicine issued by the Board of Regents of the University of the State of New York.
2. Experience in the practice of medicine.
3. Such additional qualifications as may be required by the Municipal Civil Service Commission.

COMPENSATION—

Senior Civil Service Examiner, Senior Civil Service Examiner (Engineering).

Range of annual compensation—$2940 to $3420 inclusive.
Salary rates—$2940, $3180, $3420.
Compensation per diem—$10.

Senior Civil Service Examiner (Medical):

Range of annual compensation for full-time service—$2940 to $3420 inclusive.
Salary rates—$2940, $3180, $3420.
Range of annual compensation for part-time service, aggregating not less than 18 hours a week—$2100 to $2460 inclusive.
Salary rates—$2100, $2280, $2460.
Compensation per diem—$10.

SPECIAL REGULATION GOVERNING COMPENSATION—

Beginning with the lowest rate, advancement within this grade is conditional upon appraisal under the rules of the Board of Estimate and Apportionment, indicating that the rate requested does not exceed the value of the work to be performed.

GRADE 3 (V E 3)

TITLES OF POSITIONS—

ASSISTANT CHIEF CIVIL SERVICE EXAMINER
SUPERVISING CIVIL SERVICE EXAMINER (MEDICAL)

DUTIES—

Assistant Chief Civil Service Examiner:

The duties of Assistant Chief Civil Service Examiners are to assist the Chief Civil Service Examiner in the planning, general direction and control of the examining work of the Municipal Civil Service Commission.

Supervising Civil Service Examiner (Medical):

The duties of the Supervising Civil Service Examiner (Medical), which are performed under the supervision of the Chief Civil Service Examiner, are to supervise and be responsible for the conduct of all physical examinations in accordance with the standards prescribed by the Municipal Civil Service Commission, to submit to the Commission recommendations on all debatable questions arising in connection with the rating of medical and physical examinations, and to assist, when called upon, in the selection of expert examiners and in the preparation and rating of papers for positions in or closely related to the medical field.

QUALIFICATIONS—

1. The minimum qualifications prescribed for Grade 2.
2. If appointed by promotion, not less than two years of appropriate experience in Grade 2, or if appointed as the result of an open competitive examination, experience in work of the character and standard of Grade 2.
3. Such additional qualifications as may be required by the Municipal Civil Service Commission.

COMPENSATION—

Assistant Chief Civil Service Examiner:

Range of annual compensation—$3660 to $4260 inclusive.
Salary rates—$3660, $3960, $4260.

Supervising Civil Service Examiner (Medical):

Range of annual compensation for full-time service—$3660 to $4260 inclusive.
Salary rates—$3660, $3960, $4260.

Range of annual compensation for part-time service, aggregating not less than 18 hours a week—$2700 to $3180 inclusive.
Salary rates—$2700, $2940, $3180.

SPECIAL REGULATION GOVERNING COMPENSATION—

Beginning with the lowest rate, advancement within this grade is conditional upon appraisal under the rules of the Board of Estimate and Apportionment, indicating that the rate requested does not exceed the value of the work to be performed.

GRADE 4 (V E 4)

TITLES OF POSITIONS—

CHIEF CIVIL SERVICE EXAMINER

DUTIES—

The duties of the incumbent of this position, which involve supervision of employes in Grades 1, 2 and 3, are to direct the entire work of conducting civil service examinations, including complete responsibility for the planning and satisfactory progress of examinations and the technique of examining and rating.

QUALIFICATIONS—

1. The minimum qualifications prescribed for Assistant Chief Civil Service Examiner in Grade 3.
2. If appointed by promotion, not less than one year of appropriate experience in Grade 3, or if appointed as the result of an open competitive examination, experience in work of the character and standard of Grade 3.
3. Such additional qualifications as may be required by the Municipal Civil Service Commission.

COMPENSATION—

Range of annual compensation—$4560 to $4860 inclusive.
Salary rates—$4560, $4860.

SPECIAL REGULATION GOVERNING COMPENSATION—

Beginning with the lowest rate, advancement within this grade is conditional upon appraisal under the rules of the Board of Estimate and Apportionment, indicating that the rate requested does not exceed the value of the work to be performed.

CIVIL SERVICE INVESTIGATOR GROUP

SYMBOL (V C)

The term Civil Service Investigator Group is applied to those offices or employments of the Investigational Service in which incumbents are required to investigate or to supervise the investigation of the accuracy of statements made by civil service candidates in their experience papers and character sheets, and to make such further investigations into the character, experience and career of candidates and into the improper assignment of employes in the civil service as may be required.

GRADE 1 (V C 1)

TITLES OF POSITIONS—

CIVIL SERVICE INVESTIGATOR

DUTIES—

The duties of incumbents of these positions are to investigate the accuracy of statements made by candidates in civil service examinations in their experience papers and character sheets, to make such further investigations into the character, experience and career of candidates and into the improper assignment of employes in the civil service as may be required by the Supervising Civil Service Investigator, and to make written reports of the results of their investigations.

QUALIFICATIONS—

1. Experience in investigational work for a government department, life insurance company or charitable, social or economic agency, or in other work recognized by the Municipal Civil Service Commission as qualifying.
2. Such additional qualifications as may be required by the Municipal Civil Service Commission.

COMPENSATION—

Range of annual compensation—$1500 to $1740 inclusive.
Salary rates—$1500, $1560, $1620, $1680, $1740.

SPECIAL CONDITION GOVERNING ADVANCEMENT—

The following table indicates the minimum number of years of meritorious service required at each rate before advancement to the next rate. See also page 30.

$1500	1 year
1560	1 "
1620	2 years
1680	2 "

GRADE 2 (V C 2)

TITLES OF POSITIONS—

SUPERVISING CIVIL SERVICE INVESTIGATOR

DUTIES—

The duties of the incumbent of this position, which are performed under the direction of the members of the Municipal Civil Service Commission, are to supervise the work of Civil Service Investigators and to be responsible for the accuracy of reports on statements made by candidates in experience papers and on other subjects of investigation.

QUALIFICATIONS—

1. The minimum qualifications prescribed for Grade 1.
2. If appointed by promotion, not less than three years of appropriate experience in Grade 1, or if appointed as the result of an open competitive examination, experience in work of the character and standard of Grade 1.
3. Such additional qualifications as may be required by the Municipal Civil Service Commission.

COMPENSATION—

Range of annual compensation—$2400 to $3120 inclusive.
Salary rates—$2400, $2640, $2880, $3120.

CLAIM INVESTIGATOR GROUP

SYMBOL (V K).

The term Claim Investigator Group is applied to those offices or employments of the Investigational Service in which incumbents are required to investigate and report on claims, to serve subpoenas and other legal papers, to examine records, to locate and interrogate witnesses, to be in attendance at court at time of trial, or to supervise this work, and to perform other investigational or clerical work incident to the litigation or audit of claims against the city.

GRADE 1 (V K 1)

TITLES OF POSITIONS—

CLAIM INVESTIGATOR

DUTIES—

The duties of incumbents of these positions are to investigate and report on claims, to serve subpoenas and other legal papers, to examine records, to locate and interrogate witnesses, to be in attendance at court at time of trial, and to perform other investigational or clerical work incident to the litigation or audit of claims against the city.

QUALIFICATIONS—

1. Experience in investigating for a railroad company or insurance company, or in other work recognized by the Municipal Civil Service Commission as qualifying.
2. Such additional qualifications as may be required by the Municipal Civil Service Commission.

COMPENSATION—

Range of annual compensation—$1080 to $1500 inclusive.
Salary rates—$1080, $1140, $1200, $1260, $1320, $1380, $1440, $1500.

SPECIAL REGULATION GOVERNING COMPENSATION—

Beginning with the lowest rate, advancement within this grade is conditional upon appraisal under the rules of the Board of Estimate and Apportionment, indicating that the rate requested does not exceed the value of the work to be performed.

SPECIAL CONDITION GOVERNING ADVANCEMENT—

The following table indicates the minimum number of years of meritorious service required at each rate before advancement to the next rate. See also page 30.

$1080	1 year
1140	1 "
1200	1 "
1260	1 "
1320	2 years
1380	2 "
1440	2 "

GRADE 2 (V K 2)

TITLES OF POSITIONS—

SENIOR CLAIM INVESTIGATOR

DUTIES—

The duties of incumbents of these positions are to supervise a group of employes in Grade 1 and to be responsible for a branch or division of their investigational work, or to make special investigations and reports on matters incident to the litigation and audit of claims, requiring a high order of tact, knowledge and experience.

QUALIFICATIONS—

1. The minimum qualifications prescribed for Grade 1.

2. If appointed by promotion, not less than two years of appropriate experience in Grade 1, or if appointed as the result of an open competitive examination, experience in work of the character and standard of Grade 1.

3. Such additional qualifications as may be required by the Municipal Civil Service Commission.

COMPENSATION—

Range of annual compensation—$1620 to $2280 inclusive.

Salary rates—$1620, $1740, $1920, $2100, $2280.

SPECIAL REGULATION GOVERNING COMPENSATION—

Beginning with the lowest rate, advancement within this grade is conditional upon appraisal under the rules of the Board of Estimate and Apportionment, indicating that the rate requested does not exceed the value of the work to be performed.

SPECIAL CONDITION GOVERNING ADVANCEMENT—

The following table indicates the minimum number of years of meritorious service required at each rate before advancement to the next rate. See also page 30.

$1620	1 year
1740	2 years
1920	2 "
2100	2 "

GRADE 3 (V K 3)

TITLES OF POSITIONS—

CHIEF CLAIM INVESTIGATOR

DUTIES—

The duties of the incumbent of this position, which involve supervision of groups of employes in Grades 1 and 2, are to be responsible for investigation relative to the litigation and audit in the Finance Department of claims for damages to person or property and of affirmative claims in favor of the city and to make independently the most important and responsible investigations and reports relative to claims of the above nature.

QUALIFICATIONS—

1. The minimum qualifications prescribed for Grade 2.

2. If appointed by promotion, not less than two years of appropriate experience in Grade 2, or if appointed as the result of an open competitive examination, experience in work of the character and standard of Grade 2.

3. Such additional qualifications as may be required by the Municipal Civil Service Commission.

COMPENSATION—

Range of annual compensation—$2520 to $3000 inclusive.

Salary rates—$2520, $2760, $3000.

FIRE MARSHAL GROUP

SYMBOL (V F)

The term Fire Marshal Group is applied to those offices or employments of the Investigational Service in which incumbents are required to investigate and report on the cause, circumstances and origin of fires, to examine witnesses, to report all violations of the laws and ordinances relating to fire prevention, to prepare evidence in arson cases, to be in attendance at court at time of trial, or to supervise this work, and to perform other incidental investigational or clerical work.

GRADE 1 (V F 1)

TITLES OF POSITIONS—

ASSISTANT FIRE MARSHAL

DUTIES—

The duties of incumbents of these positions, which require considerable detective ability, are to investigate and report on the cause, circumstances and origin of fires, to examine witnesses, to report all violations of the laws and ordinances relating to fire prevention, to prepare evidence in arson cases and to be in attendance at court at time of trial.

QUALIFICATIONS—

1. Experience in investigating work for a fire insurance company, or in other work recognized by the Municipal Civil Service Commission as qualifying.
2. Such additional qualifications as may be required by the Municipal Civil Service Commission.

COMPENSATION—

Range of annual compensation—$1500 to $1740 inclusive.
Salary rates—$1500, $1560, $1620, $1680, $1740.

SPECIAL CONDITION GOVERNING ADVANCEMENT—

The following table indicates the minimum number of years of meritorious service required at each rate before advancement to the next rate. See also page 30.

$1500	1 year
1560	1 "
1620	2 years
1680	2 "

GRADE 2 (V F 2)[1]

TITLES OF POSITIONS—

SENIOR ASSISTANT FIRE MARSHAL

DUTIES—

The duties of incumbents of these positions, which may or may not involve supervision of employes in Grade 1, are to perform fire investigating work of the most difficult and responsible nature requiring the highest degree of ability and experience in the detection of arson.

QUALIFICATIONS—

1. The minimum qualifications prescribed for Grade 1.
2. If appointed by promotion, not less than two years of appropriate experience in Grade 1, or if appointed as the result of an open competitive examination, experience in work of the character and standard of Grade 1.
3. Such additional qualifications as may be required by the Municipal Civil Service Commission.

COMPENSATION—

Range of annual compensation—$1920 to $2280 inclusive.
Salary rates—$1920, $2100, $2280.

---

[1]It is contemplated that very few positions in this grade will be required It is not intended that employes in Grade 1 shall graduate into Grade 2 merely as the result of long and satisfactory service. The purpose is to establish only as many positions in Grade 2 as are required for the performance of exceptionally difficult and responsible work and to fill these positions by the promotion of the most expert and trustworthy employes in Grade 1.

SPECIAL REGULATION GOVERNING COMPENSATION—

Beginning with the lowest rate, advancement within this grade is conditional upon appraisal under the rules of the Board of Estimate and Apportionment, indicating that the rate requested does not exceed the value of the work to be performed.

SPECIAL CONDITION GOVERNING ADVANCEMENT—

The following table indicates the minimum number of years of meritorious service required at each rate before advancement to the next rate. See also page 30.

$1920	2 years
2100	2 "

GRADE 3 (V F 3)

TITLES OF POSITIONS—

FIRE MARSHAL

DUTIES—

The duties of the incumbent of this position, which involve supervision of employes in Grades 1 and 2, are to act as deputy and assistant to the Chief Fire Marshal.

QUALIFICATIONS—

1. The minimum qualifications prescribed for Grade 2.
2. If appointed by promotion, not less than two years of appropriate experience in Grade 2, or if appointed as the result of an open competitive examination, experience in work of the character and standard of Grade 2.
3. Such additional qualifications as may be required by the Municipal Civil Service Commission.

COMPENSATION—

Range of annual compensation—$2520 to $3000 inclusive.

Salary rates—$2520, $2760, $3000.

SPECIAL REGULATION GOVERNING COMPENSATION—

Beginning with the lowest rate, advancement within this grade is conditional upon appraisal under the rules of the Board of Estimate and Apportionment, indicating that the rate requested does not exceed the value of the work to be performed.

GRADE 4 (V F 4)

TITLES OF POSITIONS—

CHIEF FIRE MARSHAL[1]

DUTIES—

The duties of the incumbent of this position, which require the highest order of specialized knowledge, are to supervise and be responsible for the work of a central fire investigating bureau for the whole city.

QUALIFICATIONS—

1. The minimum qualifications prescribed for Grade 3.
2. If appointed by promotion, not less than one year of appropriate experience in Grade 3, or if appointed as the result of an open competitive examination, experience in work of the character and standard of Grade 3.
3. Such additional qualifications as may be required by the Municipal Civil Service Commission.

---

[1]The present title of the position in this grade as provided in the charter is Fire Marshal. There is no legal obstacle to the use of the prefix Chief in connection with the statutory title.

COMPENSATION—

Range of annual compensation—$3600 to $4800 inclusive.
Salary rates—$3600, $3900, $4200, $4500, $4800.

SPECIAL REGULATION GOVERNING COMPENSATION—

Beginning with the lowest rate, advancement within this grade is conditional upon appraisal under the rules of the Board of Estimate and Apportionment, indicating that the rate requested does not exceed the value of the work to be performed.

MUNICIPAL EXAMINER GROUP

SYMBOL (VM)

The term Municipal Examiner Group is applied to those offices or employments of the Investigational Service in which incumbents are required to inquire into and to make critical and constructive reports on the organization, methods, procedure, results, requests for appropriations, and expenditures in the various branches of the city government, or to gather information, to make studies and reports, or to perform other investigational work in order to keep executive officials informed as to the details of administration, or to assist the Board of Estimate and Apportionment and the Board of Aldermen in reaching decisions on important projects and policies.[1]

GRADE 1 (V M 1)

TITLES OF POSITIONS—

ASSISTANT MUNICIPAL EXAMINER
ASSISTANT MUNICIPAL EXAMINER (SPECIAL)[2]

DUTIES—

The duties of incumbents of these positions are to perform, as assistants to employes in Grade 2 or independently, the less important descriptive, critical or constructive investigational work for central agencies or for executive or legislative officials of the city government.

---

[1] Much of the work outlined in this group may properly be performed either under the title of Municipal Examiner or under titles in the Accountant and Engineer Groups, and in some cases under titles in the Clerk Group. This will allow heads of departments considerable freedom in the choice of employes for investigational work. In general, the work outlined in this group will be performed by Municipal Examiners, but it will be possible for heads of departments to choose Accountants and Engineers for the same kind of work, and in exceptional cases to employ Clerks on the less important details of this work. The creation of new and peculiar titles, such as Efficiency Engineer, Efficiency Examiner, Efficiency Accountant, and other titles prefaced by the word Expert, marks an attempt to give a professional status to so-called efficiency work. Efficiency is an object of all professional or business training and is an important element in the successful practice of any profession or the transaction of any business. There appears to be no justification for the creation of special efficiency titles in the municipal civil service. In establishing a new standard classification of positions in the City of New York, an attempt has been made to avoid using any of these misleading and undescriptive titles.

[2] The title of Assistant Municipal Examiner (Special) is used to refer to exempt positions involving duties of a special or confidential nature which render it desirable that the incumbent shall be the personal choice of the appointing officer.

Examples:

Assisting in gathering data for organization charts.

Reporting on minor changes in budget lines, transfer of funds, etc., for the Board of Estimate and Apportionment.

Making minor investigations for the Commissioner of Accounts.

Gathering data under supervision for standard supply specifications.

Gathering information and statistics as to organization, methods of procedure, conditions, etc., in municipal activities in other cities.

Gathering general information bearing upon authorization of corporate stock or revenue bond issue.

Performing under supervision minor work in the preparation of the annual budget.

Assisting in gathering cost data.

Performing general utility or apprentice work involved in the conduct of a central investigating agency.

QUALIFICATIONS[1]—

1. Evidence of the completion of a standard course of instruction in a recognized college or university, including study of government or political science, or other education or experience recognized by the Municipal Civil Service Commission as the equivalent.

2. Not less than one year of professional or graduate university study or of experience in business, professional or investigational work.

3. If appointed by promotion, not less than two years of experience in other groups of the city service recognized by the Municipal Civil Service Commission as qualifying.

4. Such additional qualifications as may be required by the Municipal Civil Service Commission.

The minimum qualifications shall consist of 1, 2 and 4 or 3 and 4.

COMPENSATION—

Range of annual compensation—$1200 to $1800 inclusive.

Salary rates—$1200, $1320, $1440, $1560, $1680, $1800.

GRADE 2 (V M 2)

TITLES OF POSITIONS—

MUNICIPAL EXAMINER
MUNICIPAL EXAMINER (SPECIAL)[2]

DUTIES—

The duties of incumbents of these positions are to perform independently or under supervision important and responsible descriptive, critical or constructive investigational work for central agencies or for executive or legislative officials of the city government.

---

[1]Investigations or studies designed to bring about greater efficiency in any organization or function of municipal government, or to realize important projects and plans of the Board of Estimate and Apportionment and executive officials, are extremely varied and generally demand a certain type of investigating mind, critical ability, both analytical and constructive, general education and common sense, rather than any special kind of training. It is frequently impossible to decide that a particular kind of professional training or experience is prerequisite.

[2]The title of Municipal Examiner (Special) is used to refer to exempt positions involving duties of a special or confidential nature which render it desirable that the incumbent shall be the personal choice of the appointing officer.

Examples:

Examining into and reporting on recommendations on requests for special revenue bonds, transfer of funds affecting supplies, material, equipment and contract or open order appropriations.

Reporting on requests for corporate stock appropriations, where engineering knowledge is not essential, including a report on the necessity for the proposed expenditure, the advisability of allowing funds for the particular improvement desired and an analysis of the proposed cost.

Making investigations in the preparation of the annual budget.

Reporting on personal service matters in an assigned division, bureau or department.

Preparing record charts of the present or proper organization of departments.

Making under supervision functional studies of bureaus or divisions of city departments, for the purpose of reorganization or economy.

Installing, under the supervision of a Senior Municipal Examiner, Engineer or Accountant, proper cost accounting methods in city departments.

Making investigations in the preparation of standard specifications for supply purchases by the city.

Making studies and investigations, compiling statistics, etc., not requiring the highest degree of expert knowledge and experience, for the committees of the Board of Estimate and Apportionment, such as Committee on Social Welfare, Education, City Plan, etc.

QUALIFICATIONS—

1. The minimum qualifications prescribed for Grade 1.
2. If appointed by promotion, not less than two years of appropriate experience in Grade 1, or if appointed as the result of an open competitive examination, experience in work of the character and standard of Grade 1.
3. Such additional qualifications as may be required by the Municipal Civil Service Commission.

COMPENSATION—

Range of annual compensation—$1980 to $2820 inclusive.

Salary rates—$1980, $2160, $2340, $2580, $2820.

SPECIAL REGULATION GOVERNING COMPENSATION—

Beginning with the lowest rate, advancement within this grade is conditional upon appraisal under the rules of the Board of Estimate and Apportionment, indicating that the rate requested does not exceed the value of the work to be performed.

GRADE 3 (V M 3)

TITLES OF POSITIONS—

SENIOR MUNICIPAL EXAMINER

SENIOR MUNICIPAL EXAMINER (SPECIAL)[1]

DUTIES—

The duties of incumbents of these positions are to exercise supervision over investigations outlined in Grades 1 and 2 and to be responsible for important units or divisions of the work in investigational bureaus, or for independent investigational work requiring the highest degree of judgment and dependability.

---

[1] The title of Senior Municipal Examiner (Special) is used to refer to exempt positions involving duties of a special or confidential nature which render it desirable that the incumbent shall be the personal choice of the appointing officer.

Examples:

Taking charge of the field work on a large inquiry for the Mayor, under the supervision of the Commissioner of Accounts, such as the preparation of a descriptive work on the organization of city departments for the Constitutional Convention.

Taking charge of all personal service matters in a group of city departments.

Reporting on important corporate stock appropriations, transfer of funds, or requests for special revenue bonds.

Gathering data and reporting on recreation for the Committee on Social Welfare.

Taking charge of an analysis of expenditures, organization and methods in a bureau, division or department under the Mayor, for the purpose of reorganization, economy, or the introduction of improved methods.

QUALIFICATIONS—

1. The minimum qualifications prescribed for Grade 2.
2. If appointed by promotion, not less than two years of appropriate experience in Grade 2, or if appointed as the result of an open competitive examination, experience in work of the character and standard of Grade 2.
3. Such additional qualifications as may be required by the Municipal Civil Service Commission.

COMPENSATION—

Range of annual compensation—$3060 to $3840 inclusive.
Salary rates—$3060, $3300, $3540, $3840.

SPECIAL REGULATION GOVERNING COMPENSATION—

Persons entering this grade need not necessarily begin at the lowest rate. Fixation of the initial salary rate and advancement within this grade are conditional upon appraisal under the rules of the Board of Estimate and Apportionment, indicating that the rate requested does not exceed the value of the work to be performed.

GRADE 4 (V M 4)

TITLES OF POSITIONS[1]—

CHIEF MUNICIPAL EXAMINER
CHIEF MUNICIPAL EXAMINER (PENSIONS)
CHIEF MUNICIPAL EXAMINER (PERSONAL SERVICE)
CHIEF MUNICIPAL EXAMINER (SPECIAL)[2]

DUTIES—

Chief Municipal Examiner:

The duties of Chief Municipal Examiners, which involve supervision of employes in Grades 2 and 3, are to take charge of an important major division of an investigational bureau or to assist the head of the bureau in the conduct of its entire business, or to supervise and be responsible for an entire small investigational bureau or unit.

---

[1] The following positions are among those appraised by the Bureau of Personal Service in this grade on the basis of duties performed by present incumbents:

Chief Municipal Examiner in the office of the Commissioner of Accounts.

Chief Municipal Examiner acting as assistant to the Director of the Bureau of Personal Service.

[2] The title of Chief Municipal Examiner (Special) is used to refer to exempt positions involving duties of a special or confidential nature which render it desirable that the incumbent shall be the personal choice of the appointing officer.

Chief Municipal Examiner (Pensions):

The duties of the Chief Municipal Examiner (Pensions), which require executive ability and wide experience in pension investigations, are to supervise and be responsible for the entire staff engaged in pension work, including the study of present systems, the formulation of plans for a proper co-ordinative pension system and reporting on current pension questions.

Chief Municipal Examiner (Personal Service):

The duties of Chief Municipal Examiners (Personal Service), which involve supervision of employes in Grades 1, 2 and 3, are to assume a major responsibility for investigational work in preparing and reporting on modifications of personal service schedules in the annual tax budget, in reporting on requests for corporate stock and revenue bonds for personal service, and in the most important studies of the proper organization of the personnel of departments for purposes of budget preparation, current reporting or charter revision, and to perform such other important work relating to budget investigation as may be assigned by the Director (Bureau of Personal Service) or other executive officers.

QUALIFICATIONS—

Chief Municipal Examiner, Chief Municipal Examiner (Personal Service):

1. The minimum qualifications prescribed for Grade 3.
2. If appointed by promotion, not less than two years of appropriate experience in Grade 3, or if appointed as the result of an open competitive examination, experience in work of the character and standard of Grade 3.
3. Such additional qualifications as may be required by the Municipal Civil Service Commission.

Chief Municipal Examiner (Pensions):

1. Experience in a supervisory capacity in the investigation of pension systems or experience in independent investigation of large pension funds, or other experience in pension work recognized by the Municipal Civil Service Commission as qualifying.
2. Such additional qualifications as may be required by the Municipal Civil Service Commission.

COMPENSATION—

Range of annual compensation for full-time service—$4140 to $4740 inclusive.

Salary rates—$4140, $4440, $4740.

Range of annual compensation for part-time service, averaging not less than 18 hours a week—$2400 to $2880 inclusive.

Salary rates—$2400, $2640, $2880.

Compensation per diem for service of an occasional nature or of short duration—$15.

SPECIAL REGULATION GOVERNING COMPENSATION—

Persons entering this grade need not necessarily begin at the lowest rate. Fixation of the initial salary rate and advancement within this grade are conditional upon appraisal under the rules of the Board of Estimate and Apportionment, indicating that the rate requested does not exceed the value of the work to be performed.

GRADE 5 (V M 5)

TITLES OF POSITIONS—

DIRECTOR (BUREAU OF CONTRACT SUPERVISION)
DIRECTOR (BUREAU OF PERSONAL SERVICE)
SUPERVISING STATISTICIAN AND EXAMINER

DUTIES—

The duties of incumbents of these positions, which involve supervision of employes in Grades 1, 2, 3 and 4 of the Municipal Examiner Group and of engineers, accountants and other employes properly assigned to investigational work, are to assume responsibility for special investigations or current reporting of the widest scope as a basis for the determination of major policies of government or for current executive action.

QUALIFICATIONS—

1. The minimum qualifications prescribed for Grade 4.
2. If appointed by promotion, not less than one year of appropriate experience in Grade 4, or if appointed as the result of an open competitive examination, experience in work of the character and standard of Grade 4.
3. Such additional qualifications as may be required by the Municipal Civil Service Commission.

COMPENSATION[1]—

Range of annual compensation for full-time service—$6000 and up.

Range of annual compensation for part-time service, averaging not less than 18 hours a week—$3000 and up.

Compensation per diem for service of an occasional nature or of short duration—$20 or $25, according to the nature and responsibility of the services to be rendered and the qualifications of the appointee.

SPECIAL REGULATION GOVERNING COMPENSATION—

Persons entering this grade need not necessarily begin at the lowest rate. Fixation of the initial salary rate and advancement within this grade are conditional upon appraisal under the rules of the Board of Estimate and Apportionment, indicating that the rate requested does not exceed the value of the work to be performed.

PROBATION OFFICER GROUP

SYMBOL (V P)

The term Probation Officer Group is applied to those offices or employments of the Investigational Service in which incumbents are required to investigate and report on cases of persons awaiting disposition by the courts or the Board of Parole and to exercise helpful and authoritative supervision, subject to the direction of the courts or the Board of Parole, over persons under probation or on parole, or to direct and be responsible for the above work.

GRADE 1 (V P 1)

TITLES OF POSITIONS—

PROBATION OFFICER
PAROLE OFFICER

DUTIES—

The duties of incumbents of these positions are to investigate cases of persons awaiting disposition by the courts or by the Board of Parole, to report to the proper authorities upon such investigations, to exercise helpful and authoritative supervision over persons under probation or on parole, and to enforce orders regarding such persons.

---

[1]This range of compensation may be applied to positions as heads of the most important permanent or temporary investigational bureaus or commissions.

QUALIFICATIONS—

1. A certificate of graduation from a public high school of the State of New York, or proof of other training recognized by the Municipal Civil Service Commission as the equivalent.

2. Experience in volunteer probation work, teaching in the public schools, related settlement work, visiting for an organized charity, or other charitable or social work recognized by the Municipal Civil Service Commission as qualifying.

3. Such additional qualifications as may be required by the Municipal Civil Service Commission.

COMPENSATION—

Range of annual compensation—$1200 to $1560 inclusive.
Salary rates—$1200, $1260, $1320, $1380, $1440, $1500, $1560.

SPECIAL CONDITION GOVERNING ADVANCEMENT—

The following table indicates the minimum number of years of meritorious service required at each rate before advancement to the next rate. See also page 30.

$1200	1 year
1260	1 "
1320	1 "
1380	1 "
1440	2 years
1500	2 "

GRADE 2 (V P 2)

TITLES OF POSITIONS[1]—

SENIOR PROBATION OFFICER
SENIOR PAROLE OFFICER

DUTIES—

Senior Probation Officer:

The duties of Senior Probation Officers, which may include supervision of Probation Officers in Grade 1, are to take charge continuously in a particular part of the court, under the Chief Probation Officer, of the most difficult probation work involving the re-establishment of normal family life, the supervision of female delinquents, or other complex problems.

Senior Parole Officer:

The duties of Senior Parole Officers are to supervise and be responsible to the Chief Parole Officer for the work of Parole Officers in Grade 1, and to perform independently when required investigations requiring a high degree of ability and experience in parole work.

QUALIFICATIONS—

1. The minimum qualifications prescribed for Grade 1.

2. If appointed by promotion, not less than two years of appropriate experience in Grade 1, or if appointed as the result of an open competitive examination, experience in work of the character and standard of Grade 1.

3. Such additional qualifications as may be required by the Municipal Civil Service Commission.

---

[1] The following positions are among those appraised by the Bureau of Personal Service in this grade on the basis of duties performed by present incumbents:
Senior Probation Officer in the Children's Court.
Senior Probation Officer in the Court of Domestic Relations.
Senior Probation Officer in the Women's Night Court.

COMPENSATION—

Range of annual compensation—$1680 to $2160 inclusive.
Salary rates—$1680, $1800, $1980, $2160.

SPECIAL REGULATION GOVERNING COMPENSATION—

Beginning with the lowest rate, advancement within this grade is conditional upon appraisal under the rules of the Board of Estimate and Apportionment, indicating that the rate requested does not exceed the value of the work to be performed.

SPECIAL CONDITION GOVERNING ADVANCEMENT—

The following table indicates the minimum number of years of meritorious service required at each rate before advancement to the next rate. See also page 30.

$1680	1 year
1800	2 years
1980	2 "

GRADE 3 (V P 3)

TITLES OF POSITIONS[1]—

DEPUTY CHIEF PROBATION OFFICER

DUTIES—

Deputy Chief Probation Officer:

The duties of Deputy Chief Probation Officers, which include supervision of employes in Grades 1 and 2, are to assist the Chief Probation Officer in the general direction of all probation work or to direct and be responsible to the Chief Probation Officer for a major division of probation work in a group of courts.

QUALIFICATIONS—

1. The minimum qualifications prescribed for Grade 1 or Grade 2.
2. If appointed by promotion, not less than three years of appropriate experience in Grade 1 or two years of appropriate experience in Grade 2, or if appointed as the result of an open competitive examination, experience in work of the character and standard of Grade 2.
3. Such additional qualifications as may be required by the Municipal Civil Service Commission.

COMPENSATION—

Range of annual compensation—$2340 to $2820 inclusive.
Salary rates—$2340, $2580, $2820.

SPECIAL REGULATION GOVERNING COMPENSATION—

Persons entering this grade need not necessarily begin at the lowest rate. Fixation of the initial salary rate and advancement within this grade are conditional upon appraisal under the rules of the Board of Estimate and Apportionment, indicating that the rate requested does not exceed the value of the work to be performed.

---

[1] The following positions are among those appraised by the Bureau of Personal Service in this grade on the basis of duties performed by present incumbents:

Deputy Chief Probation Officer in the Magistrates' Court.
Deputy Chief Probation Officer in the Children's Court.

GRADE 4 (V P 4)

TITLES OF POSITIONS[1]—

CHIEF PROBATION OFFICER
CHIEF PAROLE OFFICER

DUTIES—

Chief Probation Officer:

The duties of Chief Probation Officers, which include supervision of employes in Grades 1, 2 and 3, are to direct and be responsible to magistrates or judges for the entire probation work of a group of courts.

Chief Parole Officer:

The duties of the Chief Parole Officer, which include supervision of employes in Grades 1 and 2, are to direct and be responsible to the Parole Commission for the work of Parole Officers and of employes of the Police Department assigned to co-operate in parole work and to perform personally such highly responsible parole work as may be required.

QUALIFICATIONS—

Chief Probation Officer:

1. The minimum qualifications prescribed for Grade 3.
2. If appointed by promotion, not less than one year of appropriate experience in Grade 3, or if appointed as the result of an open competitive examination, experience in work of the character and standard of Grade 3.
3. Such additional qualifications as may be required by the Municipal Civil Service Commission.

Chief Parole Officer:

1. The minimum qualifications prescribed for Grade 2.
2. If appointed by promotion, not less than two years of appropriate experience in Grade 2, or if appointed as the result of an open competitive examination, experience in work of the character and standard of Grade 2.
3. Such additional qualifications as may be required by the Municipal Civil Service Commission.

COMPENSATION[2]—

Range of annual compensation—$3060 to $4140 inclusive.
Salary rates—$3060, $3300, $3540, $3840, $4140.

SPECIAL REGULATION GOVERNING COMPENSATION—

Persons entering this grade need not necessarily begin at the lowest rate. Fixation of the initial salary rate and advancement within this grade are conditional upon appraisal under the rules of the Board of Estimate and Apportionment, indicating that the rate requested does not exceed the value of the work to be performed.

---

[1] The following positions are among those appraised by the Bureau of Personal Service in this grade on the basis of duties performed by present incumbents:

Chief Probation Officer in the Court of Special Sessions.
Chief Probation Officer in the Children's Court.
Chief Probation Officer in the Magistrates' Court.

[2] Arrangements have been made to increase gradually the number of employes under the supervision of the Chief Parole Officer to keep pace with the increasing volume of parole work. The necessary force will have been established toward the end of the current year. The minimum salary recommended for the position of Chief Parole Officer should not therefore be made effective till at least January, 1918.

SOCIAL INVESTIGATOR GROUP

SYMBOL (V V)

The term Social Investigator Group is applied to those offices or employments of the Investigational Service in which incumbents are required to perform, supervise, or direct investigation of the circumstances of persons receiving or applying for charitable relief from the City of New York and to take proper action toward relief, or to inspect and investigate private charitable institutions receiving funds from the city.

GRADE 1 (V V 1)[1]

TITLES OF POSITIONS—

CHARITY APPLICATION INVESTIGATOR

DUTIES—

The duties of incumbents of these positions are to receive applications for admission to any of the charitable institutions of the city and such applications as are referred from one institution to another, to interview applicants for institutional care, treatment and relief, to receive and interview parents seeking the commitment of, admission of, or material relief for children, and to record, index and file histories.[2]

QUALIFICATIONS—

1. Experience in investigational work for public or private charitable institutions or other experience recognized by the Municipal Civil Service Commission as qualifying.
2. Such additional qualifications as may be required by the Municipal Civil Service Commission.

COMPENSATION—

Range of annual compensation—$600 to $900 inclusive.
Salary rates—$600, $660, $720, $780, $840, $900.

SPECIAL REGULATION GOVERNING COMPENSATION—

Beginning with the lowest rate, advancement within this grade is conditional upon appraisal under the rules of the Board of Estimate and Apportionment, indicating that the rate requested does not exceed the value of the work to be performed.

GRADE 2 (V V 2)

TITLES OF POSITIONS—

SOCIAL INVESTIGATOR

DUTIES—

The duties of incumbents of these positions are to ascertain and report facts regarding the economic and social condition of persons receiving or applying for institutional or other relief from the City of New York, to suggest remedial measures and to take such action toward relief as may be directed by a superior or determined by rules or general instructions.

---

[1] The following positions are among those appraised by the Bureau of Personal Service in this grade on the basis of duties performed by present incumbents:

Charity Application Investigator in the hospital admission bureaus and in the several district offices of the Bureau of Social Investigation in the Department of Public Charities.

[2] This position is to be distinguished carefully from the position of Social Investigator in Grade 2, to which there will be no promotion from this grade. This is a special office position of a quasi-investigational character limited to the hospital bureaus and district offices of the Department of Public Charities and requiring the services of an experienced and mature woman. No field work is involved.

QUALIFICATIONS—

1. A certificate of graduation from a public high school of the State of New York or proof of other training recognized by the Municipal Civil Service Commission as the equivalent.

2. Any one of the three following alternatives:

A. A two years' course in a professional training school recognized by the Municipal Civil Service Commission as qualifying for this work, or other educational experience recognized by the Municipal Civil Service Commission as the equivalent.

B. Experience in related settlement work, visiting for an organized charity, or other charitable or social work recognized by the Municipal Civil Service Commission as qualifying.

C. A four years' college course, including instruction in economics, sociology, or related subjects, approved by the Municipal Civil Service Commission.

3. Such additional qualifications as may be required by the Municipal Civil Service Commission.

COMPENSATION—

Range of annual compenstion—$1080 to $1380 inclusive.
Salary rates—$1080, $1140, $1200, $1260, $1320, $1380.

GRADE 3 (V V 3)

TITLES OF POSITIONS[1]—

SENIOR SOCIAL INVESTIGATOR
SENIOR SOCIAL INVESTIGATOR (INSTITUTIONS)

DUTIES—

Senior Social Investigator:

The duties of Senior Social Investigators are to supervise a group of Social Investigators in Grade 1 and to be responsible for the disposition of applications for relief in a particular district or other unit, or to make independently important special investigations affecting relief requiring a high degree of ability and experience, other than investigations of institutions.

Senior Social Investigator (Institutions):

The duties of Senior Social Investigators (Institutions) are to investigate the condition and operation of plant and structures in private charitable institutions receiving funds from the City of New York and the living conditions of inmates of these institutions, including food, care, treatment, recreation, instruction and discipline.

QUALIFICATIONS—

Senior Social Investigator:

1. The minimum qualifications prescribed for Grade 2.

2. If appointed by promotion, not less than two years of appropriate experience in Grade 2, or if appointed as the result of an open competitive examination, experience in work of the character and standard of Grade 2.

3. Such additional qualifications as may be required by the Municipal Civil Service Commission.

---

[1] The following positions are among those appraised by the Bureau of Personal Service in this grade on the basis of duties performed by present incumbents:

Senior Social Investigator in charge of the Bureau of Domestic Relations in Manhattan and Brooklyn.

Senior Social Investigator in charge of social investigation in the Lower Manhattan District.

Senior Social Investigator (Institutions):

1. Experience in inspecting or investigating charitable institutions, reformatories or hospitals, or other institutional experience recognized by the Municipal Civil Service Commission as qualifying.

2. Such additional qualifications as may be required by the Municipal Civil Service Commission.

COMPENSATION—

Senior Social Investigator in Charge of a District Office:

Range of annual compensation—$1500 to $1740 inclusive.
Salary rates—$1500, $1620, $1740.

Senior Social Investigator in Charge of One of the Two Divisions of Domestic Relations:

Range of annual compensation—$1740 to $2100 inclusive.
Salary rates—$1740, $1920, $2100.

Senior Social Investigator (Institutions):

Range of annual compensation—$1500 to $1920 inclusive.
Salary rates—$1500, $1620, $1740, $1920.

SPECIAL REGULATION GOVERNING COMPENSATION—

Beginning with the lowest rate, advancement within this grade is conditional upon appraisal under the rules of the Board of Estimate and Apportionment, indicating that the rate requested does not exceed the value of the work to be performed.

SPECIAL REGULATION GOVERNING COMPENSATION—

The following table indicates the minimum number of years of meritorious service required at each rate before advancement to the next rate. See also page 30.

$1500	1 year
1620	1 "
1740	2 years
1920	2 "

GRADE 4 (V V 4)

TITLES OF POSITIONS[1]—

CHIEF SOCIAL INVESTIGATOR

DUTIES—

The duties of incumbents of these positions, which involve supervision of employes in Grades 1 and 2, are to supervise an entire important function of investigation and relief work, or to act as assistant and staff adviser to the Director of Social Investigation.

QUALIFICATIONS—

1. The minimum qualifications prescribed for Grade 3.

2. If appointed by promotion, not less than two years of appropriate experience in Grade 3, or if appointed as the result of an open competitive examination, experience in work of the character and standard of Grade 3.

3. Such additional qualifications as may be required by the Municipal Civil Service Commission.

COMPENSATION—

Range of annual compensation—$2280 to $2940 inclusive.
Salary rates—$2280, $2460, $2700, $2940.

---

[1] The following positions are among those appraised by the Bureau of Personal Service in this grade on the basis of duties performed by present incumbents:

Chief Social Investigator acting as Assistant Director of the Bureau of Social Investigation.

Chief Social Investigator in charge of the inspection and investigation of private charitable institutions.

SPECIAL REGULATION GOVERNING COMPENSATION—

Beginning with the lowest rate, advancement within this grade is conditional upon appraisal under the rules of the Board of Estimate and Apportionment, indicating that the rate requested does not exceed the value of the work to be performed.

GRADE 5 (V V 5)

TITLES OF POSITIONS—

DIRECTOR OF SOCIAL INVESTIGATION

DUTIES—

The duties of the incumbent of this position, which involve supervision of employes in Grades 1, 2, and 3, and which require a thorough practical understanding of social and economic problems and knowledge of the agencies available for their solution, are to shape the policy and direct the work of social and institutional investigation and relief under the supervision of the Commissioner of Public Charities.

QUALIFICATIONS—

1. The minimum qualifications prescribed for Grade 4.
2. If appointed by promotion, not less than two years of appropriate experience in Grade 4, or if appointed as the result of an open competitive examination, experience in work of the character and standard of Grade 4.
3. Such additional qualifications as may be required by the Municipal Civil Service Commission.

COMPENSATION—

Range of annual compensation—$3900 to $4500 inclusive.
Salary rates—$3900, $4200, $4500.

SPECIAL REGULATION GOVERNING COMPENSATION—

Persons entering this grade need not necessarily begin at the lowest rate. Fixation of the initial salary rate and advancement within this grade are conditional upon appraisal under the rules of the Board of Estimate and Apportionment, indicating that the rate requested does not exceed the value of the work to be performed.

STATISTICIAN GROUP

SYMBOL (V S)

The term Statistician Group is applied to those offices or employments of the Investigational Service in which incumbents are required to collect, classify, co-ordinate and summarize such facts concerning municipal business or other subjects of interest to officers or citizens as may be expressed numerically, to study the life history, mortality and experience of a large number of individuals or things for the purpose of establishing an average experience or rate as a guide to judgment in calculating future possibilities, and to perform other work requiring knowledge of statistical theory and practice.

GRADE 1 (V S 1)[1]—

TITLES OF POSITIONS—

JUNIOR STATISTICIAN
JUNIOR ACTUARY

---

[1] The following positions are among those appraised by the Bureau of Personal Service in this grade on the basis of duties performed by present incumbents.

Junior Actuary acting as actuarial clerk in the Pension Division of the Bureau of Personal Service.

DUTIES—

The duties of incumbents of these positions are to perform under supervision minor or apprentice statistical or actuarial work requiring knowledge of the science of statistics or of actuarial formulae.

QUALIFICATIONS—

1. Completion of a course of study in statistics or actuarial science recognized by the Municipal Civil Service Commission as qualifying, or experience in statistical or acturial work recognized by the Municipal Civil Service Commission as the equivalent.

2. Such additional qualifications as may be required by the Municipal Civil Service Commission.

COMPENSATION—

Range of annual compensation—$1200 to $1800 inclusive.
Salary rates—$1200, $1320, $1440, $1560, $1680, $1800.

GRADE 2 (V S 2)

TITLES OF POSITIONS—

ASSISTANT STATISTICIAN
ASSISTANT ACTUARY

DUTIES—

The duties of incumbents of these positions are to perform important and responsible statistical or actuarial work requiring considerable experience and the exercise of independent judgment.

QUALIFICATIONS—

1. The minimum qualifications prescribed for Grade 1.

2. If appointed by promotion, not less than two years of appropriate experience in Grade 1, or if appointed as the result of an open competitive examination, experience in work of the character and standard of Grade 1.

3. Such additional qualifications as may be required by the Municipal Civil Service Commission.

COMPENSATION—

Range of annual compensation—$1980 to $2820 inclusive.
Salary rates—$1980, $2160, $2340, $2580, $2820.

GRADE 3 (V S 3)

TITLES OF POSITIONS—

STATISTICIAN
ACTUARY

DUTIES—

The duties of incumbents of these positions, which require wide experience in statistical or actuarial work and a specialized knowledge of statistical or actuarial science, are to be responsible for the work of a less important statistical or actuarial bureau or division, or to perform independently difficult statistical or actuarial work.

QUALIFICATIONS—

1. The minimum qualifications prescribed for Grade 2.

2. If appointed by promotion, not less than two years of appropriate experience in Grade 2, or if appointed as the result of an open competitive examination, experience in work of the character and standard of Grade 2.

3. Such additional qualifications as may be required by the Municipal Civil Service Commission.

COMPENSATION—

Range of annual compensation—$3060 to $3840 inclusive.
Salary rates—$3060, $3300, $3540, $3840.

SPECIAL REGULATION GOVERNING COMPENSATION—

Persons entering this grade need not necessarily begin at the lowest rate. Fixation of the initial salary rate and advancement within this grade are conditional upon appraisal under the rules of the Board of Estimate and Apportionment, indicating that the rate requested does not exceed the value of the work to be performed.

GRADE 4 (V S 4)

TITLES OF POSITIONS—

CHIEF STATISTICIAN
CHIEF ACTUARY (PENSIONS)

DUTIES—

Chief Statistician:

The duties of Chief Statisticians, which require the widest experience in statistical work and a highly specialized knowledge of the science of statistics, are to direct and be responsible for the work of an important bureau or division of statistics, or to perform independently the most difficult statistical work.

Chief Actuary (Pensions):[1]

The duties of the Chief Actuary (Pensions), which require the widest experience in actuarial work and a highly specialized knowledge of actuarial science as applied to pensions, are to direct and be responsible for all actuarial work on pensions in the City of New York, and to prepare such reports on existing or proper pension systems as may be required.

QUALIFICATIONS—

Chief Statistician:

1. The minimum qualifications prescribed for Grade 3.
2. If appointed by promotion, not less than one year of appropriate experience in Grade 3, or if appointed as the result of an open competitive examination, experience in work of the character and standard of Grade 3.
3. Such additional qualifications as may be required by the Municipal Civil Service Commission.

Chief Actuary (Pensions):

1. Experience in a supervisory capacity in the practice of actuarial science or experience in independent and responsible actuarial work recognized by the Municipal Civil Service Commission as qualifying.
2. Such additional qualifications as may be required by the Municipal Civil Service Commission.

COMPENSATION—

Range of annual compensation—$4140 to $4740 inclusive.
Salary rates—$4140, $4440, $4740.

---

[1]This description of duties and the salary range proposed are intended only for the present reorganization of the pension system of the city.

SPECIAL REGULATION GOVERNING COMPENSATION—

Persons entering this grade need not necessarily begin at the lowest rate. Fixation of the initial salary rate and advancement within this grade are conditional upon appraisal under the rules of the Board of Estimate and Apportionment, indicating that the rate requested does not exceed the value of the work to be performed.

TAX OFFICER AND APPRAISER GROUP

SYMBOL (V T)

The term Tax Officer and Appraiser Group is applied to those offices or employments of the Investigational Service in which incumbents are required to inspect, appraise, make record of and classify land, improvements and personal property for the purpose of assessment.

GRADE 1 (V T 1)

TITLES OF POSITIONS—

DEPUTY TAX COMMISSIONER

DUTIES—

The duties of incumbents of these positions, which are performed under supervision, are to inspect, appraise, and collect and record data pertaining to real estate for the purpose of assessment, or to make inquiry into, appraise, and collect and record data pertaining to personal property for the purpose of personal assessment, acquisition, leasing, or condemnation by the city, or for evidence in litigation in which the city is a party.[1]

QUALIFICATIONS—

1. Experience in clerical work in the Department of Taxes and Assessments, or such experience in the real estate or building business as is recognized by the Municipal Civil Service Commission as qualifying.
2. Such additional qualifications as may be required by the Municipal Civil Service Commission.

COMPENSATION—

Range of annual compensation—$2400 to $3600 inclusive.
Salary rates—$2400, $2640, $2880, $3120, $3360, $3600.

GRADE 2 (V T 2)

TITLES OF POSITIONS—

SENIOR DEPUTY TAX COMMISSIONER (BOROUGH CHIEF)
SENIOR DEPUTY TAX COMMISSIONER (PERSONAL ESTATE OF BOROUGH)
SENIOR DEPUTY TAX COMMISSIONER (PERSONAL ESTATE OF CORPORATIONS)
SENIOR DEPUTY TAX COMMISSIONER (REAL ESTATE OF CORPORATIONS)

DUTIES—

Senior Deputy Tax Commissioner (Borough Chief):

The duties of Senior Deputy Tax Commissioners (Borough Chief) are to take charge of and be responsible for the assessment of real estate within a borough, other than special franchises and real estate of corporations, and in addition, in the Boroughs of The Bronx, Queens and Richmond, to take charge of and be responsible for the assessment of all personal property of natural persons and corporations.

---

[1]The existing positions of Assistant Tax Commissioner are appraised in Grade 1 of the Private Secretary Group. These positions appear to be unnecessary.

Senior Deputy Tax Commissioner (Personal Estate of Borough):

The duties of Senior Deputy Tax Commissioners (Personal Estate of Borough) are to take charge of and be responsible for the assessment of all personal property of natural persons and estates within a borough.

Senior Deputy Tax Commissioner (Personal Estate of Corporations):

The duties of Senior Deputy Tax Commissioners (Personal Estate of Corporations) are to take charge of and be responsible for the assessment of personal estate of corporations in all boroughs.

Senior Deputy Tax Commissioner (Real Estate of Corporations):

The duties of Senior Deputy Tax Commissioners (Real Estate of Corporations) are to take charge of and be responsible for the assessment of real estate of corporations in all boroughs.

QUALIFICATIONS—

1. The minimum qualifications prescribed for Grade 1.
2. If appointed by promotion, not less than four years of appropriate experience in Grade 1, or if appointed as the result of an open competitive examination, experience in work of the character and standard of Grade 1.
3. Such additional qualifications as may be required by the Municipal Civil Service Commission.

COMPENSATION—

Range of annual compensation—$3900 to $4200 inclusive.
Salary rates—$3900, $4200.

SPECIAL REGULATION GOVERNING COMPENSATION—

Beginning with the lowest rate, advancement within this grade is conditional upon appraisal under the rules of the Board of Estimate and Apportionment, indicating that the rate requested does not exceed the value of the work to be performed.

GRADE 3 (V T 3)

TITLES OF POSITIONS—

ASSISTANT CHIEF DEPUTY TAX COMMISSIONER (REAL ESTATE)

DUTIES—

The duties of the incumbent of this position are to assist the Chief Deputy Tax Commissioner (Real Estate) in the administration of the Real Estate Bureau and the Bureau of Real Estate of Corporations.

QUALIFICATIONS—

1. The minimum qualifications prescribed for Grade 2.
2. If appointed by promotion, not less than two years of appropriate experience in Grade 2, or if appointed as the result of an open competitive examination, experience in work of the character and standard of Grade 2.
3. Such additional qualifications as may be required by the Municipal Civil Service Commission.

COMPENSATION—

Range of annual compensation—$4200 to $4500 inclusive.
Salary rates—$4200, $4500.

SPECIAL REGULATION GOVERNING COMPENSATION—

Persons entering this grade need not necessarily begin at the lowest rate. Fixation of the initial salary rate and advancement within this grade are conditional upon appraisal under the rules of the Board of Estimate and Apportionment, indicating that the rate requested does not exceed the value of the work to be performed.

GRADE 4 (V T 4)

TITLES OF POSITIONS—

CHIEF DEPUTY TAX COMMISSIONER (REAL ESTATE)
CHIEF APPRAISER (REAL ESTATE)

DUTIES—

Chief Deputy Tax Commissioner (Real Estate):

The duties of the Chief Deputy Tax Commissioner (Real Estate) are to direct and be responsible to the Board of Tax Commissioners for the administration of the Real Estate Bureau of the Department of Taxes and Assessments.

Chief Appraiser (Real Estate):

The duties of the Chief Appraiser (Real Estate) are to act as adviser to the Comptroller in matters involving the appraisal of real estate, including appraisals incident to certain acquisitions and the sale of real estate by the city, condemnation proceedings or other litigations, approval of settlements in connection with the reduction of taxes and assessments, agreements on boundary lines, the straightening of highwater marks, the release of the city's interest in real property, and the handling of leases in all cases where the city is the lessee.

QUALIFICATIONS[1]—

1. The minimum qualifications prescribed for Grades 2 or 3.
2. If appointed by promotion, not less than three years of appropriate experience in Grades 2 or 3, or if appointed as the result of an open competitive examination, experience in work of the character and standard of Grades 2 or 3.
3. Such additional qualifications as may be required by the Municipal Civil Service Commission.

COMPENSATION—

Range of annual compensation—$4800 to $7200 inclusive.
Salary rates—$4800, $5220, $5640, $6060, $6600, $7200.

SPECIAL REGULATION GOVERNING COMPENSATION—

Beginning with the lowest rate, advancement within this grade is conditional upon appraisal under the rules of the Board of Estimate and Apportionment, indicating that the rate requested does not exceed the value of the work to be performed.

MISCELLANEOUS INVESTIGATOR GROUP

SYMBOL (V Z)

The term Miscellaneous Investigator Group is applied to those offices or employments of the Investigational Service in which incumbents are required to perform routine or specialized investigational work of an exceptional nature not included in the other groups of the Investigational Service.

GRADE 1 (V Z 1)

TITLES OF POSITIONS—

EXAMINER OF PLUMBERS

DUTIES—

Examiner of Plumbers:

The duties of Examiners of Plumbers are to perform the work devolving upon members of the Examining Board of Plumbers, including examination and certification of persons applying for licenses to act as master plumber and the revocation of such certificates upon due cause.

---

[1]The intention of these qualifications is to allow candidates in both Grade 2 and Grade 3 to compete for this position. For this purpose the Municipal Civil Service Commission may find it desirable to incorporate Grades 3 and 4 of the standard specifications in one civil service grade.

QUALIFICATIONS—

Examiner of Plumbers:

1. A license issued by the Examining Board of Plumbers to act as a master plumber or experience as a journeyman plumber.

2. Evidence of ability to perform the duties of the position satisfactory to the appointing officer.

COMPENSATION—

Examiner of Plumbers:

Compensation per diem—$5.

GRADE 2 (V Z 2)

TITLES OF POSITIONS—

SUPERINTENDENT (PUBLIC EMPLOYMENT BUREAU)
EXAMINER (FIRE PREVENTION)

DUTIES—

Superintendent (Public Employment Bureau):

The duties of the Superintendent (Public Employment Bureau) are to be responsible for the operation of the Public Employment Bureau, including the recording of applications for employment, the soliciting and recording of applications for employes, the placing of persons seeking employment in vacant positions and the preparation of appropriate statistics regarding employment, labor, market and social conditions.

Examiner (Fire Prevention):

The duties of Examiners (Fire Prevention) are to examine and to pass upon applicants for certificates of fitness to take charge of hazardous occupations, and to assist the Fire Commissioner in drawing up regulations governing the manufacture, sale, storage, transportation or other handling of chemicals and explosive and combustible materials.

QUALIFICATIONS—

Superintendent (Public Employment Bureau):

1. Experience in an executive capacity in a semi-public or philanthropic employment agency or in connection with the employment departments of large organizations, or in other work recognized by the Municipal Civil Service Commission as qualifying.

2. Such additional qualifications as may be required by the Municipal Civil Service Commission.

Examiner (Fire Prevention):

1. Ability to perform the duties of the position satisfactory to the appointing officer.

COMPENSATION—

Superintendent (Public Employment Bureau):

Range of annual compensation—$3000 to $3480 inclusive.
Salary rates—$3000, $3240, $3480.

Examiner (Fire Prevention):

Compensation per diem—$10.

SPECIAL REGULATION GOVERNING COMPENSATION—

Superintendent (Public Employment Bureau):

Beginning with the lowest rate, advancement within this grade is conditional upon appraisal under the rules of the Board of Estimate and Apportionment, indicating that the rate requested does not exceed the value of the work to be performed.

EDUCATIONAL SERVICE

SYMBOL (E)

The term Educational Service is applied to those offices or employments the duties of whose incumbents are to give or to supervise instruction designed to develop the mental and physical powers or to develop manual skill.[1]

INDUSTRIAL INSTRUCTOR GROUP

SYMBOL (E I)

The term Industrial Instructor Group is applied to those offices or employments of the Educational Service in which incumbents are required to instruct or to supervise the instruction of inmates of correctional or charitable institutions in handicrafts or skilled trades.

GRADE 1 (E I 1)

TITLES OF POSITIONS—

ASSISTANT INDUSTRIAL INSTRUCTOR

DUTIES—

The duties of incumbents of these positions, which may include responsibility for the custody and discipline of inmates, are to perform under supervision the routine and less responsible work involved in the industrial or vocational instruction of inmates of charitable or correctional institutions.

Examples:

Taking charge of a class engaged in weaving, rug and mat making, chair caning, sewing, shoemaking, etc.

QUALIFICATIONS[2]—

1. Evidence of ability to perform the duties of the position satisfactory to the appointing officer.
2. Such additional qualifications as may be required by the Municipal Civil Service Commission.

COMPENSATION—

Range of annual compensation with maintenance—$480 to $600 inclusive.
Salary rates—$480, $540, $600.
Range of annual compensation without maintenance—$720 to $840 inclusive.
Salary rates—$720, $780, $840.

---

[1]The Educational Service as presented includes only positions as industrial instructors, recreation instructors and other miscellaneous instructors. The service definition should later be expanded to include the Librarian Group. See footnote on page 150. The main body of teachers is at present under the control of the Board of Education and their salaries are fixed by law. In the case of teachers employed by the Department of Public Charities, upon nomination by the City Superintendent of Schools and certification by the Board of Examiners of the Department of Education, it is recommended that the same rates be paid as are paid by the Board of Education for similar work, unless maintenance and other peculiar considerations are involved. Payment of these rates and granting of increases should be conditioned on appointment from appropriate lists, adequate supervision and meeting of conditions prescribed by the Board of Education for similar action in the case of their own teaching force.

[2]Positions in this grade are classified by the Municipal Civil Service Commission as non-competitive. Incumbents of these positions may compete in open competitive examinations for positions as Industrial Instructor in Grade 2.

GRADE 2 (E I 2)

TITLES OF POSITIONS[1 2]—

INDUSTRIAL INSTRUCTOR (FARMING)
INDUSTRIAL INSTRUCTOR (HANDICRAFTS)
INDUSTRIAL INSTRUCTOR (TRADES)

DUTIES—

Industrial Instructor (Farming):

The duties of Industrial Instructors (Farming), which may include responsibility for the custody and discipline of inmates and the actual performance of farm work, are to organize, carry on and give instruction in the various activities of farm life among the inmates of correctional or charitable institutions, to supervise their work, and to order and take charge of needed supplies and equipment.

Industrial Instructor (Handicrafts):

The duties of Industrial Instructors (Handicrafts), which may include responsibility for the custody and discipline of inmates and the supervision of employes in Grade 1, are to instruct or supervise the instruction of inmates of correctional or charitable institutions in handicrafts, simple trades, or the elementary work of skilled trades, to plan and supervise their work, and to order and take charge of needed supplies and equipment.

Examples:

Supervising the instruction of several groups of inmates in basketry, weaving, rug and mat making, broom and brush making, chair caning, mattress making, wood and metal work or needlework.

Industrial Instructor (Trades):

The duties of Industrial Instructors (Trades), which may include responsibility for the custody and discipline of inmates and the supervision of employes in Grade 1, are to instruct or supervise the instruction of inmates of correctional or charitable institutions in one or more of the various skilled trades, to plan and supervise their work, and to order and take charge of needed supplies and equipment.

Examples:

Supervising the instruction of several groups of inmates in carpentry, plumbing, tailoring, printing, shoemaking, electrical work, painting, or trade dressmaking.

QUALIFICATIONS—

Industrial Instructor (Farming):

1. Completion of a standard course of training in agriculture at an agricultural college of recognized standing, or practical experience in farm work recognized by the Municipal Civil Service Commission as the equivalent.
2. Experience in supervising boys and men in agricultural or other work.
3. Such additional qualifications as may be required by the Municipal Civil Service Commission.

---

[1]The following positions are among those appraised by the Bureau of Personal Service in this grade on the basis of duties performed by present incumbents:

Industrial Instructor (Farming) at the Farm Colony.

Industrial Instructor (Trades) at the Reformatory of the Department of Correction.

[2]In case an Industrial Instructor (Trades) or Industrial Instructor (Handicrafts) is appointed for instruction in a particular trade or handicraft, the position will be designated by that trade or handicraft, as Industrial Instructor (Carpentry) or Industrial Instructor (Basketry and Weaving).

Industrial Instructor (Handicrafts):

1. Completion of a normal course of training in the industrial arts, or other training or experience recognized by the Municipal Civil Service Commission as the equivalent.

2. Such additional qualifications as may be required by the Municipal Civil Service Commission.

Industrial Instructor (Trades):

1. Practical experience in the actual work of a trade.

2. Completion of a normal course of training in the work of a trade at a technical school of recognized standing, or other training or experience recognized by the Municipal Civil Service Commission as the equivalent.

3. Such additional qualifications as may be required by the Municipal Civil Service Commission.

The minimum qualifications shall consist of 1 and 3 or 2 and 3.

COMPENSATION—

Range of annual compensation—$900 to $1500 inclusive, with or without maintenance.

Salary rates—$900, $960, $1020, $1080, $1140, $1200, $1260, $1320, $1380, $1440, $1500.

SPECIAL REGULATION GOVERNING COMPENSATION—

Persons entering this grade need not necessarily begin at the lowest rate. Fixation of the initial salary rate and advancement within this grade are conditional upon appraisal under the rules of the Board of Estimate and Apportionment, indicating that the rate requested does not exceed the value of the work to be performed.

SPECIAL CONDITION GOVERNING ADVANCEMENT—

The following table indicates the minimum number of years of meritorious service required at each rate before advancement to the next rate. See also page 30.

$900	1 year
960	1 "
1020	1 "
1080	1 "
1140	1 "
1200	1 "
1260	1 "
1320	1 "
1380	2 years
1440	2 "

GRADE 3 (E I 3)

TITLES OF POSITIONS[1]—

SUPERINTENDENT OF INDUSTRIES

DUTIES—

The duties of incumbents of these positions, which involve supervision of employes in Grades 1 and 2, and which require a thorough practical knowledge of the methods and purposes of industrial education as well as of trade processes and factory management, are to direct and be responsible for the industrial instruction and production of an entire department.

---

[1]The following positions are among those appraised by the Bureau of Personal Service in this grade on the basis of duties performed by present incumbents:

Superintendent of Industries in the Department of Correction.

QUALIFICATIONS—

1. The minimum qualifications prescribed for Grade 2.
2. If appointed by promotion, not less than three years of appropriate experience in Grade 2, or if appointed as the result of an open competitive examination, experience in work of the character and standard of Grade 2.
3. Successful experience in factory or industrial management.
4. Experience in the supervision of industrial instruction in schools or of industries in charitable or correctional institutions.
5. Such additional qualifications as may be required by the Municipal Civil Service Commission.

The minimum qualifications shall consist of 1, 2 and 5, 3 and 5, or 4 and 5.

COMPENSATION—

Range of annual compensation—$2460 to $3660 inclusive.
Salary rates—$2460, $2700, $2940, $3180, $3420, $3660.

SPECIAL REGULATION GOVERNING COMPENSATION—

Beginning with the lowest rate, advancement within this grade is conditional upon appraisal under the rules of the Board of Estimate and Apportionment, indicating that the rate requested does not exceed the value of the work to be performed.

RECREATION INSTRUCTOR GROUP

SYMBOL (E R).

The term Recreation Instructor Group is applied to those offices or employments of the Educational Service in which incumbents are required to lead, give instruction in, supervise or direct the various forms of play or recreational activity in public playgrounds, gymnasiums, farm gardens or recreation centers.

GRADE 1 (E R 1)

TITLES OF POSITIONS—

FARM GARDEN INSTRUCTOR
RECREATION INSTRUCTOR
RECREATION INSTRUCTOR (ATHLETICS)
RECREATION INSTRUCTOR (SWIMMING)

DUTIES—

Farm Garden Instructor:

The duties of Farm Garden Instructors are to give instruction in and to supervise gardening and other farm gardening activities.

Recreation Instructor:

The duties of Recreation Instructors are to direct and conduct games, dancing, ingenuity work, dramatization or other recreational activities at public playgrounds or recreation piers.

Recreation Instructor (Athletics):

The duties of Recreation Instructors (Athletics) are to give instruction in various forms of athletics and gymnastics and to conduct these activities in public gymnasiums or playgrounds.

Recreation Instructor (Swimming):

The duties of Recreation Instructors (Swimming) are to give instruction in swimming and life saving and to guard the safety of persons using public baths.

QUALIFICATIONS—

1. A certificate of graduation from a public high school of the state of New York, or proof of other training recognized by the Municipal Civil Service Commission as the equivalent.

2. A certificate granted on the completion of a one year standard course of training in recreational work at a physical culture or normal school or other specialized school of recognized standing, or proof of other training or experience recognized by the Municipal Civil Service Commission as the equivalent.

3. Such additional qualifications as may be required by the Municipal Civil Service Commission.

COMPENSATION—

Range of annual compensation—$900 to $1080 inclusive.
Salary rates—$900, $960, $1020, $1080.
Compensation per diem—$3.

GRADE 2 (E R 2)

TITLES OF POSITIONS—

HEAD FARM GARDEN INSTRUCTOR
HEAD RECREATION INSTRUCTOR

DUTIES—

Head Farm Garden Instructor:

The duties of Head Farm Garden Instructors are to supervise and be responsible for one large or several small farm gardens.

Head Recreation Instructor:

The duties of Head Recreation Instructors, which involve supervision of employes in Grade 1, are to supervise and be responsible for an entire large playground, gymnasium or recreation center, or for a group of small playgrounds or gymnasiums, or for the recreational activities on a large pier or group of small piers, or to act as field inspector of a number of playgrounds or gymnasiums.

QUALIFICATIONS—

1. The minimum qualifications prescribed for Grade 1.

2. If appointed by promotion, not less than one year of appropriate experience in Grade 1, or if appointed as the result of an open competitive examination, experience in work of the character and standard of Grade 1.

3. Such additional qualifications as may be required by the Municipal Civil Service Commission.

COMPENSATION—

Range of annual compensation—$1200 to $1440 inclusive.
Salary rates—$1200, $1320, $1440.
Compensation per diem—$4.

SPECIAL REGULATION GOVERNING COMPENSATION—

Beginning with the lowest rate, advancement within this grade is conditional upon appraisal under the rules of the Board of Estimate and Apportionment, indicating that the rate requested does not exceed the value of the work to be performed.

SPECIAL CONDITION GOVERNING ADVANCEMENT—

The following table indicates the minimum number of years of meritorious service required at each rate before advancement to the next rate. See also page 30.

$1200	1 year
1320	1 "

GRADE 3 (E R 3)

TITLES OF POSITIONS[1]—

ASSISTANT SUPERVISOR OF RECREATION
SUPERVISOR OF FARM GARDENS
SUPERVISOR (VOLUNTEER LIFE SAVING CORPS)

DUTIES—

Assistant Supervisor of Recreation:

The duties of Assistant Supervisors of Recreation, which require administrative ability and specialized knowledge, are to assist the Supervisor of Recreation in the origination, organization and administration of municipal recreational activities for boys and for girls within the borough of Manhattan or in the general supervision of recreational work in that borough.

Supervisor of Farm Gardens:

The duties of Supervisors of Farm Gardens are to supervise and be responsible for the farm garden activities within one or more boroughs, including responsibility for materials and equipment used in farm garden work.

Supervisor (Volunteer Life Saving Corps):

The duties of the Supervisor (Volunteer Life Saving Corps), which involve supervision of the members of the Life Saving Corps, are to direct and be responsible for the New York City department of the United States Volunteer Life Saving Corps, to supervise the teaching of swimming by members of the Corps at the public baths and to conduct lectures on life saving and first aid methods.

QUALIFICATIONS—

Assistant Supervisor of Recreation, Supervisor of Farm Gardens:

1. The minimum qualifications prescribed for Grade 2.
2. If appointed by promotion, not less than two years of appropriate experience in Grade 2, or if appointed as the result of an open competitive examination, experience in work of the character and standard of Grade 2.
3. Such additional qualifications as may be required by the Municipal Civil Service Commission.

Supervisor (Volunteer Life Saving Corps):

1. The minimum qualifications prescribed for Recreation Instructor (Swimming) in Grade 1.
2. If appointed by promotion, not less than three years of appropriate experience in Grade 1, or if appointed as the result of an open competitive examination, experience in work of the character and standard of Grade 1.
3. Such additional qualifications as may be required by the Municipal Civil Service Commission.

---

[1] The following positions are among those appraised by the Bureau of Personal Service in this grade on the basis of duties performed by present incumbents:

Assistant Supervisor of Recreation in charge of recreational activities for boys or for girls in the Bureau of Recreation, Manhattan.

COMPENSATION—

Range of annual compensation—$1560 to $1800 inclusive.
Salary rates—$1560, $1680, $1800.

SPECIAL REGULATION GOVERNING COMPENSATION—

Beginning with the lowest rate, advancement within this grade is conditional upon appraisal under the rules of the Board of Estimate and Apportionment, indicating that the rate requested does not exceed the value of the work to be performed.

SPECIAL CONDITION GOVERNING ADVANCEMENT—

The following table indicates the minimum number of years of meritorious service required at each rate before advancement to the next rate. See also page 30.

$1560	1 year
1680	2 years

GRADE 4 (E R 4)

TITLES OF POSITIONS—

SUPERVISOR OF RECREATION

DUTIES—

The duties of incumbents of these positions, which require administrative ability and specialized knowledge, are to supervise and be responsible for the origination, organization and administration of municipal recreational activities within one or more boroughs, including responsibility for materials and equipment used in recreational work.

QUALIFICATIONS—

1. The minimum qualifications prescribed for Grade 3.
2. If appointed by promotion, not less than two years of appropriate experience in Grade 3, or if appointed as the result of an open competitive examination, experience in work of the character and standard of Grade 3.
3. Such additional qualifications as may be required by the Municipal Civil Service Commission.

COMPENSATION—

Supervisor of Recreation, Manhattan:

Range of annual compensation—$2340 to $3300 inclusive.
Salary rates—$2340, $2580, $2820, $3060, $3300.

Supervisor of Recreation, Brooklyn:

Range of annual compensation—$1980 to $2580 inclusive.
Salary rates—$1980, $2160, $2340, $2580.

SPECIAL REGULATION GOVERNING COMPENSATION—

Beginning with the lowest rate, advancement within this grade is conditional upon appraisal under the rules of the Board of Estimate and Apportionment, indicating that the rate requested does not exceed the value of the work to be performed.

MISCELLANEOUS INSTRUCTOR GROUP

SYMBOL (E Z)

The term Miscellaneous Instructor Group is applied to those offices or employments of the Educational Service in which incumbents are required to perform routine or specialized educational work of an exceptional nature, not included in the other groups of the Educational Service.

GRADE 1 (E Z 1)

TITLES OF POSITIONS[1]—

INSTITUTIONAL INSTRUCTOR (BAND MUSIC)

DUTIES—

Institutional Instructor (Band Music):

The duties of Institutional Instructors (Band Music) are to give instruction in the playing of band instruments and to conduct bands in practice and in public appearances in city hospitals or other institutions.

QUALIFICATIONS—

Institutional Instructor (Band Music):

1. Evidence of ability to play on instruments commonly used in bands.
2. Experience in teaching the playing of band instruments or in conducting a band.
3. Such additional qualifications as may be required by the Municipal Civil Service Commission.

COMPENSATION—

Institutional Instructor (Band Music):

Range of annual compensation—$900 to $1200 inclusive.
Salary rates—$900, $960, $1020, $1080, $1140, $1200.

SPECIAL REGULATION GOVERNING COMPENSATION—

Institutional Instructor (Band Music):

Beginning with the lowest rate, advancement within this grade is conditional upon appraisal under the rules of the Board of Estimate and Apportionment, indicating that the rate requested does not exceed the value of the work to be performed.

GRADE 2 (E Z 2)

TITLES OF POSITIONS—

SUPERVISOR OF TRAINING (RANDALL'S ISLAND)

DUTIES—

Supervisor of Training (Randall's Island):

The duties of the Supervisor of Training (Randall's Island), which involve supervision of teachers, industrial instructors and recreation instructors, are to direct and to be responsible to the head of the institution for the mental, physical and industrial training of inmates of the Children's Hospitals and Schools on Randall's Island.

QUALIFICATIONS—

Supervisor of Training (Randall's Island):

1. Evidence of the completion of a normal course of training, not less than two years in length, at a normal school or other pedagogical training school of recognized standing, including courses in the training of mental defectives, or other educational qualifications recognized by the Municipal Civil Service Commission as qualifying.

---

[1] The following positions are among those appraised by the Bureau of Personal Service in this grade on the basis of duties performed by present incumbents:

Institutional Instructor (Band Music) at the New York City Children's Hospitals and Schools, Randall's Island.

2. Experience in the mental, industrial or recreational instruction of mental defectives.

3. Such additional qualifications as may be required by the Municipal Civil Service Commission.

COMPENSATION—

Supervisor of Training (Randall's Island):

Range of annual compensation—$1620 to $2100 inclusive, with or without maintenance.

Salary rates—$1620, $1740, $1920, $2100.

SPECIAL REGULATION GOVERNING COMPENSATION—

Supervisor of Training (Randall's Island):

Beginning with the lowest rate, advancement within this grade is conditional upon appraisal under the rules of the Board of Estimate and Apportionment, indicating that the rate requested does not exceed the value of the work to be performed.

SPECIAL CONDITION GOVERNING ADVANCEMENT—

Supervisor of Training (Randall's Island):

The following table indicates the minimum number of years of meritorious service required at each rate before advancement to the next rate. See also page 30.

$1620	1 year
1740	2 years
1920	2 "

CLERICAL SERVICE.

SYMBOL (C).

The term Clerical Service is applied to those offices or employments the preponderant duties of whose incumbents are to perform routine or administrative office work requiring business ability or specialized training other than office work merely incident to duties outlined in other services.

BOOKKEEPER GROUP

SYMBOL (C B)

The term Bookkeeper Group is applied to those offices or employments of the Clerical Service in which incumbents are required to perform work involving a knowledge of double entry bookkeeping and ability to compute, journalize, post and compile data in connection with bookkeeping procedure.

GRADE 1 (C B 1)

TITLES OF POSITIONS—

JUNIOR BOOKKEEPER

DUTIES—

The duties of incumbents of these positions are to make simple postings of accounting information from one book to another or from documents or schedules to accounting records, to balance or adjust accounts, to take trial balances, to make journal entries, to write statements or bills, and to perform other bookkeeping work of a similar character and standard.

Examples:

Writing up registers and cash books.
Posting detail ledgers.
Posting fund ledgers.
Locating errors in detail ledgers.
Taking trial balances.
Making journal entries.
Computing, posting or compiling data in connection with functional and unit cost accounting, budget accounting or budget estimates.
Making out vouchers or statements of accounts.
Preparing financial data or periodical reports on prepared forms.
Verifying payrolls and recapitulations.

QUALIFICATIONS—

1. Such qualifications as may be required by the Municipal Civil Service Commission.

COMPENSATION—

Range of annual compensation—$840 to $1200 inclusive.
Salary rates—$840, $960, $1080, $1200.

GRADE 2 (C B 2)

TITLES OF POSITIONS—

BOOKKEEPER

DUTIES—

The duties of incumbents of these positions, which may or may not include supervision of one or more bookkeepers in Grade 1 or of other subordinates, are to keep general ledgers and controlling accounts of subsidiary records and to prepare balance sheets and special reports.

Examples:

Making general journal entries and posting to controlling accounts.

Taking trial balances of general ledgers.

Comparing and reconciling subsidiary ledger balances with controlling accounts.

Determining accounts to which orders and vouchers are to be charged.

Preparing special financial statements or reports for department or bureau heads.

Devising or installing minor forms and methods of departmental bookkeeping.

QUALIFICATIONS—

1. The minimum qualifications prescribed for Grade 1.

2. If appointed by promotion, not less than two years of experience in Grade 1, or if appointed as the result of an open competitive examination, experience in work of the character and standard of Grade 1.

3. Such additional qualifications as may be required by the Municipal Civil Service Commission.

COMPENSATION—

Range of annual compensation—$1320 to $1800 inclusive.

Salary rates—$1320, $1440, $1560, $1680, $1800.

SPECIAL REGULATION GOVERNING COMPENSATION—

Beginning with the lowest rate, advancement within this grade is conditional upon appraisal under the rules of the Board of Estimate and Apportionment, indicating that the rate requested does not exceed the value of the work to be performed.

SPECIAL CONDITION GOVERNING ADVANCEMENT—

The following table indicates the minimum number of years of meritorious service required at each rate before advancement to the next rate. See also page 30.

$1320	1 year
1440	1 "
1560	2 years
1680	2 "

GRADE 3 (C B 3)

TITLES OF POSITIONS[1]—

SENIOR BOOKKEEPER

DUTIES—

The duties of incumbents of these positions, which require expert knowledge of bookkeeping and accounting procedure in the city service, involve the keeping of intricate financial records or the direct supervision of important bookkeeping groups.[2]

---

[1] The following positions are among those appraised by the Bureau of Personal Service in this grade on the basis of duties performed by present incumbents:

Senior Bookkeeper in charge of the bookkeeping division of the Finance Department.

Senior Bookkeeper in the Department of Street Cleaning.

[2] Positions as chiefs of the largest bookkeeping divisions where accounting knowledge and experience is required will be found in Grades 2 and 3 of the Accountant Group of the Professional Service.

QUALIFICATIONS—

1. The minimum qualifications prescribed for Grade 2.

2. If appointed by promotion, not less than two years of appropriate experience in Grade 2, or if appointed as the result of an open competitive examination, experience in work of the character and standard of Grade 2.

3. Such additional qualifications as may be required by the Municipal Civil Service Commission.

COMPENSATION—

Range of annual compensation—$1980 to $2820 inclusive.
Salary rates—$1980, $2160, $2340, $2580, $2820.

SPECIAL REGULATION GOVERNING COMPENSATION—

Beginning with the lowest rate, advancement within this grade is conditional upon appraisal under the rules of the Board of Estimate and Apportionment, indicating that the rate requested does not exceed the value of the work to be performed.

SPECIAL CONDITION GOVERNING ADVANCEMENT—

The following table indicates the minimum number of years of meritorious service required at each rate before advancement to the next rate. See also page 30.

$1980	1 year
2160	2 years
2340	2 "
2580	2 "

CLERK GROUP

SYMBOL (C C)

The term Clerk Group is applied to those offices or employments of the Clerical Service in which incumbents are required to perform routine or specialized clerical work not included in the other groups of the Clerical Service.

GRADE 1 (C C 1)

TITLES OF POSITIONS—

JUNIOR CLERK

DUTIES—

The duties of incumbents of these positions are to perform under supervision the simplest kinds of office work.

Examples:

Addressing.
Mailing.
Letter-press copying.
Indexing.
Ordinary filing.
Keeping office in order.
Running errands.
Receiving visitors.
Distributing mail.
Operating small office telephone switchboards.

QUALIFICATIONS—

1. Such qualifications as may be required by the Municipal Civil Service Commission.

COMPENSATION—

Range of annual compensation—$360 to $540 inclusive.
Salary rates—$360, $420, $480, $540.

GRADE 2 A (C C 2 A)[1]

TITLES OF POSITIONS[2]—

ASSISTANT CLERK A

DUTIES—

The duties of incumbents of these positions are to perform under supervision prescribed routine clerical work of minor consequence.

Examples:

- Plain longhand copying.
- Keeping ordinary card indices.
- Receiving and distributing routine reports and applications.
- Making out and tabulating daily, weekly and monthly reports, simple charts and statistics.
- Registering and verifying extensions and additions on orders and invoices.
- Writing, registering and scheduling vouchers.
- Simple filing of correspondence, tracings, maps, reports, etc.
- Operating tabulating machines, adding and scheduling machines and addressographs.
- Performing simple or apprentice work on Hollerith or multigraph machines.
- Verifying time sheets and payrolls.
- Writing notices and permits on prepared forms.
- Acting as information clerk for a department in outer office.

QUALIFICATIONS—

1. The minimum qualifications prescribed for Grade 1.
2. Not less than one year of appropriate experience in Grade 1.
3. Such additional qualifications as may be required by the Municipal Civil Service Commission.

COMPENSATION—

Range of annual compensation—$600 to $720 inclusive.
Salary rates—$600, $660, $720.

---

[1]For purposes of appraisal and appropriation, Grade 2 is divided into two parts, Grade 2 A and Grade 2 B. The unspecialized titles are Assistant Clerk A and Assistant Clerk B. For civil service purposes, this grade will be known simply as Grade 2, the unspecialized title being simply Assistant Clerk.

[2]The following positions are among those appraised by the Bureau of Personal Service in this grade on the basis of duties performed by present incumbents:

Assistant Clerks A acting as Bill Clerks in the Bureau of Assessments and Arrears in the Department of Finance.

Assistant Clerks A acting as Tickler Clerks in the Tenement House Department.

GRADE 2 B (C C 2 B)[1]

TITLES OF POSITIONS[2]—

ASSISTANT CLERK B
ASSISTANT CLERK (MULTIGRAPH OPERATOR)
ASSISTANT CLERK (TABULATING MACHINE OPERATOR)

DUTIES—

Assistant Clerk B:

The duties of Assistant Clerks B, which may involve limited supervision, are to perform clerical work incident to preparing, compiling, entering or verifying routine office information, reports, records and forms, and to dealing with the public on routine departmental matters.

Examples:

Keeping important official records.
Reviewing inspectors' reports.
Copying and compiling cost account records under supervision.
Calculating and scheduling penalties and arrears.
Filing and keeping in custody important papers and records.
Receiving for custody and returning property in small property divisions.
Issuing permits and notices according to prescribed regulations.
Making up and verifying payrolls.
Searching wills and corporation records.
Indexing mortgages and other legal documents.
Comparing and certifying genuineness of signatures on legal papers.
Explaining building plans to applicants.
Receiving applications and issuing certificates for commissioners of deeds.
Keeping cost record of mechanics' work.

Assistant Clerk (Multigraph Operator):

The specialized duties of Assistant Clerks (Multigraph Operator) are to operate multigraph machines in the performance of work requiring great expertness and involving considerable responsible clerical work.

Assistant Clerk (Tabulating Machine Operator):

The specialized duties of Assistant Clerks (Tabulating Machine Operator) are to operate complicated tabulating machine systems in the performance of work requiring great expertness in punching, sorting, tabulating and checking, and involving considerable responsible clerical work.

QUALIFICATIONS—

Assistant Clerk B:

1. Not less than one year of experience in Grade 2 A.

---

[1]For purposes of appraisal and appropriation, Grade 2 is divided into two parts, Grade 2 A and Grade 2 B. The unspecialized titles are Assistant Clerk A and Assistant Clerk B. For civil service purposes, this grade will be known simply as Grade 2, the unspecialized title being simply Assistant Clerk.

[2] The following positions are among those appraised by the Bureau of Personal Service in this grade on the basis of duties performed by present incumbents:

Assistant Clerks B acting as Window Clerks in the Department of Licenses.
Assistant Clerks B acting as Correspondence Clerks in the Tenement House Department.

Assistant Clerk (Multigraph Operator), Assistant Clerk (Tabulating Machine Operator):

1. Such qualifications as may be required by the Municipal Civil Service Commission.

COMPENSATION—

Assistant Clerk B:

Range of annual compensation—$840 to $1200 inclusive.
Salary rates—$840, $960, $1080, $1200.

Assistant Clerk (Multigraph Operator), Assistant Clerk (Tabulating Machine Operator):

Range of annual compensation—$720 to $960 inclusive.
Salary rates—$720, $840, $960.

SPECIAL REGULATION GOVERNING COMPENSATION—

Beginning with the lowest rate, advancement within this grade is conditional upon appraisal under the rules of the Board of Estimate and Apportionment, indicating that the rate requested does not exceed the value of the work to be performed.

GRADE 3 (C C 3)

TITLES OF POSITIONS[1]—

CLERK
CLERK (BERTILLON)
CLERK (COMPUTER)
CLERK (FINGER PRINT)

DUTIES—

Clerk:

The duties of Clerks, which may include taking charge of the clerical force in divisions and in minor departments, are to exercise continuing judgment and responsibility either in independent work or in the supervision of other employes.

Examples:

- Preparing specifications, requisitions, orders of advice of awards.
- Acting as contract clerk in the largest departments.
- Receiving and finally disposing of routine complaints.
- Summarizing reports.
- Making difficult computations of financial or cost statistics, estimates, etc.
- Collecting and computing important data for budget estimates.
- Supervising employes charged with renovations, disinfections, inventories, stores and expense accounting.
- Issuing and keeping record of electric sign licenses.
- Sealing and keeping record of corporate stock, etc.
- Preparing contracts according to prescribed specifications.
- Supervising a division in the searching of deeds, mortgages, and tax records.[2]
- Installing, revising and supervising other employes in the current administration of complex filing systems.
- Collecting rentals at city markets.
- Taking charge of a large stenographic bureau.

---

[1] The following positions are among those appraised by the Bureau of Personal Service in this grade on the basis of duties performed by present incumbents:

Clerk in charge of the central property division of the Police Department.
Clerk acting as Chief Clerk in the office of the Commissioner of Accounts.
Clerk (Computer) in the Law Department or in the Board of Assessors.

[2] See also the Title Examiner Group of the Sub-professional Service.

Clerk (Bertillon):

The specialized duties of Clerks (Bertillon) are to take and develop photographs of prisoners, to take, record and file Bertillon measurements, and to identify prisoners from measurements and photographs on file.

Clerk (Computer):

The specialized duties of Clerks (Computer) are to make computations incident to the fixing of awards and assessments for benefit in park and street opening proceedings or incident to the fixing of assessments for highway and sewer work and other public improvements.

Clerk (Finger Print):

The specialized duties of Clerks (Finger Print) are to take, classify and identify finger prints.

QUALIFICATIONS—

Clerk, Clerk (Bertillon), Clerk (Finger Print):

1. The minimum qualifications prescribed for Grade 2.
2. If appointed by promotion, not less than three years of appropriate experience in Grade 2, or if appointed as the result of an open competitive examination to the position of Clerk (Bertillon) or Clerk (Finger Print), such experience as may be required by the Municipal Civil Service Commission.
3. Such additional qualifications as may be required by the Municipal Civil Service Commission.

Clerk (Computer):

1. Experience in sub-professional engineering work, such as work in Grade 1 of the Instrumentman or Draftsman Group, or in clerical work involving the use of mathematics, or in other work recognized by the Municipal Civil Service Commission as qualifying.
2. Such additional qualifications as may be required by the Municipal Civil Service Commission.

COMPENSATION—

Range of annual compensation—$1320 to $1800 inclusive.

Salary rates—$1320, $1440, $1560, $1680, $1800.

SPECIAL REGULATION GOVERNING COMPENSATION—

Beginning with the lowest rate, advancement within this grade is conditional upon appraisal under the rules of the Board of Estimate and Apportionment, indicating that the rate requested does not exceed the value of the work to be performed.

SPECIAL CONDITION GOVERNING ADVANCEMENT—

The following table indicates the minimum number of years of meritorious service required at each rate before advancement to the next rate. See also page 30.

$1320	1 year
1440	1 "
1560	2 years
1680	2 "

GRADE 4 (C C 4)

TITLES OF POSITIONS[1]—

SENIOR CLERK
SENIOR CLERK (COMPUTER)
SENIOR CLERK (FINGER PRINT)

[1] The following positions are among those appraised by the Bureau of Personal Service in this grade on the basis of duties performed by present incumbents:

Senior Clerk acting as Chief Clerk in the Municipal Civil Service Commission.
Senior Clerk (Computer) in the Board of Assessors.
Senior Clerks acting as Clerks of the most important committees of the Board of Education.

DUTIES—

Senior Clerk:

The duties of Senior Clerks, which require a high degree of clerical knowledge and administrative ability, are to assume complete responsibility for the clerical work of entire bureaus or departments other than those mentioned in Grades 3 and 5, or to perform independently difficult, responsible or technical clerical work specifically appraised in this grade by the Board of Estimate and Apportionment.

Senior Clerk (Computer):

The specialized duties of Senior Clerks (Computer) are to supervise the work of Clerks (Computer) in Grade 3 or to perform independently and be responsible for the accuracy of all the most important calculations made in connection with fixing awards and assessments incident to condemnation proceedings.

Senior Clerk (Finger Print):

The specialized duties of Senior Clerks (Finger Print), which require a high degree of technical knowledge and ability, are to supervise the routine work of taking, classifying and identifying finger prints, and to perform exceptionally difficult finger print work requiring special skill.

QUALIFICATIONS—

Senior Clerk, Senior Clerk (Finger Print):

1. The minimum qualifications prescribed for Grade 3.
2. If appointed by promotion, not less than two years of appropriate experience in Grade 3, or if appointed as the result of an open competitive examination to the position of Senior Clerk (Finger Print), such experience as may be required by the Municipal Civil Service Commission.
3. Such additional qualifications as may be required by the Municipal Civil Service Commission.

Senior Clerk (Computer):

1. The minimum qualifications prescribed for Clerk (Computer) in Grade 3.
2. If appointed by promotion, not less than two years of appropriate experience as Clerk (Computer) in Grade 3, or if appointed as the result of an open competitive examination, experience in work of the character and standard of Clerk (Computer) in Grade 3.
3. Such additional qualifications as may be required by the Municipal Civil Service Commission.

COMPENSATION—

Senior Clerk, Senior Clerk (Finger Print):

Range of annual compensation—$1980 to $2580 inclusive.
Salary rates—$1980, $2160, $2340, $2580.

Senior Clerk (Computer):

Range of annual compensation—$1980 to $2340 inclusive.
Salary rates—$1980, $2160, $2340.

SPECIAL REGULATION GOVERNING COMPENSATION—

Beginning with the lowest rate, advancement within this grade is conditional upon appraisal under the rules of the Board of Estimate and Apportionment, indicating that the rate requested does not exceed the value of the work to be performed.

SPECIAL CONDITION GOVERNING ADVANCEMENT—

The following table indicates the minimum number of years of meritorious service required at each rate before advancement to the next rate. See also page 30.

$1980	1 year
2160	2 years
2340	2 "

GRADE 5 (C C 5)

TITLES OF POSITIONS[1]—

CHIEF CLERK
EXECUTIVE CLERK

DUTIES—

The duties of incumbents of these positions, which require the highest degree of clerical knowledge, administrative ability and experience, are to assume complete responsibility for the clerical work of departments composed of a number of important clerical units under the direction of clerks in Grades 3 and 4, or to perform independently the most difficult, responsible or technical clerical work specifically appraised in this grade by the Board of Estimate and Apportionment.

QUALIFICATIONS—

1. The minimum qualifications prescribed for Grade 4.
2. If appointed by promotion, not less than two years of appropriate experience in Grade 4, or if appointed as the result of an open competitive examination, such experience as may be required by the Municipal Civil Service Commission.
3. Such additional qualifications as may be required by the Municipal Civil Service Commission.

COMPENSATION—

Range of annual compensation—$2820 to $3540[2] inclusive.
Salary rates—$2820, $3060, $3300, $3540.

SPECIAL REGULATION GOVERNING COMPENSATION—

Beginning with the lowest rate, advancement within this grade is conditional upon appraisal under the rules of the Board of Estimate and Apportionment, indicating that the rate requested does not exceed the value of the work to be performed.

COURT CLERK GROUP

SYMBOL (C K)

The term Court Clerk Group is applied to those offices or employments of the Clerical Service in which incumbents are required to perform in courts responsible clerical work involving a knowledge of court procedure other than minor clerical work included in Grades 1, 2, 3 and 4 of the Clerk Group.

GRADE 1 (C K 1)

TITLES OF POSITIONS[3]—

ASSISTANT COURT CLERK

---

[1] The following positions are among those appraised by the Bureau of Personal Service in this grade on the basis of duties performed by present incumbents:
Chief Clerk in the Department of Health.
Chief Clerk in the Department of Water Supply, Gas and Electricity.
Chief Clerk in the Central Payroll Division of the Department of Finance.

[2] The Board of Estimate and Apportionment reserves the right to appraise certain positions in this grade at salaries of $3840 or $4140.

[3] The following positions are among those appraised by the Bureau of Personal Service in this grade on the basis of duties performed by present incumbents:
Complaint Clerk in the Magistrates' Courts.
Deputy Clerk of the Court of Special Sessions and the Children's Court.
Assistant Clerk in the City Court.
Clerk in the Court of Special Sessions, the Children's Court and the Magistrate's Court in the Boroughs of The Bronx, Queens and Richmond.
Clerk in the Municipal Court in outlying districts where the volume of work is small.

DUTIES—

The duties of incumbents of these positions are to act as assistant to the clerk of a large and important part of a court, or to perform specialized clerical work requiring knowledge of court procedure under the general supervision of such clerk, or to take charge of and be responsible for the entire clerical work of smaller and less important parts of courts.[1]

QUALIFICATIONS—

1. Experience as clerk in a court or law office, or as attendant or interpreter in a court, or other experience or education recognized by the Municipal Civil Service Commission as qualifying.
2. In the case of exempt positions or positions not classified by the Municipal Civil Service Commission, evidence of ability to perform the duties of the position satisfactory to the appointing officer.
3. Such additional qualifications as may be required by the Municipal Civil Service Commission.

The minimum qualifications shall consist of 1 and 3, or 2 and 3.

COMPENSATION—

Range of annual compensation—$1800 to $2340 inclusive.

Salary rates—$1800, $1980, $2160, $2340.

In addition to this compensation an annual compensation of $120 may be paid to Assistant Court Clerks who act as Interpreters in one or more foreign languages and who perform in this capacity work which would otherwise require the service of a Court Interpreter. Such additional compensation shall not be paid until the presiding judge of the court in which he is employed shall have certified to the usefulness of such foreign language or languages in the court and until the Assistant Court Clerk shall have been examined by the Municipal Civil Service Commission and shall have received a certificate of his ability to speak and write fluently such language or languages and to translate speech and writing from such language or languages into English, and vice versa.

SPECIAL REGULATION GOVERNING COMPENSATION—

Beginning with the lowest rate, advancement within this grade is conditional upon appraisal under the rules of the Board of Estimate and Apportionment, indicating that the rate requested does not exceed the value of the work to be performed.

SPECIAL CONDITION GOVERNING ADVANCEMENT—

The following table indicates the minimum number of years of meritorious service required at each rate before advancement to the next rate. See also page 30.

$1800	1 year
1980	2 years
2160	2 "

GRADE 2 (C K 2)

TITLES OF POSITIONS[2]—

COURT CLERK

---

[1]The majority of the Assistant Court Clerks in the Municipal Courts are appraised in Grades 3 and 4 of the Clerk Group of the Clerical Service. Only a limited number are performing the duties of Assistant Court Clerk.

[2]The following positions are among those appraised by the Bureau of Personal Service in this grade on the basis of duties performed by present incumbents:

Clerk of the Court in the Magistrates' Courts, Court of Special Sessions, Municipal Court and Children's Court.

DUTIES—

The duties of incumbents of these positions are to take charge of and be responsible to the justices and to the Chief Court Clerk for the clerical work in a large and important part of a court.

QUALIFICATIONS—

1. The minimum qualifications prescribed for Grade 1.
2. If appointed by promotion, not less than two years of appropriate experience in Grade 1, or if appointed as the result of an open competitive examination, experience in work of the character and standard of Grade 1.
3. In the case of exempt positions or positions not classified by the Municipal Civil Service Commission, evidence of ability to perform the duties of the position satisfactory to the appointing officer.
4. Such additional qualifications as may be required by the Municipal Civil Service Commission.

The minimum qualifications shall consist of 1, 2 and 4, or 3 and 4.

COMPENSATION—

Range of annual compensation—$2340 to $3300 inclusive.

Salary rates—$2340, $2580, $2820, $3060, $3300.

In addition to this compensation an annual compensation of $120 may be paid to Court Clerks who act as Interpreters in one or more foreign languages and who perform in this capacity work which would otherwise require the service of a Court Interpreter. Such additional compensation shall not be paid until the presiding judge of the court in which he is employed shall have certified to the usefulness of such foreign language or languages in the court and until the Court Clerk shall have been examined by the Municipal Civil Service Commission and shall have received a certificate of his ability to speak and write fluently such language or languages, and to translate speech and writing from such language or languages into English, and vice versa.

SPECIAL REGULATION GOVERNING COMPENSATION—

Beginning with the lowest rate, advancement within this grade is conditional upon appraisal under the rules of the Board of Estimate and Apportionment, indicating that the rate requested does not exceed the value of the work to be performed.

GRADE 3 (C K 3)

TITLES OF POSITIONS[1]—

DEPUTY CHIEF COURT CLERK

DUTIES—

The duties of incumbents of these positions are to act as deputy and assistant to the Chief Court Clerk.

QUALIFICATIONS—

1. The minimum qualifications prescribed for Grade 2.
2. If appointed by promotion, not less than two years of appropriate experience in Grade 2, or if appointed as the result of an open competitive examination, experience in work of the character and standard of Grade 2.

---

[1] The following positions are among those appraised by the Bureau of Personal Service in this grade on the basis of duties performed by present incumbents:

Deputy Chief Court Clerk in the Brooklyn, Queens and Richmond parts of the Magistrates' Courts and in the Children's Court.

3. In the case of exempt positions or positions not classified by the Municipal Civil Service Commission, evidence of ability to perform the duties of the position satisfactory to the appointing officer.

4. Such additional qualifications as may be required by the Municipal Civil Service Commission.

The minimum qualifications shall consist of 1, 2 and 4, or 3 and 4.

COMPENSATION—

Deputy Chief Court Clerk in Magistrates' Court:

Range of annual compensation—$3540 to $4140 inclusive.
Salary rates—$3540, $3840, $4140.

Deputy Chief Court Clerk in Children's Court:

Range of annual compensation—$3540 to $3840 inclusive.
Salary rates—$3540, $3840.

GRADE 4 (C K 4)

TITLES OF POSITIONS[1]—

CHIEF COURT CLERK

DUTIES—

The duties of incumbents of these positions are to take charge of and be responsible for all clerical work, including the supervision of employes, in an entire court, and to act as intermediary on all clerical matters between the judges and the employes of the court.

QUALIFICATIONS—

Chief Court Clerk in the Magistrates' Courts and the Children's Court:

1. The minimum qualifications prescribed for Grade 3.

2. If appointed by promotion, not less than two years of appropriate experience in Grade 3, or if appointed as the result of an open competitive examination, experience in work of the character and standard of Grade 3.

3. In the case of exempt positions or positions not classified by the Municipal Civil Service Commission, evidence of ability to perform the duties of the position satisfactory to the appointing officer.

4. Such additional qualifications as may be required by the Municipal Civil Service Commission.

The minimum qualifications shall consist of 1, 2 and 4, or 3 and 4.

Chief Court Clerk in the Court of Special Sessions, the Municipal Court and City Court:

1. The minimum qualifications prescribed for Grade 2.

2. If appointed by promotion, not less than two years of appropriate experience in Grade 2, or if appointed as the result of an open competitive examination, experience in work of the character and standard of Grade 2.

3. In the case of exempt positions or positions not classified by the Municipal Civil Service Commission, evidence of ability to perform the duties of the position satisfactory to the appointing officer.

4. Such additional qualifications as may be required by the Municipal Civil Service Commission.

The minimum qualifications shall consist of 1, 2 and 4, or 3 and 4.

---

[1] The following positions are among those appraised by the Bureau of Personal Service in this grade on the basis of duties performed by present incumbents:

Chief Court Clerk in the Magistrates' Court, Court of Special Sessions, Children's Court and the City Court.

COMPENSATION—

Range of annual compensation—$4140 to $5160 inclusive.
Salary rates—$4140, $4440, $4740, $5160.

SPECIAL REGULATION GOVERNING COMPENSATION—

Persons entering this grade need not necessarily begin at the lowest rate. Fixation of the initial salary rate and advancement within this grade are conditional upon appraisal under the rules of the Board of Estimate and Apportionment, indicating that the rate requested does not exceed the value of the work to be performed.

LIBRARIAN GROUP

SYMBOL (C L)

The term Librarian Group is applied to those offices or employments of the Clerical Service in which incumbents are required to perform routine, specialized, or supervisory library work in connection with the operation of a public library system, to direct and be responsible for such a system, or to classify, index and loan books, documents, periodicals, or other library material used by a department or bureau and to perform such other library services as may be required by the department or bureau.[1]

GRADE 3 (C L 3)

TITLES OF POSITIONS[2]—

DEPARTMENTAL LIBRARIAN

DUTIES—

Departmental Librarian:

The duties of Departmental Librarians, which require a technical knowledge of the activities and terminology of a department or bureau, are to classify, index and loan books, documents, periodicals, reprints and clippings, or other materials used by the department or bureau, and to perform such other library services as may be assigned.

QUALIFICATIONS—

Departmental Librarian:

1. Such training as is evidenced by a certificate granted on the completion of a standard course of library training, not less than one year in length, or other training or experience recognized by the Municipal Civil Service Commission as qualifying.
2. Such additional qualifications as may be required by the Municipal Civil Service Commission.

COMPENSATION—

Range of annual compensation—$1020 to $1260 inclusive.
Salary rates—$1020, $1080, $1140, $1200, $1260.

---

[1]Standard specifications for the personal service in the three public library systems of New York City are now being prepared by a joint committee from the libraries and the central agencies of the city government. They will be included in the above skeleton specifications for the Librarian Group if an agreement is reached between the trustees of the libraries and the Board of Estimate and Apportionment on budgetary and current control of appropriations granted by the city to the libraries. The Librarian Group should then be transferred to the Educational Service.

[2]The following positions are among those appraised by the Bureau of Personal Service in this grade on the basis of duties performed by present incumbents:

Departmental Librarian in the Research Laboratory of the Department of Health.

SPECIAL REGULATION GOVERNING COMPENSATION—

Departmental Librarian:

Persons entering this grade need not necessarily begin at the lowest rate. Fixation of the initial salary rate and advancement within this grade are conditional upon appraisal under the rules of the Board of Estimate and Apportionment, indicating that the rate requested does not exceed the value of the work to be performed.

SPECIAL CONDITION GOVERNING ADVANCEMENT—

The following table indicates the minimum number of years of meritorious service required at each rate before advancement to the next rate. See also page 30.

$1020	1 year
1080	1 "
1140	2 years
1200	2 "

GRADE 5 (C L 5)

TITLES OF POSITIONS[1]—

COURT LIBRARIAN
LAW LIBRARIAN

DUTIES—

Court Librarian:

The duties of Court Librarians, which require a considerable amount of legal knowledge, are to brief propositions of law, to maintain a system of annotations and card indices devised to show all details of library text and reports, the existing condition of all statutes and ordinances, and the titles, history and subject matter of all current cases, to advise as to additions to the library, and to perform such other related duties as may be required by the justices of the court.

Law Librarian:

The duties of the Law Librarian, which require familiarity with legal procedure, are to select for purchase books required by the Law Department, to prepare cases and points for binding, to index and digest judicial decisions, to annotate reports and statutes and to perform such other related duties as may be assigned.

QUALIFICATIONS—

1. Experience as librarian in a law library of recognized standing, or other training or experience recognized by the Municipal Civil Service Commission as qualifying.
2. Such additional qualifications as may be required by the Municipal Civil Service Commission.

COMPENSATION—

Range of annual compensation—$1980 to $2820 inclusive.

Salary rates—$1980, $2160, $2340, $2580, $2820.

An additional compensation of $600 may be paid to the Court Librarian of the City Court who, in addition to the duties described above, acts as law assistant to the justices of the court.

---

[1] The following positions are among those appraised by the Bureau of Personal Service in this grade on the basis of duties performed by present incumbents:

Law Librarian in the Law Department.
Court Librarian in the City Court of the City of New York.

SPECIAL REGULATION GOVERNING COMPENSATION—

Persons entering this grade need not necessarily begin at the lowest rate. Fixation of the initial salary rate and advancement within this grade are conditional upon appraisal under the rules of the Board of Estimate and Apportionment, indicating that the rate requested does not exceed the value of the work to be performed.

SPECIAL CONDITION GOVERNING ADVANCEMENT—

The following table indicates the minimum number of years of meritorious service required at each rate before advancement to the next rate. See also page 30.

$1980	1 year
2160	2 years
2340	2 "
2580	2 "

INTERPRETER GROUP

SYMBOL (C I)

The term Interpreter Group is applied to those offices or employments of the Clerical Service in which incumbents are required to write and speak English and one or more foreign languages fluently and to translate with clearness and accuracy speech and writing in those foreign languages into English and vice versa.

GRADE 1 (C I 1)

TITLES OF POSITIONS[1]—

INTERPRETER
COURT INTERPRETER

DUTIES—

The duties of incumbents of these positions, which are performed in connection with the official routine work of hospitals, courts or other city departments, are to converse and write fluently in foreign languages and to translate with clearness and accuracy speech and writing in these languages into English and vice versa.

QUALIFICATIONS[2]—

1. Such qualifications as may be required by the Municipal Civil Service Commission.

---

[1] The following positions are among those appraised by the Bureau of Personal Service in this grade on the basis of duties performed by present incumbents:

Interpreter in Bellevue Hospital.
Interpreter in the Bureau of Marriage Licenses in the City Clerk's office.
Interpreter in the Department of Licenses.
Court Interpreter in the City Magistrates' Courts, Municipal Courts or Court of Special Sessions.

[2] It is recommended that the Municipal Civil Service Commission hold a combined examination for the positions of Interpreter and Court Interpreter in this grade. The first part of the examination should consist of questions of less difficulty pertaining to general work as an Interpreter, while the second part should comprise questions of greater difficulty pertaining to the duties of Court Interpreter. Candidates desiring appointment to positions outside of the courts should be required to take only the first part of the examination, but candidates desiring appointment to positions as Court Interpreter should take both parts of the examination. As a result of this examination, two lists would be promulgated, one for Interpreter and one for Court Interpreter.

COMPENSATION—

Interpreter:

Range of annual compensation—$1080 to $1260 inclusive.
Salary rates—$1080, $1140, $1200, $1260.

Court Interpreter in City Magistrates' Courts, Municipal Courts or Court of Special Sessions:

Range of annual compensation—$1380 to $2100 inclusive.
Salary rates—$1380, $1500, $1620, $1740, $1920, $2100.

Court Interpreter in City Court:

Range of annual compensation—$1500 to $2280 inclusive.
Salary rates—$1500, $1620, $1740, $1920, $2100, $2280.

In addition to this compensation an annual compensation of $120 may be paid to Interpreters for each additional useful foreign language acquired, not exceeding two. A dialect of any language in which a candidate is qualified shall not be considered as an additional foreign language. Such additional compensation shall not be paid to any candidate until the head of the department in which he is employed shall have certified to the usefulness of such foreign language or languages in the department, and until the Interpreter shall have been examined by the Municipal Civil Service Commission and shall have received a certificate of his ability to speak and write fluently such language or languages and his ability to translate speech and writing in such language or languages into English and vice versa.

Persons employed temporarily as Interpreters or Court Interpreters in cases where no regular Interpreter is available shall be paid $5 per diem.

SPECIAL REGULATION GOVERNING COMPENSATION—

Court Interpreter:

Beginning with the lowest rate, advancement within this grade is conditional upon appraisal under the rules of the Board of Estimate and Apportionment, indicating that the rate requested does not exceed the value of the work to be performed.

SPECIAL CONDITION GOVERNING ADVANCEMENT—

The following table indicates the minimum number of years of meritorious service required at each rate before advancement to the next grade. See also page 30.

Interpreter:

$1080	1 year
1140	1 "
1200	2 years

Court Interpreter in City Magistrates' Courts, Municipal Courts or Court of Special Sessions:

$1380	1 year
1500	1 "
1620	1 "
1740	2 years
1920	2 "

Court Interpreter in City Court:

$1500	1 year
1620	1 "
1740	1 "
1920	2 years
2100	2 "

MESSENGER GROUP

SYMBOL (C M)

The term Messenger Group is applied to those offices or employments of the Clerical Service in which incumbents are required to serve legal notices, to receive and deliver papers, messages and valuable documents, to deposit moneys, to wait upon high city officials, and to receive and direct visitors to various bureaus or offices.

GRADE 1 (C M 1)

TITLES OF POSITIONS—

MESSENGER[1]
PROCESS SERVER

DUTIES—

Messenger:

The duties of Messengers, which require responsibility, trustworthiness and tact, are to receive and deliver moneys, valuable documents, papers and confidential messages for city departments and city officials, to meet and direct visitors to various bureaus or offices, and to perform such incidental clerical work as may be assigned by a superior.

Process Server:

The duties of Process Servers, which require the highest degree of responsibility, trustworthiness and tact and a knowledge of the law as to the service of papers, are to serve legal papers and to perform such incidental clerical work as may be assigned by a superior.

QUALIFICATIONS—

Messenger:

1. If appointed by promotion, not less than two years of appropriate experience in Grade 2 of the Clerk Group of the Clerical Service, or three years of appropriate experience in positions in the Labor Class, or if appointed as the result of an open competitive examination, such experience as may be required by the Municipal Civil Service Commission.
2. Such additional qualifications as may be required by the Municipal Civil Service Commission.

Process Server:

1. Experience in a law office or other experience recognized by the Municipal Civil Service Commission as qualifying.
2. Such additional qualifications as may be required by the Municipal Civil Service Commission.

COMPENSATION—

Range of annual compensation—$840 to $1200 inclusive.

Salary rates—$840, $900, $960, $1020, $1080, $1140, $1200.

Persons temporarily employed as Process Servers shall be paid $1.15 for each paper actually served.

An additional sum not to exceed $300 may be paid for service as Messenger to members of the Board of Estimate and Apportionment.

---

[1]These positions may also be filled by superannuated employes, such as Foremen, Caretakers, Clerks, or Inspectors, if their work has fitted them to be Messengers and if they are capable of rendering service in these positions.

SPECIAL REGULATION GOVERNING COMPENSATION—

Beginning with the lowest rate, advancement within this grade is conditional upon appraisal under the rules of the Board of Estimate and Apportionment, indicating that the rate requested does not exceed the value of the work to be performed.

PRIVATE SECRETARY GROUP

SYMBOL (C P)

The term Private Secretary Group is applied to those offices or employments of the Clerical Service in which incumbents are required to act as personal assistants to executive or administrative officials and as intermediaries between such officials and the public.[1]

GRADE 1 (C P 1)

TITLES OF POSITIONS[2]—

PRIVATE SECRETARY

DUTIES—

The duties of incumbents of these positions are to act as secretaries to heads of bureaus, less important commissions, or small departments, or to deputy commissioners in any department, and as intermediaries between them and the public, which duties involve the meeting and interviewing of visitors, the making of special investigations relating to departmental matters, and the performance of other services which relieve superiors of the details of office work.[3]

QUALIFICATIONS—

1. Ability to discharge the duties of the position satisfactory to the appointing officer.

COMPENSATION—

Range of annual compensation—$1800 to $2160 inclusive.
Salary rates—$1800, $1980, $2160.

SPECIAL REGULATION GOVERNING COMPENSATION—

Persons entering this grade need not necessarily begin at the lowest rate. Fixation of the initial salary rate and advancement within this grade are conditional upon appraisal under the rules of the Board of Estimate and Apportionment, indicating that the rate requested does not exceed the value of the work to be performed.

---

[1]No exempt position as Private Secretary shall be created where the work can be performed equally well and satisfactorily by a Stenographer in Grade 2 or a Senior Stenographer in Grade 3 of the Stenographer Group.

[2] The following positions are among those appraised by the Bureau of Personal Service in this grade on the basis of duties performed by present incumbents:

Private Secretaries to the Deputy Police Commissioners.
Private Secretary to the City Chamberlain.
Private Secretary to the Superintendent of Buildings in the Borough of Queens or the Borough of Richmond.

[3]Positions as Executive Secretaries of departments, boards, etc., will be found in the Executive Secretary Group of the Executive Service.

GRADE 2 (C P 2)

TITLES OF POSITIONS[1]—

SENIOR PRIVATE SECRETARY

DUTIES—

The duties of incumbents of these positions are to act as secretaries to heads of large city departments or commissions, and as intermediaries between them and the public, which duties involve the meeting and interviewing of visitors, the making of special investigations relating to departmental matters, and the performance of other services which relieve superiors of the details of office work.

QUALIFICATIONS—

1. Ability to discharge the duties of the position satisfactory to the appointing officer.

COMPENSATION—

Range of annual compensation—$2340 to $3540 inclusive.
Salary rates—$2340, $2580, $2820, $3060, $3300, $3540.

SPECIAL REGULATION GOVERNING COMPENSATION—

Persons entering this grade need not necessarily begin at the lowest rate. Fixation of the initial salary rate and advancement within this grade are conditional upon appraisal under the rules of the Board of Estimate and Apportionment, indicating that the rate requested does not exceed the value of the work to be performed.

GRADE 3 (C P 3)

TITLES OF POSITIONS—

EXECUTIVE PRIVATE SECRETARY

DUTIES—

The duties of incumbents of these positions are to act as secretaries to the Mayor, the President of the Board of Aldermen and the Presidents of the largest boroughs, and as intermediaries between them and the public, which duties involve the meeting and interviewing of visitors, the making of special investigations, and the performance of other services which relieve superiors of the details of office work.

QUALIFICATIONS—

1. Ability to discharge the duties of the position satisfactory to the appointing officer.

COMPENSATION—

Range of annual compensation—$3840 to $6600 inclusive.
Salary rates—$3840, $4140, $4440, $4740, $5160, $5580, $6000.

---

[1] The following positions are among those appraised by the Bureau of Personal Service in this grade on the basis of duties performed by present incumbents:

Senior Private Secretary to the Commissioner of the Police Department.
Senior Private Secretary to the Commissioner of the Department of Docks and Ferries.
Senior Private Secretary to the Commissioner of the Department of Health.
Senior Private Secretary to the Corporation Counsel.
Senior Private Secretary to the Commissioners of the Departments of Public Works in the various boroughs.
Senior Private Secretary to the Superintendent of Buildings in the Borough of Manhattan, Brooklyn or The Bronx.

SPECIAL REGULATION GOVERNING COMPENSATION—

Persons entering this grade need not necessarily begin at the lowest rate. Fixation of the initial salary rate and advancement within this grade are conditional upon appraisal under the rules of the Board of Estimate and Apportionment, indicating that the rate requested does not exceed the value of the work to be performed.

PURCHASING AGENT GROUP.

SYMBOL (C A)

The term Purchasing Agent Group is applied to those offices or employments of the Clerical Service in which incumbents are required to purchase supplies, materials and equipment in accordance with specifications, in such quantities and at such times as to meet the needs of the service and at the lowest market prices obtainable under existing conditions, or to supervise or direct this work.

GRADE 1 (C A 1)

TITLES OF POSITIONS[1]—

PURCHASING AGENT
PURCHASING AGENT AND ASSISTANT SUPERVISOR (CITY RECORD)
PURCHASING AGENT (BOOKBINDING SUPPLIES)
PURCHASING AGENT (PRINTING SUPPLIES)
PURCHASING AGENT (STATIONERY SUPPLIES)

DUTIES—

Purchasing Agent, Purchasing Agent (Bookbinding Supplies), Purchasing Agent (Printing Supplies), Purchasing Agent (Stationery Supplies):

The duties of incumbents of these positions are to carry on in departments purchasing large quantities of supplies, material and equipment, or in a central purchasing agency, the details of the work of obtaining, opening and examining bids; the preparation of contracts and ordering of supplies, materials and equipment under contract or in the open market; the supervision of deliveries to the extent of ascertaining that deliveries are made promptly and within the time limits agreed upon; the examination and approval of invoices as to agreement with the requirements of orders; and the keeping of such records and files as to provide all information connected with specifications, contractors, prices, routes, methods and rates of transportation.[2]

---

[1] The following positions are among those appraised by the Bureau of Personal Service in this grade on the basis of duties performed by present incumbents:

Purchasing Agent in the office of the President of the Borough of Manhattan or Brooklyn.

Purchasing Agent for the Department of Correction, Department of Public Charities, Bellevue and Allied Hospitals, Department of Street Cleaning, Department of Docks and Ferries or the Department of Health.

[2] The establishment of a central purchasing agency for the City of New York will result in a considerable modification of the duties of purchasing agents in the several departments. Presumably some of the present purchasing agents will become assistants to the Director of Central Purchase as specialists on the purchase of a particular line of supplies, materials or equipment. In addition, the Director of Central Purchase will probably have on his staff municipal examiners or inspectors of purchase and supplies.

The assistant of a purchasing agent in this grade, if such an assistant is required, should receive the title and compensation provided for in Grade 3 of the Clerk Group of the Clerical Service.

Purchasing Agent and Assistant Supervisor (City Record):

The duties of the Purchasing Agent and Assistant Supervisor (City Record) are to assist the Chief Purchasing Agent and Supervisor (City Record) in the supervision of the preparation and publication of the City Record and of all contracts for printing and stationery supplies for the city.

QUALIFICATIONS—

1. The minimum qualifications prescribed for Grade 3 of the Clerk Group of the Clerical Service.

2. If appointed by promotion, not less than three years of appropriate experience in Grade 3 of the Clerk Group of the Clerical Service.

3. Experience as purchasing agent or assistant purchasing agent for a large concern.

4. Such additional qualifications as may be required by the Municipal Civil Service Commission.

The minimum qualifications shall consist of 1, 2 and 4, or 3 and 4.

COMPENSATION—

Purchasing Agent, Purchasing Agent and Assistant Supervisor (City Record):

Range of annual compensation—$2100 to $2940 inclusive.
Salary rates—$2100, $2280, $2460, $2700, $2940.

Purchasing Agent (Bookbinding Supplies):

Range of annual compensation—$1800 to $2160 inclusive.
Salary rates—$1800, $1980, $2160.

Purchasing Agent (Printing Supplies), Purchasing Agent (Stationery Supplies):

Range of annual compensation—$2100 to $2700 inclusive.
Salary rates—$2100, $2280, $2460, $2700.

GRADE 2 (C A 2)

TITLES OF POSITIONS—

ASSISTANT DIRECTOR OF CENTRAL PURCHASE
PURCHASING AGENT AND ASSISTANT SUPERINTENDENT OF SCHOOL SUPPLIES (EDUCATION)

DUTIES—

Assistant Director of Central Purchase:

The duties of Assistant Director of Central Purchase are to assist the Director of Central Purchase in the devising, installation, organization and operation of a system of central purchase of all supplies purchased by the city.

Purchasing Agent and Assistant Superintendent of School Supplies (Education):

The duties of the Purchasing Agent and Assistant Superintendent of School Supplies (Education) are to assist the Chief Purchasing Agent and Superintendent of School Supplies (Education) in the supervision and direction of the purchasing, storage and distribution of all supplies, material and equipment for the Department of Education.

QUALIFICATIONS—

1. The minimum qualifications prescribed for Grade 1.

2. If appointed by promotion, not less than two years of appropriate experience in Grade 1, or if appointed as the result of an open competitive examination, experience in work of the character and standard of Grade 1.

3. Such additional qualifications as may be required by the Municipal Civil Service Commission.

COMPENSATION—

Assistant Director of Central Purchase:

Range of annual compensation—$3660 to $4260[1] inclusive.
Salary rates—$3660, $3960, $4260.

Purchasing Agent and Assistant Superintendent of School Supplies (Education):

Range of annual compensation—$3180 to $3960 inclusive.
Salary rates—$3180, $3420, $3660, $3960.

SPECIAL REGULATION GOVERNING COMPENSATION—

Persons entering this grade need not necessarily begin at the lowest rate. Fixation of the initial salary rate and advancement within this grade are conditional upon appraisal under the rules of the Board of Estimate and Apportionment, indicating that the rate requested does not exceed the value of the work to be performed.

GRADE 3 (C A 3)

TITLES OF POSITIONS—

CHIEF PURCHASING AGENT AND SUPERINTENDENT OF SCHOOL SUPPLIES (EDUCATION)
CHIEF PURCHASING AGENT AND SUPERVISOR (CITY RECORD)
DIRECTOR OF CENTRAL PURCHASE
SUPERINTENDENT OF PURCHASE AND MAINTENANCE (FIRE)

DUTIES—

Chief Purchasing Agent and Superintendent of School Supplies (Education):

The duties of the Chief Purchasing Agent and Superintendent of School Supplies (Education) are to supervise and be responsible for the purchasing, storage and distribution of all supplies, material and equipment for the Department of Education.

Chief Purchasing Agent and Supervisor (City Record):

The duties of the Chief Purchasing Agent and Supervisor (City Record) are to supervise the preparation and publication of the City Record and all contracts for printing and stationery supplies for the city.

Director of Central Purchase:

The duties of the Director of Central Purchase, which involve supervision of Purchasing Agents in Grade 1 and of other employes and which require a high degree of executive ability and specialized knowledge regarding the purchase of supplies, are to devise, install, organize and supervise the operation of a system of central purchase of all supplies purchased by the city.

Superintendent of Purchase and Maintenance (Fire):

The duties of the Superintendent of Purchase and Maintenance (Fire), which involve supervision of clerical and mechanical forces, are to direct and be responsible to the Fire Commissioner for purchasing, maintenance and repairs in the Fire Department and to perform such incidental work in the use, upkeep, locating and replacement of plant equipment and supplies as may be assigned.

---

[1]These salary rates are based upon the present unofficial and experimental character of the central purchase organization, and are subject to revision when the organization is placed on a more definite statutory basis.

QUALIFICATIONS—

Chief Purchasing Agent and Superintendent of School Supplies (Education), Chief Purchasing Agent and Supervisor (City Record), Director of Central Purchase:

1. The minimum qualifications prescribed for Grade 1 or Grade 2.
2. If appointed by promotion, not less than three years of appropriate experience in Grade 1 or one year of appropriate experience in Grade 2, or if appointed as the result of an open competitive examination, experience in work of the character and standard of Grade 1 or Grade 2.
3. Such additional qualifications as may be required by the Municipal Civil Service Commission.

Superintendent of Purchase and Maintenance (Fire):[1]

See footnote.

COMPENSATION—

Chief Purchasing Agent and Superintendent of School Supplies (Education):

Range of annual compensation—$6120 to $7200 inclusive.
Salary rates—$6120, $6600, $7200.

Chief Purchasing Agent and Supervisor (City Record):

Range of annual compensation—$4560 to $5280 inclusive.
Salary rates—$4560, $4860, $5280.

Director of Central Purchase:

Range of annual compensation—$4860 to $5700[2] inclusive.
Salary rates—$4860, $5280, $5700.

Superintendent of Purchase and Maintenance (Fire)[1]**:**

Annual compensation—$4560.

SPECIAL REGULATION GOVERNING COMPENSATION—

Director of Central Purchase:

Persons entering this grade need not necessarily begin at the lowest rate. Fixation of the initial salary rate and advancement within this grade are conditional upon appraisal under the rules of the Board of Estimate and Apportionment, indicating that the rate requested does not exceed the value of the work to be performed.

REVENUE OFFICER GROUP

SYMBOL (CR)

The term Revenue Officer Group is applied to those offices or employments of the Clerical Service in which incumbents are required to collect, receive, or disburse money and to perform clerical work directly incident thereto, or to administer offices whose principal function is the collection or disbursement of money.

---

[1] This position at present embraces a wide and somewhat unusual range of duties which has grown up during the term of the present incumbent. When the service of this incumbent terminates, reorganization and redistribution of duties will presumably follow which will change the nature of the position to such an extent that any statement of the qualifications or of a minimum salary for the position is at present omitted.

[2] These salary rates are based upon the present unofficial and experimental character of the central purchase organization and are subject to revision when the organization is placed on a more definite statutory basis.

GRADE 1 (C R 1)

TITLES OF POSITIONS—

TICKET SELLER

DUTIES—

The duties of Ticket Sellers are to sell tickets at entrances to municipal ferries or other terminals, to receive and guard money and to keep such records and make such reports as may be required.

QUALIFICATIONS—

1. Such qualifications as may be required by the Municipal Civil Service Commission.

COMPENSATION—

Regular Service Exclusive of Sundays:

Range of annual compensation—$960 to $1200 inclusive.
Salary rates—$960, $1020, $1080, $1140, $1200.

Temporary Service:

Per diem compensation—$3.25.

GRADE 2 (C R 2)

TITLES OF POSITIONS[1]—

CASHIER

DUTIES—

The duties of incumbents of these positions are to collect, receive, or disburse and to account for moneys due to or from the city, and to perform other assigned clerical work.

QUALIFICATIONS—

1. The minimum qualifications prescribed for Grade 2 of the Clerk Group.
2. If appointed by promotion, not less than three years of appropriate experience in Grade 2 of the Clerk Group, or if appointed as the result of an open competitive examination, experience in work of the character and standard of Grade 2.
3. Such additional qualifications as may be required by the Municipal Civil Service Commission.

COMPENSATION—

Range of annual compensation—$1320 to $1800 inclusive.
Salary rates—$1320, $1440, $1560, $1680, $1800.

SPECIAL REGULATION GOVERNING COMPENSATION—

Persons entering this grade need not necessarily begin at the lowest rate. Fixation of the initial salary rate and advancement within this grade are conditional upon appraisal under the rules of the Board of Estimate and Apportionment, indicating that the rate requested does not exceed the value of the work to be performed.

---

[1] The following positions are among those appraised by the Bureau of Personal Service in this grade on the basis of duties performed by present incumbents:

Cashier in the office of the Receiver of Taxes.
Cashier in the Water Register's Office, Queens.

SPECIAL CONDITION GOVERNING ADVANCEMENT—

The following table indicates the minimum number of years of meritorious service required at each rate before advancement to the next rate. See also page 30.

$1320	1 year
1440	1 "
1560	2 years
1680	2 "

GRADE 3 (C R 3)

TITLES OF POSITIONS[1]—

DEPUTY SUPERINTENDENT OF MARKETS
DEPUTY COLLECTOR OF CITY REVENUE
SENIOR CASHIER

DUTIES—

The duties of incumbents of these positions are to collect, receive, or disburse and to account for moneys amounting to large sums in the aggregate in positions involving complete independent responsibility.

QUALIFICATIONS—

1. The minimum qualifications prescribed for Grade 2.
2. If appointed by promotion, not less than two years of appropriate experience in Grade 2, or if appointed as the result of an open competitive examination, experience in work of the character and standard of Grade 2.
3. Such additional qualifications as may be required by the Municipal Civil Service Commission.

COMPENSATION—

Range of annual compensation—$1980 to $2160 inclusive.
Salary rates—$1980, $2160.

SPECIAL REGULATION GOVERNING COMPENSATION—

Persons entering this grade need not necessarily begin at the lowest rate. Fixation of the initial salary rate and advancement within this grade are conditional upon appraisal under the rules of the Board of Estimate and Apportionment, indicating that the rate requested does not exceed the value of the work to be performed.

GRADE 4 (C R 4)

TITLES OF POSITIONS[2]—

CHIEF STOCK AND BOND CLERK
CITY PAYMASTER
COLLECTOR OF CITY REVENUE AND SUPERINTENDENT OF MARKETS
DEPUTY COLLECTOR OF ASSESSMENTS AND ARREARS
DEPUTY RECEIVER OF TAXES
PENSION OFFICER

---

[1]The following positions are among those appraised by the Bureau of Personal Service in this grade on the basis of duties performed by present incumbents:

Senior Cashiers acting as deputies to the City Paymaster in the Department of Finance.
Senior Cashier in the Water Register's Office, Manhattan.
Senior Cashier in the office of the Receiver of Taxes.

[2]The following positions are among those appraised by the Bureau of Personal Service in this grade on the basis of duties performed by present incumbents:

Pension Officer in the Fire Department.

DUTIES—

The duties of incumbents of these positions are to exercise administrative control over the major divisions of the largest revenue receiving and disbursing bureaus or offices, or over small revenue receiving and disbursing bureaus or offices.

QUALIFICATIONS—

1. The minimum qualifications prescribed for Grade 3.
2. If appointed by promotion, not less than two years of appropriate experience in Grade 3, or if appointed as the result of an open competitive examination, experience in work of the character and standard of Grade 3.
3. Such additional qualifications as may be required by the Municipal Civil Service Commission.

COMPENSATION—

Range of annual compensation—$2340 to $4140 inclusive.
Salary rates—$2340, $2580, $2820, $3060, $3300, $3540, $3840, $4140.

SPECIAL REGULATION GOVERNING COMPENSATION—

Persons entering this grade need not necessarily begin at the lowest rate. Fixation of the initial salary rate and advancement within this grade are conditional upon appraisal under the rules of the Board of Estimate and Apportionment, indicating that the rate requested does not exceed the value of the work to be performed.

GRADE 5 (C R 5)

TITLES OF POSITIONS—

COLLECTOR OF ASSESSMENTS AND ARREARS
RECEIVER OF TAXES

DUTIES—

The duties of incumbents of these positions are to exercise administrative control over the largest revenue receiving or disbursing bureaus or offices.

QUALIFICATIONS—

1. The minimum qualifications prescribed for Grade 4.
2. If appointed by promotion, not less than two years of appropriate experience in Grade 4, or if appointed as the result of an open competitive examination, experience in work of the character and standard of Grade 4.
3. Such additional qualifications as may be required by the Municipal Civil Service Commission.

COMPENSATION—

Range of annual compensation—$4440 to $5160 inclusive.
Salary rates—$4440, $4740, $5160.

SPECIAL REGULATION GOVERNING COMPENSATION—

Persons entering this grade need not necessarily begin at the lowest rate. Fixation of the initial salary rate and advancement within this grade are conditional upon appraisal under the rules of the Board of Estimate and Apportionment, indicating that the rate requested does not exceed the value of the work to be performed.

STENOGRAPHER GROUP

SYMBOL (C S)

The term Stenographer Group is applied to those offices or employments of the Clerical Service in which incumbents are required to make, read and type stenographic notes and to perform such incidental typing and clerical work as may be required, or to supervise this work.

GRADE 1 (C S 1)

TITLES OF POSITIONS—

JUNIOR STENOGRAPHER
JUNIOR STENOTYPIST

DUTIES—

The duties of incumbents of these positions are to take symbolic notes of and to typewrite work which ordinarily does not include technical matter.

Examples:

Taking and transcribing routine correspondence, reports, notices and office memoranda.

Writing stereotyped communications and office forms.

QUALIFICATIONS—

1. Such qualifications as may be required by the Municipal Civil Service Commission.

COMPENSATION—

Women:

Range of annual compensation—$720 to $900 inclusive.
Salary rates—$720, $780, $840, $900.

Men[1]:

Range of annual compensation—$840 to $900 inclusive.
Salary rates—$840, $900.

GRADE 2 (C S 2)

TITLES OF POSITIONS—

STENOGRAPHER
STENOTYPIST

DUTIES—

The duties of incumbents of these positions, which may or may not involve supervision of small groups of stenographers and typists, are to perform general stenographic and typewriting work requiring ability to take and transcribe technical, scientific, legal or other matter recognized as difficult dictation, and to perform incidental clerical work.

Examples:

Disposing of important correspondence, reports and memoranda.

Taking notes of and transcribing legal briefs, opinions, agreements and statements, engineering specifications and technical communications, reports and papers.

QUALIFICATIONS—

1. The minimum qualifications prescribed for Grade 1.
2. If appointed by promotion, not less than one year of appropriate experience in Grade 1, or if appointed as the result of an open competitive examination, such qualifications as may be required by the Municipal Civil Service Commission.[2]
3. Such additional qualifications as may be required by the Municipal Civil Service Commission.

---

[1]Positions as Junior Stenographer shall be filled by men at the higher rate of $840 only when the location or nature of the position renders it impracticable that it should be filled by a woman.

[2]In open competitive examinations for positions in this grade, experience will be tested by examinations of greater difficulty than those set for Grade 1.

COMPENSATION—

Range of annual compensation—$960 to $1200 inclusive.
Salary rates—$960, $1020, $1080, $1140, $1200.

GRADE 3 (CS 3)

TITLES OF POSITIONS—

SENIOR STENOGRAPHER
SENIOR STENOTYPIST

DUTIES—

The duties of incumbents of these positions, which require a thorough acquaintance with the organization and work of the department in which they occur and a high degree of stenographic skill, accuracy and dependability, are to supervise a large stenographic bureau, to act as secretary and stenographer to the highest officials, to report and transcribe testimony at important public hearings and quasi-judicial trials, or to perform other exceptionally difficult stenographic work requiring peculiar skill and dependability not ordinarily found in Grade 2.

Examples:

Supervising the general stenographic force of a department or large bureau.
Disposing of correspondence for executives.
Meeting and interviewing visitors and performing other secretarial services.
Reporting testimony at trials of policemen and firemen by Commissioners and Deputy Commissioners.
Reporting and transcribing minutes of meetings of the Board of Estimate and Apportionment, Board of Aldermen and Board of Assessors.
Reporting public hearings before various committees of the Board of Estimate and Apportionment, such as the Committee on Franchises, City Plan, Assessments, etc.

QUALIFICATIONS—

1. The minimum qualifications prescribed for Grade 2.
2. If appointed by promotion, not less than two years of appropriate experience in Grade 2, or if appointed as the result of an open competitive examination, experience in work of the character and standard of Grade 2.
3. Such additional qualifications as may be required by the Municipal Civil Service Commission.

COMPENSATION—

Senior Stenographer or Senior Stenotypist supervising stenographic bureau or doing important reporting work:

Range of annual compensation—$1320 to $1980 inclusive.
Salary rates—$1320, $1440, $1560, $1680, $1800, $1980.

Other Senior Stenographers or Senior Stenotypists:

Range of annual compensation—$1320 to $1680 inclusive.
Salary rates—$1320, $1440, $1560, $1680.

SPECIAL REGULATION GOVERNING COMPENSATION—

Senior Stenographer or Senior Stenotypist supervising stenographic bureau:

Persons entering this grade need not necessarily begin at the lowest rate. Fixation of the initial salary rate and advancement within this grade are conditional upon appraisal under the rules of the Board of Estimate and Apportionment, indicating that the rate requested does not exceed the value of the work to be performed.

Other Senior Stenographers or Senior Stenotypists:

Beginning with the lowest rate, advancement within this grade is conditional upon appraisal under the rules of the Board of Estimate and Apportionment, indicating that the rate requested does not exceed the value of the work to be performed.

SPECIAL CONDITION GOVERNING ADVANCEMENT—

The following table indicates the minimum number of years of meritorious service required at each rate before advancement to the next rate. See also page 30.

Senior Stenographer or Senior Stenotypist supervising stenographic bureau or doing important reporting work:

$1320	1 year
1440	1 "
1560	2 years
1680	2 "
1800	2 "

Other Senior Stenographers or Senior Stenotypists:

$1320	1 year
1440	2 years
1560	2 "

GRADE 4 (C S 4)

TITLES OF POSITIONS—

COURT STENOGRAPHER

DUTIES—

The duties of incumbents of these positions, which require the highest degree of stenographic skill and a wide knowledge of court procedure, are to report and transcribe testimony at the City, Municipal, Magistrates', Special Sessions, or Children's Courts, and to do such incidental stenographic and typewriting work as may be required by the judges of these courts.

QUALIFICATIONS—

1. The minimum qualifications prescribed for Grade 3.
2. If appointed by promotion, not less than two years of appropriate experience in Grade 3, or if appointed as the result of an open competitive examination, experience in work of the character and standard of Grade 3.
3. Such additional qualifications as may be required by the Municipal Civil Service Commission.

COMPENSATION—

Range of annual compensation—$2160 to $3060 inclusive.
Salary rates—$2160, $2340, $2580, $2820, $3060.

SPECIAL REGULATION GOVERNING COMPENSATION—

Beginning with the lowest rate, advancement within this grade is conditional upon appraisal under the rules of the Board of Estimate and Apportionment, indicating that the rate requested does not exceed the value of the work to be performed.

SPECIAL CONDITION GOVERNING ADVANCEMENT—

The following table indicates the minimum number of years of meritorious service required at each rate before advancement to the next rate. See also page 30.

$2160	1 year
2340	2 years
2580	2 "
2820	2 "

TELEPHONE OPERATOR GROUP

SYMBOL (C O)

The term Telephone Operator Group is applied to those offices or employments of the Clerical Service in which incumbents are required to operate telephone switchboards, to keep records of calls and to do other incidental clerical work.

GRADE 1 (C O 1)

TITLES OF POSITIONS—

TELEPHONE OPERATOR

DUTIES—

The duties of incumbents of these positions, which require ability to facilitate the communications of a city department and knowledge of or the ability to learn the relations of a department with other departments and with the public, are to operate telephone switchboards, other than monitor or small boards which can be operated by office boys, to keep records of telephone calls, and to perform other incidental clerical work.

QUALIFICATIONS—

1. Experience in operating telephone switchboards.
2. Such additional qualifications as may be required by the Municipal Civil Service Commission.

COMPENSATION[1]—

Women:

Range of annual compensation—$600 to $1020 inclusive.
Salary rates—$600, $660, $720, $780, $840, $900, $960, $1020.

Men:

Range of annual compensation—$660 to $1020 inclusive.
Salary rates—$660, $720, $780, $840, $900, $960, $1020.

TYPIST GROUP

SYMBOL (C T)

The term Typist Group is applied to those offices or employments of the Clerical Service in which incumbents are required to operate one or more of the various kinds of typewriting machines used in city departments.

GRADE 1 (C T 1)

TITLES OF POSITIONS[2]—

JUNIOR TYPIST
JUNIOR TYPIST (DICTAPHONE)

DUTIES—

The duties of incumbents of these positions, which may involve the performance of incidental clerical work, are to make from written or typed copy or from the dictaphone on ordinary typewriting machines plain copies of information, reports, notices and memoranda.

---

[1]Positions requiring the highest ability as telephone operator, as for example in the Mayor's office, shall be filled not by appointment at a higher rate than the initial rate, but by transfer of a telephone operator from another department in the city service.

[2]The following positions are among those appraised by the Bureau of Personal Service in this grade on the basis of duties performed by present incumbents:

Junior Typist (Dictaphone) in the Bureau of Fire Prevention of the Fire Department.

Examples:

Making typed copies of information on cards or prepared forms.
Typing, listing and addressing form letters.
Doing plain routine copying on typewriter.
Typing from oral dictation.
Transcribing on the typewriter from the dictaphone.

QUALIFICATIONS—

1. Such qualifications as may be required by the Municipal Civil Service Commission.

COMPENSATION—

Junior Typist:

Women:

Range of annual compensation—$600 to $780 inclusive.
Salary rates—$600, $660, $720, $780.

Men:[1]

Range of annual compensation—$720 to $780 inclusive.
Salary rates—$720, $780.

Junior Typist (Dictaphone):[2]

Range of annual compensation—$720 to $780 inclusive.
Salary rates—$720, $780.

GRADE 2 (C T 2)

TITLES OF POSITIONS[3]**—**

TYPIST
TYPIST (DICTAPHONE)

DUTIES—

The duties of incumbents of these positions, which may or may not involve the operation of special billing machines or book-typewriters, are to perform difficult or technical work which requires judgment in rearranging, expanding, interpreting, segregating, or tabulating matter to be copied, or to perform dictaphone work requiring previous service in Grade 1.[4]

Examples:

Copying legal forms and notices.
Copying technical, scientific or statistical reports and such accounting information as requisitions, counterfoils, tax collections, schedules, recapitulations, reconciliation sheets, etc.
Computing averages on special billing machines.

---

[1]Positions as Junior Typist shall be filled by men at the higher rate of $720 only when the location or nature of the position renders it impracticable that it should be filled by a woman.

[2]These rates shall be applied only in the case of persons exclusively engaged in dictaphone work. Junior Typists (Dictaphone) may proceed by promotion to a maximum of $900 in Grade 2. See Grade 2.

[3]The following positions are among those appraised by the Bureau of Personal Service in this grade on the basis of duties performed by present incumbents:

Typist engaged in computing averages of examinations on a Moons-Hopkins machine in the Municipal Civil Service Commission.
Typist engaged in typing accounting tabulations on long carriage machines in the Department of Finance.
Typist (Dictaphone) in the Bureau of Fire Prevention of the Fire Department.

[4]Dictaphone operators shall enter the service in Grade 1 at $720 and may proceed after promotion examination to a maximum of $900 in Grade 2.

QUALIFICATIONS—

1. The minimum qualifications prescribed for Grade 1.

2. If appointed by promotion, not less than one year of appropriate experience in Grade 1, or if appointed as the result of an open competitive examination, such qualifications as may be required by the Municipal Civil Service Commission.[1]

3. Such additional qualifications as may be required by the Municipal Civil Service Commission.

COMPENSATION—

Typist:

Range of annual compensation—$840 to $1020 inclusive.
Salary rates—$840, $900, $960, $1020.

Typist (Dictaphone):

Range of annual compensation—$840 to $900 inclusive.
Salary rates—$840, $900.

GRADE 3 (C T 3)

TITLES OF POSITIONS[2]—

SENIOR TYPIST
SENIOR TYPIST (COMPUTING)

DUTIES—

Senior Typist:

The duties of Senior Typists, which require thorough acquaintance with the organization and work of the department in which they occur, are to supervise a typewriting bureau, or to perform exceptionally difficult departmental typing and clerical work requiring peculiar skill and dependability not ordinarily found in Grade 2.

Examples:

Preparing the most technical and important departmental reports, indices, etc.

Senior Typist (Computing):

The specialized duties of Senior Typists (Computing), which require some knowledge of bookkeeping or accounting, are to operate typewriting and computing machines used in the city service to record and segregate accounting information.

Examples:

Computing, segregating and tabulating special accounting data.

QUALIFICATIONS—

1. The minimum qualifications prescribed for Grade 2.

2. If appointed by promotion, not less than one year of appropriate experience in Grade 2, or if appointed as the result of an open competitive examination, experience in work of the character and standard of Grade 2.

3. Such additional qualifications as may be required by the Municipal Civil Service Commission.

---

[1]In open competitive examinations for positions in this grade, experience will be tested by examinations of greater difficulty than those set for Grade 1.

[2]The following positions are among those appraised by the Bureau of Personal Service in this grade on the basis of duties performed by present incumbents:

Senior Typist (Computing) engaged in performing the most difficult work on Wahl machines in the Department of Finance.

COMPENSATION—

Range of annual compensation—$1140 to $1380 inclusive.
Salary rates—$1140, $1260, $1380.

SPECIAL REGULATION GOVERNING COMPENSATION—

Beginning with the lowest rate, advancement within this grade is conditional upon appraisal under the rules of the Board of Estimate and Apportionment, indicating that the rate requested does not exceed the value of the work to be performed.

MISCELLANEOUS CLERK GROUP

SYMBOL (CZ)

The term Miscellaneous Clerk Group is applied to those offices or employments of the Clerical Service in which incumbents are required to perform non-professional routine or specialized clerical work of an exceptional nature not included in the other groups of the Clerical Service.

GRADE 4 (C Z 4)

TITLES OF POSITIONS—

EDITOR (CITY RECORD)

DUTIES—

Editor (City Record):

The duties of the Editor (City Record), which require a thorough knowledge of the laws relating to New York City advertising and of the functions and procedure of the various city departments, are to edit all copy for publication in the City Record and to devise methods of saving space and reducing expense in the make-up of the City Record, to keep statistical records of City Record copy, to keep books relating to advertising in newspapers other than the City Record, and to perform related correspondence, bookkeeping and recording work.

QUALIFICATIONS—

Editor (City Record):

1. Experience as Inspector of Supplies in the City Record office, Bookkeeper in Grade 2 of the Bookkeeper Group, Clerk in Grade 3 of the Clerk Group, Assistant Municipal Examiner in Grade 1 of the Municipal Examiner Group, or in other work recognized by the Municipal Civil Service Commission as qualifying.
2. Such additional qualifications as may be required by the Municipal Civil Service Commission.

COMPENSATION—

Editor (City Record):

Range of annual compensation—$2100 to $2940 inclusive.
Salary rates—$2100, $2280, $2460, $2700, $2940.

SPECIAL REGULATION GOVERNING COMPENSATION—

Editor (City Record):

Beginning with the lowest rate, advancement within this grade is conditional upon appraisal under the rules of the Board of Estimate and Apportionment, indicating that the rate requested does not exceed the value of the work to be performed,

INSPECTIONAL SERVICE

SYMBOL (I).

The term Inspectional Service is applied to those offices or employments the duties of whose incumbents are to observe and report on facts and conditions, or to supervise such observation and reporting and to take appropriate official action, in order to insure compliance with regulations, standards or specifications governing public health or safety, honest trade, or the verification of work performed or things purchased for the city, other than observation and reporting requiring professional training or merely incident to police duty or to the work outlined in other services.

INSPECTOR OF BUILDINGS GROUP

(SYMBOL I B)

The term Inspector of Buildings Group is applied to those offices or employments of the Inspectional Service in which incumbents are required to inspect and report on or to supervise and be responsible for the inspection of and reporting on the construction, alteration, maintenance and use of public and private buildings and other structures, including plumbing, plastering, elevators, amusement devices, etc., and steel work in buildings, bridges, or other structures, in order to insure compliance with the provisions of the building and plastering code, the labor and tenement house laws and regulations, the rules and regulations of the Board of Standards and Appeals and other established regulations and principles governing public health and safety.

GRADE 1 (I B 1)

TITLES OF POSITIONS—

BUILDING INSPECTOR[1,2]
BUILDING INSPECTOR (ELEVATORS)
BUILDING INSPECTOR (FIRE PREVENTION)
BUILDING INSPECTOR (HEATING)
BUILDING INSPECTOR (IRON AND STEEL)
BUILDING INSPECTOR (PIERS)
BUILDING INSPECTOR (PLASTERING)
BUILDING INSPECTOR (PLUMBING AND SANITATION)
BUILDING INSPECTOR (TENEMENTS)

---

[1]Building Inspectors who have served one year in this grade are eligible for promotion to Plan Examiner in Grade 2 of the Draftsman Group of the Sub-professional Service.

[2]The former title of Inspector of Repairs will be covered under the general title Building Inspector, unless the inspection is of specialized repairs, in which case the proper specialized title should be used.

DUTIES—

Building Inspector:

The duties of Building Inspectors are to inspect and report on construction, alteration or maintenance work on buildings and other structures, as to authorization, materials, compliance with the building code and with the regulations and principles of public health and safety, to make surveys of old buildings or buildings thought to be unsafe, to inspect and report on places of public assemblage, theatres, amusement devices, etc., as to their fitness to be licensed and used, and on hotels as to their compliance with the provisions of the Raines Law.[1]

Building Inspector (Elevators):

The duties of Building Inspectors (Elevators) are to inspect and report on elevators or escalators as to their mechanism and compliance with the provisions of the building code and with the established principles of public safety and health.

Building Inspector (Fire Prevention):

The duties of Building Inspectors (Fire Prevention) are to inspect and report on construction, alteration, occupancy and use of buildings, factories and other structures as to compliance with the laws and regulations governing fire prevention, and to make such other inspections and investigations relating to fire prevention, fire risks and dangers as may be assigned by the Chief of the Bureau of Fire Prevention.

Building Inspector (Heating):

The duties of Building Inspectors (Heating) are to inspect and report on construction or alteration work on heating plants or appliances in buildings.

Building Inspector (Iron and Steel):

The duties of Building Inspectors (Iron and Steel) are to inspect and report on iron and steel construction, alteration or maintenance in order to insure compliance with contract specifications or with the provisions of the building code, including the examination of materials delivered on the site of the work and the inspection of and reporting on the assembling, erection, riveting, bolting and painting of all iron and steel structures and parts.

Building Inspector (Piers):

The duties of Building Inspectors (Piers) are to inspect and report on construction, alteration or maintenance work on piers, bulkheads and other waterfront structures in order to insure compliance with contract specifications and with the regulations of the Department of Docks and Ferries and to inspect and report on waterfront structures erected by private persons under permit from the Department of Docks and Ferries.

Building Inspector (Plastering):

The duties of Building Inspectors (Plastering) are to examine and report on plastering and fireproofing processes as to their compliance with the provisions of the plastering code and the laws of the State of New York governing plastering work.

---

[1]The duties set forth are those at present performed by inspectors in the Bureaus of Buildings in the offices of the various borough presidents, and include such other inspections of buildings as do not require specialized knowledge of or work in particular limited phases of building inspection, such as plumbing, plastering, etc. In the case of such positions, a specialized title in brackets should be added to the group title of Building Inspector.

It is thought that this title will also cover the work of inspectors working under the present titles of Inspector of Masonry and Carpentry, without adding any specialized titles in brackets.

Building Inspector (Plumbing and Sanitation):

The duties of Building Inspectors (Plumbing and Sanitation) are to inspect and report on plumbing and general sanitation as to their compliance with the provisions of the plumbing code, tenement house regulations and the established principles of public health, and to make tests of plumbing, drainage and gas systems.[1]

Building Inspector (Tenements):

The duties of Building Inspectors (Tenements) are to inspect and report on construction, alteration or maintenance work on tenement houses as to compliance with tenement house laws and regulations.

QUALIFICATIONS[2]—

Building Inspector:

1. Not less than five years of experience as Architect, Engineer, Mason, Carpenter, Plumber, Iron Worker, or Plasterer.
2. Such additional qualifications as may be required by the Municipal Civil Service Commission.

Building Inspector (Elevators):

1. Practical experience in construction and inspection of elevators.
2. Such additional qualifications as may be required by the Municipal Civil Service Commission.

Building Inspector (Fire Prevention):

1. Training or experience either in general building construction work or as an inspector or investigator for fire underwriters, or in other work related to building inspection and fire prevention work recognized by the Municipal Civil Service Commission as qualifying.
2. Such additional qualifications as may be required by the Municipal Civil Service Commission.

Building Inspector (Heating):

1. Training or experience in general building construction, including specialized experience in maintenance or inspection of heating plants and appliances.
2. Such additional qualifications as may be required by the Municipal Civil Service Commission.

Building Inspector (Iron and Steel):

1. Not less than five years of experience as Architect, Engineer, or Iron Worker.
2. Such additional qualifications as may be required by the Municipal Civil Service Commission.

Building Inspector (Piers):

1. Practical experience in pier building.
2. Such additional qualifications as may be required by the Municipal Civil Service Commission.

---

[1]There is a considerable amount of similarity between some of the duties performed by these inspectors and those performed by Health Inspectors. At the present time there is confusion and overlapping of inspectional work. A proper line of division between the work of Health Inspectors and that of Tenement House or Building Inspectors is that Health Inspectors are inspecting for unsanitary and unhealthful conditions of food and sanitation not primarily due to structural defects, while Building and Tenement House Inspectors are inspecting for the compliance of building and equipment with laws and regulations governing their structure. See the Health Inspector Group of the Inspectional Service.

[2]For the positions of Building Inspector, Building Inspector (Iron and Steel), Building Inspector (Plastering), and Building Inspector (Plumbing and Sanitation), the first qualification mentioned is a charter requirement.

Building Inspector (Plastering):

1. Not less than ten years of experience as a journeyman in the plastering trade.

2. Such additional qualifications as may be required by the Municipal Civil Service Commission.

Building Inspector (Plumbing and Sanitation):

1. Not less than five years of training or experience in sanitary science or as journeyman in the plumbing trade.

2. A license issued by the Examining Board of Plumbers to work as a licensed plumber.

3. Such additional qualifications as may be required by the Municipal Civil Service Commission.

Building Inspector (Tenements):

1. Training or experience in general building construction, engineering or architectural work, sanitary work, or other work related to building sanitation recognized by the Municipal Civil Service Commission as qualifying.

2. Such additional qualifications as may be required by the Municipal Civil Service Commission.

COMPENSATION—

Range of annual compensation—$1200 to $1500 inclusive.
Salary rates—$1200, $1260, $1320, $1380, $1440, $1500.

SPECIAL CONDITION GOVERNING ADVANCEMENT—

The following table indicates the minimum number of years of meritorious service required at each rate before advancement to the next rate. See also page 30.

$1200	1 year
1260	1 "
1320	1 "
1380	2 years
1440	2 "

GRADE 2 (I B 2)

TITLES OF POSITIONS—

SENIOR BUILDING INSPECTOR
SENIOR BUILDING INSPECTOR (ELEVATORS)
SENIOR BUILDING INSPECTOR (FIRE PREVENTION)
SENIOR BUILDING INSPECTOR (IRON AND STEEL)
SENIOR BUILDING INSPECTOR (PLUMBING AND SANITATION)
SENIOR BUILDING INSPECTOR (TENEMENTS)

DUTIES—

The duties of incumbents of these positions are to supervise the work of Building Inspectors in Grade 1 or to perform independently the most difficult and responsible technical inspections.

QUALIFICATIONS—

1. The minimum qualifications prescribed for Grade 1.

2. If appointed by promotion, not less than two years of appropriate experience in Grade 1, or if appointed as the result of an open competitive examination, experience in work of the character and standard of Grade 1.

3. Such additional qualifications as may be required by the Municipal Civil Service Commission.

COMPENSATION—

Range of annual compensation—$1620 to $1920 inclusive.
Salary rates—$1620, $1740, $1920.

SPECIAL REGULATION GOVERNING COMPENSATION—

Beginning with the lowest rate, advancement within this grade is conditional upon appraisal under the rules of the Board of Estimate and Apportionment, indicating that the rate requested does not exceed the value of the work to be performed.

SPECIAL CONDITION GOVERNING ADVANCEMENT—

The following table indicates the minimum number of years of meritorious service required at each rate before advancement to the next rate. See also page 30.

$1620	1 year
1740	2 years

GRADE 3 (I B 3)

TITLES OF POSITIONS—

ASSISTANT CHIEF BUILDING INSPECTOR (BUREAU OF BUILDINGS, THE BRONX OR BROOKLYN)[1]
ASSISTANT SUPERINTENDENT (BUREAU OF BUILDINGS, QUEENS OR RICHMOND)
CHIEF BUILDING INSPECTOR (BUREAU OF BUILDINGS, QUEENS OR RICHMOND)[1]
CHIEF BUILDING INSPECTOR (FIRE PREVENTION)[1]
CHIEF BUILDING INSPECTOR (TENEMENTS)[1]

DUTIES—

Assistant Chief Building Inspector (Bureau of Buildings, The Bronx or Brooklyn)
Assistant Superintendent (Bureau of Buildings, Queens or Richmond)
Chief Building Inspector (Bureau of Buildings, Queens or Richmond):

The duties of incumbents of these positions are to assist the Chief Inspector in the entire supervision of inspectional work in the largest Bureaus of Buildings, or to act as Chief Inspector and to be responsible for the supervision of all inspectional work in the smaller Bureaus of Buildings.

Chief Building Inspector (Fire Prevention):

The duties of Chief Building Inspectors (Fire Prevention), which involve supervision of a large group of Building Inspectors in Grades 1 and 2, are to be responsible for the inspectional work in a major division of the Bureau of Fire Prevention.

Chief Building Inspector (Tenements):

The duties of Chief Building Inspectors (Tenements) are to be responsible for the supervision of all inspectional work in the largest units of the Tenement House Department.[2]

---

[1]These positions may be filled by the appointment of an Assistant Engineer in Grade 3 of the Engineer Group, or of an Assistant Architect in Grade 3 of the Architect Group of the Professional Service.

[2]At the present time, there are but two examples of inspectional work of this character, namely, the supervision of tenement house inspection in the Boroughs of Manhattan and Brooklyn.

The positions of Superintendents in the Tenement House Department are in the exempt class at the present time. They are appraised in Grade 4 of the Clerk Group of the Clerical Service. These positions should all be in the competitive class.

QUALIFICATIONS—

1. Such qualifications as are set forth in the Charter of the City of New York.
2. The minimum qualifications prescribed for Grade 2.
3. If appointed by promotion, not less than two years of appropriate experience in Grade 2, or if appointed as the result of an open competitive examination, experience in work of the character and standard of Grade 2.
4. Such additional qualifications as may be required by the Municipal Civil Service Commission.

COMPENSATION—

Assistant Chief Building Inspector (Bureau of Buildings, The Bronx or Brooklyn)

Assistant Superintendent (Bureau of Buildings, Queens or Richmond)

Chief Building Inspector (Bureau of Buildings, Queens or Richmond), Chief Building Inspector (Tenements):

Range of annual compensation—$2100 to $2940 inclusive.
Salary rates—$2100, $2280, $2460, $2700, $2940.

Chief Building Inspector (Fire Prevention, Manhattan, The Bronx and Richmond):

Range of annual compensation—$2100 to $2700 inclusive.
Salary rates—$2100, $2280, $2460, $2700.

Chief Building Inspector (Fire Prevention, Brooklyn and Queens):

Annual compensation—$2100.

SPECIAL REGULATION GOVERNING COMPENSATION—

Assistant Chief Building Inspector (Bureau of Buildings, The Bronx or Brooklyn)

Assistant Superintendent (Bureau of Buildings, Queens or Richmond)

Chief Building Inspector (Bureau of Buildings, Queens or Richmond):

Persons entering this grade need not necessarily begin at the lowest rate. Fixation of the initial salary rate and advancement within this grade are conditional upon appraisal under the rules of the Board of Estimate and Apportionment, indicating that the rate requested does not exceed the value of the work to be performed.

Chief Building Inspector (Fire Prevention):

Beginning with the lowest rate, advancement within this grade is conditional upon appraisal under the rules of the Board of Estimate and Apportionment, indicating that the rate requested does not exceed the value of the work to be performed.

SPECIAL CONDITION GOVERNING ADVANCEMENT—

The following table indicates the minimum number of years of meritorious service required at each rate before advancement to the next rate. See also page 30.

Assistant Chief Building Inspector (Bureau of Buildings, The Bronx or Brooklyn)

Assistant Superintendent (Bureau of Buildings, Queens or Richmond)

Chief Building Inspector (Bureau of Buildings, Queens or Richmond)

Chief Building Inspector (Tenements):

$2100	1 year
2280	1 "
2460	2 years
2700	2 "

Chief Building Inspector (Fire Prevention):

$2100	1 year
2280	1 "
2460	2 years

GRADE 4 (I B 4)

TITLES OF POSITIONS—

ASSISTANT CHIEF (BUREAU OF FIRE PREVENTION)[1]

ASSISTANT SUPERINTENDENT (BUREAU OF BUILDINGS, MANHATTAN, THE BRONX OR BROOKLYN)

CHIEF BUILDING INSPECTOR (BUREAU OF BUILDINGS, MANHATTAN, THE BRONX OR BROOKLYN)[2]

SUPERINTENDENT (BUREAU OF BUILDINGS, QUEENS OR RICHMOND)[3]

DUTIES—

Assistant Chief (Bureau of Fire Prevention):

The duties of Assistant Chiefs (Bureau of Fire Prevention) are to assist the Chief in the entire administration of the Bureau of Fire Prevention.

Assistant Superintendent (Bureau of Buildings, Manhattan, The Bronx or Brooklyn)

Chief Building Inspector (Bureau of Buildings, Manhattan, The Bronx or Brooklyn)

Superintendent (Bureau of Buildings, Queens or Richmond):

The duties of incumbents of these positions are to be responsible for all inspectional work in the smaller Bureaus of Buildings or to assist the Superintendents of the larger Bureaus of Buildings in the entire administration of these Bureaus.

QUALIFICATIONS—

1. Such qualifications as are set forth in the Charter of the City of New York.
2. The minimum qualifications prescribed for Grade 3.
3. If appointed by promotion, not less than one year of appropriate experience in Grade 3, or if appointed as the result of an open competitive examination, experience in work of the character and standard of Grade 3.
4. Such additional qualifications as may be required by the Municipal Civil Service Commission.

COMPENSATION—

Assistant Chief (Bureau of Fire Prevention):

Range of annual compensation—$3180 to $3660 inclusive.

Salary rates $3180, $3420, $3660.

Assistant Superintendent (Bureau of Buildings, Manhattan, The Bronx or Brooklyn)

Chief Building Inspector (Bureau of Buildings, Manhattan, The Bronx or Brooklyn)

Superintendent (Bureau of Buildings, Queens or Richmond):

Range of annual compensation—$3180 to $4260 inclusive.

Salary rates—$3180, $3420, $3660, $3960, $4260.

---

[1]The present titles of the incumbents of this position are Deputy Chief of the Bureau and Chief Inspector.

[2]This position may be filled by the appointment of a Senior Assistant Engineer in Grade 4 of the Engineer Group or of an Architect in Grade 4 of the Architect Group of the Professional Service.

[3]At present these positions are in the exempt class.

SPECIAL REGULATION GOVERNING COMPENSATION—

Assistant Superintendent (Bureau of Buildings, Manhattan, The Bronx or Brooklyn)

Chief Building Inspector (Bureau of Buildings, Manhattan, The Bronx or Brooklyn)

Superintendent (Bureau of Buildings, Queens or Richmond):

Persons entering this grade need not necessarily begin at the lowest rate. Fixation of the initial salary rate and advancement within this grade are conditional upon appraisal under the rules of the Board of Estimate and Apportionment, indicating that the rate requested does not exceed the value of the work to be performed.

GRADE 5 (I B 5)

TITLES OF POSITIONS—

SUPERINTENDENT (BUREAU OF BUILDINGS, MANHATTAN, THE BRONX OR BROOKLYN)[1]

CHIEF (BUREAU OF FIRE PREVENTION)

DUTIES—

Superintendent (Bureau of Buildings, Manhattan, The Bronx or Brooklyn):

The duties of the Superintendent (Bureau of Buildings, Manhattan, The Bronx or Brooklyn) are to be responsible for the entire administration of the largest Bureaus of Buildings.

Chief (Bureau of Fire Prevention):

The duties of the Chief (Bureau of Fire Prevention) are to be responsible to the Fire Commissioner for the entire administration of the Bureau of Fire Prevention.

QUALIFICATIONS—

1. Such qualifications as are set forth in the Charter of the City of New York.
2. The minimum qualifications prescribed for Grade 4.
3. If appointed by promotion, not less than one year of appropriate experience in Grade 4, or if appointed as the result of an open competitive examination, experience in work of the character and standard of Grade 4.
4. Such additional qualifications as may be required by the Municipal Civil Service Commission.

COMPENSATION—

Superintendent (Bureau of Buildings, Manhattan, The Bronx or Brooklyn):

Range of annual compensation—$4560 to $6120 inclusive.
Salary rates—$4560, $4860, $5280, $5700, $6120.

Chief (Bureau of Fire Prevention):

Range of annual compensation—$4560 to $5280 inclusive.
Salary rates—$4560, $4860, $5280.

GRADE 6 (I B 6)

TITLES OF POSITIONS—

CHAIRMAN (BOARD OF STANDARDS AND APPEALS)

MEMBER (BOARD OF STANDARDS AND APPEALS)

DUTIES—

Chairman (Board of Standards and Appeals):

The duties of the Chairman (Board of Standards and Appeals), which include supervision of the detailed work of the office, are to act as executive and administrative head of the Board of Standards and Appeals.

---

[1]At present this position is in the exempt class.

Member (Board of Standards and Appeals):

The duties of Members (Board of Standards and Appeals) are as members of the Board of Standards to test building materials for approval, to make, amend and repeal rules and regulations for the purpose of carrying into effect laws and ordinances relating to building construction and alteration, with the exception of laws and ordinances relating to tenement houses; as Members of the Board of Appeals, to hear appeals from rules, orders and decisions of the Superintendent of Buildings and the Fire Commissioner and to make such inspections and investigations as may be required in the performance of the above duties.

QUALIFICATIONS—

1. In the case of three Members, other than the Chairman, 10 years of experience as an architect, 10 years of experience as a structural engineer, and 10 years of practical experience as a builder, respectively; and in the case of the Chairman, 15 years of experience as an architect or structural engineer.

2. Ability to discharge the duties of the position satisfactory to the appointing officer.

COMPENSATION—

Chairman (Board of Standards and Appeals):

Range of annual compensation—$7200 to $8400 inclusive.
Salary rates—$7200, $7800, $8400.

Member (Board of Standards and Appeals):

$10 for each session and for each inspection or investigation.

INSPECTOR OF COMBUSTIBLES AND BLASTING GROUP

SYMBOL (I C)

The term Inspector of Combustibles and Blasting Group is applied to those offices or employments of the Inspectional Service in which incumbents are required to make inspection, to make recommendations as to the issuance of permits and to enforce rules and regulations relative to the manufacture, storage, sale, use and transportation of combustibles and explosives, or to supervise such work.

GRADE 1 (I C 1)

TITLES OF POSITIONS—

INSPECTOR OF COMBUSTIBLES
INSPECTOR OF BLASTING

DUTIES—

Inspector of Combustibles:

The duties of Inspectors of Combustibles are to inspect and report on the premises where explosives, chemicals and combustibles are manufactured, stored, sold or used, to make recommendations as to the issuance of permits for the use of combustibles and explosives, to examine plans of buildings where combustibles and explosives are kept, especially their mechanical protective appliances, and other premises of extraordinary fire hazard.

Inspector of Blasting:

The duties of Inspectors of Blasting are to make all inspections and to enforce all rules and regulations relative to the storage, sale, use and transportation of explosives used in blasting operations.

QUALIFICATIONS—

Inspector of Combustibles:

1. Experience in the technical use or inspection of combustibles, such as experience in a chemical laboratory or in a drug or explosives factory, or other experience recognized by the Municipal Civil Service Commission as qualifying.
2. Such additional qualifications as may be required by the Municipal Civil Service Commission.

Inspector of Blasting:

1. Experience in blasting and in the handling of explosives.
2. Training or experience as a mining engineer.
3. Such additional qualifications as may be required by the Municipal Civil Service Commission.

The minimum qualifications shall consist of 1 and 3 or 2 and 3.

COMPENSATION—

Range of annual compensation—$1200 to $1500 inclusive.
Salary rates—$1200, $1260, $1320, $1380, $1440, $1500.

SPECIAL CONDITION GOVERNING ADVANCEMENT—

The following table indicates the minimum number of years of meritorious service required at each rate before advancement to the next rate. See also page 30.

$1200	1 year
1260	1 "
1320	1 "
1380	2 years
1440	2 "

GRADE 2 (I C 2)

TITLES OF POSITIONS—

SENIOR INSPECTOR OF COMBUSTIBLES
SENIOR INSPECTOR OF BLASTING

DUTIES—

The duties of incumbents of these positions are to supervise and be responsible for a group of inspectors in Grade 1, or to be responsible for a small division of inspectional work, or to perform independently the most difficult and responsible technical inspections.

QUALIFICATIONS—

1. The minimum qualifications prescribed for Grade 1.
2. If appointed by promotion, not less than two years of appropriate experience in Grade 1, or if appointed as the result of an open competitive examination, experience in work of the character and standard of Grade 1.
3. Such additional qualifications as may be required by the Municipal Civil Service Commission.

COMPENSATION—

Range of annual compensation—$1620 to $1920 inclusive.
Salary rates—$1620, $1740, $1920.

SPECIAL REGULATION GOVERNING COMPENSATION—

Beginning with the lowest rate, advancement within this grade is conditional upon appraisal under the rules of the Board of Estimate and Apportionment, indicating that the rate requested does not exceed the value of the work to be performed.

SPECIAL CONDITION GOVERNING ADVANCEMENT—

The following table indicates the minimum number of years of meritorious service required at each rate before advancement to the next rate. See also page 30.

$1620	1 year
1740	2 years

GRADE 3 (I C 3)

TITLES OF POSITIONS—

CHIEF INSPECTOR OF COMBUSTIBLES AND BLASTING[1]

DUTIES—

The duties of the incumbent of this position are to act as head of a division or bureau for the inspection of combustibles and blasting.

QUALIFICATIONS—

1. The minimum qualifications prescribed for Grade 2.
2. If appointed by promotion, not less than one year of appropriate experience in Grade 2, or if appointed as the result of an open competitive examination, experience in work of the character and standard of Grade 2.
3. Such additional qualifications as may be required by the Municipal Civil Service Commission.

COMPENSATION—

Manhattan, The Bronx and Richmond:

Range of annual compensation—$2460 to $3420 inclusive.
Salary rates—$2460, $2700, $2940, $3180, $3420.

Brooklyn and Queens:

Range of annual compensation—$2100 to $2460 inclusive.
Salary rates—$2100, $2280, $2460.

SPECIAL REGULATION GOVERNING COMPENSATION—

Persons entering this grade need not necessarily begin at the lowest rate. Fixation of the initial salary rate and advancement within this grade are conditional upon appraisal under the rules of the Board of Estimate and Apportionment, indicating that the rate requested does not exceed the value of the work to be performed.

SPECIAL CONDITION GOVERNING ADVANCEMENT—

The following table indicates the minimum number of years of meritorious service required at each rate before advancement to the next rate. See also page 30.

Manhattan, The Bronx and Richmond:

$2460	1 year
2700	2 years
2940	2 "
3180	2 "

Brooklyn and Queens:

$2100	1 year
2280	2 years

---

[1]This position may also be filled by the appointment of an Assistant Engineer in Grade 3 of the Engineer Group of the Professional Service. In this case it might be necessary to add in that grade a specialized title of Assistant Engineer (Combustibles).

INSPECTOR OF ELECTRICITY GROUP

SYMBOL (I E)

The term Inspector of Electricity Group is applied to those offices or employments of the Inspectional Service in which incumbents are required to inspect and report on or to supervise and be responsible for the inspection of and reporting on electrical repairs and supplies and the proper installation, maintenance, use and service of electrical equipment.

GRADE 1 (I E 1)

TITLES OF POSITIONS[1]—

INSPECTOR OF ELECTRICITY[2]

DUTIES—

The duties of Inspectors of Electricity are to inspect and report on electrical repairs and supplies and the proper installation and maintenance of electrical equipment in city buildings or streets, to inspect electrical installations in buildings and places other than those owned by the city in order to insure compliance with the provisions of the electrical code, and to inspect overhead and underground electrical conductors in order to insure conformity with the provisions of franchises granted by the city, and in the case of conductors installed by the city, to insure conformity with contract specifications.

Examples:

Making inspections of electrical installations in private buildings or of installations of plants in public buildings in order to insure conformity with contract specifications.
Making routine inspections of maintenance and repair.
Making inspections of installations of the new fire alarm system or inspecting maintenance on the old system.

QUALIFICATIONS—

1. Experience as an electrician or other experience recognized by the Municipal Civil Service Commission as qualifying.
2. Such additional qualifications as may be required by the Municipal Civil Service Commission.

COMPENSATION—

Range of annual compensation—$1200 to $1500 inclusive.
Salary rates—$1200, $1260, $1320, $1380, $1440, $1500.[3]

Assigned on outage work:

Annual compensation—$1200.

---

[1]The following positions are among those appraised by the Bureau of Personal Service in this grade on the basis of duties performed by present incumbents:

Inspector of Electricity engaged in inspecting fire alarm boxes in the Fire Alarm Bureau of the Fire Department.

[2]These positions may also be filled by the appointment of an Engineering Assistant in Grade 1 or a Junior Engineer in Grade 2 of the Engineer Group of the Professional Service.

[3]In private employment, inspectors performing independently difficult technical electrical inspections are paid a slightly higher rate than the maximum for this grade. Provision for a limited number of such positions is made in the following grade. See specifications for Grade 2.

SPECIAL CONDITION GOVERNING ADVANCEMENT—

The following table indicates the minimum number of years of meritorious service required at each rate before advancement to the next rate. See also page 30.

$1200	1 year
1260	1 "
1320	1 "
1380	2 years
1440	2 "

GRADE 2 (I E 2)

TITLES OF POSITIONS—

SENIOR INSPECTOR OF ELECTRICITY[1]

DUTIES—

The duties of Senior Inspectors of Electricity are to supervise and be responsible for a group of Inspectors of Electricity in Grade 1, or to be responsible for less important divisions of electrical inspection in the smaller boroughs, or to perform independently the most difficult and responsible technical inspections.[2]

Examples:

Directing field inspections.

Revising inspectors' reports and preparing constructive criticisms for superiors.

Arbitrating disputes between contractors, citizens and inspectors.

Making inspections and conducting tests of important electrical machines and plants.

Supervising the examination of and granting of licenses to moving picture operators.

QUALIFICATIONS—

1. The minimum qualifications prescribed for Grade 1.
2. If appointed by promotion, not less than two years of appropriate experience in Grade 1, or if appointed as the result of an open competitive examination, experience in work of the character and standard of Grade 1.
3. Such additional qualifications as may be required by the Municipal Civil Service Commission.

COMPENSATION—

Range of annual compensation—$1620 to $1920 inclusive.

Salary rates—$1620, $1740, $1920.

SPECIAL CONDITION GOVERNING ADVANCEMENT—

The following table indicates the minimum number of years of meritorious service required at each rate before advancement to the next rate. See also page 30.

$1620	1 year
1740	2 years

---

[1]These positions may also be filled by the appointment of a Junior Engineer at the higher rates in Grade 2 of the Engineer Group of the Professional Service.

[2]It is the intention to provide in this grade for a small number of particularly skilled and experienced Senior Inspectors of Electricity to perform the most difficult independent work. The inspectors in Grade 1 may therefore look forward to promotion to a limited number of positions in Grade 2 which are not supervisory.

GRADE 3 (I E 3)

TITLES OF POSITIONS[1]—

CHIEF INSPECTOR OF ELECTRICITY[2]

DUTIES—

The duties of incumbents of these positions are to supervise and be responsible for the largest divisions of inspection of electricity and lighting involving the supervision of electrical inspection, testing or maintenance, or the preparation, analysis and criticism of estimates and specifications and other related work.

QUALIFICATIONS—

1. The minimum qualifications prescribed for Grade 2.
2. If appointed by promotion, not less than one year of appropriate experience in Grade 2, or if appointed as the result of an open competitive examination, experience in work of the character and standard of Grade 2.
3. Such additional qualifications as may be required by the Municipal Civil Service Commission.

COMPENSATION—

Range of annual compensation—$2100 to $2940 inclusive.

Salary rates—$2100, $2280, $2460, $2700, $2940.

SPECIAL CONDITION GOVERNING ADVANCEMENT—

The following table indicates the minimum number of years of meritorious service required at each rate before advancement to the next rate. See also page 30.

$2100	1 year
2280	1 "
2460	2 years
2700	2 "

HEALTH INSPECTOR GROUP

SYMBOL (I H)

The term Health Inspector Group is applied to those offices or employments of the Inspectional Service in which incumbents are required to perform services in the inspection of conditions of sanitation and hygiene affecting the public health, and in the prevention, correction and abatement of such conditions or practices as may be dangerous to public health or in violation of the laws of the State of New York, the ordinances of the City of New York, or the regulations of the Department of Health, or to supervise or direct this work.

GRADE 1 (I H 1)

TITLES OF POSITIONS—

HEALTH INSPECTOR[3]
HEALTH INSPECTOR (DRUGS)
HEALTH INSPECTOR (FOOD)
HEALTH INSPECTOR (MILK)
HEALTH INSPECTOR (SANITATION)

---

[1]The following positions are among those appraised by the Bureau of Personal Service in this grade on the basis of duties performed by present incumbents:

Chief Inspector of Electricity in charge of outage work in all boroughs.

[2]In the future, positions in this grade should be filled by the appointment of Assistant Electrical Engineers in Grade 3 of the Engineer Group of the Professional Service. Senior Inspectors in Grade 2, in order to advance beyond their grade, should be required to pass promotional examinations to positions as Assistant Electrical Engineer.

[3]It is intended in the future to fill positions in this grade, as far as possible, only under the general title Health Inspector. The specialized titles, Health Inspector (Milk), etc., are intended to cover mainly the present incumbents who are not prepared to enter the whole field of public health inspection.

DUTIES[1]—

Health Inspector:

The duties of Health Inspectors are to perform under supervision definite details of work in the inspection of conditions of sanitation and hygiene affecting the public health, and in the reporting, prevention, correction and abatement of such conditions or practices as may be dangerous to public health or in violation of the laws of the State of New York, the ordinances of the City of New York, or the regulations of the Department of Health.

Examples:

Making routine inspection and investigating complaints relative to the sanitation of dwellings, stables, factories, work-shops, stores, mercantile establishments and other buildings or places.

Making routine inspection of foods and drugs.

Procuring samples of food for analysis.

Investigating complaints relative to the production, manufacture, storage, handling and sale of foods and drugs.

Making inspections of and scoring dairies, pasteurizing plants, wholesale food establishments and food manufacturing plants.

Performing specialized work relative to the inspection and regulation of offensive trades, such as glue-making, or relative to the prevention of smoke, fly, mosquito or other nuisances.

Health Inspector (Drugs):

The duties of Health Inspectors (Drugs) are to make routine inspections of drugs, to investigate complaints relative to the production, manufacture, storage, handling and sale of drugs, and to report, prevent, correct and abate such conditions or practices as may be dangerous to public health or in violation of the laws of the State of New York, the ordinances of the City of New York, or the regulations of the Department of Health.

Health Inspector (Food):

The duties of Health Inspectors (Food) are to make routine inspections of foods, wholesale and retail food establishments, food manufacturing plants and slaughter houses, to procure samples of food for analysis, to investigate complaints relative to the production, manufacture, storage, handling and sale of foods, and to report, prevent, correct and abate such conditions or practices as may be dangerous to public health or in violation of the laws of the State of New York, the ordinances of the City of New York, or the regulations of the Department of Health.

Health Inspector (Milk):

The duties of Health Inspectors (Milk) are to make inspections of and score dairies, pasteurizing plants and places where milk is stored, handled or sold, to investigate complaints and to report, prevent, correct and abate such conditions or practices as may be dangerous to public health or in violation of the laws of the State of New York, the ordinances of the City of New York, or the regulations of the Department of Health.

---

[1]For inspection of tenement houses, see the Inspector of Buildings Group of the Inspectional Service.

For departmental inspection of foods or inspection for audit by the Finance Department, see the Inspector of Supplies Group and the Miscellaneous Inspector Group of the Inspectional Service.

For inspection of plumbing and general sanitation see Building Inspector (Plumbing and Sanitation) in Grade 1 of the Inspector of Buildings Group.

Health Inspector (Sanitation):

The duties of Health Inspectors (Sanitation) are to make routine inspections and investigate complaints relative to the sanitation of dwellings, stables, factories, work-shops, stores, mercantile establishments, lodging-houses, bath-houses and other buildings or places and to report, prevent, correct and abate such conditions or practices as may be dangerous to public health or in violation of the laws of the State of New York, the ordinances of the City of New York, or the regulations of the Department of Health.

QUALIFICATIONS[1]—

1. Such qualifications as may be required by the Municipal Civil Service Commission.

COMPENSATION—

Range of annual compensation for full-time service—$1200 to $1500 inclusive.
Salary rates—$1200, $1260, $1320, $1380, $1440, $1500.

SPECIAL CONDITION GOVERNING ADVANCEMENT—

The following table indicates the minimum number of years of meritorious service required at each rate before advancement to the next rate. See also page 30.

$1200	1 year
1260	1 "
1320	1 "
1380	2 years
1440	2 "

GRADE 2 (I H 2)

TITLES OF POSITIONS—

SENIOR HEALTH INSPECTOR
SENIOR HEALTH INSPECTOR (FOOD)
SENIOR HEALTH INSPECTOR (MILK)
SENIOR HEALTH INSPECTOR (SANITATION)

DUTIES[2]—

Senior Health Inspector:

The duties of Senior Health Inspectors are to supervise the work of groups or squads of Health Inspectors in Grade 1, or to perform independently the most difficult and responsible investigations requiring specialized knowledge of hygiene, sanitation and food manufacture or production.

---

[1]There are few persons qualified by training for the specific kind of work required of a Health Inspector. General business experience in the handling or sale of food, milk or drugs is a logical but not in practice a satisfactory preparation for health inspection in the city service. On the other hand, it is often preferable to recruit for this work young men who have had a good general education and are alert and honest, who have had no experience in this specialized kind of work but who can easily be trained to become first class Inspectors. It is therefore recommended that the Municipal Civil Service Commission require either specialized training relating to health inspection or a High School or college education and possibly some general business experience. It is strongly recommended that the more important positions in this grade be filled by Junior Chemists, Pharmacists and Veterinarians.

[2]See also Grades 1 and 2 of the Chemist and Physicist Group, Grades 2 and 3 of the Pharmacist Group and Grade 1 of the Veterinarian Group of the Professional Service.

Senior Health Inspector (Food):

The duties of Senior Health Inspectors (Food) are to supervise the work of groups or squads of Health Inspectors (Food) in Grade 1, or to perform independently the most difficult and responsible investigations requiring specialized knowledge of food manufacture or production.

Senior Health Inspector (Milk):

The duties of Senior Health Inspectors (Milk) are to supervise the work of groups or squads of Health Inspectors (Milk) in Grade 1, or to perform independently the most difficult and responsible investigations requiring specialized knowledge of the production and handling of milk and the process of pasteurization.

Senior Health Inspector (Sanitation):

The duties of Senior Health Inspectors (Sanitation) are to supervise the work of groups or squads of Health Inspectors (Sanitation) in Grade 1, or to perform independently the most difficult and responsible investigations requiring specialized knowledge of sanitation.

QUALIFICATIONS—

1. The minimum qualifications prescribed for Grade 1.
2. If appointed by promotion, not less than two years of appropriate experience in Grade 1, or if appointed as the result of an open competitive examination, experience in work of the character and standard of Grade 1.
3. Such additional qualifications as may be required by the Municipal Civil Service Commission.

COMPENSATION—

Range of annual compensation for full-time service—$1620 to $1920 inclusive.
Salary rates—$1620, $1740, $1920.

SPECIAL REGULATION GOVERNING COMPENSATION—

Beginning with the lowest rate, advancement within this grade is conditional upon appraisal under the rules of the Board of Estimate and Apportionment, indicating that the rate requested does not exceed the value of the work to be performed.

SPECIAL CONDITION GOVERNING ADVANCEMENT—

The following table indicates the minimum number of years of meritorious service required at each rate before advancement to the next rate. See also page 30.

$1620	1 year
1740	2 years

GRADE 3 (I H 3)

TITLES OF POSITIONS—

CHIEF HEALTH INSPECTOR (FOOD)
CHIEF HEALTH INSPECTOR (SANITATION)

DUTIES[1]—

The duties of incumbents of these positions are to supervise the work of a division within the Bureau of Food Inspection or the Bureau of Sanitary Inspection of the Department of Health.

---

[1]See also Grade 3 of the Chemist and Physicist Group and Grade 2 of the Veterinarian Group of the Professional Service.

QUALIFICATIONS—

1. The minimum qualifications prescribed for Grade 2.
2. If appointed by promotion, not less than one year of appropriate experience in Grade 2, or if appointed as the result of an open competitive examination, experience in work of the character and standard of Grade 2.
3. Such additional qualifications as may be required by the Municipal Civil Service Commission.

COMPENSATION—

Range of annual compensation for full-time service—$2100 to $2700 inclusive.
Salary rates—$2100, $2280, $2460, $2700.

SPECIAL REGULATION GOVERNING COMPENSATION—

Beginning with the lowest rate, advancement within this grade is conditional upon appraisal under the rules of the Board of Estimate and Apportionment, indicating that the rate requested does not exceed the value of the work to be performed.

SPECIAL CONDITION GOVERNING ADVANCEMENT—

The following table indicates the minimum number of years of meritorious service required at each rate before advancement to the next rate. See also page 30.

$2100	1 year
2280	1 "
2460	2 years

GRADE 4 (I H 4)

TITLES OF POSITIONS—

ASSISTANT HEALTH DIRECTOR (BUREAU OF FOOD INSPECTION)
ASSISTANT HEALTH DIRECTOR (BUREAU OF SANITARY INSPECTION)

DUTIES—

The duties of incumbents of these positions, which require a high degree of executive ability and specialized knowledge of public health work, are to act as assistant to the Director of the Bureau of Food Inspection or the Director of the Bureau of Sanitary Inspection of the Department of Health and to perform the duties of that director in his absence.

QUALIFICATIONS—

1. The minimum qualifications prescribed for Grade 3.
2. If appointed by promotion, not less than one year of appropriate experience in Grade 3, or if appointed as the result of an open competitive examination, experience in work of the character and standard of Grade 3.
3. Such additional qualifications as may be required by the Municipal Civil Service Commission.

COMPENSATION—

Range of annual compensation—$2940 to $3420 inclusive.
Salary rates—$2940, $3180, $3420.

SPECIAL REGULATION GOVERNING COMPENSATION—

Beginning with the lowest rate, advancement within this grade is conditional upon appraisal under the rules of the Board of Estimate and Apportionment, indicating that the rate requested does not exceed the value of the work to be performed.

GRADE 5 (I H 5)

TITLES OF POSITIONS—

HEALTH DIRECTOR (FOOD INSPECTION)

DUTIES—

The duties of the incumbent of this position, which require the highest degree of executive ability and specialized knowledge of public health work, are to direct and assume complete responsibility for the work of the Bureau of Food Inspection of the Department of Health.[1]

QUALIFICATIONS—

1. The minimum qualifications prescribed for Grade 4.
2. If appointed by promotion, not less than two years of appropriate experience in Grade 4, or if appointed as the result of an open competitive examination, experience in work of the character and standard of Grade 4.
3. Such additional qualifications as may be required by the Municipal Civil Service Commission.

COMPENSATION—

Range of annual compensation for full-time service—$5100 to $5940 inclusive.
Salary rates—$5100, $5520, $5940.

SPECIAL REGULATION GOVERNING COMPENSATION—

Beginning with the lowest rate, advancement within this grade is conditional upon appraisal under the rules of the Board of Estimate and Apportionment, indicating that the rate requested does not exceed the value of the work to be performed.

INSPECTOR OF LICENSES GROUP

SYMBOL (I L)

The term Inspector of Licenses Group is applied to those offices or employments of the Inspectional Service in which incumbents are required to observe and report or to supervise the observation and reporting of facts necessary to official action in connection with the issuing and revoking of or operation under licenses granted by the Department of Licenses, to conduct trials relative to the violation of license regulations and to render judgment thereon.

GRADE 1 (I L 1)

TITLES OF POSITIONS—

INSPECTOR OF LICENSES
INSPECTOR OF LICENSED VEHICLES

DUTIES—

Inspector of Licenses:

The duties of Inspectors of Licenses are to investigate application for, operation under and revoking of all licenses issued by the Department of Licenses other than those pertaining to vehicles and to collect and report facts necessary to official action thereon, to summon persons operating without licenses or violating regulations and to appear against them at hearings or in court.

---

[1]For the position of Health Director (Sanitary Superintendent) at the head of the Bureau of Sanitary Inspection, see Grade 6 of the Physician Group of the Professional Service.

Examples:

Inspecting relative to the terms of licenses for employment agencies, moving picture theatres, vendors' stands, etc.

Investigating and reporting on complaints regarding employment agencies, moving picture theatres, vendors' stands, etc.

Inspector of Licensed Vehicles:

The duties of Inspectors of Licensed Vehicles are to investigate application for, operation under and revoking of all licenses issued by the Department of Licenses pertaining to vehicles and to collect and report facts necessary to official action thereon, to summon persons operating without licenses or violating regulations and to appear against them at hearings or in court.

Examples:

Inspecting relative to the terms of licenses for taxicabs, hacks, etc.

Investigating and reporting on complaints regarding taxicabs, hacks, etc.

QUALIFICATIONS[1]—

1. Training or experience recognized by the Municipal Civil Service Commission as qualifying for this work.
2. Such additional qualifications as may be required by the Municipal Civil Service Commission.

COMPENSATION—

Range of annual compensation—$1200 to $1500 inclusive.
Salary rates—$1200, $1260, $1320, $1380, $1440, $1500.

SPECIAL CONDITION GOVERNING ADVANCEMENT—

The following table indicates the minimum number of years of meritorious service required at each rate before advancement to the next rate. See also page 30.

$1200	1 year
1260	1 "
1320	1 "
1380	2 years
1440	2 "

GRADE 2 (I L 2)

TITLES OF POSITIONS[2]—

SENIOR INSPECTOR OF LICENSES

---

[1]There are few persons qualified by training for the specific kind of work required of an Inspector of Licenses or an Inspector of Licensed Vehicles. General investigational or detective work is a logical preparation for license inspection in the city service. On the other hand, it is often preferable to recruit for this work young men who have had a good general education and are alert and honest, who have had no experience in this specialized kind of work, but who can easily be trained to become first class inspectors. It is therefore recommended that the Municipal Civil Service Commission require either specialized training relating to the inspection of licenses or a High School or college education and possibly some general business experience.

[2]The following positions are among those appraised by the Bureau of Personal Service in this grade on the basis of duties performed by present incumbents:

Senior Inspector of Licenses engaged in timing, testing and sealing taximeters in the laboratory of the Bureau of Weights and Measures.

DUTIES—

The duties of incumbents of these positions are to supervise the work of Inspectors in Grade 1, to make assignments and to receive and pass upon reports of violations, complaints, and the issuing or revoking of licenses, or to perform independently the most difficult and responsible inspections requiring a high order of specialized knowledge and judgment.

QUALIFICATIONS—

1. The minimum qualifications prescribed for Grade 1.
2. If appointed by promotion, not less than two years of appropriate experience in Grade 1, or if appointed as the result of an open competitive examination, experience in work of the character and standard of Grade 1.
3. Such additional qualifications as may be required by the Municipal Civil Service Commission.

COMPENSATION—

Range of annual compensation—$1620 to $1920 inclusive
Salary rates—$1620, $1740, $1920.

SPECIAL REGULATION GOVERNING COMPENSATION—

Beginning with the lowest rate, advancement within this grade is conditional upon appraisal under the rules of the Board of Estimate and Apportionment, indicating that the rate requested does not exceed the value of the work to be performed.

SPECIAL CONDITION GOVERNING ADVANCEMENT—

The following table indicates the minimum number of years of meritorious service required at each rate before advancement to the next rate. See also page 30.

$1620	1 year
1740	2 years

GRADE 3 (I L 3)

TITLES OF POSITIONS—

CHIEF INSPECTOR OF LICENSES[1]
CHIEF INSPECTOR OF LICENSED VEHICLES

DUTIES—

The duties of incumbents of these positions are to supervise the work of an important division in the Department of Licenses of which there is no deputy commissioner in immediate charge, to conduct trials relative to the violation of license regulations and to render judgments thereon.

QUALIFICATIONS—

1. The minimum qualifications prescribed for Grade 2.
2. If appointed by promotion, not less than one year of appropriate experience in Grade 2, or if appointed as the result of an open competitive examination, experience in work of the character and standard of Grade 2.
3. Such additional qualifications as may be required by the Municipal Civil Service Commission.

COMPENSATION—

Chief Inspector of Licenses:

Range of annual compensation—$2100 to $2700 inclusive.
Salary rates—$2100, $2280, $2460, $2700.

---

[1]At the present time there is but one incumbent of this position, namely, the Chief Inspector in charge of the Brooklyn office.

Chief Inspector of Licensed Vehicles:

Range of annual compensation—$2280 to $3180 inclusive.
Salary rates—$2280, $2460, $2700, $2940, $3180.

SPECIAL REGULATION GOVERNING COMPENSATION—

Beginning with the lowest rate, advancement within this grade is conditional upon appraisal under the rules of the Board of Estimate and Apportionment, indicating that the rate requested does not exceed the value of the work to be performed.

SPECIAL CONDITION GOVERNING ADVANCEMENT—

The following table indicates the minimum number of years of meritorious service required at each rate before advancement to the next rate. See also page 30.

Chief Inspector of Licenses:

$2100	1 year
2280	1 "
2460	2 years

Chief Inspector of Licensed Vehicles:

$2280	1 year
2460	1 "
2700	2 years

INSPECTOR OF METERS GROUP

SYMBOL (I T)

The term Inspector of Meters Group is applied to those offices or employments of the Inspectional Service in which incumbents are required to read, test and report on conditions of water meters and their installation, to make surveys of buildings for water consuming installation, to be in attendance when connections are made between city and service mains and between city mains and buildings, to locate and prevent leaks and waste of water, or to supervise such work.

GRADE 1 (I T 1)

TITLES OF POSITIONS—

INSPECTOR OF METERS

DUTIES—

The duties of incumbents of these positions are to read, test and report on conditions of water meters and their installation, to make surveys of buildings for water consuming installation, to be in attendance when connections are made between city and service mains and between city mains and buildings and to locate and prevent leaks and waste of water.

QUALIFICATIONS—

1. Such qualifications as may be required by the Municipal Civil Service Commission.

COMPENSATION—

Range of annual compensation—$1020 to $1200 inclusive.
Salary rates—$1020, $1080, $1140, $1200.

SPECIAL CONDITION GOVERNING ADVANCEMENT—

The following table indicates the minimum number of years of meritorious service required at each rate before advancement to the next rate. See also page 30.

$1020	1 year
1080	2 years
1140	2 "

GRADE 2 (I T 2)

TITLES OF POSITIONS—

SENIOR INSPECTOR OF METERS

DUTIES—

The duties of incumbents of these positions are to supervise a group of Inspectors of Meters in Grade 1 and to perform independently the most difficult and responsible inspections.

QUALIFICATIONS—

1. The minimum qualifications prescribed for Grade 1.
2. If appointed by promotion, not less than two years of appropriate experience in Grade 1, or if appointed as the result of an open competitive examination, experience in work of the character and standard of Grade 1.
3. Such additional qualifications as may be required by the Municipal Civil Service Commission.

COMPENSATION—

Range of annual compensation—$1320 to $1560 inclusive.
Salary rates—$1320, $1440, $1560.

SPECIAL CONDITION GOVERNING ADVANCEMENT—

The following table indicates the minimum number of years of meritorious service required at each rate before advancement to the next rate. See also page 30.

$1320	1 year
1440	2 years

GRADE 3 (I T 3)

TITLES OF POSITIONS—

CHIEF INSPECTOR OF METERS

DUTIES—

The duties of incumbents of these positions, which involve supervision of employes in Grades 1 and 2 and of other employes, are to supervise and be responsible for the work of the largest divisions of meter inspection.[1]

QUALIFICATIONS—

1. The minimum qualifications prescribed for Grade 2.
2. If appointed by promotion, not less than two years of appropriate experience in Grade 2, or if appointed as the result of an open competitive examination, experience in work of the character and standard of Grade 2.
3. Such additional qualifications as may be required by the Municipal Civil Service Commission.

COMPENSATION—

Range of annual compensation—$1680 to $2340 inclusive.
Salary rates—$1680, $1800, $1980, $2160, $2340.

SPECIAL REGULATION GOVERNING COMPENSATION—

Persons entering this grade need not necessarily begin at the lowest rate. Fixation of the initial salary rate and advancement within this grade are conditional upon appraisal under the rules of the Board of Estimate and Apportionment, indicating that the rate requested does not exceed the value of the work to be performed.

---

[1]At the present time there are but two examples of inspectional work of this character, namely the supervision of meter inspection in the Boroughs of Manhattan and Brooklyn.

SPECIAL CONDITION GOVERNING ADVANCEMENT—

The following table indicates the minimum number of years of meritorious service required at each rate before advancement to the next rate. See also page 30.

$1680	1 year
1800	1 "
1980	2 years
2160	2 "

INSPECTOR OF PUBLIC WORKS GROUP

SYMBOL (I P)

The term Inspector of Public Works Group is applied to those offices or employments of the Inspectional Service in which incumbents are required to inspect and to report on construction or maintenance work other than that connected with buildings, to report on traffic and street conditions and the occupancy and use of city property for construction and other purposes, to report on water pressure and water waste or to supervise such work.

GRADE 1 (I P 1)

TITLES OF POSITIONS[1]—

INSPECTOR OF PUBLIC WORKS[2]
INSPECTOR OF PUBLIC WORKS (DREDGING)[2]
INSPECTOR OF PUBLIC WORKS (HIGHWAYS)[2]
INSPECTOR OF PUBLIC WORKS (SEWERS)[2]
INSPECTOR OF PUBLIC WORKS (WATER MAINS)[2]

---

[1]The new title of Inspector of Public Works (Highways) includes the old titles of Inspectors of Encumbrances, Complaints, Regulating Grading and Paving, Street Openings, Vaults, etc.

The new title of Inspector of Public Works (Sewers) includes the old titles of Inspectors of Sewers, Sewers and Basins, Sewer Construction, Sewer Connections, etc.

The new title of Inspector of Public Works (Water Mains) includes the old titles of Inspectors of Pipe Laying, Pipe Laying Pipes and Hydrants, etc.

It is recommended that the Municipal Civil Service Commission hold a single examination for all positions in this grade as Inspector of Public Works. Candidates should be required to state in their experience papers the particular position or positions for which they wish to qualify. The experience ratings may be given in accordance with these statements. The mental examination should include a number of questions common to all positions, followed by groups of specialized questions on highways, sewers and masonry, water mains, etc. In order to qualify under one or more of the four specialized titles, candidates should be required to pass an examination on the appropriate group of specialized questions. In order to qualify under the general title of Inspector of Public Works, candidates should be required to select a stated number of questions from each one of the specialized groups. Such an examination would result in the certification of a number of eligible lists under specialized titles where these are required.

[2]The work outlined in this grade need not necessarily be performed by Inspectors of Public Works. It may also be performed by Engineering Assistants acting as apprentices and by Junior Engineers in Grades 1 and 2 of the Engineer Group of the Professional Service.

Inspectors of Public Works who have served one year in this grade are eligible for promotion to Plan Examiner in Grade 2 of the Draftsman Group of the Subprofessional Service.

DUTIES—

Inspector of Public Works:

The duties of Inspectors of Public Works, which require a general knowledge of the duties of all the specialized inspectorships above mentioned, are to perform under assignment general inspectional and utility work covering the whole field of public works excepting meters and water consumption.

Inspector of Public Works (Dredging):

The duties of Inspectors of Public Works (Dredging) are to be in attendance on dredging or waterfront work in order to insure its performance in accordance with contract specifications or orders, to direct the location of dredges, to take soundings, to keep notes of the progress of the work, to measure materials in and to report to the Supervisor of the Harbor the departure of scows and to inspect such waterfront work as may be assigned.

Inspector of Public Works (Highways):

The duties of Inspectors of Public Works (Highways) are to be in attendance on construction or maintenance work on highways in order to insure its performance in accordance with contract specifications or orders, to examine materials delivered on site of work, to report on pedestrian and vehicular traffic, to patrol the streets and sidewalks for the purpose of ascertaining their condition and to exercise control over street openings, proper restoration of pavements and the occupancy and use of city property for construction and other purposes, including encumbrances and sidewalk vaults.

Inspector of Public Works (Sewers):

The duties of Inspectors of Public Works (Sewers) are to be in attendance on construction or maintenance work on sewers and appurtenances, in order to insure its performance in accordance with contract specifications or orders, to examine materials delivered on site of work, to report on pedestrian and vehicular traffic, to exercise control over street openings, location and construction of subsurface structures, proper restoration of pavements and the occupancy and use of city property for construction and other purposes.

Inspector of Public Works (Water Mains):

The duties of Inspectors of Public Works (Water Mains) are to be in attendance on construction or maintenance work on water mains in order to insure its performance in accordance with contract specifications or orders, or examine materials delivered on site of work, to exercise control over street openings, location and construction of subsurface structures, proper restoration of pavements and the occupancy and use of city property for construction and other purposes.

QUALIFICATIONS—

1. Training, either educational or practical, in specialized or general public works or other related work recognized by the Municipal Civil Service Commission as qualifying.

2. Such additional qualifications as may be required by the Municipal Civil Service Commission.

COMPENSATION[1]—

Assigned on construction work:

Range of annual compensation—$1200 to $1500 inclusive.

Salary rates—$1200, $1260, $1320, $1380, $1440, $1500.

---

[1]Appropriate deductions from salary will be made in the case of Inspectors receiving part or full maintenance.

Assigned on routine or patrol work:
Range of annual compensation[1]—$1200 to $1380 inclusive.
Salary rates—$1200, $1260, $1320, $1380.
Per diem compensation[2]—$4.50.
Monthly compensation[3]—$100.

SPECIAL CONDITION GOVERNING ADVANCEMENT—

The following table indicates the minimum number of years of meritorious service required at each rate before advancement to the next rate. See also page 28.

$1200	1 year
1260	1 "
1320	1 "
1380	2 years
1440	2 "

GRADE 2 (I P 2)

TITLES OF POSITIONS—

SENIOR INSPECTOR OF PUBLIC WORKS[4]
SENIOR INSPECTOR OF PUBLIC WORKS (HIGHWAYS)[4]
SENIOR INSPECTOR OF PUBLIC WORKS (SEWERS)[4]
SENIOR INSPECTOR OF PUBLIC WORKS (SHOP AND FOUNDRY)[4]
SENIOR INSPECTOR OF PUBLIC WORKS (WATER MAINS)[4]

DUTIES—

Senior Inspector of Public Works, Senior Inspector of Public Works (Highways), Senior Inspector of Public Works (Sewers), Senior Inspector of Public Works (Water Mains):

The duties of incumbents of these positions, which are performed under the immediate direction of the engineer or higher official in charge, are to supervise a group of Inspectors in Grade 1, or to perform independently the most difficult and responsible technical inspections requiring a high order of specialized knowledge, initiative and judgment.

Senior Inspector of Public Works (Shop and Foundry):

The duties of Senior Inspectors of Public Works (Shop and Foundry), which may or may not be supervisory, are to be in attendance at the shop or foundry to determine that methods of fabrication, materials used and products are in accordance with specifications, to supervise tests of materials, to take samples or test bars for examination or analysis, to pass on machine work and to test finished products.

QUALIFICATIONS—

1. The minimum qualifications prescribed for Grade 1.
2. If appointed by promotion, not less than two years of appropriate experience in Grade 1, or if appointed as the result of an open competitive examination, experience in work of the character and standard of Grade 1.
3. Such additional qualifications as may be required by the Municipal Civil Service Commission.

---

[1]Where work will last continuously throughout the year, the annual rate shall be paid.

[2]Where work is temporary and will not last continuously for a period measurable by months, the daily rate shall be paid.

[3]Where work is temporary and will not last continuously throughout the year, but is measurable by months, the monthly rate shall be paid.

[4]These positions may also be filled by the appointment of Engineering Assistants and Junior Engineers in Grades 1 and 2 of the Engineer Group of the Professional Service.

COMPENSATION[1]—

Range of annual compensation—$1620 to $1920 inclusive.
Salary rates—$1620, $1740, $1920.

SPECIAL REGULATION GOVERNING COMPENSATION—

Beginning with the lowest rate, advancement within this grade is conditional upon appraisal under the rules of the Board of Estimate and Apportionment, indicating that the rate requested does not exceed the value of the work to be performed.

SPECIAL CONDITION GOVERNING ADVANCEMENT—

The following table indicates the minimum number of years of meritorious service required at each rate before advancement to the next rate. See also page 30.

$1620	1 year
1740	2 years

GRADE 3 (I P 3)

TITLES OF POSITIONS—

SUPERINTENDENT OF PUBLIC WORKS
SUPERINTENDENT OF PUBLIC WORKS (ASPHALT PLANT)[2]

DUTIES—

Superintendent of Public Works:

The duties of Superintendents of Public Works are to supervise and be responsible for the maintenance of sewers or highways, or both, in an entire borough.[3]

Superintendent of Public Works (Asphalt Plant):

The duties of the Superintendent of Public Works (Asphalt Plant) are to supervise and be responsible for the maintenance and operation of a large municipal asphalt plant.

QUALIFICATIONS—

1. The minimum qualifications prescribed for Grade 2.
2. If appointed by promotion, not less than one year of appropriate experience in Grade 2, or if appointed as the result of an open competitive examination, experience in work of the character and standard of Grade 2.
3. Such additional qualifications as may be required by the Municipal Civil Service Commission.

COMPENSATION—

Range of annual compensation—$2100 to $3180 inclusive.
Salary rates—$2100, $2280, $2460, $2700, $2940, $3180.

---

[1]Appropriate deductions from salary will be made in the case of Senior Inspectors receiving part or full maintenance.

[2]This position may also be filled by the appointment of an Assistant Engineer in Grade 3 of the Engineer Group of the Professional Service.

[3]There are highly paid engineers in the Department of Public Works in all boroughs who are responsible for construction, operation and maintenance work. It is very doubtful whether a position of Superintendent of Public Works is required at all in any borough. There is no such position at the present time in the borough of Manhattan. Certainly no position other than one involving supervision of maintenance is required and no salary higher than $3180 is justified. It is recommended that in future this work be in charge of an Assistant Engineer in Grade 3 of the Engineer Group of the Professional Service.

SPECIAL REGULATION GOVERNING COMPENSATION—

Persons entering this grade need not necessarily begin at the lowest rate. Fixation of the initial salary rate and advancement within this grade are conditional upon appraisal under the rules of the Board of Estimate and Apportionment, indicating that the rate requested does not exceed the value of the work to be performed.

SPECIAL CONDITION GOVERNING ADVANCEMENT—

The following table indicates the minimum number of years of meritorious service required at each rate before advancement to the next rate. See also page 30.

$2100	1 year
2280	1 "
2460	2 years
2700	2 "
2940	2 "

INSPECTOR OF SUPPLIES GROUP

SYMBOL (I S)

The term Inspector of Supplies Group is applied to those offices or employments of the Inspectional Service in which incumbents are required to inspect supplies, or to supervise the inspection of repairs and supplies.

GRADE 1 (I S 1)

TITLES OF POSITIONS[1,2]—

INSPECTOR OF SUPPLIES
INSPECTOR OF SUPPLIES (EGG CANDLER)

DUTIES—

Inspector of Supplies:

The duties of Inspectors of Supplies are to inspect supplies for the purpose of enforcing contract and open market order specifications and reporting the quantity and quality of supplies, and to ascertain qualities and processes of manufacture, prices, trade customs and conditions.

Inspector of Supplies (Egg Candler):

The duties of Inspectors of Supplies (Egg Candler) are to candle eggs in order to ascertain their freshness and fitness for use.

QUALIFICATIONS—

1. Experience in the purchasing, storage, inspection or other handling of supplies of the kind described in the title of the position.
2. Such additional qualifications as may be required by the Municipal Civil Service Commission.

COMPENSATION—

Range of annual compensation—$1200 to $1500 inclusive.
Salary rates—$1200, $1260, $1320, $1380, $1440, $1500.

---

[1]In the case of Inspectors of Supplies who specialize in some particular kind of supplies, the specialized title will be added in brackets.

[2]The former title of Inspector of Repairs will be covered under the general title Building Inspector, unless the inspection is of specialized repairs, in which case the proper specialized title should be used. See the Inspector of Buildings Group.

SPECIAL CONDITION GOVERNING ADVANCEMENT—

The following table indicates the minimum number of years of meritorious service required at each rate before advancement to the next rate. See also page 30.

$1200	1 year
1260	1 "
1320	1 "
1380	2 years
1440	2 "

GRADE 2 (I S 2)

TITLES OF POSITIONS[1]—

SENIOR INSPECTOR OF SUPPLIES

DUTIES—

The duties of incumbents of these positions are to supervise groups of Inspectors of Supplies in Grade 1, or to supervise and be responsible for a small division or bureau of supplies, where the preponderance of duties is of an inspectional nature, or to perform independently the most difficult and responsible technical inspections.[2]

QUALIFICATIONS—

1. The minimum qualifications prescribed for Grade 1.
2. If appointed by promotion, not less than two years of appropriate experience in Grade 1, or if appointed as the result of an open competitive examination, experience in work of the character and standard of Grade 1.
3. Such additional qualifications as may be required by the Municipal Civil Service Commission.

COMPENSATION—

Range of annual compensation—$1620 to $1920 inclusive.
Salary rates—$1620, $1740, $1920.

SPECIAL REGULATION GOVERNING COMPENSATION—

Beginning with the lowest rate, advancement within this grade is conditional upon appraisal under the rules of the Board of Estimate and Apportionment, indicating that the rate requested does not exceed the value of the work to be performed.

---

[1]The former title of Senior Inspector of Repairs will be covered under the general title Senior Building Inspector, unless the inspection is of specialized repairs, in which case the proper specialized title should be used. See the Inspector of Buildings Group.

[2]At the present time, the functions of Purchasing Agents, Storekeepers and Inspectors of Supplies are not clearly differentiated. The majority of Purchasing Agents also perform storekeeping and inspectional duties. Similarly, there are Storekeepers who perform incidentally duties as Purchasing Agents or Inspectors and there are heads of divisions of repairs and supplies who receive requisitions for supplies and inspect buildings to see whether repairs are necessary, order the supplies and supervise the making of repairs, and in some cases, inspect to see whether supplies and repairs comply with specifications. It is impossible to set up titles which will cover the mixture of functions at present performed by individual employes. For the time being, such employes must be graded according to the preponderance of duties, *i. e.*, the employe whose larger or more important functions are those of a Purchasing Agent should be rated as a Purchasing Agent, the employe whose principal functions and qualifications are those of an Inspector or Senior Inspector should be rated as such, the employe whose principal functions are those of Storekeeper should be rated as a Storekeeper.

See also Inspector of Public Works (Shop and Foundry).

SPECIAL CONDITION GOVERNING ADVANCEMENT—

The following table indicates the minimum number of years of meritorious service required at each rate before advancement to the next rate. See also page 30.

$1620	1 year
1740	2 years

GRADE 3 (I S 3)

TITLES OF POSITIONS[1]—

CHIEF INSPECTOR OF REPAIRS AND SUPPLIES

DUTIES—

The duties of incumbents of these positions are to supervise and be responsible for the entire administration of a large bureau of repairs and supplies where the preponderance of duties is of an inspectional nature.

QUALIFICATIONS—

1. The minimum qualifications prescribed for Grade 2.
2. If appointed by promotion, not less than two years of appropriate experience in Grade 2, or if appointed as the result of an open competitive examination, experience in work of the character and standard of Grade 2.
3. Such additional qualifications as may be required by the Municipal Civil Service Commission.

COMPENSATION—

Range of annual compensation—$2100 to $3660 inclusive.

Salary rates—$2100, $2280, $2460, $2700, $2940, $3180, $3420, $3660.

SPECIAL REGULATION GOVERNING COMPENSATION—

Persons entering this grade need not necessarily begin at the lowest rate. Fixation of the initial salary rate and advancement within this grade are conditional upon appraisal under the rules of the Board of Estimate and Apportionment, indicating that the rate requested does not exceed the value of the work to be performed.

WATERSHED INSPECTOR GROUP

SYMBOL (I W)

The term Watershed Inspector Group is applied to those offices or employments the duties of whose incumbents are to patrol assigned districts of the watershed for the purpose of conserving the purity of water impounded for the City of New York, and to observe, remove, disinfect or report any form of nuisance or source of pollution, or to supervise this work.

GRADE 1 (I W 1)

TITLES OF POSITIONS—

WATERSHED INSPECTOR

DUTIES—

The duties of incumbents of these positions are to patrol assigned districts of the watershed for the purpose of conserving the purity of water impounded for the City of New York, and to observe, remove, disinfect or report any form of nuisance or source of pollution.

---

[1]The following positions are among those appraised by the Bureau of Personal Service in this grade on the basis of duties performed by present incumbents:

Chief Inspector of Repairs and Supplies in the Bureau of Audit in the Finance Department.

See note on Grade 2.

QUALIFICATIONS—

1. Such qualifications as may be required by the Municipal Civil Service Commission.

COMPENSATION—

Range of annual compensation—$900 to $1020 inclusive.
Salary rates—$900, $960, $1020.

SPECIAL CONDITION GOVERNING ADVANCEMENT—

The following table indicates the minimum number of years of meritorious service required at each rate before advancement to the next rate. See also page 30.

$900	1 year
960	2 years

GRADE 2 (I W 2)

TITLES OF POSITIONS—

SENIOR WATERSHED INSPECTOR

DUTIES—

The duties of the incumbent of this position are to supervise and to be responsible for the work of Watershed Inspectors in Grade 1, including the assignment of patrols, the issuing of instructions and the checking of reports.

QUALIFICATIONS—

1. The minimum qualifications prescribed for Grade 1.
2. If appointed by promotion, not less than two years of appropriate experience in Grade 1, or if appointed as the result of an open competitive examination, experience in work of the character and standard of Grade 1.
3. Such additional qualifications as may be required by the Municipal Civil Service Commission.

COMPENSATION—

Range of annual compensation—$1140 to $1500 inclusive.
Salary rates—$1140, $1260, $1380, $1500.

INSPECTOR OF WEIGHTS AND MEASURES GROUP

SYMBOL (I M)

The term Inspector of Weights and Measures Group is applied to those offices or employments of the Inspectional Service in which incumbents are required to exercise regulative and restraining control over all weighing and measuring instruments used for buying and selling in the City of New York.

GRADE 1 (I M 1)

TITLES OF POSITIONS—

INSPECTOR OF WEIGHTS AND MEASURES

DUTIES—

The duties of incumbents of these positions are to inspect, to seal, or to condemn and destroy scales, weights, measures and packages, to examine scales, weights and measures in mechanical stations, and to approve and serialize the types of instruments which may be sold in the City of New York.

QUALIFICATIONS[1]—

1. Training or experience recognized by the Municipal Civil Service Commission as qualifying for this work.
2. Such additional qualifications as may be required by the Municipal Civil Service Commission.

COMPENSATION—

Range of annual compensation—$1200 to $1500 inclusive.
Salary rates—$1200, $1260, $1320, $1380, $1440, $1500.

SPECIAL CONDITION GOVERNING ADVANCEMENT—

The following table indicates the minimum number of years of meritorious service required at each rate before advancement to the next rate. See also page 30.

$1200	1 year
1260	1 "
1320	1 "
1380	2 years
1440	2 "

GRADE 2 (I M 2)

TITLES OF POSITIONS—

SENIOR INSPECTOR OF WEIGHTS AND MEASURES[2]
SENIOR INSPECTOR OF WEIGHTS AND MEASURES (MECHANICAL)[2,3]

DUTIES—

Senior Inspector of Weights and Measures:

The duties of the Senior Inspector of Weights and Measures are to exercise immediate supervision under the Chief of the Bureau over all field inspections of weights and measures.

Senior Inspector of Weights and Measures (Mechanical):

The duties of the Senior Inspector of Weights and Measures (Mechanical), which require specialized scientific knowledge of weighing and measuring instruments, are to take charge of all mechanical stations involving the serialization and testing of scales, weights and measures.

QUALIFICATIONS—

1. The minimum qualifications prescribed for Grade 1.
2. If appointed by promotion, not less than two years of appropriate experience in Grade 1, or if appointed as the result of an open competitive examination, experience in work of the character and standard of Grade 1.
3. Such additional qualifications as may be required by the Municipal Civil Service Commission.

---

[1]There are few persons qualified by training for the specific kind of work required of an Inspector of Weights and Measures. Mechanical work in the service of manufacturers of scales would be a logical preparation for weights and measures inspection in the city service. On the other hand, it is often preferable to recruit for this work young men who have a good general education and who are alert and honest, who have had no experience in this specialized kind of work, but who can easily be trained to become first class inspectors. It is therefore recommended that the Municipal Civil Service Commission require either specialized training relating to the inspection of weights and measures, or a High School or college education and possibly some general business experience.

[2]This title with the accompanying range of salary is to be employed only in the case of supervisory positions.

[3]Should this position become vacant, it would be advisable to fill it under the title of Physicist in Grade 3 with the qualifications set forth in the Chemist and Physicist Group of the Professional Service. The present title should then be abolished.

COMPENSATION—

Senior Inspector of Weights and Measures:

Range of annual compensation—$1620 to $1920 inclusive.
Salary rates—$1620, $1740, $1920.

Senior Inspector of Weights and Measures (Mechanical):

Range of annual compensation—$1920 to $2460 inclusive.
Salary rates—$1920, $2100, $2280, $2460.

SPECIAL CONDITION GOVERNING ADVANCEMENT—

The following table indicates the minimum number of years of meritorious service required at each rate before advancement to the next rate. See also page 30.

Senior Inspector of Weights and Measures:

$1620	1 year
1740	2 years

Senior Inspector of Weights and Measures (Mechanical):

$1920	1 year
2100	2 years
2280	2 "

MISCELLANEOUS INSPECTOR GROUP

SYMBOL (I Z)

The term Miscellaneous Inspector Group is applied to those offices or employments of the Inspectional Service in which incumbents are required to perform routine or specialized inspectional work of an exceptional nature not included in the other groups of the Inspectional Service.

GRADE 1 (I Z 1)

TITLES OF POSITIONS—

INSPECTOR OF BOILER AND PIPE COVERING[1]
INSPECTOR OF BOILERS
INSPECTOR OF GAS[2]

DUTIES—

Inspector of Boilers:

The duties of Inspectors of Boilers are to inspect and report on the strength and safety of stationary or marine boilers.

Inspector of Gas:

The duties of Inspectors of Gas are to inspect by chemical, photometric or other tests the candle power, pressure, specific gravity and general quality of gas and to make such records and reports as may be required.

QUALIFICATIONS—

Inspector of Boilers:

1. Experience as journeyman in a boiler shop or as stationary or marine engineman or other experience recognized by the Municipal Civil Service Commission as qualifying.

---

[1]There is but one position in the city service under the title Inspector of Boiler and Pipe Covering, and upon the occurrence of a vacancy, the title and position will be abolished. It is not therefore to be included in the classification.

[2]The title of Inspector of Gas is provided only to cover the present incumbents of these positions. In the future, this title should be abolished and these positions should be filled by Junior Chemists in Grade 1 of the Chemist and Physicist Group of the Professional Service, if necessary, under the specialized title of Junior Chemist (Gas).

2. Such additional qualifications as may be required by the Municipal Civil Service Commission.

Inspector of Gas:

1. A degree in science granted on the completion of a standard course of instruction with chemistry as the major subject in a college or technical school of recognized standing, or practical experience in the analysis and testing of gas, or other training or experience recognized by the Municipal Civil Service Commission as qualifying.

2. Such additional qualifications as may be required by the Municipal Civil Service Commission.

COMPENSATION—

Inspector of Boilers, Inspector of Boiler and Pipe Covering:

Range of annual compensation—$1200 to $1500 inclusive.
Salary rates—$1200, $1260, $1320, $1380, $1440, $1500.

Inspector of Gas:

Range of annual compensation—$1200 to $1260 inclusive.
Salary rates—$1200, $1260.

SPECIAL CONDITION GOVERNING ADVANCEMENT—

The following table indicates the minimum number of years of meritorious service required at each rate before advancement to the next rate. See also page 30.

Inspector of Boilers:

$1200	1 year
1260	1 "
1320	1 "
1380	2 years
1440	2 "

Inspector of Gas:

$1200	1 year

CUSTODIAL SERVICE

SYMBOL (K)

The term Custodial Service is applied to those offices or employments the duties of whose incumbents are to have custody of city property, to assist and keep order among persons visiting or making use of such property and to perform incidental operating, technical, or clerical work.

ANIMAL KEEPER GROUP

SYMBOL (K A)

The term Animal Keeper Group is applied to those offices or employments of the Custodial Service in which incumbents are required to feed, care for, guard, exhibit and breed mammals, birds, reptiles and fishes on exhibition in menageries, zoological parks and aquaria, or to supervise and be responsible for this work.[1]

GRADE 1 (K A 1)

TITLES OF POSITIONS—

ANIMAL KEEPER
AQUARIUM ATTENDANT

DUTIES—

The duties of incumbents of these positions are to feed, care for, guard and exhibit mammals, birds, reptiles or fishes, and to clean living quarters and equipment used.

Examples:

Preparing food and feeding animals.
Keeping living quarters of animals secure and sanitary.
Safeguarding the public.
Grooming, washing and oiling animals.

QUALIFICATIONS—

1. Experience in animal keeping.
2. Such additional qualifications as may be required by the Municipal Civil Service Commission.

COMPENSATION—

Range of annual compensation—$900 to $1080 inclusive.
Salary rates—$900, $960, $1020, $1080.

SPECIAL CONDITION GOVERNING ADVANCEMENT—

The following table indicates the minimum number of years of meritorious service required at each rate before advancement to the next rate. See also page 30.

$900	1 year
960	1 "
1020	2 years

[1]The salaries paid persons employed in the New York Zoological Park and the New York Aquarium are under the control of the New York Zoological Society and are paid from lump sums appropriated by the Board of Estimate and Apportionment. It is suggested that the salaries recommended in this group be taken into consideration in fixing salaries for the corresponding lower positions under the control of the New York Zoological Society. No provision is made in this group for the positions of Curator and Assistant Curator of the Zoological Park and the position of Director of the Aquarium.

GRADE 2 (K A 2)

TITLES OF POSITIONS—

HEAD ANIMAL KEEPER
HEAD AQUARIUM ATTENDANT

DUTIES—

The duties of incumbents of these positions, which involve supervision of employes in Grade 1, are to exercise special skill in and to be responsible for the custody, care, feeding, breeding and exhibition of a group or groups of animals.

Examples:

Taking charge of primates, reptiles, birds or deer.

QUALIFICATIONS—

1. The minimum qualifications prescribed for Grade 1.
2. If appointed by promotion, not less than two years of appropriate experience in Grade 1, or if appointed as the result of an open competitive examination, experience in work of the character and standard of Grade 1.
3. Such additional qualifications as may be required by the Municipal Civil Service Commission.

COMPENSATION—

Range of annual compensation—$1140 to $1380 inclusive.
Salary rates—$1140, $1200, $1260, $1320, $1380.

SPECIAL CONDITION GOVERNING ADVANCEMENT—

The following table indicates the minimum number of years of meritorious service required at each rate before advancement to the next rate. See also page 30.

$1140	1 year
1200	1 "
1260	1 "
1320	2 years

GRADE 3 (K A 3)

TITLES OF POSITIONS[1]—

MENAGERIE SUPERINTENDENT
AQUARIST

DUTIES—

The duties of incumbents of these positions, which involve supervision of employes in Grades 1 and 2, are to exercise the highest degree of skill in and to be completely responsible for the maintenance of a large number of mammals, birds, reptiles or fishes of various classes, including their feeding, breeding, observation, treatment, caging and exhibition, and their exchange, sale and purchase in accordance with prescribed regulations.

QUALIFICATIONS—

1. The minimum qualifications prescribed for Grade 2.
2. If appointed by promotion, not less than three years of appropriate experience in Grade 2, or if appointed as the result of an open competitive examination, experience in work of the character and standard of Grade 2.
3. Such additional qualifications as may be required by the Municipal Civil Service Commission.

---

[1]The following positions are among those appraised by the Bureau of Personal Service in this grade on the basis of duties performed by present incumbents:

Menagerie Superintendent in Central Park, Department of Parks, Manhattan.

COMPENSATION—

Range of annual compensation—$1800 to $2580 inclusive.
Salary rates—$1800, $1980, $2160, $2340, $2580.

SPECIAL REGULATION GOVERNING COMPENSATION—

Beginning with the lowest rate, advancement within this grade is conditional upon appraisal under the rules of the Board of Estimate and Apportionment, indicating that the rate requested does not exceed the value of the work to be performed.

BRIDGETENDER GROUP

SYMBOL (K B)

The term Bridgetender Group is applied to those offices or employments of the Custodial Service in which incumbents are required to guard, maintain, clean, and assist in the operation of bridges owned or controlled by the city.

GRADE 1 (K B 1)

TITLES OF POSITIONS—

BRIDGETENDER

DUTIES—

The duties of incumbents of these positions, which are performed under the direction of a Head Bridgetender or Engineman, are to regulate the traffic over and to clean and patrol the draw span of a bridge, and to assist in its operation.

QUALIFICATIONS—

1. Such qualifications as may be required by the Municipal Civil Service Commission.

COMPENSATION—

Regular Service Exclusive of Sundays:

Range of annual compensation—$876 to $984 inclusive.
Salary rates—$876, $912, $948, $984.

Temporary Service:

Per diem compensation—$2.75.

GRADE 2 (K B 2)

TITLES OF POSITIONS[1]—

HEAD BRIDGETENDER

DUTIES—

The duties of incumbents of these positions, which involve supervision of the work of all other employes on the bridge, including all shifts, are to take charge of and operate a small bridge not requiring the services of an Engineman.

QUALIFICATIONS—

1. The minimum qualifications prescribed for Grade 1.
2. If appointed by promotion, not less than two years of appropriate experience in Grade 1, or if appointed as the result of an open competitive examination, experience in work of the character and standard of Grade 1.
3. Such additional qualifications as may be required by the Municipal Civil Service Commission.

---

[1]The following positions are among those appraised by the Bureau of Personal Service in this grade on the basis of duties performed by present incumbents:

Head Bridgetender in charge of a small bridge over the Wallabout Canal.

COMPENSATION—

Range of annual compensation—$1020 to $1200 inclusive.
Salary rates—$1020, $1080, $1140, $1200.

SPECIAL CONDITION GOVERNING ADVANCEMENT—

The following table indicates the minimum number of years of meritorious service required at each rate before advancement to the next rate. See also page 30.

$1020	1 year
1080	1 "
1140	2 years

CARETAKER GROUP

SYMBOL (K C)

The term Caretaker Group is applied to those offices or employments of the Custodial Service in which incumbents are required to be responsible for the maintenance, heating, cleaning, general care and protection of buildings or other structures owned or controlled by the city or to assist, keep order among and give information to persons passing through or visiting public places or buildings.

GRADE 1 (K C 1)

TITLES OF POSITIONS[2,3]—

CARETAKER
ASSISTANT CUSTODIAN

DUTIES—

Caretaker:

The duties of Caretakers are to maintain, clean, and, where required, heat buildings owned or controlled by the city having a floor area not exceeding 6,000 square feet, and to make minor repairs to heating, electrical equipment and plumbing, or to maintain, heat, clean, and make minor repairs in or about baths, cottages, comfort stations, ferry houses, piers and other similar structures owned or controlled by the city, and to assist and keep order among persons visiting these places.

Assistant Custodian:

The duties of Assistant Custodians are to care for, exhibit and give information regarding pictures, furniture and other articles of historic or other special interest contained in public buildings.

---

[1]It is intended that the janitorial positions in the Department of Education shall be appraised in the various grades in this group. In Grades 3, 4 and 5, standard titles for the higher janitorial positions in the Department of Education are included, together with notes on the minimum and maximum salaries. No definitions of duties, qualifications, conditions governing advancement, or specific appraisals are included at the present time. These should be added at an early date when the survey of janitorial work in the Department of Education has been completed. It is intended that these specifications shall cover positions under the indirect as well as the direct payment plan.

Positions as Armorers, Assistant Armorers and Janitors in the Armories of the National Guard have not been considered in connection with the Caretaker Group.

[2]The following positions are among those appraised by the Bureau of Personal Service in this grade on the basis of duties performed by present incumbents:

Assistant Custodian in the Governor's Room in City Hall.

[3]The old title Attendant does not appear in the standard specifications. As formerly applied to Attendants on bridges and at baths and comfort stations, it is replaced in the standard specifications by the title Caretaker. See also Guard in Grade 1 of the Miscellaneous Custodian Group and Messenger in Grade 1 of the Messenger Group of the Clerical Service.

QUALIFICATIONS—

1. Such qualifications as may be required by the Municipal Civil Service Commission.

COMPENSATION—

Men:

Regular Service Exclusive of Sundays:

Range of annual compensation—$840 to $984 inclusive.
Salary rates—$840, $876, $912, $948, $984.

Temporary Service:

Per diem compensation[1]—$2.75.

Women:

Regular Service Exclusive of Sundays:

Range of annual compensation—$660 to $840 inclusive.
Salary rates—$660, $696, $732, $768, $804, $840.

Temporary Service:

Per diem compensation[1]—$2.25.

GRADE 2 (K C 2)

TITLES OF POSITIONS[2]—

HEAD CARETAKER
CUSTODIAN

DUTIES—

Head Caretaker:

The duties of Head Caretakers are to direct and assist the force engaged in the heating, cleaning, maintenance and operation of public baths or of buildings owned or controlled by the city having a floor area of over 6,000 square feet and not exceeding 50,000 square feet, and to make minor repairs to heating, electrical equipment and plumbing where no engineman is employed.

Custodian:

The duties of Custodians are to be responsible for the care of public buildings of historic or other special interest and for the pictures, furniture and other articles contained therein and to exhibit these articles to persons visiting the building.

QUALIFICATIONS—

1. The minimum qualifications prescribed for Grade 1.
2. If appointed by promotion, not less than three years of appropriate experience in Grade 1, or if appointed as the result of an open competitive examination, experience in work of the character and standard of Grade 1.
3. Such additional qualifications as may be required by the Municipal Civil Service Commission.

COMPENSATION—

Range of annual compensation—$1020 to $1200 inclusive.
Salary rates—$1020, $1080, $1140, $1200.
Custodians in charge of the Jumel Mansion and Dyckman House may receive lodging in addition to salary.

---

[1]The daily rate shall be paid only where work is temporary and will not last continuously for a period measurable by years.

[2]The following positions are among those appraised by the Bureau of Personal Service in this grade on the basis of duties performed by present incumbents:

Custodian of the Jumel Mansion.

SPECIAL REGULATION GOVERNING COMPENSATION—

Beginning with the lowest rate, advancement within this grade is conditional upon appraisal under the rules of the Board of Estimate and Apportionment, indicating that the rate requested does not exceed the value of the work to be performed.

SPECIAL CONDITION GOVERNING ADVANCEMENT—

The following table indicates the minimum number of years of meritorious service required at each rate before advancement to the next rate. See also page 30.

$1020	1 year
1080	1 "
1140	2 years

GRADE 3 (K C 3)

TITLES OF POSITIONS—

JANITOR
JANITOR-ENGINEMAN[1]
SUPERVISOR OF CARETAKERS

DUTIES—

Janitor:

The duties of Janitors are to direct the force engaged in the heating, cleaning, and maintenance of buildings owned or controlled by the city, having a floor area of over 50,000 square feet and not exceeding 250,000 square feet, or to direct the cleaning force in buildings having a floor area exceeding 250,000 square feet.[2]

Supervisor of Caretakers:

The duties of Supervisors of Caretakers are to supervise the work of employes in Grades 1 and 2 and of Janitors in Grade 3, to be responsible to the Superintendent or Assistant Superintendent of Public Buildings and Offices for the operation, maintenance and cleaning of public buildings, including comfort stations, baths and markets, to investigate and report on methods of work, to enforce rules and regulations, and to perform such other investigational, inspectional or clerical work as may be required.[3]

QUALIFICATIONS—

Janitor, Supervisor of Caretakers:

1. The minimum qualifications prescribed for Grade 2.
2. If appointed by promotion, not less than two years of appropriate experience in Grade 2, or if appointed as the result of an open competitive examination, experience in work of the character and standard of Grade 2.
3. Such additional qualifications as may be required by the Municipal Civil Service Commission.

---

[1]This title includes Janitors in charge of high pressure school plants, excepting the largest high school and other plants included in Grade 4. No definition of duties, qualifications, condition governing advancement, or specific appraisals under this title are included at the present time. It is, however, assumed that the minimum salary for the least important position will be not less than $1320 and that the maximum salary for the most important position will not exceed $1980.

[2]For the present position of Stationary Engineman in buildings with a high pressure plant, see the Engineman Group of the Skilled Trades Service.

[3]The old title of this position was Inspector. While the duties of this position are partly inspectional, it is thought desirable, because of the supervisory functions involved, to include the position here rather than in the Inspectional Service.

COMPENSATION—

Janitor, Supervisor of Caretakers:

Range of annual compensation—$1320 to $1800 inclusive.
Salary rates—$1320, $1440, $1560, $1680, $1800.

SPECIAL REGULATION GOVERNING COMPENSATION—

Janitor, Supervisor of Caretakers:

Beginning with the lowest rate, advancement within this grade is conditional upon appraisal under the rules of the Board of Estimate and Apportionment, indicating that the rate requested does not exceed the value of the work to be performed.

SPECIAL CONDITION GOVERNING ADVANCEMENT—

The following table indicates the minimum number of years of meritorious service required at each rate before advancement to the next rate. See also page 30.

Janitor, Supervisor of Caretakers:

$1320	1 year
1440	1 "
1560	2 years
1680	2 "

GRADE 4 (K C 4)

TITLES OF POSITIONS—

ASSISTANT CHIEF SUPERVISOR OF JANITORS[1]
SENIOR JANITOR-ENGINEMAN[2]

GRADE 5 (K C 5)

TITLES OF POSITIONS—

ASSISTANT SUPERINTENDENT OF PUBLIC BUILDINGS AND OFFICES (MANHATTAN)
CHIEF SUPERVISOR OF JANITORS
SUPERINTENDENT OF PUBLIC BUILDINGS AND OFFICES (QUEENS OR RICHMOND)

DUTIES—

Assistant Superintendent of Public Buildings and Offices (Manhattan), Superintendent of Public Buildings and Offices (Queens or Richmond):

The duties of incumbents of these positions are to be responsible for the operation, care and maintenance, construction and reconstruction of all public buildings in the smaller boroughs, including baths, comfort stations and markets, involving the supervision of employes and the purchase of necessary supplies, material and equipment, or to assist the Superintendent of Public Buildings and Offices in the administration of the largest bureaus of public buildings and offices, and to be immediately responsible for all investigational and inspectional work and for the supervision of the employes in the bureau.

---

[1]It is probable that these positions will be abolished when the work of janitorial supervision is reorganized. No definition of duties, qualifications or conditions governing advancement are included at the present time. If these positions are retained, a salary range from $1980 to $2580 is recommended.

[2]Under this title the janitors in charge of the largest high schools and grade schools are included. No definition of duties, qualifications, conditions governing advancement, or specific appraisals are included under this title at the present time. It is contemplated that the minimum salary for the least important position in this grade will be not less than $2160 and that the maximum salary for the most important position will not exceed $2580.

Chief Supervisor of Janitors:

The duties of the Chief Supervisor of Janitors are to be responsible for the care of school buildings, including heating, cleaning and minor repairs; to assign and supervise the work of Janitors, Enginemen and other employes; to draw up rules and regulations, and advise principals and teachers regarding care of school buildings, and to promote economy in the use of fuel, gas and electricity.

QUALIFICATIONS—

1. The minimum qualifications prescribed for Grade 3.
2. If appointed by promotion, not less than one year of appropriate experience as Supervisor of Caretakers in Grade 3, or if appointed as the result of an open competitive examination, experience in other administrative work recognized by the Municipal Civil Service Commission as qualifying.
3. Such additional qualifications as may be required by the Municipal Civil Service Commission.

COMPENSATION—

Range of annual compensation—$2820 to $3540 inclusive.
Salary rates—$2820, $3060, $3300, $3540.

SPECIAL REGULATION GOVERNING COMPENSATION—

Persons entering this grade need not necessarily begin at the lowest rate. Fixation of the initial salary rate and advancement within this grade are conditional upon appraisal under the rules of the Board of Estimate and Apportionment, indicating that the rate requested does not exceed the value of the work to be performed.

GRADE 6 (KC6)

TITLES OF POSITIONS—

SUPERINTENDENT OF PUBLIC BUILDINGS AND OFFICES (MANHATTAN, BROOKLYN OR THE BRONX)

DUTIES—

The duties of incumbents of these positions are to be responsible for the operation, care and maintenance, construction and reconstruction of all public buildings in a borough, including baths, comfort stations and markets, involving the supervision of employes and the purchase of necessary supplies, material and equipment.

QUALIFICATIONS—

1. Administrative experience in civil engineering or in other work recognized by the Municipal Civil Service Commission as qualifying.
2. Such additional qualifications as may be required by the Municipal Civil Service Commission.

COMPENSATION—

Range of annual compensation—$3840 to $5160 inclusive.
Salary rates—$3840, $4140, $4440, $4740, $5160.

SPECIAL REGULATION GOVERNING COMPENSATION—

Persons entering this grade need not necessarily begin at the lowest rate. Fixation of the initial salary rate and advancement within this grade are conditional upon appraisal under the rules of the Board of Estimate and Apportionment, indicating that the rate requested does not exceed the value of the work to be performed.

COURT AND LEGISLATIVE ATTENDANT GROUP

SYMBOL (K K)

The term Court and Legislative Attendant Group is applied to those offices or employments of the Custodial Service in which incumbents are required to maintain order in court rooms or legislative chambers, to keep in custody persons awaiting trial, and to assist justices and clerks of the court or members of the legislative body in routine clerical work and procedure.

GRADE 1 (K K 1)

TITLES OF POSITIONS—

COURT ATTENDANT[1]
ASSISTANT SERGEANT-AT-ARMS[1,2]

DUTIES—

The duties of incumbents of these positions are to maintain order in court rooms or legislative chambers, to keep in custody persons awaiting trial, and to assist justices and clerks of the court or members of the legislative body in routine clerical work and procedure.

QUALIFICATIONS—

1. Such qualifications as may be required by the Municipal Civil Service Commission.

COMPENSATION—

Court Attendant:

Range of annual compensation—$1080 to $1380 inclusive.
Salary rates—$1080, $1140, $1200, $1260, $1320, $1380.

Assistant Sergeant-at-Arms:

Range of annual compensation—$1020 to $1200 inclusive.
Salary rates—$1020, $1080, $1140, $1200.

SPECIAL REGULATION GOVERNING COMPENSATION—

Beginning with the lowest rate, advancement within this grade is conditional upon appraisal under the rules of the Board of Estimate and Apportionment, indicating that the rate requested does not exceed the value of the work to be performed.

SPECIAL CONDITION GOVERNING ADVANCEMENT—

The following table indicates the minimum number of years of meritorious service required at each rate before advancement to the next rate. See also page 30.

Court Attendant:

$1080	1 year
1140	1 "
1200	1 "
1260	2 years
1320	2 "

Assistant Sergeant-at-Arms:

$1020	1 year
1080	1 "
1140	2 years

---

[1]These positions may also be filled by superannuated employes, such as Laborers, Foremen, Caretakers, Clerks and Inspectors, if their work has fitted them for these positions, and if they are capable of rendering the necessary service.

[2]This position is not at present classified by the Municipal Civil Service Commission.

GRADE 2 (K K 2)

TITLES OF POSITIONS—

SERGEANT-AT-ARMS[1]

DUTIES—

The duties of the incumbent of this position are to supervise the Assistant Sergeants-at-Arms, to be responsible to the presiding officer for the maintenance of order in the legislative chambers and to render such other services as may be required.

QUALIFICATIONS—

1. The minimum qualifications prescribed for Grade 1.
2. If appointed by promotion, not less than one year of appropriate experience in Grade 1, or if appointed as the result of an open competitive examination, experience in work of the character and standard of Grade 1.
3. Such additional qualifications as may be required by the Municipal Civil Service Commission.

COMPENSATION—

Range of annual compensation—$1320 to $1440 inclusive.
Salary rates—$1320, $1440.

SPECIAL CONDITION GOVERNING ADVANCEMENT—

The following table indicates the minimum number of years of meritorious service required at each rate before advancement to the next rate. See also page 30.

$1320 .... 2 years

DOCKMASTER GROUP

SYMBOL (K D)

The term Dockmaster Group is applied to those offices or employments of the Custodial Service in which incumbents are required to take charge of the open piers and bulkheads in a prescribed water front district, to supervise the berthing of vessels, to collect the statutory wharfage fees, and to exercise judgment in the use, care and maintenance of docks, piers and adjacent thoroughfares, or to supervise this work.

GRADE 1 (K D 1)

TITLES OF POSITIONS—

DOCKMASTER

DUTIES—

The duties of incumbents of these positions are to collect the statutory wharfage fees, to patrol daily and to be responsible for the care and preservation of all docks, piers, bulkheads and adjacent thoroughfares in a prescribed waterfront district, to assign berths to vessels, and to enforce the laws, rules and regulations of the Department of Docks and Ferries.

QUALIFICATIONS—

1. Experience in a supervisory capacity in work involving a knowledge of shipping.
2. Such additional qualifications as may be required by the Municipal Civil Service Commission.

---

[1]This position is not at present classified by the Municipal Civil Service Commission.

COMPENSATION—

Range of annual compensation—$1800 to $2160 inclusive.
Salary rates—$1800, $1980, $2160.

SPECIAL REGULATION GOVERNING COMPENSATION—

Beginning with the lowest rate, advancement within this grade is conditional upon appraisal under the rules of the Board of Estimate and Apportionment, indicating that the rate requested does not exceed the value of the work to be performed.

SPECIAL CONDITION GOVERNING ADVANCEMENT—

The following table indicates the minimum number of years of meritorious service required at each rate before advancement to the next rate. See also page 30.

$1800	2 years
1980	2 "

GRADE 2 (K D 2)

TITLES OF POSITIONS—

SUPERINTENDENT OF DOCKS

DUTIES—

The duties of the incumbent of this position are to supervise and be responsible for the work of employes in Grade 1 and of other employes and for the care of all docks, piers, bulkheads and adjacent thoroughfares, and to assist the Commissioner of Docks and Ferries in the issuing of permits.

QUALIFICATIONS—

1. The minimum qualifications prescribed for Grade 1.
2. If appointed by promotion, not less than two years of appropriate experience in Grade 1, or if appointed as the result of an open competitive examination, experience recognized by the Municipal Civil Service Commission as qualifying.
3. Such additional qualifications as may be required by the Municipal Civil Service Commission.

COMPENSATION—

Range of annual compensation—$3000 to $3780 inclusive.
Salary rates—$3000, $3240, $3480, $3780.

SPECIAL REGULATION GOVERNING COMPENSATION—

Beginning with the lowest rate, advancement within this grade is conditional upon appraisal under the rules of the Board of Estimate and Apportionment, indicating that the rate requested does not exceed the value of the work to be performed.

ELEVATOR OPERATOR GROUP

SYMBOL (K E)

The term Elevator Operator Group is applied to those offices or employments of the Custodial Service in which incumbents are required to operate or to supervise the operation of passenger or freight elevators in public buildings.

GRADE 1 (K E 1)

TITLES OF POSITIONS—

ELEVATOR OPERATOR

DUTIES—

The duties of incumbents of these positions are to operate passenger or freight elevators.

QUALIFICATIONS—

1. Such qualifications as may be required by the Municipal Civil Service Commission.

COMPENSATION—

Regular Service Exclusive of Sundays:

Range of annual compensation—$840 to $984 inclusive.

Salary rates—$840, $876, $912, $948, $984.

Temporary Service:

Per diem compensation—$2.75.

GRADE 2 (K E 2)

TITLES OF POSITIONS—

ELEVATOR STARTER

DUTIES—

The duties of incumbents of these positions, which require a knowledge of the traffic conditions of buildings and alertness, decision and executive ability, are to supervise wholly or in part the operation of passenger elevators and to direct visitors to various bureaus or offices.

QUALIFICATIONS—

1. The minimum qualifications prescribed for Grade 1.
2. If appointed by promotion, not less than one year of appropriate experience in Grade 1, or if appointed as the result of an open competitive examination, experience in work of the character and standard of Grade 1.
3. Such additional qualifications as may be required by the Municipal Civil Service Commission.

COMPENSATION—

Range of annual compensation—$1020 to $1080 inclusive.[1]

Salary rates—$1020, $1080.

GRADE 3 (K E 3)

TITLES OF POSITIONS—

ELEVATOR DESPATCHER[2]

DUTIES—

The duties of incumbents of these positions, which require the highest degree of alertness, decision and accuracy, are to supervise, either wholly or in part, the operation of a system of passenger elevators by mechanical and electrical indicator equipment.

QUALIFICATIONS—

1. If appointed by promotion, not less than one year of appropriate experience in Grade 1 of the Telephone Operator Group of the Clerical Service, or if appointed as the result of an open competitive examination, experience recognized by the Municipal Civil Service Commission as qualifying.
2. Such additional qualifications as may be required by the Municipal Civil Service Commission.

---

[1]It may be desirable to raise the maximum rate in this grade in the case of Starters in the Municipal Building when the present system of running the elevators entirely from the tower of the Municipal Building is changed and the Starters control the elevators from the ground floor with the assistance of a dial on each elevator, with or without advice from the despatchers on the top floor.

[2]This position may ultimately be abolished when the present system of running elevators from the tower of the Municipal Building is changed.

COMPENSATION—

Range of annual compensation—$1140 to $1200 inclusive.
Salary rates—$1140, $1200.

STOREKEEPER GROUP

SYMBOL (K S)

The term Storekeeper Group is applied to those offices or employments of the Custodial Service in which incumbents are required to maintain stock within prescribed limits, to receive, inspect, store, issue on approved requisitions, classify and account for, according to prescribed methods and procedure, supplies, materials and equipment.

GRADE 1 (K S 1)

TITLES OF POSITIONS[1]—

STORES FOREMAN

DUTIES—

The duties of incumbents of these positions are to make requisitions necessary to maintain stock within prescribed limits, to receive, inspect, store, issue on approved requisitions, classify and account for, according to prescribed methods and procedure, supplies, materials and equipment in isolated supply depots, yards or rooms under the supervision of a Storekeeper or Senior Storekeeper, or to act as assistant to a Storekeeper or Senior Storekeeper in a main or central storehouse, sub-storehouse or yard.[2]

QUALIFICATIONS—

1. Experience in storekeeping or in the handling of supplies, materials and equipment.
2. Such additional qualifications as may be required by the Municipal Civil Service Commission.

COMPENSATION—

Range of annual compensation—$960 to $1200 inclusive.
Salary rates—$960, $1020, $1080, $1140, $1200.

GRADE 2 (K S 2)

TITLES OF POSITIONS[3]—

STOREKEEPER

---

[1]The following positions are among those appraised by the Bureau of Personal Service in this grade on the basis of duties performed by present incumbents:

Stores Foreman in the ward yards of the Borough of Queens.
Yard Storekeepers in the Department of Water Supply, Gas and Electricity.

[2]See also the position of Assistant Steward in Grade 2 of the Institutional Supervisor Group of the Institutional Service.

[3]The following positions are among those appraised by the Bureau of Personal Service in this grade on the basis of duties performed by present incumbents

Storekeeper in the Department of Parks, Manhattan and Richmond.
Storekeeper for the borough of Manhattan.
Storekeeper for the borough of Queens.
Storekeeper in the Department of Water Supply, Gas and Electricity.

DUTIES—

The duties of incumbents of these positions, which may or may not be supervisory in character, are to make requisitions necessary to maintain stock within prescribed limits, to receive, inspect, store, issue on approved requisitions, classify and account for, according to prescribed methods and procedure, supplies, materials and equipment in a large storehouse, sub-storehouse or yard, or for a group of small storehouses, sub-storehouses or yards.[1]

QUALIFICATIONS—

1. The minimum qualifications prescribed for Grade 1.
2. If appointed by promotion, not less than two years of appropriate experience in Grade 1, or if appointed as the result of an open competitive examination, experience in work of the character and standard of Grade 1.
3. Such additional qualifications as may be required by the Municipal Civil Service Commission.

COMPENSATION—

Range of annual compensation—$1320 to $1800 inclusive.
Salary rates—$1320, $1440, $1560, $1680, $1800.

SPECIAL REGULATION GOVERNING COMPENSATION—

Beginning with the lowest rate, advancement within this grade is conditional upon appraisal under the rules of the Board of Estimate and Apportionment, indicating that the rate requested does not exceed the value of the work to be performed.

SPECIAL CONDITION GOVERNING ADVANCEMENT—

The following table indicates the minimum number of years of meritorious service required at each rate before advancement to the next rate. See also page 30.

$1320	1 year
1440	1 "
1560	2 years
1680	2 "

GRADE 3 (K S 3)

TITLES OF POSITIONS[2]—

SENIOR STOREKEEPER

DUTIES—

The duties of incumbents of these positions are to make requisitions necessary to maintain stock within prescribed limits, to receive, inspect, store, issue on approved requisitions, classify and account for, according to prescribed methods and procedure, the supplies, materials and equipment of an entire department handling a large quantity and variety of stores or of a large interdepartmental storehouse or of a major division of a general stores department.

QUALIFICATIONS—

1. The minimum qualifications prescribed for Grade 2.
2. If appointed by promotion, not less than two years of appropriate experience in Grade 2, or if appointed as the result of an open competitive examination, experience in work of the character and standard of Grade 2.
3. Such additional qualifications as may be required by the Municipal Civil Service Commission.

---

[1]See also the position of Steward in Grade 3 of the Institutional Supervisor Group of the Institutional Service.

[2]The following positions are among those appraised by the Bureau of Personal Service in this grade on the basis of duties performed by present incumbents:

Senior Storekeeper of the Blackwell's Island Storehouse for the Department of Public Charities.

COMPENSATION—

Range of annual compensation—$1980 to $2580 inclusive.
Salary rates—$1980, $2160, $2340, $2580.

SPECIAL REGULATION GOVERNING COMPENSATION—

Beginning with the lowest rate, advancement within this grade is conditional upon appraisal under the rules of the Board of Estimate and Apportionment, indicating that the rate requested does not exceed the value of the work to be performed.

WATCHMAN GROUP

SYMBOL (K W)

The term Watchman Group is applied to those offices or employments of the Custodial Service in which incumbents are required to exercise care in the protection of property owned or controlled by or in the custody of the city from theft, fire or other injury or danger.

GRADE 1 (K W 1)

TITLES OF POSITIONS—

WATCHMAN[1]

DUTIES—

The duties of incumbents of these positions, which may include cleaning or other light laboring work when so directed, are to exercise care in the protection of property owned or controlled by or in the custody of the city from theft, fire or other injury or danger.

QUALIFICATIONS—

1. Such qualifications as may be required by the Municipal Civil Service Commission.

COMPENSATION—

Regular Service Exclusive of Sundays:

Range of annual compensation—$792 to $888 inclusive.
Salary rates—$792, $816, $840, $864, $888.

Temporary Service:

Per diem compensation—$2.50.

MISCELLANEOUS CUSTODIAN GROUP

SYMBOL (K Z)

The term Miscellaneous Custodian Group is applied to those offices or employments of the Custodial Service in which incumbents are required to perform routine or specialized custodial work of an exceptional nature not included in the other groups of the Custodial Service.

---

[1]It is recommended that persons be appointed to perform the duties of this position under the title Watchman only when the work is regular and cannot be satisfactorily performed by the temporary assignment of laborers or cleaners or by the appointment of laborer-watchmen. See Grade 1 of the Laborer Group of the Unskilled Service.

GRADE 1 (K Z 1)

TITLES OF POSITIONS[1]—

GUARD
LIFE GUARD
MONITOR

DUTIES—

Guard:

The duties of Guards are to attend and accompany bank messengers, deputy city paymasters and other persons entrusted with the custody and disbursement of large sums of money in order to assist them in the safeguarding of these funds and to protect them in the discharge of their duty.

Life Guard:

The duties of Life Guards are to patrol public beaches and adjacent waters for the purpose of observing and warning or rescuing persons who are in danger of drowning.

Monitor:

The duties of Monitors are to be in attendance at civil service examinations, to distribute papers and other material, to guard against dishonest practices and to perform such incidental clerical work as may be required.

QUALIFICATIONS—

Guard, Life Guard, Monitor:

1. Such qualifications as may be required by the Municipal Civil Service Commission.

COMPENSATION—

Guard:

Range of annual compensation—$900 to $1200 inclusive.
Salary rates—$900, $960, $1020, $1080, $1140, $1200.

Life Guard:

Per diem compensation—$3.

Monitor:

Per diem compensation—$4.

---

[1]The following positions are among those appraised by the Bureau of Personal Service in this grade on the basis of duties performed by present incumbents:

Guard in the City Paymaster's office.

INSTITUTIONAL SERVICE

SYMBOL (N)

The term Institutional Service is applied to those offices or employments the duties of whose incumbents are to perform non-professional work incident to the maintenance and operation of city hospitals or charitable or correctional institutions and to the care of patients or inmates.

CORRECTION OFFICER GROUP

SYMBOL (N O)

The term Correction Officer Group is applied to those offices or employments of the Institutional Service in which incumbents are required to exercise custodial and correctional supervision over persons committed to correctional institutions or persons temporarily in custody in connection with the administration of justice.

GRADE 1 (N O 1)

TITLES OF POSITIONS[1]—

CORRECTION OFFICER
CORRECTION MATRON
POLICE MATRON

DUTIES—

Correction Officer, Correction Matron:

The duties of incumbents of these positions are to guard, discipline, care for and instruct inmates of correctional institutions.

Police Matron:

The duties of Police Matrons are to guard and care for women and children brought to or detained in station houses and to perform such other police duties as may be assigned by the captain of the precinct.

QUALIFICATIONS—

1. Such qualifications as may be required by the Municipal Civil Service Commission.

COMPENSATION—

Correction Officer:

Range of annual compensation—$960 to $1320 inclusive.
Salary rates—$960, $1020, $1080, $1140, $1200, $1260, $1320.

Correction Matron, Police Matron:

Range of annual compensation—$720 to $960 inclusive.
Salary rates—$720, $780, $840, $900, $960.

---

[1]The following positions are among those appraised by the Bureau of Personal Service in this grade on the basis of duties performed by present incumbents:

Correction Officer in the Penitentiary.
Correction Matron in the Workhouse.

GRADE 2 (N O 2)

TITLES OF POSITIONS[1]—

HEAD CORRECTION OFFICER
HEAD CORRECTION MATRON

DUTIES—

The duties of incumbents of these positions are to supervise the work of Correction Officers and Matrons in Grade 1 and to perform such other services as may be incident to the maintenance of discipline and the enforcement of rules governing the action of keepers, the custody of inmates and the maintenance of quarters under their jurisdiction.

QUALIFICATIONS—

1. The minimum qualifications prescribed for Grade 1.
2. If appointed by promotion, not less than two years of appropriate experience in Grade 1, or if appointed as the result of an open competitive examination, experience in work of the character and standard of Grade 1.
3. Such additional qualifications as may be required by the Municipal Civil Service Commission.

COMPENSATION—

Head Correction Officer:

Range of annual compensation—$1440 to $1800 inclusive.
Salary rates—$1440, $1560, $1680, $1800

Head Correction Matron:

Range of annual compensation—$1080 to $1440 inclusive.
Salary rates—$1080, $1200, $1320, $1440.

SPECIAL REGULATION GOVERNING COMPENSATION—

Beginning with the lowest rate, advancement within this grade is conditional upon appraisal under the rules of the Board of Estimate and Apportionment, indicating that the rate requested does not exceed the value of the work to be performed.

SPECIAL CONDITION GOVERNING ADVANCEMENT—

The following table indicates the minimum number of years of meritorious service required at each rate before advancement to the next rate. See also page 30.

Head Correction Officer:

$1440	1 year
1560	2 years
1680	2 "

Head Correction Matron:

$1080	1 year
1200	2 years
1320	2 "

---

[1]The following positions are among those appraised by the Bureau of Personal Service in this grade on the basis of duties performed by present incumbents:

Head Correction Officer in charge of a hall in the City Prison, Manhattan or Brooklyn.

Head Correction Officer in charge of a small district prison, as the 2d District Prison (Jefferson Market).

GRADE 3 (NO3)

TITLES OF POSITIONS[1]—

ASSISTANT SUPERINTENDENT OF REFORMATORY
ASSISTANT SUPERINTENDENT OF WOMEN (CORRECTION)
DEPUTY WARDEN

DUTIES—

Assistant Superintendent of Reformatory:

The duties of Assistant Superintendents of Reformatories, which involve responsibility for the work of employes in Grades 1 and 2, are to direct and be responsible for the whole of a small reformatory, or to assist the superintendent in the direction of a large reformatory.

Assistant Superintendent of Women (Correction):

The duties of Assistant Superintendents of Women (Correction), which involve responsibility for the work of employes in Grades 1 and 2, are to assist the Warden in the direction of that division of a large correctional institution set aside for women.

Deputy Warden:

The duties of Deputy Wardens, which involve responsibility for the work of employes in Grades 1 and 2, are to direct and be responsible for the whole of a small correctional institution or to assist the Warden in the direction of a large correctional institution.

QUALIFICATIONS—

1. The minimum qualifications prescribed for Grade 2.
2. If appointed by promotion, not less than two years of appropriate experience in Grade 2, or if appointed as the result of an open competitive examination, experience in work of the character and standard of Grade 2.
3. Such additional qualifications as may be required by the Municipal Civil Service Commission.

COMPENSATION—

Range of annual compensation—$1920 to $2280 inclusive.
Salary rates—$1920, $2100, $2280.

SPECIAL REGULATION GOVERNING COMPENSATION—

Beginning with the lowest rate, advancement within this grade is conditional upon appraisal under the rules of the Board of Estimate and Apportionment, indicating that the rate requested does not exceed the value of the work to be performed.

SPECIAL CONDITION GOVERNING ADVANCEMENT—

The following table indicates the minimum number of years of meritorious service required at each rate before advancement to the next rate. See also page 30.

$1920	1 year
2100	2 years

---

[1]The following positions are among those appraised by the Bureau of Personal Service in this grade on the basis of duties performed by present incumbents:

Deputy Warden of the Penitentiary.
Deputy Warden of the City Prison in Manhattan or Brooklyn.
Deputy Warden of the Workhouse on Blackwell's Island.
Assistant Superintendent of Women (Correction) at the Workhouse.
Deputy Warden in charge of Branch Workhouse on Riker's Island.

GRADE 4 (N O 4)

TITLES OF POSITIONS[1]—

SUPERINTENDENT OF REFORMATORY
SUPERINTENDENT OF WOMEN'S FARM
WARDEN

DUTIES—

The duties of incumbents of these positions, which involve entire responsibility for the work of employes in Grades 1, 2 and 3, are to direct and be responsible for one large or several small correctional institutions.

QUALIFICATIONS—

1. The minimum qualifications prescribed for Grade 3.
2. If appointed by promotion, not less than one year of appropriate experience in Grade 3, or if appointed as the result of an open competitive examination, experience in work of the character and standard of Grade 3.
3. Such additional qualifications as may be required by the Municipal Civil Service Commission.

COMPENSATION—

Range of annual compensation—$2520 to $3480 inclusive.
Salary rates—$2520, $2760, $3000, $3240, $3480.

SPECIAL REGULATION GOVERNING COMPENSATION—

Beginning with the lowest rate, advancement within this grade is conditional upon appraisal under the rules of the Board of Estimate and Apportionment, indicating that the rate requested does not exceed the value of the work to be performed.

CULINARY WORKER GROUP

SYMBOL (N Q)

The term Culinary Worker Group is applied to those offices or employments of the Institutional Service in which incumbents are required to prepare or to supervise the preparation of foods for inmates and employes in city institutions, steamboats or other structures in which maintenance or part maintenance is provided, to inspect foods for fitness and quality, and to perform other related duties in kitchens, bake shops or butcher shops.

---

[1]The following positions are among those appraised by the Bureau of Personal Service in this grade on the basis of duties performed by present incumbents:

Warden in charge of the Penitentiary.
Warden in charge of all District Prisons.
Warden in charge of the City Prison in Manhattan, Brooklyn or Queens.
Warden in charge of the Workhouse on Blackwell's Island.
Warden in charge of the Branch Workhouse on Hart's Island.

GRADE 1 (N Q 1)

TITLES OF POSITIONS[1]—

BAKER[2]
BUTCHER
COOK A
COOK B
COOK C

DUTIES—

Baker:

The duties of Bakers, which may or may not involve supervision of inmates, helpers, or other employes, are to mix, work and prepare dough for baking, to attend one or more ovens, and to perform other related duties.

Butcher:

The duties of Butchers, which may or may not involve supervision of inmates, helpers, or other employes, are to receipt for, weigh and inspect all meat received, to cut up upon requisition all sides, quarters and other cuts of meats, and to supervise and assist in cleaning and maintaining premises where meat is kept.

Cook:

The duties of Cooks, which may or may not involve supervision of inmates, helpers, or other employes, are to requisition and receipt for all necessary kitchen supplies, under the direction of a head cook or dietitian in the larger institutions, or independently in the smaller institutions, to prepare for immediate or future table use all varieties of foods and beverages, and to supervise and assist in kitchens, pantries and supply rooms in the performance of all cooking operations and routine kitchen work.

QUALIFICATIONS—

1. Evidence of ability to perform the duties of the position satisfactory to the appointing officer.
2. Such additional qualifications as may be required by the Municipal Civil Service Commission.

COMPENSATION—

Baker:

Range of annual compensation without maintenance—$1080 to $1200 inclusive.
Annual salary rates—$1080, $1140, $1200.
Range of annual compensation with full maintenance—$840 to $960 inclusive.
Annual salary rates—$840, $900, $960.
Range of monthly compensation without maintenance—$90 to $100 inclusive.
Monthly salary rates—$90, $95, $100.
Range of monthly compensation with full maintenance—$70 to $80 inclusive.
Monthly salary rates—$70, $75, $80.

---

[1]For convenience in designation Cooks in this grade will be known as Cook A, Cook B and Cook C. These titles will bear the following significance: Cook A refers to cooks in residences of Medical Superintendents; Cook B refers to assistant cooks in Nurses' residences, in general kitchens of small hospitals, and in general kitchens of workhouses and prisons; Cook C refers to head cooks in Nurses' residences, excepting Bellevue and in smallest hospitals, and first assistant cooks in general kitchens of largest hospitals. Persons employed under these three titles will receive the various rates of compensation indicated above.

[2]It is open to question whether the positions as Baker and Head Baker belong in the Institutional Service or in the Skilled Trades Service. It has been decided to place them in the Institutional Service on account of their close relation to other positions in the Culinary Worker Group. The rates of compensation, however, are based upon the prevailing rates for Bakers.

Butcher:

Range of annual compensation without maintenance—$660 to $840 inclusive.
Annual salary rates—$660, $690, $720, $750, $780, $810, $840.
Range of annual compensation with full maintenance—$420 to $600 inclusive.
Annual salary rates—$420, $450, $480, $510, $540, $570, $600.
Range of monthly compensation without maintenance—$55 to $70 inclusive.
Monthly salary rates—$55, $57.50, $60, $62.50, $65, $67.50, $70.
Range of monthly compensation with full maintenance—$35 to $50 inclusive.
Monthly salary rates—$35, $37.50, $40, $42.50, $45, $47.50, $50.

Cook A[1] (Cooks in residences of Medical Superintendents):

Range of annual compensation with maintenance—$360 to $420 inclusive.
Annual salary rates—$360, $390, $420.
Range of monthly compensation with maintenance—$30 to $35 inclusive.
Monthly salary rates—$30, $32.50, $35.

Cook B (Assistant Cooks in Nurses' residences, in general kitchens of small hospitals, and in general kitchens of work houses and prisons):

Range of annual compensation with maintenance—$480 to $660 inclusive.
Annual salary rates—$480, $510, $540, $570, $600, $630, $660.
Range of monthly compensation with maintenance—$40 to $55 inclusive.
Monthly salary rates—$40, $42.50, $45, $47.50, $50, $52.50, $55.

---

[1]The following tentative close appraisals are based upon present conditions and are being used currently by the Bureau of Personal Service in its reports to the Committee on Salaries and Grades of the Board of Estimate and Apportionment. The value of these positions, as of many others, must naturally be subject to reappraisal from time to time in accordance with changing conditions.

$360 to $420 with maintenance—

Cook in residence of:

General Medical Superintendent of Bellevue and Allied Hospitals.
Superintendent of Kings County Hospital.
Superintendent of Metropolitan Hospital.
Superintendent of Sea View Hospital.

$480 to $660 with maintenance—

2nd Assistant Cook—Main Kitchen—Bellevue.
Assistant Cook—Male or Female Division—Otisville.
Assistant Cook—Mills Training School.
Assistant Cook at Work Houses and Prisons.
Assistant Cook—Gouverneur, Harlem and Fordham Hospitals.
Assistant Cook in Nurses' Residence at:

Bellevue Hospital.
Metropolitan Hospital.
Kings County Hospital.
Harlem Hospital.
City Hospital.

$600 to $720 with maintenance—

Head Cook, Nurses' Residence—Metropolitan, City or Kings County Hospital.
1st Assistant Cook—Main Kitchen—Metropolitan Hospital.
1st Assistant Cook—Main Kitchen—Bellevue Hospital.
Head Cook—Neponsit Beach Hospital.
Cook—Mills Training School.

Cook C (Head Cooks in Nurses' residences, excepting Bellevue and in smallest hospitals and first Assistant Cooks in general kitchens of largest hospitals):

Range of annual compensation with maintenance—$600 to $720 inclusive.
Annual salary rates—$600, $630, $660, $690, $720.
Range of monthly compensation with maintenance—$50 to $60 inclusive.
Monthly salary rates—$50, $52.50, $55, $57.50, $60.

SPECIAL CONDITION GOVERNING ADVANCEMENT—

The following table indicates the minimum number of years of meritorious service required at each rate before advancement to the next rate. See also page 30.

Baker:

$1080	$840	$90	$70	1 year
1140	900	95	75	1 "

Butcher:

$650	$420	$55.00	$35.00	¼ year
690	450	57.50	37.50	¾ "
720	480	60.00	40.00	1 "
750	510	62.50	42.50	1 "
780	540	65.00	45.00	1 "
810	570	67.50	47.50	1 "

Cook A (Cooks in residences of Medical Superintendents):

$360	$30.00	¼ year
390	32.50	¾ "

Cook B (Assistant Cooks in Nurses' residences, in general kitchens of small hospitals, and in general kitchens of work houses and prisons):

$480	$40.00	¼ year
510	42.50	¾ "
540	45.00	1 "
570	47.50	1 "
600	50.00	1 "
630	52.50	1 "

Cook C (Head Cooks in Nurses' residences, excepting Bellevue and in smallest hospitals and first Assistant Cooks in general kitchens of largest hospitals):

$600	$50.00	¼ year
630	52.50	¾ "
660	55.00	1 "
690	57.50	1 "

GRADE 2 (N Q 2)

TITLES OF POSITIONS[1]—

HEAD BAKER[2]
HEAD BUTCHER
HEAD COOK

DUTIES—

Head Baker:

The duties of Head Bakers, which involve supervision of Bakers in Grade 1 and of helpers, are to be responsible for all baking for distribution to a group of institutions in a large city department or departments.

Head Butcher:

The duties of Head Butchers, which involve supervision of Butchers in Grade 1 and of helpers, are to be responsible for all butchering work for a group of institutions, or for the receipt and inspection of meat in one large institution.

Head Cook:

The duties of Head Cooks, which involve supervision of Cooks in Grade 1 and of helpers, are similar to those performed by Cooks in Grade 1, but include responsibility for the preparation of meals for large groups of inmates, patients or employes.

QUALIFICATIONS—

1. The minimum qualifications prescribed for Grade 1.
2. If appointed by promotion, appropriate experience in Grade 1, or if appointed as the result of non-competitive examination, evidence of ability to perform the duties of the position satisfactory to the appointing officer.
3. Such additional qualifications as may be required by the Municipal Civil Service Commission.

---

[1]The following positions are among those appraised by the Bureau of Personal Service in this grade on the basis of duties performed by present incumbents:

Head Baker in the Blackwell's Island Bakery of the Department of Public Charities.
Head Butcher at Kings County Hospital, Sea View Hospital, or Bellevue and Allied Hospitals.
Head Cook at:
Brooklyn Home for Aged and Infirm.
New York City Home for Aged and Infirm.
Willard Parker Hospital.
Kingston Avenue Hospital.
Riverside Hospital.
Work House—Hart's Island.
City Prisons—Manhattan and Brooklyn.
Reformatory—New Hampton.
Male or Female Division—Otisville.
Main Kitchen—Nurses' Residence—Bellevue Hospital.
Kings County Hospital.
Sea View Hospital.
City Hospital.
Metropolitan Hospital.
New York City Children's Hospitals and Schools.

[2]See note on Baker in Grade 1 of this Group.

COMPENSATION—

Head Baker:

Range of annual compensation without maintenance—$1260 to $1380 inclusive.
Annual salary rates—$1260, $1320, $1380.
Range of monthly compensation without maintenance—$105 to $115 inclusive.
Monthly salary rates—$105, $110, $115.

Head Butcher:

Range of annual compensation without maintenance—$900 to $1140 inclusive.
Annual salary rates—$900, $930, $960, $990, $1020, $1050, $1080, $1110, $1140.
Range of annual compensation with full maintenance—$660 to $900 inclusive.
Annual salary rates—$660, $690, $720, $750, $780, $810, $840, $870, $900.
Range of monthly compensation without maintenance—$75 to $95 inclusive.
Monthly salary rates—$75, $77.50, $80, $82.50, $85, $87.50, $90, $92.50, $95.
Range of monthly compensation with full maintenance—$55 to $75 inclusive.
Monthly salary rates—$55, $57.50, $60, $62.50, $65, $67.50, $70, $72.50, $75.

Head Cook:

Range of annual compensation without maintenance—$1020 to $1140 inclusive.
Annual salary rates—$1020, $1050, $1080, $1110, $1140.
Range of annual compensation with maintenance—$780 to $900 inclusive.
Annual salary rates—$780, $810, $840, $870, $900.
Range of monthly compensation without maintenance—$85 to $95 inclusive.
Monthly salary rates—$85, $87.50, $90, $92.50, $95.
Range of monthly compensation with maintenance—$65 to $75 inclusive.
Monthly salary rates—$65, $67.50, $70, $72.50, $75.

SPECIAL REGULATION GOVERNING COMPENSATION—

Head Cook:

Persons entering this grade need not necessarily begin at the lowest rate. Fixation of the initial salary rate and advancement within this grade are conditional upon appraisal under the rules of the Board of Estimate and Apportionment, indicating that the rate requested does not exceed the value of the work to be performed.

SPECIAL CONDITION GOVERNING ADVANCEMENT—

The following table indicates the minimum number of years of meritorious service required at each rate before advancement to the next rate. See also page 30.

Head Baker:

$1260	$105	1 year
1320	110	1 "

Head Butcher:

$900	$660	$75.00	$55.00	¼ year
930	690	77.50	57.50	¾ "
960	720	80.00	60.00	1 "
990	750	82.50	62.50	1 "
1020	780	85.00	65.00	1 "
1050	810	87.50	67.50	1 "
1080	840	90.00	70.00	1 "
1110	870	92.50	72.50	1 "

Head Cook:

$1020	$780	$85.00	$65.00	¼ year
1050	810	87.50	67.50	¾ "
1080	840	90.00	70.00	1 "
1110	870	92.50	72.50	1 "

DIETITIAN GROUP

SYMBOL (N D)

The term Dietitian Group is applied to those offices or employments of the Institutional Service in which incumbents are required to supervise and be responsible for the planning of diets, the requisition, storage, preparation and serving of foods, and the work of cooks, waitresses and other dietary helpers.

GRADE 1 (N D I)

TITLES OF POSITIONS[1]—

PUPIL DIETITIAN

DUTIES—

The duties of incumbents of these positions are to receive such instruction and to perform under supervision such general apprentice work in the practice of dietetics as is incident to training for the position of Dietitian.

QUALIFICATIONS—

1. A diploma or certificate granted on the completion of a one-year standard course of instruction in domestic science, including courses in physiological chemistry and dietetics or nutrition, at a technical school of recognized standing, or proof of other training or experience recognized by the Municipal Civil Service Commission as the equivalent.
2. Evidence of ability to perform the duties of the position satisfactory to the appointing officer.

COMPENSATION—

Annual compensation—$120 with maintenance.

GRADE 2 (N D 2)

TITLES OF POSITIONS[2]—

DIETITIAN

DUTIES—

The duties of incumbents of these positions are to perform such definite details of dietary work in a large hospital as may be assigned by the head dietitian and to supervise the work of pupil dietitians, or to direct and be responsible for the dietary work in a small hospital or in a large charitable institution for children or the aged.[3]

QUALIFICATIONS—

1. A diploma or certificate granted on the completion of a one-year standard course of instruction in domestic science, including courses in physiological chemistry and dietetics or nutrition, at a technical school of recognized standing, or proof of other training or experience recognized by the Municipal Civil Service Commission as the equivalent.
2. Experience in the practice of dietetics.
3. Such additional qualifications as may be required by the Municipal Civil Service Commission.

---

[1]The following positions are among those appraised by the Bureau of Personal Service in this grade on the basis of duties performed by present incumbents:

Pupil Dietitians at Kings County Hospital, Metropolitan Hospital and City Hospital.

[2]The following positions are among those appraised by the Bureau of Personal Service in this grade on the basis of duties performed by present incumbents:

Dietitian in charge of the dietary work of the Coney Island Hospital or the New York City Children's Hospitals and Schools.

Dietitian at Bellevue Hospital.

[3]See Grades 1 and 2 of the Supervisor Group of the Institutional Service.

COMPENSATION—

Range of annual compensation—$720 to $900 inclusive, with maintenance.
Salary rates—$720, $780, $840, $900.

GRADE 3 (N D 3)

TITLES OF POSITIONS[1]—

HEAD DIETITIAN

DUTIES—

The duties of incumbents of these positions are to direct and be responsible for the dietary work in a large hospital, or to direct and be responsible for the dietary work in a training school for nurses and to instruct the nurses in dietetics.

QUALIFICATIONS—

1. The minimum qualifications prescribed for Grade 2.
2. If appointed by promotion, not less than three years of appropriate experience in Grade 2, or if appointed as the result of an open competitive examination, experience in work of the character and standard of Grade 2.
3. Such additional qualifications as may be required by the Municipal Civil Service Commission.

COMPENSATION—

Range of annual compensation—$1020 to $1380 inclusive, with maintenance.
Salary rates—$1020, $1140, $1260, $1380.

GRADE 4 (N D 4)

TITLES OF POSITIONS[2]—

DEPARTMENTAL DIETITIAN

DUTIES—

The duties of incumbents of these positions, which require the highest order of specialized knowledge of dietetics, are to direct and be responsible for the dietary work of an entire city department.

QUALIFICATIONS—

1. The minimum qualifications prescribed for Grade 3.
2. If appointed by promotion, not less than two years of appropriate experience in Grade 3, or if appointed as the result of an open competitive examination, experience in work of the character and standard of Grade 3.
3. Such additional qualifications as may be required by the Municipal Civil Service Commission.

COMPENSATION—

Range of annual compensation—$1800 to $2820 inclusive, with or without maintenance.
Salary rates—$1800, $1980, $2160, $2340, $2580, $2820.

---

[1]The following positions are among those appraised by the Bureau of Personal Service in this grade on the basis of duties performed by present incumbents:
Head Dietitian at Bellevue Hospital or City Hospital.

[2]The following positions are among those appraised by the Bureau of Personal Service in this grade on the basis of duties performed by present incumbents:
Departmental Dietitian for the Department of Health.

SPECIAL REGULATION GOVERNING COMPENSATION—

Persons entering this grade need not necessarily begin at the lowest rate. Fixation of the initial salary rate and advancement within this grade are conditional upon appraisal under the rules of the Board of Estimate and Apportionment, indicating that the rate requested does not exceed the value of the work to be performed.

HELPER GROUP

SYMBOL (N H)

The term Helper Group is applied to those offices or employments of the Institutional Service in which incumbents are required to perform domestic or other minor manual work about buildings and grounds, incident to the maintenance of city hospitals or charitable or correctional institutions, other than the duties performed by persons in the Hospital Attendant Group.

GRADE 1 (N H 1)

TITLES OF POSITIONS—

JUNIOR HOSPITAL HELPER

DUTIES—

The duties of incumbents of these positions are to perform the least important and responsible domestic or other manual work incident to the maintenance of city hospitals or charitable institutions, other than contagious disease or emergency hospitals.[1]

Examples:

Performing general utility work of minor consequence.
Assisting in any activity mentioned in Grade 2.

QUALIFICATIONS—

1. Evidence of ability to perform the duties of the position satisfactory to the appointing officer.
2. Such additional qualifications as may be required by the Municipal Civil Service Commission.

COMPENSATION—

Range of annual compensation with maintenance—$120 to $150 inclusive.
Annual salary rates—$120, $150.
Range of monthly compensation with maintenance—$10 to $12.50 inclusive.
Monthly salary rates—$10, $12.50.

SPECIAL CONDITION GOVERNING ADVANCEMENT—

The following table indicates the minimum number of years of meritorious service required at each rate before advancement to the next rate. See also page 30.

$120 .... $10 .... ¼ year

[1]The number of persons in this grade should be carefully restricted. It provides for patients or inmates whose services require a small compensation, but who do not render the continuous and effective service required in Grade 2. At the present time this grade is required only in the following institutions: Otisville, Riverside, the tuberculosis service of Metropolitan Hospital and other tuberculosis hospitals, Homes for the Aged and Infirm and the Municipal Lodging House.

GRADE 2 (N H 2)

TITLES OF POSITIONS[1]—

HOSPITAL HELPER A
HOSPITAL HELPER B
HOSPITAL HELPER C
PRISON HELPER A
PRISON HELPER B
SEAMSTRESS

DUTIES—

The duties of incumbents of these positions are to perform responsible domestic or other manual work incident to the maintenance of city hospitals or charitable or correctional institutions.

QUALIFICATIONS—

1. Evidence of ability to perform the duties of the position satisfactory to the appointing officer.
2. Such additional qualifications as may be required by the Municipal Civil Service Commission.

COMPENSATION—

Men:

Hospital Helper A (Men employed as Cleaners, Kitchen Helpers, Waiters, Helpers in drug-rooms, storehouses, bakeries, stables, clothes and mending rooms, etc., transporters of patients, less responsible Watchmen and Elevator Operators, or Helpers engaged in performing minor handicraft or mechanical work about grounds, plant, buildings and equipment), Prison Helper A:

Range of annual compensation without maintenance—$528 to $600 inclusive.
Annual salary rates—$528, $552, $576, $600.
Range of annual compensation with full maintenance—$288 to $360 inclusive.
Annual salary rates—$288, $312, $336, $360.
Range of monthly compensation without maintenance—$44 to $50 inclusive.
Monthly salary rates—$44, $46, $48, $50.
Range of monthly compensation with full maintenance—$24 to $30 inclusive.
Monthly salary rates—$24, $26, $28, $30.

---

[1]For convenience in designation, Hospital Helpers in this grade will be known as Hospital Helper A, Hospital Helper B and Hospital Helper C, and Prison Helpers as Prison Helper A and Prison Helper B. These titles will bear the following significance: Hospital Helper A refers to men employed as Cleaners, Kitchen Helpers, Waiters, Helpers in drug-rooms, storehouses, bakeries, stables, clothes and mending rooms, etc., transporters of patients, less responsible Watchmen and Elevator Operators, or Helpers engaged in performing minor handicraft or mechanical work about grounds, plant, buildings and equipment; Hospital Helper B refers to women employed as Waitresses, Chambermaids in nurses' homes and in staff residences, Helpers in diet kitchens; Hospital Helper C refers to women employed as Cleaners, Pantry and Kitchen Helpers, Chambermaids other than those employed in nurses' homes and staff residences, and other women helpers performing work of similar standard; Prison Helper A refers to men; Prison Helper B refers to women. Persons employed under these five titles will receive the various rates of compensation indicated above.

Women:

Hospital Helper B (Women employed as Waitresses, Chambermaids in nurses' homes and in staff residences, Helpers in diet kitchens), Prison Helper B, Seamstress:

Range of annual compensation without maintenance—$504 to $576 inclusive.
Annual salary rates—$504, $528, $552, $576.
Range of annual compensation with full maintenance—$264 to $336 inclusive.
Annual salary rates—$264, $288, $312, $336.
Range of monthly compensation without maintenance—$42 to $48 inclusive.
Monthly salary rates—$42, $44, $46, $48.
Range of monthly compensation with full maintenance—$22 to $28 inclusive.
Monthly salary rates—$22, $24, $26, $28.

Hospital Helper C (Women employed as Cleaners, Pantry and Kitchen Helpers, Chambermaids other than those employed in nurses' homes and staff residences, and other women helpers performing work of similar standard):

Range of annual compensation without maintenance—$480 to $552 inclusive.
Annual salary rates—$480, $504, $528, $552.
Range of annual compensation with full maintenance—$240 to $312 inclusive.
Annual salary rates—$240, $264, $288, $312.
Range of monthly compensation without maintenance—$40 to $46 inclusive.
Monthly salary rates—$40, $42, $44, $46.
Range of monthly compensation with full maintenance—$20 to $26 inclusive.
Monthly salary rates—$20, $22, $24, $26.

SPECIAL CONDITION GOVERNING ADVANCEMENT—

The following table indicates the minimum number of years of meritorious service required at each rate before advancement to the next rate. See also page 30.

Men:

Hospital Helper A (Men employed as Cleaners, Kitchen Helpers, Waiters, Helpers in drug-rooms, storehouses, bakeries, stables, clothes and mending rooms, etc., transporters of patients, less responsible Watchmen and Elevator Operators, or Helpers engaged in performing minor handicraft or mechanical work about grounds, plant, buildings and equipment), Prison Helper A:

$528	$288	$44	$24	¼ year
552	312	46	26	¾ "
576	336	48	28	1 "

Women:

Hospital Helper B (Women employed as Waitresses, Chambermaids in nurses' homes and in staff residences, Helpers in diet kitchens), Prison Helper B, Seamstress:

$504	$264	$42	$22	¼ year
528	288	44	24	¾ "
552	312	46	26	1 "

Hospital Helper C (Women employed as Cleaners, Pantry and Kitchen Helpers, Chambermaids other than those employed in nurses' homes and staff residences, and other women helpers performing work of similar standard):

$480	$240	$40	$20	¼ year
504	264	42	22	¾ "
528	288	44	24	1 "

GRADE 3 (N H 3)

TITLES OF POSITIONS[1]—

SENIOR HOSPITAL HELPER A
SENIOR HOSPITAL HELPER B
SENIOR PRISON HELPER A
SENIOR PRISON HELPER B
HEAD SEAMSTRESS

DUTIES—

The duties of incumbents of these positions are to perform domestic or other manual work of a more difficult or supervisory nature and requiring considerable trustworthiness or independent and responsible handicraft or mechanical work incident to the maintenance of city hospitals or charitable or correctional institutions.

Examples:

Supervising a group of helpers or inmates engaged in cleaning wards, dormitories, halls and buildings; in serving and distributing foods; in manufacturing linen goods; in marking, repairing and distributing clothing; in fumigating clothing; in the operation of a piggery.

Performing independently more difficult work, such as polishing floors, barbering, repairing mattresses and chairs.

Performing independently responsible work requiring knowledge of carpentry, plumbing, gardening, repairing of machinery, painting, electrical work, oiling, firing, tinsmithing, locksmithing, steamfitting.

Operating ice machines.

Driving morgue, garbage and delivery wagons.

QUALIFICATIONS—

1. Evidence of ability to perform the duties of the position satisfactory to the appointing officer.

2. Such additional qualifications as may be required by the Municipal Civil Service Commission.

COMPENSATION—

Men:

Senior Hospital Helper A, Senior Prison Helper A:

Range of annual compensation without maintenance—$630 to $780 inclusive.
Annual salary rates—$630, $660, $690, $720, $750, $780.
Range of annual compensation with full maintenance—$390 to $540 inclusive.
Annual salary rates—$390, $420, $450, $480, $510, $540.
Range of monthly compensation without maintenance—$52.50 to $65 inclusive.
Monthly salary rates—$52.50, $55, $57.50, $60, $62.50, $65.
Range of monthly compensation with full maintenance—$32.50 to $45 inclusive.
Monthly salary rates—$32.50, $35, $37.50, $40, $42.50, $45.

---

[1]For convenience in designation, Helpers in this grade will be known as Senior Hospital Helper A and Senior Prison Helper A, referring to men, and Senior Hospital Helper B and Senior Prison Helper B, referring to women.

Women:

Head Seamstress, Senior Hospital Helper B, Senior Prison Helper B:

Range of annual compensation without maintenance—$600 to $690 inclusive.
Annual salary rates—$600, $630, $660, $690.
Range of annual compensation with full maintenance—$360 to $450 inclusive.
Annual salary rates—$360, $390, $420, $450.
Range of monthly compensation without maintenance—$50 to $57.50 inclusive.
Monthly salary rates—$50, $52.50, $55, $57.50.
Range of monthly compensation with full maintenance—$30 to $37.50 inclusive.
Monthly salary rates—$30, $32.50, $35, $37.50.

SPECIAL CONDITION GOVERNING ADVANCEMENT—

The following table indicates the minimum number of years of meritorious service required at each rate before advancement to the next rate. See also page 30.

Men:

Senior Hospital Helper A, Senior Prison Helper A:

$630	$390	$52.50	$32.50	¼ year
660	420	55.00	35.00	¾ "
690	450	57.50	37.50	1 "
720	480	60.00	40.00	1 "
750	510	62.50	42.50	1 "

Women:

Head Seamstress, Senior Hospital Helper B, Senior Prison Helper B:

$600	$360	$50.00	$30.00	¼ year
630	390	52.50	32.50	¾ "
660	420	55.00	35.00	1 "

HOSPITAL ATTENDANT GROUP

SYMBOL (N A)

The term Hospital Attendant Group is applied to those offices or employments of the Institutional Service in which incumbents are required to perform under supervision duties not requiring registration as a graduate nurse, incident to the nursing, care and comfort of patients or inmates in city hospitals or charitable or correctional institutions.

GRADE 1 (N A 1)

TITLES OF POSITIONS—

PUPIL HOSPITAL ATTENDANT

DUTIES—

The duties of incumbents of these positions are to receive instruction in the nursing and care of patients and to render such assistance to nurses and physicians as may be required.

QUALIFICATIONS—

1. Evidence of ability to perform the duties of the position satisfactory to the appointing officer.
2. Such additional qualifications as may be required by the Municipal Civil Service Commission.

COMPENSATION—

Annual compensation—$180 with maintenance.

GRADE 2 (N A 2)

TITLES OF POSITIONS[1,2]—

HOSPITAL ATTENDANT A
HOSPITAL ATTENDANT B
HOSPITAL ATTENDANT C
NURSES' ASSISTANT

DUTIES—

Hospital Attendant:

The duties of Hospital Attendants, which require considerable skill and experience in practical nursing, but no professional training, are to perform under professional supervision those duties not requiring registration as a graduate nurse which are incident to the nursing, care and comfort of patients or inmates in city hospitals, clinics or charitable or correctional institutions.

Nurse's Assistant:

The duties of Nurses' Assistants are to assist Nurses at milk stations of the Department of Health in interviewing mothers at the stations, in the weighing of infants, and in the care and distribution of milk, to make visits to mothers of infants for the purpose of securing their attendance at the milk stations and to render such other assistance to milk station Nurses as may be required.

QUALIFICATIONS—

1. Evidence of ability to perform the duties of the position satisfactory to the appointing officer.
2. Such additional qualifications as may be required by the Municipal Civil Service Commission.

COMPENSATION—

Hospital Attendant A (Hospital Attendants in tuberculosis wards for primary and secondary cases, except when the employe is a tuberculosis case, and in all other services except those mentioned below):

Range of annual compensation without maintenance—$600 to $780 inclusive.
Annual salary rates—$600, $630, $660, $690, $720, $750, $780.
Range of annual compensation with full maintenance—$360 to $540 inclusive.
Annual salary rates—$360, $390, $420, $450, $480, $510, $540.
Range of monthly compensation without maintenance—$50 to $65 inclusive.
Monthly salary rates—$50, $52.50, $55, $57.50, $60, $62.50, $65.
Range of monthly compensation with full maintenance—$30 to $45 inclusive.
Monthly salary rates—$30, $32.50, $35, $37.50, $40, $42.50, $45.

---

[1]For convenience in designation, Hospital Attendants in this grade will be known as Hospital Attendant A, Hospital Attendant B, Hospital Attendant C. These titles will bear the following significance: Hospital Attendant A refers to Hospital Attendants in tuberculosis wards for primary and secondary cases except when the employe is a tuberculosis case, and in all other services excepting those mentioned below; Hospital Attendant B refers to Hospital Attendants in wards for genito-urinary, luetic and erysipelas cases, for tuberculosis cases in a tertiary stage, in psychopathic wards and in the contagious wards in the hospitals of the Department of Health; Hospital Attendant C refers to Attendants who are themselves tuberculosis cases in tuberculosis wards for primary and secondary cases. Persons employed under these three titles will receive the various rates of compensation indicated above.

[2]It is intended to limit the title Nurse to registered graduate Nurses. The titles Pupil Hospital Attendant and Hospital Attendant will cover employes not entitled to registration as graduate nurses (male employes in the majority of cases), who are receiving training in a school for Hospital Attendants or who are so-called "practical nurses," whether graduates of a school for Hospital Attendants or not.

Hospital Attendant B (Hospital Attendants in wards for genito-urinary, luetic and erysipelas cases, for tuberculosis cases in a tertiary stage, in psychopathic wards and in the contagious wards of the hospitals of the Department of Health):

Range of annual compensation without maintenance—$720 to $900 inclusive.
Annual salary rates—$720, $750, $780, $810, $840, $870, $900.
Range of annual compensation with full maintenance—$480 to $660 inclusive.
Annual salary rates—$480, $510, $540, $570, $600, $630, $660.
Range of monthly compensation without maintenance—$60 to $75 inclusive.
Monthly salary rates—$60, $62.50, $65, $67.50, $70, $72.50, $75.
Range of monthly compensation with full maintenance—$40 to $55 inclusive.
Monthly salary rates—$40, $42.50, $45, $47.50, $50, $52.50, $55.

Hospital Attendant C (Hospital Attendants who are themselves tuberculosis cases in tuberculosis wards for primary and secondary cases):

Range of annual compensation without maintenance—$540 to $720 inclusive.
Annual salary rates—$540, $570, $600, $630, $660, $690, $720.
Range of annual compensation with full maintenance—$300 to $480 inclusive.
Annual salary rates—$300, $330, $360, $390, $420, $450, $480.
Range of monthly compensation without maintenance—$45 to $60 inclusive
Monthly salary rates—$45, $47.50, $50, $52.50, $55, $57.50, $60.
Range of monthly compensation with full maintenance—$25 to $40 inclusive
Monthly salary rates—$25, $27.50, $30, $32.50, $35, $37.50, $40.

Nurse's Assistant:

Range of annual compensation for services averaging not less than 28 hours a week—$420 to $540 inclusive.

Salary rates—$420, $450, $480, $510, $540.

SPECIAL CONDITION GOVERNING ADVANCEMENT—

The following table indicates the minimum number of years of meritorious service required at each rate before advancement to the next rate. See also page 30.

Hospital Attendant A:

$600	$360	$50.00	$30.00	¼ year
630	390	52.50	32.50	¾ "
660	420	55.00	35.00	1 "
690	450	57.50	37.50	1 "
720	480	60.00	40.00	1 "
750	510	62.50	42.50	1 "

Hospital Attendant B:

$720	$480	$60.00	$40.00	¼ year
750	510	62.50	42.50	¾ "
780	540	65.00	45.00	1 "
810	570	67.50	47.50	1 "
840	600	70.00	50.00	1 "
870	630	72.50	52.50	1 "

Hospital Attendant C:

$540	$300	$45.00	$25.00	¼ year
570	330	47.50	27.50	¾ "
600	360	50.00	30.00	1 "
630	390	52.50	32.50	1 "
660	420	55.00	35.00	1 "
690	450	57.50	37.50	1 "

Nurse's Assistant:

$420	1 year
450	1 "
480	1 "
510	1 "

INSTITUTIONAL CLERK GROUP

SYMBOL (N C)

The term Institutional Clerk Group is applied to those offices or employments of the Institutional Service in which incumbents are required to perform prescribed routine or specialized clerical work of minor consequence in city hospitals or charitable or correctional institutions.

GRADE 1 A (N C 1 A)[1]

TITLES OF POSITIONS—

ASSISTANT INSTITUTIONAL CLERK A

DUTIES—

The duties of incumbents of these positions are to perform, under supervision, in city hospitals or charitable or correctional institutions, clerical work of the character and standard of Grade 2A of the Clerk Group of the Clerical Service, including work of corresponding grade in other groups of the Clerical Service.

Examples:

Plain longhand copying.
Keeping card indices.
Recording, indexing and filing correspondence.
Receiving and distributing routine reports and applications.
Making out and tabulating daily, weekly and monthly reports, simple charts and statistics.
Registering and verifying extensions and additions on orders and invoices.
Writing, registering and scheduling vouchers.
Operating correspondence and tickler files.
Operating tabulating machines, adding and scheduling machines, addressographs, multigraphs and mimeographs.

QUALIFICATIONS—

1. Evidence of ability to perform the duties of the position satisfactory to the appointing officer.
2. Such qualifications as may be required by the Municipal Civil Service Commission.

If the position is classified as non-competitive, the minimum qualifications shall consist of 1 and 2; if competitive, the minimum qualifications shall consist of 2.

---

[1]This grade covers clerical positions in institutions at salaries below $600 with maintenance, which are placed by the Civil Service Commission in the non-competitive class and positions without maintenance at salary rates from $600 to $720, which are generally placed by the Civil Service Commission in the competitive class, but which are filled by certification from a special list for Assistant Institutional Clerk. In a few cases these latter positions will be placed by the Civil Service Commission in the non-competitive class. See also Grade 1B.

Clerical work requiring a higher degree of responsibility and ability than is indicated in this group should be performed by employes in the Clerk Group and other groups of the Clerical Service.

COMPENSATION—

Range of annual compensation without maintenance—$600 to $720 inclusive.
Annual salary rates—$600, $660, $720.
Range of annual compensation with full maintenance—$360 to $540 inclusive.
Annual salary rates—$360, $420, $480, $540.

SPECIAL CONDITION GOVERNING ADVANCEMENT—

The following table indicates the minimum number of years of meritorious service required at each rate before advancement to the next rate. See also page 30.

$600	$360	1 year
660	420	1 "
	480	1 "

GRADE 1 B (N C 1 B)[1]

TITLES OF POSITIONS—

ASSISTANT INSTITUTIONAL CLERK B

DUTIES—

The duties of incumbents of these positions, which may involve limited supervision, are to perform in city hospitals or charitable or correctional institutions clerical work of the character and standard of Grade 2 B of the Clerk Group of the Clerical Service, including work of corresponding grade in other groups of the Clerical Service.

Examples:

Keeping important official records.
Copying and compiling cost account records under supervision.
Filing and keeping in custody important papers and records.
Receiving for custody and returning property in small property divisions.
Making up and verifying payrolls.
Filing and indexing medical records.

QUALIFICATIONS—

1. Evidence of ability to perform the duties of the position satisfactory to the appointing officer.
2. Such qualifications as may be required by the Municipal Civil Service Commission.

If the position is classified as non-competitive, the minimum qualifications shall consist of 1 and 2; if competitive, the minimum qualifications shall consist of 2.

COMPENSATION—

Range of annual compensation without maintenance—$840 to $1200 inclusive.
Salary rates—$840, $960, $1080, $1200.
Range of annual compensation with maintenance—$600 to $960 inclusive.
Salary rates—$600, $720, $840, $960.

SPECIAL CONDITION GOVERNING ADVANCEMENT—

The following table indicates the minimum number of years of meritorious service required at each rate before advancement to the next rate. See also page 30.

$840	$600	1 year
960	720	1 "
1080	840	1 "

[1]Positions in this grade are generally placed by the Civil Service Commission in the competitive class, but are filled by certification from a special list for Assistant Institutional Clerk. In a few cases these positions will be placed by the Civil Service Commission in the non-competitive class.

INSTITUTIONAL SUPERVISOR GROUP

SYMBOL (N S)

The term Institutional Supervisor Group is applied to those offices or employments of the Institutional Service in which incumbents are required to supervise and be responsible for household administration including in some cases dietary work, the maintenance of grounds, buildings and other property, and the non-professional care of patients and inmates in city hospitals and charitable institutions.

GRADE 1 (N S 1)

TITLES OF POSITIONS[1]—

MATRON
OVERSEER

DUTIES—

Matron:

The duties of Matrons, which involve supervision of the work of inmates, helpers and other employes, are to be responsible for general household administration, including in some cases dietary work, and non-professional care of patients or inmates in a small hospital or charitable institution, or for one or both of these functions in a unit of a large hospital or charitable institution.

Overseer:

The duties of Overseers, which involve supervision of the work of inmates, helpers and other employes, are to be responsible for the maintenance of grounds, buildings and equipment or for non-professional care of male patients or inmates in a small hospital or charitable institution, or for one or both of these functions in a unit of a large hospital or charitable institution.

QUALIFICATIONS—

1. Such qualifications as may be required by the Municipal Civil Service Commission.

COMPENSATION—

Matron, Overseer:

Range of annual compensation—$600 to $780 inclusive, with maintenance.
Annual salary rates—$600, $660, $720, $780.
Range of monthly compensation—$50 to $65 inclusive, with maintenance.
Monthly salary rates—$50, $55, $60, $65.

Matrons Acting also as Working Dietitians in Institutions Employing no Trained Dietitian:

Range of annual compensation—$660 to $780 inclusive.
Salary rates—$660, $720, $780.

SPECIAL CONDITION GOVERNING ADVANCEMENT—

The following table indicates the minimum number of years of meritorious service required at each rate before advancement to the next rate. See also page 30.

$600	$50	1 year
660	55	1 "
720	60	2 years

[1]The following positions are among those appraised by the Bureau of Personal Service in this grade on the basis of duties performed by present incumbents:
Matron at Greenpoint Hospital.
Matron at Cumberland Street Hospital.
Matron at Fordham Hospital.

GRADE 2 (N S 2)

TITLES OF POSITIONS[1]—

EMPLOYMENT AGENT
HEAD MATRON
HEAD OVERSEER
ASSISTANT STEWARD

DUTIES—

Employment Agent:

The duties of Employment Agents are to interview and investigate the records of persons seeking employment at city institutions, to select and employ suitable persons and to perform such additional work related to employment as may be required.

Head Matron:

The duties of Head Matrons, which involve supervision of the work of inmates, helpers and other employes, are to be responsible for general household administration, including in some cases dietary work, or for non-professional care of patients or inmates, or for both of these functions, in a large hospital or charitable institution.[2]

Head Overseer:

The duties of Head Overseers, which involve supervision of the work of inmates, helpers and other employes, are to be responsible for the maintenance of grounds, buildings and equipment or for non-professional care of male patients or inmates in a large hospital or charitable institution.

Assistant Steward:

The duties of Assistant Stewards are to order, receipt for, distribute and account for all supplies and equipment in a small hospital or charitable institution and to exercise direct supervision over the preparation and serving of food.[2]

QUALIFICATIONS—

Employment Agent:

1. Experience in public or private employment agencies or in connection with the employment departments of innstitutions or business organizations, or other experience recognized by the Municipal Civil Service Commission as qualifying.

2. Such additional qualifications as may be required by the Municipal Civil Service Commission.

Head Matron, Head Overseer:

1. The minimum qualifications prescribed for Grade 1.

2. If appointed by promotion, not less than two years of appropriate experience in Grade 1, or if appointed as the result of an open competitive examination, experience in work of the character and standard of Grade 1.

3. Such additional qualifications as may be required by the Municipal Civil Service Commission.

---

[1]The following positions are among those appraised by the Bureau of Personal Service in this grade on the basis of duties performed by present incumbents:

Head Matron in Bellevue Hospital.
Head Matron in the New York City Home for the Aged and Infirm, Blackwell's Island.
Head Matrons in Willard Parker, Riverside and Kingston Avenue Hospitals.
Head Overseers in Kings County Hospital.

[2]See also the Dietitian Group of the Institutional Service.

Assistant Steward:

1. Such qualifications as may be required by the Municipal Civil Service Commission.

COMPENSATION—

Employment Agent, Head Matron, Head Overseer, Assistant Steward:

Range of annual compensation—$840 to $1020 inclusive, with maintenance.
Salary rates—$840, $900, $960, $1020.

Head Matrons Acting also as Working Dietitians in Institutions Employing no Trained Dietitian:

Range of annual compensation—$900 to $1020 inclusive, with maintenance.
Salary rates—$900, $960, $1020.

SPECIAL CONDITION GOVERNING ADVANCEMENT—

The following table indicates the minimum number of years of meritorious service required at each rate before advancement to the next rate. See also page 30.

$840	1 year
900	2 years
960	2 "

GRADE 3 (N S 3)

TITLES OF POSITIONS[1]—

DEPUTY LAY SUPERINTENDENT
STEWARD

DUTIES—

Deputy Lay Superintendent:

The duties of Deputy Lay Superintendents, which involve responsibility for the work of employes in Grades 1 and 2, and of inmates, helpers and other employes, are to assist the Lay or Medical Superintendent in the general lay administration of a large hospital or charitable institution or to direct independently and be responsible for the general lay administration of a small hospital or charitable institution, including all household administration, maintenance of grounds, buildings and equipment and non-professional care of patients or inmates.

Steward:

The duties of Stewards are to order, receipt for, distribute and account for all supplies and equipment in a large hospital or charitable institution and to exercise direct supervision over the preparation and serving of foods.[2]

QUALIFICATIONS—

1. The minimum qualifications prescribed for Grade 2.
2. If appointed by promotion, not less than two years of appropriate experience in Grade 2, or if appointed as the result of an open competitive examination, experience in work of the character and standard of Grade 2.
3. Such additional qualifications as may be required by the Municipal Civil Service Commission.

---

[1]The following positions are among those appraised by the Bureau of Personal Service in this grade on the basis of duties performed by present incumbents:

Deputy Lay Superintendent of City Hospital.
Deputy Lay Superintendent of Sea View Hospital.
Deputy Lay Superintendent at Farm Colony.

[2]See also the Dietitian Group of the Institutional Service.

COMPENSATION—

Deputy Lay Superintendent:

Range of annual compensation—$1080 to $1800 inclusive, with maintenance.
Salary rates—$1080, $1200, $1320, $1440, $1560, $1680, $1800.

Steward:

Range of annual compensation—$1080 to $1560 inclusive, with maintenance.
Salary rates—$1080, $1200, $1320, $1440, $1560.

SPECIAL REGULATION GOVERNING COMPENSATION—

Persons entering this grade need not necessarily begin at the lowest rate. Fixation of the initial salary rate and advancement within this grade are conditional upon appraisal under the rules of the Board of Estimate and Apportionment, indicating that the rate requested does not exceed the value of the work to be performed.

SPECIAL CONDITION GOVERNING ADVANCEMENT—

The following table indicates the minimum number of years of meritorious service required at each rate before advancement to the next rate. See also page 30.

$1080	1 year
1200	1 "
1320	1 "
1440	2 years
1560	2 "
1680	2 "

GRADE 4 (N S 4)

TITLES OF POSITIONS[1]—

LAY SUPERINTENDENT
DEPARTMENTAL STEWARD

DUTIES—

Lay Superintendent:

The duties of Lay Superintendents, which involve entire responsibility for the work of employes in Grades 1, 2 and 3, and of inmates, helpers and other employes, are to direct and be responsible for the general lay administration of a large hospital or charitable institution, including all household administration, maintenance of grounds, building and equipment and the non-professional care of inmates.

Departmental Steward:

The duties of Departmental Stewards are to order, receipt for, distribute and account for all supplies and equipment in an entire city department and to exercise general supervision over the preparation and serving of foods in the institutions of that department.[2]

---

[1]The following positions are among those appraised by the Bureau of Personal Service in this grade on the basis of duties performed by present incumbents:

Lay Superintendent of Municipal Lodging House.
Lay Superintendent of New York City Farm Colony.
Lay Superintendent of New York City Home for the Aged and Infirm, Blackwell's Island.
Lay Superintendent of Harlem Hospital (with no Medical Superintendent).
Lay Superintendent of Bellevue Hospital.

[2]See also Departmental Dietitian in the Dietitian Group of the Institutional Service.

QUALIFICATIONS—

1. The minimum qualifications prescribed for Grade 3.

2. If appointed by promotion, not less than one year of appropriate experience in Grade 3, or if appointed as the result of an open competitive examination, experience in work of the character and standard of Grade 3.

3. Such additional qualifications as may be required by the Municipal Civil Service Commission.

COMPENSATION—

Lay Superintendent:

Range of annual compensation—$2100 to $2940 inclusive, with maintenance.

Salary rates—$2100, $2280, $2460, $2700, $2940.

Departmental Steward:

Range of annual compensation—$1920 to $2940 inclusive, with or without maintenance.

Salary rates—$1920, $2100, $2280, $2460, $2700, $2940.

In the case of Departmental Stewards receiving maintenance, the salary rate shall not exceed $1920.

SPECIAL REGULATION GOVERNING COMPENSATION—

Persons entering this grade need not necessarily begin at the lowest rate. Fixation of the initial salary rate and advancement within this grade are conditional upon appraisal under the rules of the Board of Estimate and Apportionment, indicating that the rate requested does not exceed the value of work to be performed.

GRADE 5 (N S 5)

TITLES OF POSITIONS[1]—

GENERAL LAY SUPERINTENDENT

DUTIES—

The duties of incumbents of these positions, which involve supervision of Lay Superintendents, Medical Superintendents, or both, are to direct and control the administration of a group of hospitals and charitable institutions.

QUALIFICATIONS—

1. The minimum qualifications prescribed for Grade 4.

2. If appointed by promotion, not less than one year of appropriate experience in Grade 4, or if appointed as the result of an open competitive examination, experience in work of the character and standard of Grade 4.

3. Such additional qualifications as may be required by the Municipal Civil Service Commission.

COMPENSATION—

Range of annual compensation—$3180 and up, with maintenance.

Salary rates—$3180, $3420, $3660, $3960, $4260.[2]

SPECIAL REGULATION GOVERNING COMPENSATION—

Persons entering this grade need not necessarily begin at the lowest rate. Fixation of the initial salary rate and advancement within this grade are conditional upon appraisal under the rules of the Board of Estimate and Apportionment, indicating that the rate requested does ot exceed the value of the work to be performed.

---

[1]The following positions are among those appraised by the Bureau of Personal Service in this grade on the basis of duties performed by present incumbents:

General Lay Superintendent of Sea View Hospital and the New York City Farm Colony on Staten Island.

[2]No recommendation is made above $4260.

LAUNDRYMAN GROUP

SYMBOL (N L)

The term Laundryman Group is applied to those offices or employments of the Institutional Service in which incumbents are required to perform or to supervise the performance of laundry work in city hospitals or charitable or correctional institutions.

GRADE 1 (N L 1)

TITLES OF POSITIONS[1]—

LAUNDRY HELPER A
LAUNDRY HELPER B
LAUNDRY HELPER C

DUTIES—

The duties of incumbents of these positions are to perform the less difficult or less responsible work involved in the operation of an institutional laundry.

QUALIFICATIONS—

1. Evidence of ability to perform the duties of the position satisfactory to the appointing officer.
2. Such additional qualifications as may be required by the Municipal Civil Service Commission.

COMPENSATION—

Laundry Helper A (Women employed as Manglers, Counters, Markers and Sorters of ward linen, Shakers and Folders):

Range of annual compensation without maintenance—$480 to $552 inclusive.
Annual salary rates—$480, $504, $528, $552.
Range of annual compensation with full maintenance—$240 to $312 inclusive.
Annual salary rates—$240, $264, $288, $312.
Range of monthly compensation without maintenance—$40 to $46 inclusive.
Monthly salary rates—$40, $42, $44, $46.
Range of monthly compensation with full maintenance—$20 to $26 inclusive.
Monthly salary rates—$20, $22, $24, $26.

Laundry Helper B (Women employed as Starchers, Packers, Hand and Machine Ironers and Press Machine Operators and Men employed as Drying Room Attendants):

Range of annual compensation without maintenance—$504 to $576 inclusive.
Annual salary rates—$504, $528, $552, $576.
Range of annual compensation with full maintenance—$264 to $336 inclusive.
Annual salary rates—$264, $288, $312, $336.
Range of monthly compensation without maintenance—$42 to $48 inclusive.
Monthly salary rates—$42, $44, $46, $48.
Range of monthly compensation with full maintenance—$22 to $28 inclusive.
Monthly salary rates—$22, $24, $26, $28.

---

[1]For convenience in designation, Laundry Helpers in this grade will be known as Laundry Helper A, Laundry Helper B and Laundry Helper C. These titles will bear the following significance: Laundry Helper A refers to women employed as Manglers, Counters. Markers and Sorters of ward linen, Shakers and Folders; Laundry Helper B refers to women employed as Starchers, Packers, Hand and Machine Ironers and Press Machine Operators, and men employed as Drying Room Attendants; Laundry Helper C refers to Markers and Sorters of staff linen, men employed as Body Ironers and other men performing work of similar standard. Persons employed under these three titles will receive the various rates of compensation indicated above.

Laundry Helper C (Markers and Sorters of staff linen, Men employed as Body Ironers and other men performing work of similar standard):

Range of annual compensation without maintenance—$528 to $600 inclusive.
Annual salary rates—$528, $552, $576, $600.
Range of annual compensation with full maintenance—$288 to $360 inclusive.
Annual salary rates—$288, $312, $336, $360.
Range of monthly compensation without maintenance—$44 to $50 inclusive.
Monthly salary rates—$44, $46, $48, $50.
Range of monthly compensation with full maintenance—$24 to $30 inclusive.
Monthly salary rates—$24, $26, $28, $30.

SPECIAL CONDITION GOVERNING ADVANCEMENT—

The following table indicates the minimum number of years of meritorious service required at each rate before advancement to the next rate. See also page 30.

Laundry Helper A (Women employed as Manglers, Counters, Markers and Sorters of ward linen, Shakers and Folders):

$480	$240	$40	$20	¼ year
504	264	42	22	¾ "
528	288	44	24	1 "

Laundry Helper B (Women employed as Starchers, Packers, Hand and Machine Ironers and Press Machine Operators and Men employed as Drying Room Attendants):

$504	$264	$42	$22	¼ year
528	288	44	24	¾ "
552	312	46	26	1 "

Laundry Helper C (Markers and Sorters of staff linen, Men employed as Body Ironers and other men performing work of similar standard):

$528	$288	$44	$24	¼ year
552	312	46	26	¾ "
576	336	48	28	1 "

GRADE 2 (N L 2)

TITLES OF POSITIONS[1]—

SENIOR LAUNDRY HELPER A
SENIOR LAUNDRY HELPER B

DUTIES—

The duties of incumbents of these positions are to perform the more difficult or more responsible work involved in the operation of an institutional laundry.

Examples:

Operating washing machine.
Working at the extractor.

QUALIFICATIONS—

1. Evidence of ability to perform the duties of the position satisfactory to the appointing officer.
2. Such additional qualifications as may be required by the Municipal Civil Service Commission.

[1]For convenience in designation, Senior Laundry Helpers in this grade will be known as Senior Laundry Helper A and Senior Laundry Helper B. These titles will bear the following significance: Senior Laundry Helper A refers to Extractormen, Head Sorters and Head Markers and Forewomen in charge; Senior Laundry Helper B refers to men engaged in operating a washing machine.

COMPENSATION—

Senior Laundry Helper A (Extractorman, Head Sorter and Head Marker, and Floorwoman in charge):

Range of annual compensation without maintenance—$630 to $780 inclusive.
Annual salary rates—$630, $660, $690, $720, $750, $780.
Range of annual compensation with full maintenance—$390 to $540 inclusive.
Annual salary rates—$390, $420, $450, $480, $510, $540.
Range of monthly compensation without maintenance—$52.50 to $65 inclusive.
Monthly salary rates—$52.50, $55, $57.50, $60, $62.50, $65.
Range of monthly compensation with full maintenance—$32.50 to $45 inclusive.
Monthly salary rates—$32.50, $35, $37.50, $40, $42.50, $45.

Senior Laundry Helper B (Engaged in operating a washing machine):

Range of annual compensation without maintenance—$690 to $840 inclusive.
Annual salary rates—$690, $720, $750, $780, $810, $840.
Range of annual compensation with full maintenance—$450 to $600 inclusive.
Annual salary rates—$450, $480, $510, $540, $570, $600.
Range of monthly compensation without maintenance—$57.50 to $70 inclusive.
Monthly salary rates—$57.50, $60, $62.50, $65, $67.50, $70.
Range of monthly compensation with full maintenance—$37.50 to $50 inclusive.
Monthly salary rates—$37.50, $40, $42.50, $45, $47.50, $50.

SPECIAL CONDITION GOVERNING ADVANCEMENT—

The following table indicates the minimum number of years of meritorious service required at each rate before advancement to the next rate. See also page 30.

Senior Laundry Helper A (Extractorman, Head Sorter and Head Marker, and Floorwoman in charge):

$630	$390	$52.50	$32.50	¼ year
660	420	55.00	35.00	¾ "
690	450	57.50	37.50	1 "
720	480	60.00	40.00	1 "
750	510	62.50	42.50	1 "

Senior Laundry Helper B (Engaged in operating a washing machine):

$690	$450	$57.50	$37.50	¼ year
720	480	60.00	40.00	¾ "
750	510	62.50	42.50	1 "
780	540	65.00	45.00	1 "
810	570	67.50	47.50	1 "

GRADE 3 (N L 3)

TITLES OF POSITIONS[1 2]—

LAUNDRYMAN

DUTIES—

The duties of incumbents of these positions are to assist the Head Laundryman in the operation of a laundry in a large institution or to take charge of the operation of a laundry in a small institution.

[1]The following positions are among those appraised by the Bureau of Personal Service in this grade on the basis of duties performed by present incumbents:
Laundryman at Coney Island Hospital.
Laundryman at Cumberland Street Hospital.
Laundryman at Greenpoint Hospital.

[2]Positions of Laundryman in this grade are classified by the Municipal Civil Service Commission in the non-competitive class.

QUALIFICATIONS—

1. Evidence of ability to perform the duties of the position satisfactory to the appointing officer.

2. Such additional qualifications as may be required by the Municipal Civil Service Commission.

COMPENSATION—

Range of annual compensation without maintenance—$840 to $900 inclusive. Salary rates—$840, $870, $900.

Range of annual compensation with full maintenance—$600 to $660 inclusive. Salary rates—$600, $630, $660.

Range of monthly compensation without maintenance—$70 to $75 inclusive. Monthly salary rates—$70, $72.50, $75.

Range of monthly compensation with full maintenance—$50 to $55 inclusive. Monthly salary rates—$50, $52.50, $55.

SPECIAL CONDITION GOVERNING ADVANCEMENT—

The following table indicates the minimum number of years of meritorious service required at each rate before advancement to the next rate. See also page 30.

$840	$600	$70.00	$50.00	¼ year
870	630	72.50	52.00	¾ "

GRADE 4 (N L 4)

TITLES OF POSITIONS[1]—

HEAD LAUNDRYMAN

DUTIES—

The duties of incumbents of these positions are to take charge of a large institutional laundry.

QUALIFICATIONS—

1. The minimum qualifications prescribed for Grade 3.

2. If appointed by promotion, not less than three years of appropriate experience in Grade 3, or if appointed as the result of an open competitive examination, experience in work of the character and standard of Grade 3.

3. Such additional qualifications as may be required by the Municipal Civil Service Commission.

COMPENSATION[2]—

Range of annual compensation without maintenance—$960 to $1440 inclusive. Salary rates—$960, $1020, $1080, $1140, $1200, $1260, $1320, $1380, $1440.

Range of annual compensation with full maintenance—$720 to $1200 inclusive. Salary rates—$720, $780, $840, $900, $960, $1020, $1080, $1140, $1200.

---

[1]Positions as Head Laundrymen are classified by the Municipal Civil Service Commission in the competitive class.

[2]The following tentative close appraisals are based upon present conditions and are being used currently by the Bureau of Personal Service in its reports to the Committee on Salaries and Grades of the Board of Estimate and Apportionment. The value of these positions, as of many others, must naturally be subject to reappraisal from time to time in accordance with changing conditions.

	With Maintenance.	Without Maintenance.
Head Laundryman for Department of Public Charities, Blackwell's Island	$840-1200	$1080-1440
Head Laundryman at Kings County Hospital	720-1080	960-1320
Head Laundryman at Sea View Hospital	720-1080	960-1320
Head Laundryman at New York City Children's Hospitals and Schools, Randall's Island	720-1080	960-1320

SPECIAL REGULATION GOVERNING COMPENSATION—

Persons entering this grade need not necessarily begin at the lowest rate. Fixation of the initial salary rate and advancement within this grade are conditional upon appraisal under the rules of the Board of Estimate and Apportionment, indicating that the rate requested does not exceed the value of the work to be performed.

SPECIAL CONDITION GOVERNING ADVANCEMENT—

The following table indicates the minimum number of years of meritorious service required at each rate before advancement to the next rate. See also page 30.

$960	$720	1 year
1020	780	1 "
1080	840	1 "
1140	900	1 "
1200	960	1 "
1260	1020	1 "
1320	1080	1 "
1380	1140	2 years

GRADE 5 (N L 5)

TITLES OF POSITIONS[1]—

SUPERINTENDENT OF LAUNDRIES

DUTIES—

The duties of incumbents of these positions are to supervise and be responsible for all institutional laundries in a department, involving supervision of employes in Grade 1 and other employes, and responsibility for equipment, materials, supplies and the operation and maintenance of plants.

QUALIFICATIONS—

1. The minimum qualifications prescribed for Grade 4.
2. If appointed by promotion, not less than three years of appropriate experience in Grade 4, or if appointed as the result of an open competitive examination, experience in work of the character and standard of Grade 4.
3. Such additional qualifications as may be required by the Municipal Civil Service Commission.

COMPENSATION—

Range of annual compensation—$1800 to $2580 inclusive.
Salary rates—$1800, $1980, $2160, $2340, $2580.

SPECIAL REGULATION GOVERNING COMPENSATION—

Persons entering this grade need not necessarily begin at the lowest rate. Fixation of the initial salary rate and advancement within this grade are conditional upon appraisal under the rules of the Board of Estimate and Apportionment, indicating that the rate requested does not exceed the value of the work to be performed.

SPECIAL CONDITION GOVERNING ADVANCEMENT—

The following table indicates the minimum number of years of meritorious service required at each rate before advancement to the next rate. See also page 30.

$1800	1 year
1980	1 "
2160	2 years
2340	2 "

[1]The following positions are among those appraised by the Bureau of Personal Service in this grade on the basis of duties performed by present incumbents:
Superintendent of Laundries in the Department of Public Charities.

MASSEUR GROUP

SYMBOL (N M)

The term Masseur Group is applied to those offices or employments of the Institutional Service in which incumbents are required to administer treatment to the sick in the form of massage, medical gymnastics and muscle training, or to supervise and give instruction in this treatment.

GRADE 1 (N M 1)

TITLES OF POSITIONS—

MASSEUR

DUTIES—

The duties of incumbents of these positions are to administer to the sick under supervision routine treatment in the form of massage, medical gymnastics and muscle training.

QUALIFICATIONS—

1. Evidence of the completion of a course in medical gymnastics and massage at an institution of recognized standing.
2. Experience in the practice of massage.
3. Such additional qualifications as may be required by the Municipal Civil Service Commission.

COMPENSATION—

Range of annual compensation for full-time service—$960 to $1140 inclusive.

Salary rates—$960, $1020, $1080, $1140.

Range of annual compensation for part-time service, averaging not less than 18 hours a week—$600 to $720 inclusive.

Salary rates—$600, $660, $720.

GRADE 2 (N M 2)

TITLES OF POSITIONS—

CHIEF MASSEUR

DUTIES—

The duties of incumbents of these positions, which involve supervision of the work of employes in Grade 1 and instruction of Pupil Nurses, are to supervise and give instruction in massage, medical gymnastics and muscle training in a group of hospitals.

QUALIFICATIONS—

1. The minimum qualifications prescribed for Grade 1.
2. If appointed by promotion, not less than one year of appropriate experience in Grade 1, or if appointed as the result of an open competitive examination, experience in work of the character and standard of Grade 1.
3. Such additional qualifications as may be required by the Municipal Civil Service Commission.

COMPENSATION—

Range of annual compensation for full-time service—$1200 to $1440 inclusive.

Salary rates—$1200, $1260, $1320, $1380, $1440.

Range of annual compensation for part-time service, averaging not less than 18 hours a week—$900 to $1080 inclusive.

Salary rates—$900, $960, $1020, $1080.

MORTUARY KEEPER GROUP

SYMBOL (N K)

The term Mortuary Keeper Group is applied to those offices or employments of the Institutional Service in which incumbents are required to assist in or be responsible for the maintenance and operation of an institutional, borough, or central city mortuary, including the receipt, care and proper disposition of bodies, the meeting and interviewing of visitors, the keeping of necessary records and the cleaning of the mortuary.

GRADE 1 (N K 1)

TITLES OF POSITIONS—

MORTUARY HELPER

DUTIES—

The duties of incumbents of these positions are to perform the less responsible routine work involved in the maintenance and operation of an institutional, borough, or central city mortuary.

QUALIFICATIONS—

1. Evidence of ability to perform the duties of the position satisfactory to the appointing officer.
2. Such additional qualifications as may be required by the Municipal Civil Service Commission.

COMPENSATION[1]—

Range of annual compensation without maintenance—$792 to $888 inclusive.
Annual salary rates—$792, $816, $840, $864, $888.
Range of monthly compensation without maintenance—$66 to $74 inclusive.
Monthly salary rates—$66, $68, $70, $72, $74.

SPECIAL CONDITION GOVERNING ADVANCEMENT—

The following table indicates the minimum number of years of meritorious service required at each rate before advancement to the next rate: See also page —.

Annual	Monthly	Years
$792	$66	¼ year
816	68	¾ "
840	70	1 "
864	72	1 "

GRADE 2 (N K 2)

TITLES OF POSITIONS—

MORTUARY KEEPER

DUTIES—

The duties of incumbents of these positions are to receive, care for and deliver bodies in a large institutional mortuary, to meet and interview visitors, to keep necessary records, to be responsible for the cleanliness of the building and to perform incidentally such other institutional work of the same general grade and character as may be assigned by the head of the institution.

QUALIFICATIONS—

1. Such qualifications as may be required by the Municipal Civil Service Commission.

---

[1]For rates in institutions with maintenance, see Senior Hospital Helper A in Grade 3 of the Helper Group.

COMPENSATION—

Range of annual compensation without maintenance—$900 to $1020 inclusive.
Salary rates—$900, $960, $1020.
Range of annual compensation with full maintenance—$660 to $780 inclusive.
Salary rates—$660, $720, $780.

GRADE 3 (N K 3)

TITLES OF POSITIONS—

HEAD MORTUARY KEEPER

DUTIES—

The duties of incumbents of these positions are to be responsible for the maintenance and operation of a large borough mortuary, or to assist the superintendent in the maintenance and operation of the central city mortuary, including the receipt, care and proper disposition of bodies, the meeting and interviewing of visitors, the keeping of necessary records and the cleaning of the mortuary.

QUALIFICATIONS

1. The minimum qualifications prescribed for Grade 2.
2. If appointed by promotion, not less than three years of appropriate experience in Grade 2, or if appointed as the result of an open competitive examination, experience in work of the character and standard of Grade 2.
3. Such additional qualifications as may be required by the Municipal Civil Service Commission.

COMPENSATION—

Range of annual compensation without maintenance—$1080 to $1200 inclusive.
Salary rates—$1080, $1140, $1200.
Range of annual compensation with full maintenance—$840 to $960 inclusive.
Salary rates—$840, $900, $960.

SPECIAL REGULATION GOVERNING COMPENSATION—

Beginning with the lowest rate, advancement within this grade is conditional upon appraisal under the rules of the Board of Estimate and Apportionment, indicating that the rate requested does not exceed the value of the work to be performed.

SPECIAL CONDITION GOVERNING ADVANCEMENT—

The following table indicates the minimum number of years of meritorious service required at each rate before advancement to the next rate. See also page 30.

$1080	$840	1 year
1140	900	2 years

GRADE 4 (N K 4)

TITLES OF POSITIONS—

SUPERINTENDENT OF MORTUARY

DUTIES—

The duties of incumbents of these positions are to be responsible for the maintenance and operation of the central city mortuary, including the receipt, care and proper disposition of bodies, the meeting and interviewing of visitors, the keeping of necessary records and the cleaning of the mortuary.

QUALIFICATIONS—

1. Administrative experience in institutional or social work, or other experience recognized by the Municipal Civil Service Commission as qualifying.
2. Such additional qualifications as may be required by the Municipal Civil Service Commission.

COMPENSATION—

Range of annual compensation—$1980 to $2160 inclusive.
Salary rates—$1980, $2160.

SPECIAL CONDITION GOVERNING ADVANCEMENT—

The following table indicates the minimum number of years of meritorious service required at each rate before advancement to the next rate. See also page 30.

$1980 .... 2 years

TAILOR GROUP

SYMBOL (N T)

The term Tailor Group is applied to those offices or employments of the Institutional Service in which incumbents are required to cut cloth for and direct inmates and helpers in the making of garments and household linen used in city institutions or to supervise and be responsible for this work in an entire institutional department.

GRADE 1 (N T 1)

TITLES OF POSITIONS—

TAILOR

DUTIES—

The duties of incumbents of these positions, which involve supervision and incidental instruction of inmates and helpers, are to cut cloth for and direct inmates and helpers in the making of garments and household linen used in city institutions.

QUALIFICATIONS—

1. Experience in tailoring.
2. Such additional qualifications as may be required by the Municipal Civil Service Commission.

COMPENSATION—

Range of annual compensation without maintenance—$720 to $1020 inclusive.
Salary rates—$720, $780, $840, $900, $960, $1020.
Range of annual compensation with full maintenance—$480 to $780 inclusive.
Salary rates—$480, $540, $600, $660, $720, $780.
There shall be no initial rate for Tailors above $900.

SPECIAL REGULATION GOVERNING COMPENSATION—

Persons entering this grade need not necessarily begin at the lowest rate. Fixation of the initial salary rate and advancement within this grade are conditional upon appraisal under the rules of the Board of Estimate and Apportionment, indicating that the rate requested does not exceed the value of the work to be performed.

GRADE 2 (N T 2)

TITLES OF POSITIONS—

HEAD TAILOR

DUTIES—

The duties of incumbents of these positions, which involve supervision of employes in Grade 1 and of inmates and helpers, are to supervise and be responsible for the making of garments and household linen in the central sewing rooms of an entire institutional department.

QUALIFICATIONS—

1. The minimum qualifications prescribed for Grade 1.
2. If appointed by promotion, not less than one year of appropriate experience in Grade 1, or if appointed as the result of an open competitive examination, experience in work of the character and standard of Grade 1.
3. Such additional qualifications as may be required by the Municipal Civil Service Commission.

COMPENSATION—

Range of annual compensation—$1140 to $1260 inclusive.
Salary rates—$1140, $1200, $1260.

SPECIAL CONDITION GOVERNING ADVANCEMENT—

The following table indicates the minimum number of years of meritorious service required at each rate before advancement to the next rate. See also page 30.

$1140	1 year
1200	2 years

MISCELLANEOUS INSTITUTIONAL WORKER GROUP

SYMBOL (N Z)

The term Miscellaneous Institutional Worker Group is applied to those offices or employments of the Institutional Service in which incumbents are required to perform non-professional routine or specialized institutional work of an exceptional nature not included in the other groups of the Institutional Service.

GRADE 1 (N Z 1)

TITLES OF POSITIONS[1]—

COFFEE ROASTER
FARMER
FIRE OFFICER

DUTIES—

Coffee Roaster:

The duties of Coffee Roasters are to operate a coffee roasting machine and to supply roasted coffee to city hospitals or other institutions.

Farmer:

The duties of Farmers, which involve supervision of the work of inmates, helpers and laborers, are to cultivate the soil, to raise vegetables and other farm products, to care for live stock and farm implements and to perform other related work on farms connected with city institutions.[2]

---

[1]The following positions are among those appraised by the Bureau of Personal Service in this grade on the basis of duties performed by present incumbents:

Coffee Roaster at the general storehouse of the Department of Public Charities, Blackwell's Island.
Farmer at the Farm Colony of the Department of Public Charities.
Fire Officer at Bellevue Hospital.

[2]The title of Farmer is provided for persons acting as working farmers or supervising farm work. Persons whose work is primarily instruction in farm work are provided for in the Industrial Instructor Group of the Educational Service.

Fire Officer:

The duties of Fire Officers are to instruct inmates of city hospitals or other institutions in fire drills and the use of fire fighting apparatus, to inspect buildings as to means of egress and conditions hazardous in the case of or liable to cause fires, to inspect and be responsible for the condition of fire fighting apparatus and to make such reports as may be required.

QUALIFICATIONS—

Coffee Roaster:

1. Experience in the operation of a coffee roaster.
2. Such additional qualifications as may be required by the Municipal Civil Service Commission.

Farmer:

1. Experience in farming.
2. Such additional qualifications as may be required by the Municipal Civil Service Commission.

Fire Officer:

1. Administrative experience in the work of fire prevention, fire fighting, or other work recognized by the Municipal Civil Service Commission as qualifying.
2. Such additional qualifications as may be required by the Municipal Civil Service Commission.

COMPENSATION—

Coffee Roaster:

Range of annual compensation—$900 to $1080 inclusive.
Salary rates—$900, $960, $1020, $1080.

Farmer:

Range of annual compensation—$720 to $900 inclusive, with maintenance.
Salary rates—$720, $780, $840, $900.

Fire Officer:

Range of annual compensation—$840 to $960 inclusive, with maintenance.
Salary rates—$840, $900, $960.

SPECIAL REGULATION GOVERNING COMPENSATION—

Fire Officer:

Persons entering this grade need not necessarily begin at the lowest rate. Fixation of the initial salary rate and advancement within this grade are conditional upon appraisal under the rules of the Board of Estimate and Apportionment, indicating that the rate requested does not exceed the value of the work to be performed.

POLICE SERVICE

SYMBOL (P)

The term Police Service is applied to those offices or employments the duties of whose incumbents are to enforce laws and ordinances, to prevent crime and apprehend criminals, to guard property, to control traffic and to perform other inspectional, investigational or regulative duties incident to the protection of persons and property.[1]

[1]Tentative specifications for this service were submitted by the Bureau of Personal Service in August, 1916. As these specifications have not as yet received adequate discussion, they are not included in the present volume.

FIRE SERVICE

SYMBOL (F)

The term Fire Service is applied to those offices or employments the duties of whose incumbents are to enforce laws and ordinances and rules and regulations regarding the extinguishment of fires and to perform other inspectional, investigational or regulative duties incident to the prevention or extinguishment of fires.

STREET CLEANING SERVICE

SYMBOL (S)

The term Street Cleaning Service is applied to those offices or employments the duties of whose incumbents are to perform routine, supervisory or administrative work incident to the cleaning of streets, the collection, removal and disposal of refuse and related work.

MOTOR REFUSE COLLECTOR GROUP

SYMBOL (S M)

The term Motor Refuse Collector Group is applied to those offices or employments of the Street Cleaning Service in which incumbents are required to load or to supervise the loading of collection equipment and to drive and care for motor-driven equipment.[1]

GRADE 1 (S M 1)

TITLES OF POSITIONS—

LOADER (DEPARTMENT OF STREET CLEANING)

DUTIES—

The duties of incumbents of these positions are to load refuse collection equipment and in case of emergency to perform temporarily such other duties as may be assigned.

QUALIFICATIONS—

1. A certificate of fitness to perform the duties of Loader, issued by the School for Recruits of the Department of Street Cleaning.

COMPENSATION—

Range of annual compensation—$864 to $936 inclusive.
Salary rates—$864, $888, $912, $936.

---

[1]This group provides for new positions necessitated by the establishment of a model street cleaning district and by the beginning of the motorization of the Street Cleaning Department. Each motor will be in charge of a Driver who will so far as possible supervise the work of Loaders. Provision is, however, made for the designation of a Chief of Loaders, who will receive an additional compensation of $24 per annum. The Municipal Civil Service Commission will classify positions as Motor Truck Driver in the Labor Class for the present. As far as possible, positions as Motor Truck Driver will be filled by the assignment of Drivers and other uniformed employes after a period of apprenticeship in the School for Recruits. Drivers, Sweepers, or other uniformed employes may be assigned to the School for Recruits for the purpose of training as Motor Truck Drivers. While serving under the office title of Recruit Motor Truck Drivers, they will receive the per diem wage fixed for their regular positions. After a period of trial not exceeding three months, Recruit Motor Truck Drivers whose work has been satisfactory will receive from the School for Recruits a certificate of fitness to perform the duties of regular Motor Truck Drivers. The Civil Service Commission will then hold a practical examination for change of title. Those whose work has been unsatisfactory will return to their former positions. Uniformed employes or others who have received a certificate of fitness to act as Motor Truck Drivers and have passed the civil service examination may be assigned temporarily or appointed permanently as Motor Truck Drivers. While serving on a temporary basis as Motor Truck Drivers they will receive 1-313 of the minimum rate prescribed for the permanent position of Motor Truck Driver.

Persons temporarily employed as Loaders, designated as Extra Loaders, shall receive a per diem rate of 1-313 of the minimum annual rate prescribed for the position of Loader.

$24 in addition to the rate which he is receiving may be paid to one of each gang of Loaders who is assigned as leader of the gang.

Loaders assigned in charge of section stations or yards and employed every day in the year shall receive a flat rate of $840.

SPECIAL CONDITION GOVERNING ADVANCEMENT—

The following table indicates the minimum number of years of meritorious service required at each rate before advancement to the next rate. See also page 30.

$864	1 year
888	1 "
912	2 years

GRADE 2 (S M 2)

TITLES OF POSITIONS—

RECRUIT MOTOR TRUCK DRIVER (DEPARTMENT OF STREET CLEANING)[1]
MOTOR TRUCK DRIVER (DEPARTMENT OF STREET CLEANING)
MOTOR TRUCK DRIVER (BUREAU OF STREET CLEANING, RICHMOND)

DUTIES—

Recruit Motor Truck Driver (Department of Street Cleaning):

The duties of Recruit Motor Truck Drivers (Department of Street Cleaning) are to receive such instruction and to perform such work as may be required in the School for Recruits of the Department of Street Cleaning, relative to the driving and operation of motor-driven equipment, the supervision of the collection of refuse, the delivery of refuse at a dump, transfer or disposal point, and the care of equipment.

Motor Truck Driver (Department of Street Cleaning), Motor Truck Driver (Bureau of Street Cleaning, Richmond):

The duties of Motor Truck Drivers (Department of Street Cleaning) and Motor Truck Drivers (Bureau of Street Cleaning, Richmond) are to drive and operate motor-driven collection equipment, to collect or to supervise the collection of refuse, to deliver refuse at a dump, transfer or disposal point, and to care for equipment in their charge, or in case of emergency to perform temporarily such other duties as may be assigned.

QUALIFICATIONS—

Recruit Motor Truck Driver (Department of Street Cleaning), Motor Truck Driver (Bureau of Street Cleaning, Richmond):

1. Service in Grade 1 of the Street Cleaner, Refuse Collector, or Refuse Disposer Groups of the Street Cleaning Service.
2. The minimum qualifications prescribed for Grade 1 of the Motor Driver Group of the Skilled Trades Service.
3. Such additional qualifications as may be required by the Municipal Civil Service Commission.

The minimum qualifications shall consist of 1 and 3 or 2 and 3.

---

[1]Recruit Motor Truck Driver (Department of Street Cleaning) is an office title for employes under assignment from positions in Grade 1 of the Street Cleaner, Refuse Collector or Refuse Disposer ,Groups of the Street Cleaning Service.

Motor Truck Driver (Department of Street Cleaning):

1. A certificate of fitness to perform the duties of Motor Truck Driver issued by the School for Recruits of the Department of Street Cleaning.

COMPENSATION[1]—

Recruit Motor Truck Driver (Department of Street Cleaning):

For a uniformed employe of the Department of Street Cleaning on assignment, the rate paid in the regular position from which the employe was assigned.

Motor Truck Driver (Department of Street Cleaning), Motor Truck Driver (Bureau of Street Cleaning, Richmond):

Range of annual compensation—$960 to $996 inclusive.

Salary rates—$960, $996.

Persons temporarily employed as Motor Truck Drivers, designated as Extra Motor Truck Drivers, shall receive a per diem rate of 1-313 of the minimum annual rate prescribed for the position of Motor Truck Driver.

SPECIAL CONDITION GOVERNING ADVANCEMENT—

The following table indicates the minimum number of years of meritorious service required at each rate before advancement to the next rate. See also page 30.

Motor Truck Driver (Department of Street Cleaning), Motor Truck Driver (Bureau of Street Cleaning, Richmond):

$960 .... 1 year

RECRUIT GROUP

SYMBOL (S R)

The term Recruit Group is applied to those offices or employments of the Street Cleaning Service in which incumbents are trained for work in one or more of the specialized branches of the Street Cleaning Service.[2]

GRADE 1 (S R 1)

TITLES OF POSITIONS—

RECRUIT (DEPARTMENT OF STREET CLEANING)

DUTIES—

The duties of incumbents of these positions, which involve the performance of actual street cleaning work, are to receive training in the School for Recruits of the Department of Street Cleaning preparatory for work in one or more of the specialized branches of the Street Cleaning Service.

---

[1]It will be noted that the maximum rate for Motor Truck Drivers in the Department of Street Cleaning and the Bureau of Street Cleaning, Richmond, is lower than the maximum rate proposed for Motor Truck Drivers in other departments. (See the Motor Driver Group of the Skilled Trades Service.) The nature of the work, the training required and the limited competition have been considered in fixing the street cleaning rate. It may be desirable in future, as street cleaning motorization proceeds, to raise this maximum.

[2]Recruits for the Department of Street Cleaning will be qualified by the Municipal Civil Service Commission. After a period of trial not exceeding three months in the School for Recruits, Recruits whose work has been satisfactory will receive certificates of fitness to perform the duties of the positions of Sweeper, Driver, Loader or Boardman. Those whose work has been unsatisfactory will be dismissed from the department. Assignment to extra or permanent positions will be made according to the needs of the service.

QUALIFICATIONS—

1. The minimum qualifications prescribed by the Municipal Civil Service Commission for candidates for positions as Sweeper, Loader, Driver or Boardman in the Street Cleaning Service.

PERIOD OF TRIAL—

Not more than three months.

COMPENSATION—

A per diem rate of 1-313 of the minimum annual rate prescribed for the position for which the Recruit is in training.

REFUSE COLLECTOR GROUP

SYMBOL (S K)

The term Refuse Collector Group is applied to those offices or employments of the Street Cleaning Service in which incumbents are required to drive and care for horses, to collect refuse, to operate and care for horse-drawn equipment, or to supervise the operation of a stable.

GRADE 1 (S K 1)

TITLES OF POSITIONS—

DRIVER (DEPARTMENT OF STREET CLEANING)
DRIVER (BUREAU OF STREET CLEANING, QUEENS)
DRIVER (BUREAU OF STREET CLEANING, RICHMOND)
HOSTLER (DEPARTMENT OF STREET CLEANING)
HOSTLER (BUREAU OF STREET CLEANING, QUEENS)
HOSTLER (BUREAU OF STREET CLEANING, RICHMOND)
STABLEMAN (DEPARTMENT OF STREET CLEANING)
STABLEMAN (BUREAU OF STREET CLEANING, QUEENS)
STABLEMAN (BUREAU OF STREET CLEANING, RICHMOND)

DUTIES—

Driver:

The duties of Drivers are to drive and care for horses while outside of the stable, to collect refuse and deliver it at a dump, transfer or disposal point, to operate and care for equipment, and in case of emergency to perform temporarily such other duties as may be assigned.[1]

Hostler:

The duties of Hostlers are to care for, clean, feed and bed horses and when required to clean stables.[2]

Stableman:

The duties of Stablemen are to clean stables, to clean and care for equipment and to perform such other service in stables as may be required.[2]

---

[1]Employes in the Bureaus of Street Cleaning in the boroughs of Queens and Richmond acting as assistants to Drivers in the loading of horse-drawn collection vehicles will continue to be employed and compensated as unskilled laborers.

[2]Positions of Hostler and Stableman in other departments and bureaus will be found in the Unskilled Service. The same range of salary is recommended in all departments.

QUALIFICATIONS—

Driver (Department of Street Cleaning), Hostler (Department of Street Cleaning), Stableman (Department of Street Cleaning):

1. A certificate of fitness to perform the duties of Driver, issued by the School for Recruits of the Department of Street Cleaning.

Driver (Bureau of Street Cleaning, Queens), Driver (Bureau of Street Cleaning, Richmond), Hostler (Bureau of Street Cleaning, Queens), Hostler (Bureau of Street Cleaning, Richmond), Stableman (Bureau of Street Cleaning, Queens), Stableman (Bureau of Street Cleaning, Richmond):

1. Such qualifications as may be required by the Municipal Civil Service Commission.

COMPENSATION—

Driver:

Range of annual compensation—$840 to $936 inclusive.
Salary rates—$840, $864, $888, $912, $936.

Hostler:

Range of annual compensation—$816 to $912 inclusive.
Salary rates—$816, $840, $864, $888, $912.

Stableman:

Range of annual compensation—$792 to $888 inclusive.
Salary rates—$792, $816, $840, $864, $888.

Persons temporarily employed as Drivers, Hostlers or Stablemen, designated as Extra Drivers, Hostlers or Stablemen, shall receive a per diem rate of 1-313 of the minimum annual rate prescribed for the position in question.

Drivers, Hostlers and Stablemen assigned in charge of section stations or yards and employed every day in the year shall receive a flat rate of $840.

SPECIAL CONDITION GOVERNING ADVANCEMENT—

The following table indicates the minimum number of years of meritorious service required at each rate before advancement to the next rate. See also page 30.

Driver:

$840	1 year
864	1 "
888	2 years
912	2 "

Hostler:

$816	1 year
840	1 "
864	2 years
888	2 "

Stableman:

$792	1 year
816	1 "
840	2 years
864	2 "

GRADE 2 (S K 2)

TITLES OF POSITIONS[1]—

ASSISTANT STABLE FOREMAN (DEPARTMENT OF STREET CLEANING)
ASSISTANT STABLE FOREMAN (BUREAU OF STREET CLEANING, QUEENS)

DUTIES—

The duties of incumbents of these positions are to execute definite instructions from Stable Foremen relative to the care, maintenance and operation of a stable, the supervision of Drivers, Hostlers and Stablemen while in the stable, the care of horses and equipment and the keeping of necessary records, and to perform the duties of Stable Foremen in their absence.

QUALIFICATIONS—

1. The minimum qualifications prescribed for Grade 1 of the Refuse Collector, Refuse Disposer or Street Cleaner Group, or for Motor Truck Driver in Grade 2 of the Motor Refuse Collector Group.
2. Not less than three years of appropriate experience in Grade 1 of the Refuse Collector, Refuse Disposer or Street Cleaner Group, or as Motor Truck Driver in Grade 2 of the Motor Refuse Collector Group.
3. Such additional qualifications as may be required by the Municipal Civil Service Commission.

COMPENSATION—

Assistant Stable Foreman (Department of Street Cleaning):

Range of annual compensation—$1020 to $1140 inclusive.
Salary rates—$1020, $1080, $1140.

Assistant Stable Foreman (Bureau of Street Cleaning, Queens):

Range of annual compensation—$1020 to $1080 inclusive.
Salary rates—$1020, $1080.

SPECIAL CONDITION GOVERNING ADVANCEMENT—

The following table indicates the minimum number of years of meritorious service required at each rate before advancement to the next rate. See also page 30.

$1020	1 year
1080	2 years

GRADE 3 (S K 3)

TITLES OF POSITIONS—

STABLE FOREMAN (DEPARTMENT OF STREET CLEANING)
STABLE FOREMAN (BUREAU OF STREET CLEANING, QUEENS)
STABLE FOREMAN (BUREAU OF STREET CLEANING, RICHMOND)

DUTIES—

The duties of incumbents of these positions, which involve responsibility for the care, maintenance and operation of a stable, are to execute definite instructions from District Superintendents relative to the supervision of Drivers, Hostlers and Stablemen while in the stable, the care of horses, equipment and supplies, and the keeping of necessary records, or for Stable Foremen (Department of Street Cleaning) on assignment, to act as Assistant District Superintendent.

---

[1]Assistant Stable Foremen are not required in the Bureau of Street Cleaning, Richmond.

QUALIFICATIONS—

1. The minimum qualifications prescribed for Grade 2 of the Refuse Collector, Refuse Disposer or Street Cleaner Group.

2. Not less than one year of appropriate experience in Grade 2 of the Refuse Collector, Refuse Disposer or Street Cleaner Group.

3. Such additional qualifications as may be required by the Municipal Civil Service Commission.

COMPENSATION—

Stable Foreman (Department of Street Cleaning):

Range of annual compensation—$1200 to $1620 inclusive.
Salary rates—$1200, $1260, $1320, $1380, $1440, $1500, $1560, $1620.[1]

Stable Foreman (Department of Street Cleaning) assigned as Assistant District Superintendent:

Range of annual compensation—$1620 to $1740 inclusive.
Salary rates—$1620, $1740.

Stable Foreman (Bureau of Street Cleaning, Queens), Stable Foreman (Bureau of Street Cleaning, Richmond):

Range of annual compensation—$1140 to $1440 inclusive.
Salary rates—$1140, $1200, $1260, $1320, $1380, $1440.

SPECIAL CONDITION GOVERNING ADVANCEMENT—

The following table indicates the minimum number of years of meritorious service required at each rate before advancement to the next rate. See also page 30.

Stable Foreman (Department of Street Cleaning):

$1200	1 year
1260	1 "
1320	1 "
1380	1 "
1440	2 years
1500	2 "
1560	2 "

Stable Foreman (Bureau of Street Cleaning, Queens), Stable Foreman (Bureau of Street Cleaning, Richmond):

$1140	1 year
1200	1 "
1260	1 "
1320	1 "
1380	1 "

REFUSE DISPOSER GROUP

SYMBOL (S D)

The term Refuse Disposer Group is applied to those offices or employments of the Street Cleaning Service in which incumbents are required to assist in or to direct, supervise or report on the operation of a dump, transfer or disposal point.

---

[1]The rates of $1560 and $1620 are to be paid only to Foremen in charge of the largest stables.

GRADE 1 (S D 1)

TITLES OF POSITIONS—

BOARDMAN (DEPARTMENT OF STREET CLEANING)
BOARDMAN (BUREAU OF STREET CLEANING, QUEENS)

DUTIES—

Boardman (Department of Street Cleaning):

The duties of Boardmen (Department of Street Cleaning) are to assist in and to record minor information relative to the operation of dumps, transfer or disposal points and in case of emergency to perform temporarily such other duties as may be assigned.

Boardman (Bureau of Street Cleaning, Queens):

The duties of Boardmen (Bureau of Street Cleaning, Queens), are to perform or to supervise the work of leveling and disinfecting dumps, transfer or disposal points and to direct the unloading of carts.

QUALIFICATIONS—

Boardman (Department of Street Cleaning):

1. A certificate of fitness to perform the duties of Boardman, issued by the School for Recruits of the Department of Street Cleaning.

Boardman (Bureau of Street Cleaning, Queens):

1. Such qualifications as may be required by the Municipal Civil Service Commission.

COMPENSATION—

Range of annual compensation—$840 to $936 inclusive.
Salary rates—$840, $864, $888, $912, $936.

Persons temporarily employed as Boardmen, designated as Extra Boardmen, shall receive a per diem rate of 1-313 of the minimum annual rate prescribed for the position of Boardman.

Boardmen assigned in charge of section stations or yards and employed every day in the year shall receive a flat rate of $840.

SPECIAL CONDITION GOVERNING ADVANCEMENT—

The following table indicates the minimum number of years of meritorious service required at each rate before advancement to the next rate. See also page 30.

$840	1 year
864	1 "
888	2 years
912	2 "

GRADE 2 (S D 2)

TITLES OF POSITIONS—

ASSISTANT DUMP INSPECTOR (DEPARTMENT OF STREET CLEANING)
ASSISTANT DUMP INSPECTOR (BUREAU OF STREET CLEANING, QUEENS)

DUTIES—

Assistant Dump Inspector (Department of Street Cleaning):

The duties of Assistant Dump Inspectors (Department of Street Cleaning) are to execute definite instructions from Dump Inspectors relative to the operation of a dump, transfer or disposal point, or relative to the recording of information, and to perform the duties of Dump Inspectors in their absence.

Assistant Dump Inspector (Bureau of Street Cleaning, Queens):

The duties of Assistant Dump Inspectors (Bureau of Street Cleaning, Queens) are to execute definite instructions from Dump Inspectors relative to the inspection of a dump, transfer or disposal point, and to all reporting incident to its operation.

QUALIFICATIONS—

1. The minimum qualifications prescribed for Grade 1 of the Refuse Collector, Refuse Disposer or Street Cleaner Group, or for Motor Truck Driver in Grade 2 of the Motor Refuse Collector Group.

2. Not less than three years of appropriate experience in Grade 1 of the Refuse Collector, Refuse Disposer or Street Cleaner Group, or as Motor Truck Driver in Grade 2 of the Motor Refuse Collector Group.

3. Such additional qualifications as may be required by the Municipal Civil Service Commission.

COMPENSATION—

Assistant Dump Inspector (Department of Street Cleaning):

Range of annual compensation—$1020 to $1140 inclusive.
Salary rates—$1020, $1080, $1140.

Assistant Dump Inspector (Bureau of Street Cleaning, Queens):

Range of annual compensation—$1020 to $1080 inclusive.
Salary rates—$1020, $1080.

SPECIAL CONDITION GOVERNING ADVANCEMENT—

The following table indicates the minimum number of years of meritorious service required at each rate before advancement to the next rate. See also page 30.

$1020	1 year
1080	2 years

GRADE 3 (S D 3)

TITLES OF POSITIONS—

DUMP INSPECTOR (DEPARTMENT OF STREET CLEANING)
DUMP INSPECTOR (BUREAU OF STREET CLEANING, QUEENS)

DUTIES—

Dump Inspector (Department of Street Cleaning):

The duties of Dump Inspectors (Department of Street Cleaning), which involve responsibility for the operation of a dump, transfer or disposal point, are to execute definite instructions relative to the supervision, inspection and recording of the dumping of loads and the loading, shifting, recording and removing of scows or other conveyances, or on assignment, to act as Assistant District Superintendent.

Dump Inspector (Bureau of Street Cleaning, Queens):

The duties of Dump Inspectors (Bureau of Street Cleaning, Queens) are to inspect dumps, transfer or disposal points, and to make reports as to their general condition, the men on duty and the kind of material deposited.

QUALIFICATIONS—

1. The minimum qualifications prescribed for Grade 2 of the Refuse Collector, Refuse Disposer or Street Cleaner Group.

2. Not less than one year of appropriate experience in Grade 2 of the Refuse Collector, Refuse Disposer or Street Cleaner Group.

3. Such additional qualifications as may be required by the Municipal Civil Service Commission.

COMPENSATION—

Dump Inspector (Department of Street Cleaning):

Range of annual compensation—$1200 to $1500 inclusive.
Salary rates—$1200, $1260, $1320, $1380, $1440, $1500.

Dump Inspector (Department of Street Cleaning) assigned as Assistant District Superintendent:

Range of annual compensation—$1620 to $1740 inclusive.
Salary rates—$1620, $1740.

Dump Inspector (Bureau of Street Cleaning, Queens):

Range of annual compensation—$1140 to $1440 inclusive.
Salary rates—$1140, $1200, $1260, $1320, $1380, $1440.

SPECIAL CONDITION GOVERNING ADVANCEMENT—

The following table indicates the minimum number of years of meritorious service required at each rate before advancement to the next rate. See also page 30.

Dump Inspector (Department of Street Cleaning):

$1200	1 year
1260	1 "
1320	1 "
1380	1 "
1440	2 years

Dump Inspector (Bureau of Street Cleaning, Queens):

$1140	1 year
1200	1 "
1260	1 "
1320	1 "
1380	1 "

STREET CLEANER GROUP

SYMBOL (S C)

The term Street Cleaner Group is applied to those offices or employments of the Street Cleaning Service in which incumbents are required to clean streets, to separate, collect and remove refuse or to collect and remove dirt and snow, or to supervise, inspect or report on this work.

GRADE 1 (S C 1)

TITLES OF POSITIONS—

SWEEPER (DEPARTMENT OF STREET CLEANING)
SWEEPER (BUREAU OF STREET CLEANING, QUEENS)
SWEEPER (BUREAU OF STREET CLEANING, RICHMOND)

DUTIES—

The duties of incumbents of these positions are to clean the streets, to remove dirt, refuse and snow by the use of brooms, hand scrapers, hose or other equipment, and in case of emergency to perform temporarily such other duties as may be assigned.

In addition the duties of Sweepers (Bureau of Street Cleaning, Richmond) include the making of light repairs on macadam roads.

QUALIFICATIONS—

Sweeper (Department of Street Cleaning):

1. A certificate of fitness to perform the duties of Sweeper, issued by the School for Recruits of the Department of Street Cleaning.

Sweeper (Bureau of Street Cleaning, Queens), Sweeper (Bureau of Street Cleaning, Richmond):

1. Such qualifications as may be required by the Municipal Civil Service Commission.

COMPENSATION—

Range of annual compensation—$792 to $888 inclusive.

Salary rates—$792, $816, $840, $864, $888.

Persons temporarily employed as Sweepers, designated as Extra Sweepers, shall receive a per diem rate of 1-313 of the minimum annual rate prescribed for the position of Sweeper.

Sweepers employed on flushing work shall receive an additional compensation of 15c. per diem.

Sweepers assigned in charge of section stations or yards and employed every day in the year shall receive a flat rate of $840.

SPECIAL CONDITION GOVERNING ADVANCEMENT—

The following table indicates the minimum number of years of meritorious service required at each rate before advancement to the next rate. See also page 30.

$792	1 year
816	1 "
840	2 years
864	2 "

GRADE 2 (S C 2)

TITLES OF POSITIONS—

ASSISTANT SECTION FOREMAN (DEPARTMENT OF STREET CLEANING)
ASSISTANT SECTION FOREMAN (BUREAU OF STREET CLEANING, QUEENS)

DUTIES—

The duties of incumbents of these positions are to execute definite instructions from Section Foremen relative to the supervision, inspection and reporting of the cleaning of streets, the separation, collection and removal of refuse, or the collection and removal of dirt and snow, and to perform the duties of Section Foremen in their absence.

In addition the duties of Assistant Section Foremen (Bureau of Street Cleaning, Queens) include the supervision, inspection and reporting of the disposal of dirt, refuse and snow.

QUALIFICATIONS—

1. The minimum qualifications prescribed for Grade 1 of the Refuse Collector, Refuse Disposer or Street Cleaner Group, or for Motor Truck Driver in Grade 2 of the Motor Refuse Collector Group.
2. Not less than three years of appropriate experience in Grade 1 of the Refuse Collector, Refuse Disposer or Street Cleaner Group, or as Motor Truck Driver in Grade 2 of the Motor Refuse Collector Group.
3. Such additional qualifications as may be required by the Municipal Civil Service Commission.

COMPENSATION—

Assistant Section Foreman (Department of Street Cleaning):

Range of annual compensation—$1020 to $1140 inclusive.
Salary rates—$1020, $1080, $1140.

Assistant Section Foreman (Bureau of Street Cleaning, Queens):

Range of annual compensation—$1020 to $1080 inclusive.
Salary rates—$1020, $1080.

SPECIAL CONDITION GOVERNING ADVANCEMENT—

The following table indicates the minimum number of years of meritorious service required at each rate before advancement to the next rate. See also page 30.

$1020	1 year
1080	2 years

GRADE 3 (S C 3)

TITLES OF POSITIONS—

SECTION FOREMAN (DEPARTMENT OF STREET CLEANING)
SECTION FOREMAN (BUREAU OF STREET CLEANING, QUEENS)
SECTION FOREMAN (BUREAU OF STREET CLEANING, RICHMOND)

DUTIES—

The duties of incumbents of these positions, which involve responsibility for all the work of a street cleaning section, are to execute definite instructions from District Superintendents relative to the supervision, inspection and reporting of the cleaning of streets, the separation, collection and removal of refuse and the collection and removal of dirt and snow, or for Section Foremen (Department of Street Cleaning) on assignment, to act as Assistant District Superintendent.

In addition the duties of Section Foremen (Bureau of Street Cleaning, Queens) include the supervision, inspection and reporting of the disposal of dirt, refuse and snow.

The duties of Section Foremen (Bureau of Street Cleaning, Richmond) include the general duties outlined above with the exception of the collection and removal of refuse other than sweepings and dirt.

QUALIFICATIONS—

1. The minimum qualifications prescribed for Grade 2 of the Refuse Collector, Refuse Disposer or Street Cleaner Group.
2. Not less than one year of appropriate experience in Grade 2 of the Refuse Collector, Refuse Disposer or Street Cleaner Group.
3. Such additional qualifications as may be required by the Municipal Civil Service Commission.

COMPENSATION—

Section Foreman (Department of Street Cleaning):

Range of annual compensation—$1200 to $1500 inclusive.
Salary rates—$1200, $1260, $1320, $1380, $1440, $1500.

Section Foreman (Department of Street Cleaning) assigned as Assistant District Superintendent:

Range of annual compensation—$1620 to $1740 inclusive.
Salary rates—$1620, $1740.

Section Foreman (Bureau of Street Cleaning, Queens), Section Foreman (Bureau of Street Cleaning, Richmond):

Range of annual compensation—$1140 to $1440 inclusive.
Salary rates—$1140, $1200, $1260, $1320, $1380, $1440.

SPECIAL CONDITION GOVERNING ADVANCEMENT—

The following table indicates the minimum number of years of meritorious service required at each rate before advancement to the next rate. See also page 30.

Section Foreman (Department of Street Cleaning):

$1200	1 year
1260	1 "
1320	1 "
1380	1 "
1440	2 years

Section Foreman (Bureau of Street Cleaning, Queens), Section Foreman (Bureau of Street Cleaning, Richmond):

$1140	1 year
1200	1 "
1260	1 "
1320	1 "
1380	1 "

SUPERVISOR GROUP

SYMBOL (S S)

The term Supervisor Group is applied to those offices or employments of the Street Cleaning Service in which incumbents are required to supervise either a specialized function or the routine work of the Department of Street Cleaning, or of the Bureau of Street Cleaning in Queens or Richmond, within the limits of a district, a borough, or the city, including the cleaning of streets, the collection, removal, transfer and disposal of refuse or snow, the removal of encumbrances from streets, and the inspection and care of all property belonging to the department.

GRADE 1 (S S 1)

TITLES OF POSITIONS—

DISTRICT SUPERINTENDENT (BUREAU OF STREET CLEANING, QUEENS)

DISTRICT SUPERINTENDENT (BUREAU OF STREET CLEANING, RICHMOND)[1]

DUTIES—

District Superintendent (Bureau of Street Cleaning, Queens):

The duties of District Superintendents (Bureau of Street Cleaning, Queens) are to be responsible for the regular operations of the Bureau of Street Cleaning within the limits of a district, including the supervision, inspection and reporting of the work of cleaning streets, the separation, collection, removal and dumping of dirt, refuse or snow, and the inspection and care of property belonging to the department, except in so far as any of the above work shall be assigned to other officers.

---

[1]The former title of the District Superintendent (Bureau of Street Cleaning, Richmond) was Inspector.

District Superintendent (Bureau of Street Cleaning, Richmond):

The duties of District Superintendents (Bureau of Street Cleaning, Richmond) are to be responsible for the regular operations of the Bureau of Street Cleaning within the limits of a district, including the supervision, inspection and reporting of the work of cleaning streets, the collection, removal and dumping of sweepings, dirt and snow, the removal of encumbrances from the streets, and the inspection and care of property belonging to the department, except in so far as any of the above work shall be assigned to other officers; or when so assigned, to take charge of the operation of stables, the collection and removal of refuse other than sweepings or dirt and special work on destructors.

QUALIFICATIONS—

1. Such qualifications as may be required by the Municipal Civil Service Commission.

COMPENSATION—

District Superintendent (Bureau of Street Cleaning, Queens):

Range of annual compensation—$1620 to $1920 inclusive.
Salary rates—$1620, $1740, $1920.

District Superintendent (Bureau of Street Cleaning, Richmond):

Range of annual compensation—$1500 to $1740 inclusive.
Salary rates—$1500, $1620, $1740.

SPECIAL REGULATION GOVERNING COMPENSATION—

Beginning with the lowest rate, advancement within this grade is conditional upon appraisal under the rules of the Board of Estimate and Apportionment, indicating that the rate requested does not exceed the value of the work to be performed.

SPECIAL CONDITION GOVERNING ADVANCEMENT—

The following table indicates the minimum number of years of meritorious service required at each rate before advancement to the next rate. See also page 30.

District Superintendent (Bureau of Street Cleaning, Queens):

$1620	1 year
1740	2 years

District Superintendent (Bureau of Street Cleaning, Richmond):

$1500	1 year
1620	2 years

GRADE 2 (SS2)

TITLES OF POSITIONS—

DISTRICT SUPERINTENDENT (DEPARTMENT OF STREET CLEANING)
ASSISTANT SUPERINTENDENT OF FINAL DISPOSITION (DEPARTMENT OF STREET CLEANING)
ASSISTANT SUPERINTENDENT OF SNOW REMOVAL (DEPARTMENT OF STREET CLEANING)
ASSISTANT SUPERINTENDENT (BUREAU OF STREET CLEANING, RICHMOND)

DUTIES—

District Superintendent (Department of Street Cleaning):

The duties of District Superintendents (Department of Street Cleaning) are to be responsible for the regular operations of the Department of Street Cleaning within the limits of a district, including the supervision, inspection and reporting of the work of cleaning streets, the separation, collection, removal and dumping of dirt, refuse or snow, the removal of encumbrances from the streets, and the inspection and care of property belonging to the department, except in so far as any of the above work shall be assigned to other officers; or when under special assignment, to act as Borough Superintendent in The Bronx, to assist the Deputy Commissioner in charge of that borough in all matters of policy in the operations of the Department of Street Cleaning and to be responsible for the routine operations of the department within the limits of that borough; or to act as Superintendent of Inspection and Instruction and to be responsible for the investigation and inspection of the routine work of the Department of Street Cleaning and for the instruction of department forces in routine or special operations carried on by the department, including the management of the School for Recruits; or to act as Assistant to the Superintendent of Inspection and Instruction.

Assistant Superintendent of Final Disposition (Department of Street Cleaning):

The duties of the Assistant Superintendent of Final Disposition (Department of Street Cleaning) are to assist the Superintendent of Final Disposition, to be responsible for the performance of assigned duties and to carry on the work of the Superintendent of Final Disposition during his absence.

Assistant Superintendent of Snow Removal (Department of Street Cleaning):

The duties of the Assistant Superintendent of Snow Removal (Department of Street Cleaning), which are performed in the central office and are subject to the direction of the Superintendent of Snow Removal, are to be responsible for routine operations involved in the direction and recording of the work of snow fighting and snow removal, to perform the duties of the Superintendent of Snow Removal during his absence and to assist him in all matters relating to such work, including the preparation, assignment, distribution and recording of special equipment or supplies used in snow removal, the transmission of orders, the receiving and recording of reports, the calculation of quantities and the supervision of the central office force engaged in the above work.[1]

Assistant Superintendent (Bureau of Street Cleaning, Richmond):

The duties of the Assistant Superintendent (Bureau of Street Cleaning, Richmond) are to assist the Superintendent (Bureau of Street Cleaning, Richmond), to be responsible for the performance of assigned duties, and to carry on the work of the Superintendent during his absence.

QUALIFICATIONS—

District Superintendent (Department of Street Cleaning), Assistant Superintendent of Final Disposition (Department of Street Cleaning), Assistant Superintendent of Snow Removal (Department of Street Cleaning):

1. The minimum qualifications prescribed for Grade 3 of the Refuse Collector, Refuse Disposer or Street Cleaner Groups.

2. If appointed by promotion, not less than one year of appropriate experience in Grade 3 of the Refuse Collector, Refuse Disposer or Street Cleaner Groups, or if appointed as the result of an open competitive examination, experience in work of the character and standard of those grades.

3. Such additional qualifications as may be required by the Municipal Civil Service Commission.

---

[1]A Section Foreman, Stable Foreman or Dump Inspector may be designated to assist the Assistant Superintendent of Snow Removal (Department of Street Cleaning) in recording facts regarding snow fighting and snow removal, distributing special stationery and acting for the Assistant Superintendent of Snow Removal in his absence.

Assistant Superintendent (Bureau of Street Cleaning, Richmond):

1. The minimum qualifications prescribed for Grade 1.
2. If appointed by promotion, not less than one year of appropriate experience in Grade 1, or if appointed as the result of an open competitive examination, experience in work of the character and standard of Grade 1.
3. Such additional qualifications as may be required by the Municipal Civil Service Commission.

COMPENSATION—

Range of annual compensation—$1920 to $2460 inclusive.

Salary rates—$1920, $2100, $2280, $2460.

A special rate of $2580 shall be paid to the District Superintendent (Department of Street Cleaning) who is assigned as Borough Superintendent of The Bronx and to the District Superintendent (Department of Street Cleaning) who is assigned as Superintendent of Inspection and Instruction.

SPECIAL REGULATION GOVERNING COMPENSATION—

Beginning with the lowest rate, advancement within this grade is conditional upon appraisal under the rules of the Board of Estimate and Apportionment, indicating that the rate requested does not exceed the value of the work to be performed.

SPECIAL CONDITION GOVERNING ADVANCEMENT—

The following table indicates the minimum number of years of meritorious service required at each rate before advancement to the next rate. See also page 30.

$1920	1 year
2100	2 years
2280	2 "

GRADE 3 (S S 3)

TITLES OF POSITIONS—

ASSISTANT GENERAL SUPERINTENDENT (DEPARTMENT OF STREET CLEANING)

BOROUGH SUPERINTENDENT (DEPARTMENT OF STREET CLEANING, BROOKLYN)

SUPERINTENDENT OF FINAL DISPOSITION (DEPARTMENT OF STREET CLEANING)

SUPERINTENDENT (BUREAU OF STREET CLEANING, QUEENS)[1]

SUPERINTENDENT (BUREAU OF STREET CLEANING, RICHMOND)[1]

DUTIES—

Assistant General Superintendent (Department of Street Cleaning):

The duties of the Assistant General Superintendent (Department of Street Cleaning) are to assist the General Superintendent (Department of Street Cleaning) in the work devolving upon him as head of the uniformed force and in the supervision of all operations of the Department of Street Cleaning within the Borough of Manhattan.

Borough Superintendent (Department of Street Cleaning, Brooklyn):

The duties of the Borough Superintendent (Department of Street Cleaning, Brooklyn) are to assist the Deputy Commissioner in charge of the Borough of Brooklyn in all matters of policy in the operations of the Department of Street Cleaning and to be responsible for the routine operations of the department within the limits of that borough.

---

[1]This position is at present exempt. It is recommended that it be placed in the competitive class.

Superintendent of Final Disposition (Department of Street Cleaning):

The duties of the Superintendent of Final Disposition (Department of Street Cleaning) are to be responsible for the proper removal and disposal of refuse delivered at dumping or disposal points and for the supervising, recording and reporting of disposal work done by the department or by contractors.

Superintendent (Bureau of Street Cleaning, Queens):

The duties of the Superintendent (Bureau of Street Cleaning, Queens) are to be responsible for the routine operations of the bureau within that borough, including the supervision, inspection and reporting of the work of cleaning streets, the separation, collection, removal and disposal of dirt, refuse or snow, the inspection and care of property belonging to the bureau, and the investigation of complaints, except in so far as any of the above work shall be assigned to other officers.

Superintendent (Bureau of Street Cleaning, Richmond):

The duties of the Superintendent (Bureau of Street Cleaning, Richmond) include those outlined above for Superintendent (Bureau of Street Cleaning, Queens) and in addition, the removal of encumbrances from streets.

QUALIFICATIONS—

Assistant General Superintendent (Department of Street Cleaning), Borough Superintendent (Department of Street Cleaning, Brooklyn), Superintendent of Final Disposition (Department of Street Cleaning):

1. The minimum qualifications prescribed for Grade 2.
2. If appointed by promotion, not less than one year of appropriate experience in Grade 2, or if appointed as the result of an open competitive examination, experience in work of the character and standard of Grade 2.
3. Such additional qualifications as may be required by the Municipal Civil Service Commission.

Superintendent (Bureau of Street Cleaning, Queens), Superintendent (Bureau of Street Cleaning, Richmond):

1. Such qualifications as are outlined in the Charter of the City of New York.
2. Ability to discharge the duties of the position satisfactory to the appointing officer.
3. Such qualifications as may be required by the Municipal Civil Service Commission.

If the position is classified as exempt, the minimum qualifications shall consist of 1 and 2.

If the position is classified as competitive in accordance with the recommendations of the Bureau of Personal Service, the minimum qualifications shall consist of 1 and 3.

COMPENSATION—

Assistant General Superintendent (Department of Street Cleaning), Borough Superintendent (Department of Street Cleaning, Brooklyn), Superintendent of Final Disposition (Department of Street Cleaning):

Range of annual compensation—$2700 to $2940 inclusive.

Salary rates—$2700, $2940.

Superintendent (Bureau of Street Cleaning, Queens), Superintendent (Bureau of Street Cleaning, Richmond):

Range of annual compensation—$2940 to $3180 inclusive.[1]

Salary rates—$2940, $3180.

---

[1]The rates, $2940 to $3180, for Superintendent (Bureau of Street Cleaning, Queens) and Superintendent (Bureau of Street Cleaning, Richmond) apply as long as these bureaus remain units separate from the Department of Street Cleaning. The higher rates are recommended because of the greater independent responsibility of the Superintendent under the borough government.

SPECIAL REGULATION GOVERNING COMPENSATION—

Persons entering this grade need not necessarily begin at the lowest rate. Fixation of the initial salary rate and advancement within this grade are conditional upon appraisal under the rules of the Board of Estimate and Apportionment indicating that the rate requested does not exceed the value of the work to be performed.

GRADE 4 (S S 4)

TITLES OF POSITIONS—

GENERAL SUPERINTENDENT (DEPARTMENT OF STREET CLEANING)

DUTIES—

The duties of the incumbent of this position are to be responsible for work devolving upon him as head of the uniformed force of the Department of Street Cleaning, to act as Borough Superintendent of the Borough of Manhattan and to assist the Commissioner in all matters of policy concerning the uniformed force and in the preparation, transmission and enforcement of orders, charges and instructions.

QUALIFICATIONS—

1. The minimum qualifications prescribed for Grade 3.
2. Not less than one year of appropriate experience in Grade 3, or if appointed as the result of an open competitive examination, experience in work of the character and standard of Grade 3.
3. Such additional qualifications as may be required by the Municipal Civil Service Commission.

COMPENSATION—

Range of annual compensation—$3180 to $3660 inclusive.
Salary rates—$3180, $3420, $3660.

SKILLED TRADES SERVICE

SYMBOL (T)

The term Skilled Trades Service is applied to those offices or employments the duties of whose incumbents are to perform manual work requiring experience and skill in a recognized trade or handicraft or to assist in or supervise the performance of such work.

BOOKBINDER GROUP

SYMBOL (T D)

The term Bookbinder Group is applied to those employments of the Skilled Trades Service in which incumbents are required to bind and repair books or to perform other duties peculiar to the bookbinding trade.

GRADE 1 (T D 1)

TITLES OF POSITIONS—

BOOKBINDER

DUTIES—

The duties of incumbents of these positions are to fold, sew and finish book work, to bind loose leaves, to repair broken binding and torn leaves, to mount maps, to patch and rebind old records, to rule paper, to make filing boxes, on special work to do marbling, gilt-edging and lettering, and to perform such other work as may properly be required of bookbinders.

QUALIFICATIONS—

1. Service as apprentice during the length of time locally stipulated by the trade.
2. Such additional qualifications as may be required by the Municipal Civil Service Commission.

COMPENSATION—

Range of annual compensation—$1140 to $1320 inclusive.
Salary rates—$1140, $1200, $1260, $1320.[1]

SPECIAL REGULATION GOVERNING COMPENSATION—

Beginning with the lowest rate, advancement within this grade is conditional upon appraisal under the rules of the Board of Estimate and Apportionment, indicating that the rate requested does not exceed the value of the work to be performed.

BUILDER GROUP

SYMBOL (T B)

The term Builder Group is applied to those employments of the Skilled Trades Service in which incumbents are required to perform duties pertaining to the bricklaying, cement-mason, flagging, glazing, marble-setting, paving, plastering, ramming, stone-cutting and stone-mason trades.

---

[1]The rates of $1260 and $1320 are established as maximum rates for Bookbinders who perform independently the most difficult and responsible work, such as being responsible for all the work of an important plant.

GRADE 1 (T B 1)

TITLES OF POSITIONS—

BRICKLAYER
CEMENT-MASON
FLAGGER
GLAZIER
MARBLE-SETTER
PAVER
PLASTERER
RAMMERMAN
STONE-CUTTER
STONE-MASON

DUTIES—

Bricklayer:

The duties of Bricklayers are to lay bricks to line and grade in or upon any structure or form of work; to do fireproofing, block arching, terra cotta cutting and setting; to lay and cut tile, plaster, mineral wool and cork blocks or any substitute therefor; to cut, rub and grind brick; to set cut stone trimmings of brick buildings; to perform such other work as may properly be required of bricklayers.

Cement-mason:

The duties of Cement-masons are to lay out, grade and lay cement floors, pavements and sidewalks; to perform such other work as may properly be required of cement-masons.

Flagger:

The duties of Flaggers are to set, reset and firmly bed curbs and flags; to lay cross walks and pavement to line and grade; to perform such other work as may properly be required of flaggers.

Glazier:

The duties of Glaziers are to cut and fit glass for sash, picture and map frames; to install glass, sash cord and sash chains; to putty and re-putty sash whenever necessary; to perform such other work as may properly be required of glaziers.

Marble-setter:

The duties of Marble-setters are to set marble, slate stone, glass and artificial imitations of the same; to set the interior marble work in buildings; to perform such other work as may properly be required of marble-setters.

Paver:

The duties of Pavers are to lay pavement; to keep the course of stone or wood blocks even and straight; to break joints properly and to make closure; to fit pavement around manholes and water gates; to regulate sand cushions to the required crown of street; to perform such other work as may properly be required of pavers.

Plasterer:

The duties of Plasterers are to do interior or exterior plastering, plain or ornamental, with stucco, cement and lime mortars or patent materials; to do artificial marble work and composition work in all its branches; to cover walls, ceilings, piers, columns, or any part of a construction with any plastic material; to perform such other work as may properly be required of plasterers.

Rammerman:

The duties of Rammermen are to ram down stone to a solid base; to regulate the finished surface; to give all necessary assistance to the paver; to perform such other work as may properly be required of rammermen.

Stone-cutter:

The duties of Stone-cutters are to cut, dress, joint and set granite, limestone or other hard stone for curbs, sills, walls, steps, arches, lintels and building blocks; to perform other repair or new work, including street work and rock faced ashlar; to do polishing; to make up, sharpen or dress tools by hand or machine; to perform such other work as may properly be required of stone-cutters.

Stone-mason:

The duties of Stone-masons are to lay rubble work with or without mortar; to set cut stone, marble, slate or manufactured stone; to cut shoddies or roughly dressed ashlar; to dress jambs, corner stones and ringstones; to clean and point stone work; to cut, set and point cement blocks or artificial stone; to do repair work; to perform such other work as may properly be required of stone-masons.

QUALIFICATIONS—

1. Service as apprentice during the length of time locally stipulated by the respective trade.
2. Such additional qualifications as may be required by the Municipal Civil Service Commission.

COMPENSATION—

The per diem compensation for work performed in this grade shall be the prevailing rate of wages for these occupations as provided by Section 3 of Article 2 of the New York State Labor Law. The following rates appear to be the prevailing rates at the present time:[1]

Bricklayer	$6.00	per	day,	8 hours
Cement-mason	5.30	"	"	"
Flagger	4.50	"	"	"
Glazier	4.00	"	"	"
Marble-setter	5.50	"	"	"
Paver	5.00	"	"	"
Plasterer	5.50	"	"	"
Rammerman	4.00	"	"	"
Stone-cutter	5.00	"	"	"
Stone-mason	5.00	"	"	"

DIVER GROUP

SYMBOL (T V)

The term Diver Group is applied to those employments of the Skilled Trades Service in which incumbents are required to perform or to assist in the performance of submarine investigation or other work requiring the use of a diver's equipment.

GRADE 1 (T V 1)

TITLES OF POSITIONS—

ASSISTANT DIVER

DUTIES—

The duties of incumbents of these positions are to adjust, remove and under direction to repair diver's apparatus; to hold the air supply pipe; to receive from and convey to the diver, while under water, by means of signal rope any instructions necessary; and to supervise the work of employes operating the air pump.

[1]Persons working under these titles may be paid the prevailing rate only when employed on the duties prescribed above.

QUALIFICATIONS—

1. Experience in operating air pumps for divers.

2. Such additional qualifications as may be required by the Municipal Civil Service Commission.

COMPENSATION—

Per diem rate—$3.50.

GRADE 2 (T V 2)

TITLES OF POSITIONS—

DIVER

DUTIES—

The duties of incumbents of these positions, which are performed under the direction of chief divers or engineers, are to explore or gather objects under water; to handle a suction pump for removing debris; to arrange explosives for blasting; to place materials for foundations; to perform such other work as may properly be required of divers.

QUALIFICATIONS—

1. The minimum qualifications prescribed for Grade 1.

2. If appointed by promotion, not less than two years of appropriate experience in Grade 1, or if appointed as the result of an open competitive examination, experience in work of the character and standard of Grade 1.

3. Such additional qualifications as may be required by the Municipal Civil Service Commission.

COMPENSATION—

Hourly rate—$1.25.

GRADE 3 (T V 3)

TITLES OF POSITIONS—

CHIEF DIVER

DUTIES—

The duties of incumbents of these positions are to assign and supervise the work of employes in Grades 1 and 2, to inspect and oversee the purchase of divers' apparel, to arrange explosives and when necessary to perform independently the most difficult and responsible submarine investigations.

QUALIFICATIONS—

1. The minimum qualifications prescribed for Grade 2.

2. If appointed by promotion, not less than three years of appropriate experience in Grade 2, or if appointed as the result of an open competitive examination, experience in work of the character and standard of Grade 2.

3. Such additional qualifications as may be required by the Municipal Civil Service Commission.

COMPENSATION—

Range of annual compensation—$1620 to $1920 inclusive.
Salary rates—$1620, $1740, $1920.

SPECIAL REGULATION GOVERNING COMPENSATION—

Beginning with the lowest rate, advancement within this grade is conditional upon appraisal under the rules of the Board of Estimate and Apportionment, indicating that the rate requested does not exceed the value of the work to be performed.

SPECIAL CONDITION GOVERNING ADVANCEMENT—

The following table indicates the minimum number of years of meritorious service required at each rate before advancement to the next rate. See also page 30.

$1620	2 years
1740	2 "

ELECTRICAL WORKER GROUP

SYMBOL (T E)

The term Electrical Worker Group is applied to those employments of the Skilled Trades Service in which incumbents are required to perform work not requiring professional education or training in the installation, operation and repair of electrical equipment.

GRADE 1 (T E 1)

TITLES OF POSITIONS[1]—

BATTERYMAN
CRANEMAN
LINEMAN
WIREMAN

DUTIES—

Batteryman:

The duties of Batterymen are to charge and repair storage batteries, fire alarm boxes and other batteries.

Craneman:

The duties of Cranemen are to operate and make minor repairs to electric cranes.

Lineman:

The duties of Linemen are to erect, climb and remove poles and to run cables and wires overhead or underground.

Wireman:

The duties of Wiremen are to do wiring for electric bells, lights and motors and other interior wire and conduit work.

QUALIFICATIONS—

1. Service as apprentice during the length of time locally stipulated by the trade.
2. Such additional qualifications as may be required by the Municipal Civil Service Commission.

---

[1]The incumbents of a number of positions as Lineman, Wireman and Batteryman are at present performing the duties of Electricians. The positions of Lineman, Wireman and Batteryman are classified by the Municipal Civil Service Commission in the labor class. The position of Electrician is a higher position in the competitive class. In order to perform work proper to their titles and to receive the prevailing rate for Electricians, it will be necessary for Linemen, Wiremen and Batterymen who perform Electricians' work to take a promotion examination for Electrician. Three years of service in the labor class is required before promotion to the competitive class. It is not desirable in future to fill existing positions or create new positions as Wireman.

COMPENSATION—

Regular Service Exclusive of Sundays:

Batteryman, Lineman, Wireman:

Range of annual compensation—$960 to $1140 inclusive.
Salary rates—$960, $1020, $1080, $1140.

Craneman:

Range of annual compensation—$900 to $1080 inclusive.
Salary rates—$900, $960, $1020, $1080.

Temporary Service:

Batteryman, Craneman, Lineman, Wireman:

Per diem compensation—$3.

GRADE 2 (T E 2)

TITLES OF POSITIONS[1]—

BATTERY CONSTRUCTOR
CABLE SPLICER
ELECTRICIAN
FOREMAN LINEMAN

DUTIES—

Battery Constructor:

The duties of Battery Constructors, which require a thorough knowledge of automobile and other types of batteries, are to construct and repair starting, lighting and ignition batteries.

Cable Splicer:

The duties of Cable Splicers are to splice electric cables, to assist in their installation and to perform such other work as may properly be required of Cable Splicers.

Electrician:

The duties of Electricians are to install electric appliances, to set and repair meters, to install and repair motors, dynamos, switchboards, electric fans and other electric fixtures, to assemble and repair electric machines and to perform such other work as may properly be required of Electricians.

Foreman Lineman:

The duties of Foremen Linemen, which involve supervision of the work of Linemen in Grade 1 and of other employes, are to be responsible for the erection and removal of poles and the stringing of wires and cables.

QUALIFICATIONS—

1. The minimum qualifications prescribed for Grade 1.
2. If appointed by promotion, not less than three years of appropriate experience in Grade 1, or if appointed as the result of an open competitive examination, experience in work of the character and standard of Grade 1.
3. Such additional qualifications as may be required by the Municipal Civil Service Commission.

COMPENSATION—

Regular Service Exclusive of Sundays:

Cable Splicer, Foreman Lineman:

Range of annual compensation—$1260 to $1440 inclusive.
Salary rates—$1260, $1320, $1380, $1440.

---

[1]See note on Grade 1.

Regular Service Exclusive of Sundays, Holidays and Saturday Afternoons:

Cable Splicer, Foreman Lineman:

Range of annual compensation—$1140 to $1320 inclusive.

Salary rates—$1140, $1200, $1260, $1320.

Per Diem Rates:

Battery Constructor, Electrician:

The per diem compensation for work performed in this grade shall be the prevailing rate of wages for these occupations as provided by Section 3 of Article 2 of the New York State Labor Law. The following rates appear to be the prevailing rates at the present time:[1]

Battery Constructor	$5.00 per day, 8 hours
Electrician	5.20 " " "

GRADE 3 (T E 3)

TITLES OF POSITIONS—

FOREMAN CABLE SPLICER
FOREMAN ELECTRICIAN

DUTIES—

Foreman Cable Splicer:

The duties of Foremen Cable Splicers, which involve supervision of Cable Splicers in Grade 2, are to be responsible for the proper splicing and installation of electric cables.

Foreman Electrician:

The duties of Foremen Electricians, which involve supervision of the work of employes in Grades 1 and 2, are to be responsible for the proper installation, maintenance and repair of electric appliances, machinery, wires and equipment.

QUALIFICATIONS—

1. The minimum qualifications prescribed for Grade 2.
2. If appointed by promotion, not less than three years of appropriate experience in Grade 2, or if appointed as the result of an open competitive examination, experience in work of the character and standard of Grade 2.
3. Such additional qualifications as may be required by the Municipal Civil Service Commission.

COMPENSATION—

Foreman Cable Splicer, Foreman Electrician:

Regular Service Every Day in the Year:

Annual compensation[2]—$1920.

Regular Service Exclusive of Sundays:

Annual compensation[2]—$1680.

Regular Service Exclusive of Sundays, Holidays and Saturday Afternoons:

Annual compensation[2]—$1500.

Foreman Electrician:

Temporary Service:

Per diem compensation[3]—$5.50.

---

[1]Persons working under these titles may be paid the prevailing rates only when employed on the duties prescribed above.

[2]Where work will last continuously throughout the year, the annual rate shall be paid.

[3]Where work is temporary and will not last continuously throughout the year, the daily rate shall be paid.

ENGINEMAN GROUP

SYMBOL (T G)

The term Engineman Group is applied to those employments of the Skilled Trades Service in which incumbents are required to operate and repair all machinery used in the production of light, heat and power for buildings, power for steam rollers, large cranes, or for hoisting and pile driving, or to supervise such work.[1]

GRADE 1 (T G 1)

TITLES OF POSITIONS—

FIREMAN
OILER

DUTIES—

Fireman:

The duties of Firemen are to maintain proper pressure in boilers; to do such cleaning and painting work as is required to keep the boilers and boiler room in proper condition; to see that the proper quantity of water is pumped into the boilers; to perform such other related work as may be assigned by the Engineman.

Oiler:

The duties of Oilers are to oil and clean machinery, to clean engine rooms, to assist in repair work and to perform such other related work as may be assigned by the Engineman.

QUALIFICATIONS—

1. Such qualifications as may be required by the Municipal Civil Service Commission.

COMPENSATION—

The per diem compensation for work performed in this grade shall be the prevailing rate of wages for these occupations as provided by Section 3 of Article 2 of the New York State Labor Law. The following rates appear to be the prevailing rates at the present time:[2]

Fireman	$3.00 per day,	8 hours
Fireman employed on pile driving[3]	3.50 " "	8 "
Oiler	3.00 " "	8 "

GRADE 2 (T G 2)

TITLES OF POSITIONS—

ENGINEMAN
ENGINEMAN (PILE DRIVING AND HOISTING)
ENGINEMAN (STEAM ROLLER)

DUTIES—

Engineman:

The duties of Enginemen, which involve supervision of firemen or laborers, are to operate and repair boilers, engines or other equipment used in the lighting, heating, ventilating, refrigeration and elevator service of a building, or in the development of power for a pumping station, or in hoisting or drilling.

[1]See also Janitor-Engineman and Senior Janitor-Engineman in Grades 3 and 4 of the Caretaker Group of the Custodial Service.

[2]Persons working under these titles may be paid the prevailing rate only when employed on the duties prescribed above.

[3]The higher rate of $3.50 per day for Firemen employed on pile-driving work is recommended because of the seasonal character of the work.

Engineman (Pile Driving and Hoisting):

The duties of Enginemen (Pile Driving and Hoisting) are to operate and repair engines, boilers and pumps used in pile driving and to operate boilers with drill or hoister attachment.

Engineman (Steam Roller):

The duties of Enginemen (Steam Roller) are to operate and repair steam rollers used in the construction and maintenance of asphalt and macadam roads.

QUALIFICATIONS—

1. A license granted by the State of New York to work as a licensed stationary engineer.

2. Such additional qualifications as may be required by the Municipal Civil Service Commission.

COMPENSATION—

The per diem compensation for work performed in this grade shall be the prevailing rate of wages for these occupations as provided by Section 3 of Article 2 of the New York State Labor Law. The following rates appear to be the prevailing rates at the present time:[1]

Engineman	$4.50	per day,	8	hours
Engineman (Pile Driving and Hoisting)	5.50	" "	8	"
Engineman (Steam Roller)	5.50	" "	8	"

GRADE 3 (T G 3)

TITLES OF POSITIONS[2]—

SUPERVISING ENGINEMAN

DUTIES—

The duties of incumbents of these positions, which involve supervision of at least two or more Enginemen in Grade 2, and of firemen, stokers, artisans, helpers and other employes, and which may or may not involve covering one shift, are to supervise and be responsible for the installation, operation and maintenance of boilers, engines and other equipment used in the lighting, heating, ventilating, refrigeration, sewage and elevator service of the largest buildings or groups of buildings, and where required to be responsible for the care and upkeep of institutional buildings and grounds or for the development of power in the largest pumping stations, or in small groups of pumping stations.[3]

---

[1]Persons working under these titles may be paid the prevailing rate only when employed on the duties prescribed above.

[2]The following positions are among those appraised by the Bureau of Personal Service in this grade on the basis of duties performed by present incumbents:

- Supervising Engineman in the Municipal Building.
- Supervising Engineman in the Hall of Records.
- Supervising Engineman in the Kingston Avenue Hospital, Kings County Hospital, Metropolitan Hospital, City Hospital.
- Supervising Engineman in charge of the Ridgewood Station or in charge of pumping stations of the Department of Water Supply, Gas and Electricity, in the Borough of Richmond. (When Catskill water is furnished to all boroughs, this position may be abolished. The last three phrases of the duties definition may then be omitted, as no pumping stations will be required.)

[3]See also Janitor-Engineman and Senior Janitor-Engineman in Grades 3 and 4 of the Caretaker Group of the Custodial Service.

QUALIFICATIONS—

1. The minimum qualifications prescribed for Grade 2.

2. If appointed by promotion, not less than one year of appropriate experience in Grade 2, or if appointed as the result of an open competitive examination, experience in work of the character and standard of Grade 2.

3. Such additional qualifications as may be required by the Municipal Civil Service Commission.

COMPENSATION—

Supervising Engineman in Charge of a Large Plant or Institution Not Covering a Shift:

Range of annual compensation without maintenance—$1740 to $2100 inclusive.
Salary rates—$1740, $1920, $2100.
Range of annual compensation with maintenance—$1320 to $1560 inclusive.
Salary rates—$1320, $1440, $1560.

Supervising Engineman Covering One Shift in a Smaller Building or Institution:

Range of annual compensation without maintenance—$1620 to $1920 inclusive.
Salary rates—$1620, $1740, $1920.
Range of annual compensation with maintenance—$1200 to $1440 inclusive.
Salary rates—$1200, $1320, $1440.

Supervising Engineman in Charge of a Large Pumping Station or a Small Group of Pumping Stations:

Range of annual compensation without maintenance—$1620 to $2100 inclusive.
Salary rates—$1620, $1740, $1920, $2100.

SPECIAL REGULATION GOVERNING COMPENSATION—

Beginning with the lowest rate, advancement within this grade is conditional upon appraisal under the rules of the Board of Estimate and Apportionment, indicating that the rate requested does not exceed the value of the work to be performed.

SPECIAL CONDITION GOVERNING ADVANCEMENT—

The following table indicates the minimum number of years of meritorious service required at each rate before advancement to the next rate. See also page 30.

Supervising Engineman in Charge of a Large Plant or Institution Not Covering a Shift:

$1740	$1320	1 year
1920	1440	2 years

Supervising Engineman Covering One Shift in a Smaller Building or Institution:

$1620	$1200	1 year
1740	1320	2 years

Supervising Engineman in Charge of a Large Pumping Station or a Small Group of Pumping Stations:

$1620	1 year
1740	2 years
1920	2 "

GRADE 4 (T G 4)[1]

TITLES OF POSITIONS—

CHIEF ENGINEMAN

DUTIES—

The duties of incumbents of these positions, which involve supervision of employes in Grades 1, 2 and 3, are to supervise and be responsible for the installation, operation and maintenance of boilers, engines and other equipment used in the development of power in a large number of pumping stations.

QUALIFICATIONS—

1. The minimum qualifications prescribed for Grade 3.
2. If appointed by promotion, not less than one year of appropriate experience in Grade 3, or if appointed as the result of an open competitive examination, experience in work of the character and standard of Grade 3.
3. Such additional qualifications as may be required by the Municipal Civil Service Commission.

COMPENSATION—

Range of annual compensation—$2280 to $2460 inclusive.
Salary rates—$2280, $2460.

SPECIAL REGULATION GOVERNING COMPENSATION—

Beginning with the lowest rate, advancement within this grade is conditional upon appraisal under the rules of the Board of Estimate and Apportionment, indicating that the rate requested does not exceed the value of the work to be performed.

SPECIAL CONDITION GOVERNING ADVANCEMENT—

The following table indicates the minimum number of years of meritorious service required at each rate before advancement to the next rate. See also page 30.

$2280 .... 2 years

FIRE TELEGRAPH DESPATCHER GROUP

SYMBOL (T H)

The term Fire Telegraph Despatcher Group is applied to those offices or employments of the Skilled Trades Service in which incumbents are required to receive and despatch fire alarms and other orders incident to the movement of fire companies and equipment and to keep the fire alarm telegraph plant in working order, or to supervise such work.

GRADE 1 (T H 1)

TITLES OF POSITIONS—

FIRE TELEGRAPH DESPATCHER

DUTIES—

The duties of incumbents of these positions are to assist in receiving and despatching fire alarms and other orders incident to the movement of fire companies and fire fighting equipment and in keeping the fire alarm plant in working order.

---

[1]This grade should be abolished when the Catskill aqueduct has been in operation long enough to demonstrate its reliability as a source of water supply. No pumping stations will then be necessary.

QUALIFICATIONS—

1. Evidence of ability to use the Morse telegraphic code and of familiarity with the principles of electric wiring and the installation of electrical apparatus, satisfactory to the Municipal Civil Service Commission.

2. Such additional qualifications as may be required by the Municipal Civil Service Commission.

COMPENSATION—

Manhattan, Brooklyn:

Range of annual compensation—$1200 to $1500 inclusive.
Salary rates—$1200, $1260, $1320, $1380, $1440, $1500.

The Bronx, Queens, Richmond:

Range of annual compensation—$1200 to $1440 inclusive.
Salary rates—$1200, $1260, $1320, $1380, $1440.

SPECIAL REGULATION GOVERNING COMPENSATION—

Beginning with the lowest rate, advancement within this grade is conditional upon appraisal under the rules of the Board of Estimate and Apportionment, indicating that the rate requested does not exceed the value of the work to be performed.

SPECIAL CONDITION GOVERNING ADVANCEMENT—

The following table indicates the minimum number of years of meritorious service required at each rate before advancement to the next rate. See also page 30

$1200	1 year
1260	1 "
1320	1 "
1380	2 years
1440	2 "

GRADE 2 (T H 2)

TITLES OF POSITIONS—

SENIOR FIRE TELEGRAPH DESPATCHER

DUTIES—

The duties of incumbents of these positions, which involve supervision of employes in Grade 1, are to be responsible during a tour for receiving and despatching fire alarms and other orders incident to the movement of fire companies and fire fighting equipment, and for assisting in keeping the fire alarm plant in working order in an entire borough, or to be responsible for the entire receiving and despatching system in the boroughs of The Bronx, Queens and Richmond.

QUALIFICATIONS—

1. The minimum qualifications prescribed for Grade 1.

2. If appointed by promotion, not less than two years of appropriate experience in Grade 1, or if appointed as the result of an open competitive examination, experience in work of the character and standard of Grade 1.

3. Such additional qualifications as may be required by the Municipal Civil Service Commission.

COMPENSATION—

In Charge of Tour, Manhattan, Brooklyn:

Range of annual compensation—$1620 to $1920 inclusive.
Salary rates—$1620, $1740, $1920.

In Charge of Tour, The Bronx, Queens, Richmond:

Range of annual compensation—$1560 to $1680 inclusive.
Salary rates—$1560, $1680.

In Charge of Entire Borough, The Bronx, Queens and Richmond:

Range of annual compensation—$1800 to $1980 inclusive.
Salary rates—$1800, $1980.

SPECIAL REGULATION GOVERNING COMPENSATION—

Beginning with the lowest rate, advancement within this grade is conditional upon appraisal under the rules of the Board of Estimate and Apportionment, indicating that the rate requested does not exceed the value of work to be performed.

SPECIAL CONDITION GOVERNING ADVANCEMENT—

The following table indicates the minimum number of years of meritorious service required at each rate before advancement to the next rate. See also page 30.

$1560	2 years
1620	2 "
1740	2 "
1800	2 "

GRADE 3 (T H 3)

TITLES OF POSITIONS—

CHIEF FIRE TELEGRAPH DESPATCHER

DUTIES—

The duties of incumbents of these positions, which involve supervision of employes in Grades 1 and 2, are to be responsible for the proper despatching of fire alarms and orders incident to the movement of the fire companies and fire fighting equipment of the boroughs of Manhattan and Brooklyn, and for keeping the fire alarm plant in working order, or to transmit necessary signals at sight of large fires and to act as instructor of the fire telegraph despatchers in the department, or to be responsible for the maintenance of the entire fire telegraph system.[1]

QUALIFICATIONS—

1. The minimum qualifications prescribed for Grade 2.
2. If appointed by promotion, not less than two years of appropriate experience in Grade 2, or if appointed as the result of an open competitive examination, experience in work of the character and standard of Grade 2.
3. Such additional qualifications as may be required by the Municipal Civil Service Commission.

COMPENSATION—

Range of annual compensation—$2100 to $2280 inclusive.
Salary rates—$2100, $2280.

SPECIAL REGULATION GOVERNING COMPENSATION—

Beginning with the lowest rate, advancement within this grade is conditional upon appraisal under the rules of the Board of Estimate and Apportionment, indicating that the rate requested does not exceed the value of the work to be performed.

---

[1]The duties of the Chief Fire Telegraph Despatcher in charge of maintenance may also be performed under the title of Superintendent of Maintenance in Grade 4 of the Laborer Group of the Unskilled Service.

SPECIAL CONDITION GOVERNING ADVANCEMENT—

The following table indicates the minimum number of years of meritorious service required at each rate before advancement to the next rate. See also page 30.

$2100 .... 2 years

JOURNEYMAN'S HELPER GROUP

SYMBOL (T J)

The term Journeyman's Helper Group is applied to those employments of the Skilled Trades Service in which incumbents are required to render such assistance to journeymen in skilled trades and to perform such independent work in the trades as may properly be performed by helpers.[1]

GRADE 1 (T J 1)

TITLES OF POSITIONS—

BLACKSMITH'S HELPER
BOOKBINDER'S HELPER
ELECTRICIAN'S HELPER
ELEVATOR MECHANIC'S HELPER
HORSESHOER'S HELPER
MACHINIST'S HELPER
MARBLE-SETTER'S HELPER
MASON'S HELPER
MECHANIC'S HELPER
PLUMBER'S HELPER
STEAMFITTER'S HELPER

DUTIES—

The duties of incumbents of these positions are to assist journeymen in their respective trades and to perform such independent work in those trades as may properly be performed by helpers.

QUALIFICATIONS—

1. Such qualifications as may be required by the Municipal Civil Service Commission.

COMPENSATION—

Range of per diem compensation—$2.80 to $3 inclusive.
Wage rates—$2.80, $2.90, $3.

SPECIAL REGULATION GOVERNING COMPENSATION—

Persons entering this grade need not necessarily begin at the lowest rate. Fixation of the initial salary rate and advancement within this grade are conditional upon appraisal under the rules of the Board of Estimate and Apportionment, indicating that the rate requested does not exceed the value of the work to be performed.

---

[1]No provision is made in these specifications for apprentices, on the assumption that no apprentices are required in the city service and that the city departments are not equipped as training schools for apprentices.

LEATHER WORKER GROUP

SYMBOL (T L)

The term Leather Worker Group is applied to those employments of the Skilled Trades Service in which incumbents are required to perform duties pertaining to the harness-making and shoemaking trades.

GRADE 1 (T L 1)

TITLES OF POSITIONS—

HARNESSMAKER
SHOEMAKER

DUTIES—

Harnessmaker:

The duties of Harnessmakers are to make and repair harness, saddles, collars, horse-boots, or anything made of leather or other fabric which a horse wears; to blacken, grease and rub up harness and saddle parts; to gum and put together harness; to trim gig-saddles and parts; to die out and finish harness and saddle parts; to cut and sew leather and operate a machine; to make halters, lines and traces; to re-line collars; to perform such other work as may properly be required of harnessmakers.

Shoemaker:

The duties of Shoemakers, which may include supervision of the work of inmates of institutions or other helpers, are to heel, sole, patch, mend, or otherwise repair shoes, to make slippers and to perform such other work as may properly be required of shoemakers.

QUALIFICATIONS—

1. Service as apprentice during the length of time locally stipulated by the trade.
2. Such additional qualifications as may be required by the Municipal Civil Service Commission.

COMPENSATION—

The per diem compensation for work performed in this grade shall be the prevailing rate of wages for these occupations as provided by Section 3 of Article 2 of the New York State Labor Law. The following rates appear to be the prevailing rates at the present time:[1]

Harnessmaker	$4.00 per	day,	8 hours
Shoemaker	3.50 "	"	8 "

MARINE ENGINEMAN GROUP

SYMBOL (T N)

The term Marine Engineman Group is applied to those employments of the Skilled Trades Service in which incumbents are required to operate or to assist in the operation of the engineering equipment of steamboats.

---

[1]Persons working under these titles may be paid the prevailing rate only when employed on the duties prescribed above.

GRADE 1 (T N 1)

TITLES OF POSITIONS—

MARINE OILER
MARINE STOKER
MARINE WATER TENDER

DUTIES—

Marine Oiler:

The duties of Marine Oilers are to oil and clean machinery, to clean engine rooms, to assist in repair work and to perform such other related work as may be assigned by a superior officer.

Marine Stoker:

The duties of Marine Stokers are to maintain the proper pressure in steamboat boilers and, when necessary, to do such cleaning and painting work as is required to keep the boilers, boiler rooms and bilges in proper condition; to see that the proper quantity of water is pumped into the boilers; to perform such other related work as may be assigned by a superior officer.

Marine Water Tender:

The duties of Marine Water Tenders are to attend to the water in boilers, to assist and supervise the Marine Stokers in the municipal ferry service and to perform such other related work as may be assigned by a superior officer.

QUALIFICATIONS—

Marine Stoker:

1. Experience as Fireman, or in other work recognized by the Municipal Civil Service Commission as qualifying.
2. Such additional qualifications as may be required by the Municipal Civil Service Commission.

Marine Oiler, Marine Water Tender:

1. Experience as Marine Stoker, or in other work recognized by the Municipal Civil Service Commission as qualifying.
2. Such additional qualifications as may be required by the Municipal Civil Service Commission.

COMPENSATION—

The per diem compensation for work performed in this grade shall be the prevailing rate of wages for these occupations as provided by Section 3 of Article 2 of the New York State Labor Law. The following rates appear to be the prevailing rates at the present time:[1]

Marine Oiler	$3.20	per day,	8 hours
Marine Stoker	3.00	" "	8 "
Marine Water Tender	3.20	" "	8 "

---

[1]Persons working under these titles may be paid the prevailing rate only when employed on the duties prescribed above.

GRADE 2 (T N 2)

TITLES OF POSITIONS—

MARINE ENGINEMAN

DUTIES—

The duties of incumbents of these positions are to take charge of and assume entire responsibility for the engineering department of steamboats other than the largest ferries and boats of corresponding tonnage mentioned in Grade 3, or to assist the Chief Marine Engineman in taking charge during a tour of duty of the engineering department of steamboats mentioned in Grade 3, requiring this position, including the operation of engineering equipment, the supervision of employes in Grade 1, the care of and the making of minor and emergency repairs on all machinery and the preservation of general order and cleanliness.

QUALIFICATIONS—

1. The license for this position issued by the United States Steamboat Inspectors.
2. Such additional qualifications as may be required by the Municipal Civil Service Commission.

COMPENSATION—

Regular Service Every Day in the Year:

Range of annual compensation—$1440 to $1680 inclusive.
Salary rates—$1440, $1560, $1680.

Regular Service Exclusive of Sundays:

Range of annual compensation—$1260 to $1500 inclusive.
Salary rates—$1260, $1380, $1500.

SPECIAL CONDITION GOVERNING ADVANCEMENT—

The following table indicates the minimum number of years of meritorious service required at each rate before advancement to the next rate. See also page 30.

$1440	$1260	1 year
1560	1380	2 years

SPECIAL REGULATION GOVERNING COMPENSATION—

Persons entering this grade need not necessarily begin at the lowest rate. Fixation of the initial salary rate and advancement within this grade are conditional upon appraisal under the rules of the Board of Estimate and Apportionment, indicating that the rate requested does not exceed the value of the work to be performed.

GRADE 3 (T N 3)

TITLES OF POSITIONS[1]—

CHIEF MARINE ENGINEMAN

---

[1]The following positions are appraised at the present time in this grade:

Chief Marine Engineman on Staten Island and 39th Street ferries of the Department of Docks and Ferries.

Chief Marine Engineman on the Thomas S. Brennan of the Department of Public Charities.

Chief Marine Engineman on the Correction of the Department of Correction.

The Board of Estimate and Apportionment will list specifically by departments such additional positions as it considers properly appraised in this grade.

DUTIES—

The duties of incumbents of these positions are to take charge of and assume entire responsibility for the engineering department of the largest ferries and of other steamboats of corresponding tonnage during a tour of duty, including the operation of engineering equipment, the supervision of employes in Grades 1 and 2, the care of and the making of minor and emergency repairs on all machinery and the preservation of general order and cleanliness.

QUALIFICATIONS—

1. The minimum qualifications prescribed for Grade 1 or Grade 2.
2. If appointed by promotion, not less than one year of appropriate experience in Grade 1 or Grade 2 when holding an engineer's license or, if appointed as the result of an open competitive examination, experience in work of the character and standard of Grade 1 or Grade 2.
3. The license for this position, covering the tonnage, issued by the United States Steamboat Inspectors.
4. Such additional qualifications as may be required by the Municipal Civil Service Commission.

COMPENSATION—

Regular Service Every Day in the Year:

Annual compensation—$1800.

Regular Service Exclusive of Sundays:

Annual compensation—$1560.

MARINE OFFICER GROUP

SYMBOL (T O)

The term Marine Officer Group is applied to those offices or employments of the Skilled Trades Service in which incumbents are required to navigate or to assist in the navigation of vessels.

GRADE 1 (T O 1)

TITLES OF POSITIONS—

DECKHAND

DUTIES—

The duties of incumbents of these positions are to operate gates and gangplanks, to regulate passenger traffic, to load and unload freight, to handle lines, to clean boats, to act as lookout and to do such other related work as may be assigned.

QUALIFICATIONS—

1. Such qualifications as may be required by the Municipal Civil Service Commission.

COMPENSATION—

Regular Service Exclusive of Sundays:

Range of annual compensation—$792 to $888 inclusive.
Salary rates—$792, $816, $840, $864, $888.

Temporary Service:

Per diem compensation—$2.50.

SPECIAL CONDITION GOVERNING ADVANCEMENT—

The following table indicates the minimum number of years of meritorious service required at each rate before advancement to the next rate. See also page 30.

$792	1 year
816	1 "
840	2 years
864	2 "

GRADE 2 (T O 2)

TITLES OF POSITIONS—

MATE

DUTIES—

The duties of incumbents of these positions are to supervise and assist deck-hands in their work, to manipulate the steering wheel and signal apparatus when required and to assist the captain or pilot in the general management of the boat, including, on large passenger steamboats and ferryboats, all the duties ordinarily performed by quartermasters.

QUALIFICATIONS—

1. A Pilot's license issued by the United States Steamboat Inspectors with the necessary endorsement and authorization to act as Mate.
2. Such additional qualifications as may be required by the Municipal Civil Service Commission.

COMPENSATION—

Mates Acting as Quartermasters on Passenger Steamboats or Ferryboats of Over 1000 Gross Tons:[1]

Range of annual compensation—$984 to $1080 inclusive.
Salary rates—$984, $1032, $1080.

Other Mates:

Range of annual compensation—$936 to $1032 inclusive.
Salary rates—$936, $984, $1032.

Temporary Service:

Per diem compensation—$3.

SPECIAL CONDITION GOVERNING ADVANCEMENT—

The following table indicates the minimum number of years of meritorious service required at each rate before advancement to the next rate. See also page 30.

Mates Acting as Quartermasters on Passenger Steamboats or Ferryboats of Over 1000 Gross Tons:

$984	1 year
1032	2 years

Other Mates:

$936	1 year
984	2 years

---

[1]Mates promoted to the work of Quartermaster on such boats shall receive the salary rate nearest to that received before promotion and involving no decrease.

GRADE 3 (T O 3)

TITLES OF POSITIONS[1]—

CAPTAIN
FIRE PILOT

DUTIES—

Captain:

The duties of Captains are to take command of steamboats, requiring under the laws of the United States the services of a licensed pilot or master, to manipulate the steering wheel and signal apparatus, and to assume entire responsibility for the management of the boat, the conduct of the crew and the safety of passengers and property.

Fire Pilot:

The duties of Fire Pilots are to steer fireboats used for fire extinguishment, to land them at the point or place designated by the officers in command and to perform such other work as may be assigned by these officers under the rules of the Fire Department.

QUALIFICATIONS—

1. A Pilot's or Master's license covering the tonnage of the boat to be operated issued by the United States Steamboat Inspectors.
2. Such additional qualifications as may be required by the Municipal Civil Service Commission.

COMPENSATION—

Captain:

On steamboats other than the largest ferries and boats of corresponding tonnage:

Range of annual compensation for regular service every day in the year—$1500 to $1740 inclusive.

Salary rates—$1500, $1620, $1740.

Range of annual compensation for regular service exclusive of Sundays—$1320 to $1560.

Salary rates—$1320, $1440, $1560.

On the largest ferries and boats of corresponding tonnage:

Annual compensation for regular service every day in the year—$1920.

Annual compensation for regular service exclusive of Sundays—$1620.

Fire Pilot:

Range of annual compensation—$1500 to $1620 inclusive.

Salary rates—$1500, $1560, $1620.

SPECIAL REGULATION GOVERNING COMPENSATION—

Captain:

Persons entering this grade need not necessarily begin at the lowest rate. Fixation of the initial salary rate and advancement within this grade are conditional upon appraisal under the rules of the Board of Estimate and Apportionment, indicating that the rate requested does not exceed the value of the work to be performed.

---

[1]The following positions are appraised at the present time in this grade:

Captain on Staten Island and 39th Street Ferries of the Department of Docks and Ferries.

Captain on the Brennan of the Department of Public Charities.

Captain on the Correction of the Department of Correction.

The Board of Estimate and Apportionment will list specifically by departments such additional positions as it considers properly appraised in this grade.

GRADE 4 (T O 4)

TITLES OF POSITIONS—

SUPERINTENDENT OF FERRIES

DUTIES--

The duties of the incumbent of this position, which involve supervision of employes in the Marine Officer and Marine Engineman Groups and of other employes in the ferry service, are to be responsible for the operation, care and maintenance of municipal boats and terminals, the preparation of time tables and the proper operation of the ferry schedule in a large bureau of ferries.

QUALIFICATIONS—

1. The minimum qualifications prescribed for Grade 3.
2. If appointed by promotion, not less than two years of appropriate experience in Grade 3, or if appointed as the result of an open competitive examination, executive experience in the operation of boats for ferry or freight service for a railroad or transportation company, or in other work recognized by the Municipal Civil Service Commission as qualifying.
3. Such additional qualifications as may be required by the Municipal Civil Service Commission.

COMPENSATION—

Range of annual compensation—$3600 to $4500 inclusive.
Salary rates—$3600, $3900, $4200, $4500.

SPECIAL REGULATION GOVERNING COMPENSATION—

Beginning with the lowest rate, advancement within this grade is conditional upon appraisal under the rules of the Board of Estimate and Apportionment, indicating that the rate requested does not exceed the value of the work to be performed.

MECHANIC GROUP

SYMBOL (T K)

The term Mechanic Group is applied to those employments of the Skilled Trades Service in which incumbents are required to perform duties pertaining to the caulking, clock repairing, hose and tire repairing, machinist, mechanic, rigging, saw filing, ship caulking, tapping and welding trades.

GRADE 1 (T K 1)

TITLES OF POSITIONS—

CAULKER
CLOCK REPAIRER
HOSE AND TIRE REPAIRER
INSTRUMENT MAKER
MACHINIST
MACHINIST (AUTOMOBILE)
MECHANIC (ADDING MACHINE)
MECHANIC (ELEVATOR)
MECHANIC (LABORATORY)
ORTHOPEDIC MECHANIC
RIGGER
SAW FILER
SHIP CAULKER
TAPPER
WELDER

DUTIES—

Caulker:

The duties of Caulkers are to cut cast iron pipe; to yarn the joints; to run with lead and caulk the joints; to search for leaks; to shut off water in the distribution system; to take proper measurements for fitting and repairing pipes; to repair valves and hydrants where making of new parts is not required; to perform such other work as may properly be required of caulkers.

Clock Repairer:

The duties of Clock Repairers are to clean and repair clocks and to keep them in proper running condition.

Hose and Tire Repairer:

The duties of Hose and Tire Repairers are to test hose by pressure and physical test; to operate hose expanders and rubber testing machines; to adjust mending sleeves on hose; to place brass patches on small bursts in hose; to repair hose used for hydrant and suction connections; to repair and set new tires for motor vehicles; to repair and vulcanize tubes; to perform such other work as may properly be required of hose and tire repairers.

Instrument Maker:

The duties of Instrument Makers are to make springs, rubber insulators and parts for fire telegraph instruments; to examine, repair, clean, remodel and adjust fire telegraph instruments; and to make up wood and metal patterns for experimental and demonstration purposes.

Machinist:

The duties of Machinists are to erect, assemble or dismantle machinery or parts of machinery, with or without drawings; to make operating nuts, valve stems, drip cups, nozzles, and caps; to repair valves, boiler nests, pumps, stanchions, brakes, shafts, crank-pins, bearings, crank-shafts, connecting rods, steam pistons, axles, ladders, pumps and blowers; to operate lathes, planers, drill presses, milling machines and other tools used in machine work; to perform such other work as may properly be required of machinists.

Machinist (Automobile):

The duties of Machinists (Automobile) are to repair automobiles, including the overhauling and testing of gears, brakes and motors and the assembling or dismantling of automobiles, and to perform such other automobile repair work as may properly be required of automobile machinists.

Mechanic (Adding Machine):

The duties of Mechanics (Adding Machine) are to clean and repair adding machines and to keep them in proper running condition.

Mechanic (Elevator):

The duties of Mechanics (Elevator), which require knowledge of and experience in the construction and repair of elevators, including the electrical and other machinery in common use on elevators, are to repair and replace wire ropes, pulleys, brakes, motors, oil cups and lubricating devices, and such other machinery or parts of machinery as may be necessary for safe and easy operation.

Mechanic (Laboratory):

The duties of Mechanics (Laboratory) are to operate and keep in repair the mechanical equipment in laboratories, to prepare physical samples for testing and to perform such other work as may properly be required of laboratory mechanics.

Orthopedic Mechanic:

The duties of Orthopedic Mechanics are to make and repair steel and iron braces for crippled or deformed persons, stretchers, arched foot-plates, splints for hip diseases and other appliances required in the treatment of cripples.

Rigger:

The duties of Riggers are to rig up derricks, pile drivers and other hoisting machinery with wire cables, ropes, blocks and sheaves; to splice, worm, parcel and adjust rope and wire cables; to set up and take down scaffolding, ladders, riggings, tents and rope attachments to flag poles; to repair tents, flag swings, canvas covers and other appliances requiring the services of a rigger; to perform such other work as may properly be required of riggers.

Saw Filer:

The duties of Saw Filers are to file saws and to keep them in good repair.

Ship Caulker:

The duties of Ship Caulkers are to drive cotton and oakum and to apply pitch, marine glue or red lead paint in the seams and butts of wood construction on boats, scows, pile drivers and derricks, in order to make the same water-tight; to recopper and place sheet lead and galvanized sheet iron on hulls of vessels constructed of wood; to caulk floors of stables and fire engine and truck houses; to perform such other work as may properly be required of ship caulkers.

Tapper:

The duties of Tappers, which require general knowledge as to water mains and their pipe connections with premises, are to insert taps in city water mains; to withdraw old or abandoned taps and insert plugs in their places; to take correct measurements of the location of taps and plugs and report thereon; to perform such other work as may properly be required of tappers.

Welder:

The duties of Welders are to repair machinery, to straighten channel bars and side bars of engines by the oxygen acetylene process, or to repair lanterns, lamps, oil cups and gauges and to perform such other similar welding or repair work as may properly be required of welders.

QUALIFICATIONS—

1. Service as apprentice during the length of time locally stipulated by the respective trade.
2. Such additional qualifications as may be required by the Municipal Civil Service Commission.

COMPENSATION—

Instrument Maker, Mechanic (Laboratory):

Range of annual compensation—$1200 to $1320 inclusive.
Salary rates—$1200, $1260, $1320.

Caulker, Clock Repairer, Hose and Tire Repairer, Machinist, Machinist (Automobile), Mechanic (Adding Machine), Mechanic (Elevator), Orthopedic Mechanic, Rigger, Saw Filer, Ship Caulker, Tapper, Welder:

The per diem compensation for work performed in this grade shall be the prevailing rate of wages for these occupations as provided by Section 3 of Article 2 of the New York State Labor Law. The following rates appear to be the prevailing rates at the present time:[1]

Caulker	$4.50	per	day,	8	hours
Clock Repairer	4.00	"	"	"	"
Hose and Tire Repairer	4.00	"	"	"	"
Machinist	5.00	"	"	"	"
Machinist (Automobile)	5.00	"	"	"	"
Mechanic (Adding Machine)	.50	"	hour		
Mechanic (Elevator)	5.28	"	day,	"	"
Orthopedic Mechanic	4.50	"	"	"	"
Rigger	4.00	"	"	"	"
Saw Filer	4.00	"	"	"	"
Ship Caulker	4.00	"	"	"	"
Tapper	4.50	"	"	"	"
Welder	4.50	"	"	"	"

GRADE 2 (T K 2)

TITLES OF POSITIONS—

FOREMAN MACHINIST
FOREMAN MACHINIST (AUTOMOBILE)
FOREMAN MECHANIC
FOREMAN RIGGER

DUTIES—

The duties of incumbents of these positions are to supervise and be responsible for the work of a number of employes in Grade 1 and of helpers in their own or related trades, including the planning and estimating of the cost of work, the requisition of and accounting for materials used, and the care of machinery, tools, and equipment, and to perform the work of journeymen when required.

QUALIFICATIONS—

1. The minimum qualifications prescribed for Grade 1.
2. If appointed by promotion, not less than three years of appropriate experience in Grade 1, or if appointed as the result of an open competitive examination, experience in work of the character and standard of Grade 1.
3. Such additional qualifications as may be required by the Municipal Civil Service Commission.

COMPENSATION—

Foreman Machinist, Foreman Machinist (Automobile), Foreman Mechanic:

Regular Service Every Day in the Year:

Annual Compensation[2]—$1920.

Regular Service Exclusive of Sundays:

Annual Compensation[2]—$1680.

---

[1]Persons working under these titles may be paid the prevailing rate only when employed on the duties prescribed above.

[2]Where work will last continuously throughout the year, the annual rate shall be paid.

Regular Service Exclusive of Sundays, Holidays and Saturday Afternoons:
Annual compensation[1]—$1500.

Temporary Service:
Per diem compensation[2]—$5.50.

Foreman Rigger:

Regular Service Every Day in the Year:
Annual compensation[1]—$1560.

Regular Service Exclusive of Sundays:
Annual compensation[1]—$1320.

Regular Service Exclusive of Sundays, Holidays and Saturday Afternoons:
Annual compensation[1]—$1200.

Temporary Service:
Per diem compensation[2]—$4.50.

METAL WORKER GROUP

SYMBOL (T M)

The term Metal Worker Group is applied to those employments of the Skilled Trades Service in which incumbents are required to perform duties pertaining to the blacksmithing, boilermaking, brass finishing, bridge mechanic, riveting, coremaking, horseshoeing, housesmithing, moulding, nickel plating and sheet metal working trades.

GRADE 1 (T M 1)

TITLES OF POSITIONS—

BLACKSMITH
BOILERMAKER
BRASS FINISHER
BRIDGE MECHANIC AND RIVETER
COREMAKER
HORSESHOER
HOUSESMITH
MOULDER
NICKEL PLATER
SHEET METAL WORKER

DUTIES—

Blacksmith:

The duties of Blacksmiths are to forge and shape axles, braces, tires, turn buckles, springs, lathes, planes and minor tools, chisels, radio bars, crank-shafts, clip-chocks, skidding irons, angles, plates, upsetting bars, pins, nuts, drills, crowbars, washers, ball bearings, iron rods, stone drills, wrenches and bolts; to set tires; to repair iron parts of fire engines, trucks, hose wagons, automobiles, carts, sweepers, sprinklers and other vehicles; to perform such other work as may properly be required of blacksmiths.

---

[1]Where work will last continuously throughout the year, the annual rate shall be paid.

[2]Where work is temporary and will not last continuously throughout the year, the daily rate shall be paid.

Boilermaker:

The duties of Boilermakers are to make repairs to marine and stationary boilers; to install new boilers; to make plates and shapes of articles used for boilers; to examine boilers and ascertain what repairs are necessary; to install soft patches on boilers; to replace or repair boiler tubes, fire boxes, staybolts, furnaces, bearing bars and boiler braces; to perform such other work as may properly be required of boilermakers.

Brass Finisher:

The duties of Brass Finishers are to make brass fittings used for fire engines, hose, nozzles and other fire apparatus, pipe holders, pressure regulators, hose reducers, couplings for standpipes, bells, suction and cup caps and miscellaneous fittings; to repair all brass fittings; to perform such other work as may properly be required of brass finishers.

Bridge Mechanic and Riveter:

The duties of Bridge Mechanics and Riveters are to make repairs and replacements in steel work on structures and buildings; to repair and replace cables, suspenders, truss-chords, posts, diagonals, counters and pins, floor beams, stringers, promenade beams, railing, roadway curbs, columns, stairways, roofs, skylights, steam heating plants and piping, water and compressed air lines, plumbing and leaders, steel shutters and doors; to care for air tools and riveter shop power tools; to perform such other work as may properly be required of bridge mechanics and riveters.

Coremaker:

The duties of Coremakers, which require a practical knowledge of the mixing of raw sand and its conversion into forms, are to make ready the core for the moulds; to prepare all cores according to patterns furnished by the pattern maker; to perform such other work as may properly be required of coremakers.

Horseshoer:

The duties of Horseshoers are to work as firemen at the forge; to heat the metal and properly shape the shoe; to pare the horse's hoof; to fit the shoe to the horse's foot; to drive or nail the shoe to the foot; to perform such other work as may properly be required of horseshoers.

Housesmith:

The duties of Housesmiths are to erect and repair various kinds of iron work, except sheet metal, used in buildings; to repair cast and wrought iron railings and fences, park bridges, iron gates, iron columns and other ornamental iron work; to perform such other work as may properly be required of housesmiths.

Moulder:

The duties of Moulders, which involve responsibility for the condition of castings, are to operate any machine, squeezer, or other mechanical device used for moulding castings in sand; to set the sand in beds; to adjust patterns in position; to mix metals, to pour molten metal into moulds; to perform such other work as may properly be required of moulders.

Nickel Plater:

The duties of Nickel Platers are to do buffing on a rag wheel; to do polishing on bull-neck wheels, wooden wheels with leather cover, felt wheels, and hard stone or emery wheels; to do plating; to perform such other work as may properly be required of nickel platers.

Sheet Metal Worker:

The duties of Sheet Metal Workers are to do sheet metal work in connection with buildings, structures and vessels, hollow metal sashes, frames, doors and trim, skylights, cornices, crestings, awnings, heating and ventilating apparatus; to set registers; to erect metal ceilings, side walls, lockers, tanks and other light sheet metal work; to do tinning, furring, sheathing, soldering and the glazing of metal work; to repair metal roofs, leaders, gutters, street-cleaning, paper and fruit skin cans and sprinkling wagons; to perform such other work as may properly be required of sheet metal workers.

QUALIFICATIONS—

1. Service as apprentice during the length of time locally stipulated by the respective trade.
2. Such additional qualifications as may be required by the Municipal Civil Service Commission.

COMPENSATION—

The per diem compensation for work performed in this grade shall be the prevailing rate of wages for these occupations as provided by Section 3 of Article 2 of the New York State Labor Law. The following rates appear to be the prevailing rates at the present time:[1]

Blacksmith	$4.50	per	day,	8 hours
Boilermaker	4.50	"	"	"
Brass Finisher	4.00	"	"	"
Bridge Mechanic and Riveter	5.50	"	"	"
Coremaker	4.25	"	"	"
Horseshoer	4.50	"	"	"
Housesmith	5.50	"	"	"
Moulder	4.25	"	"	"
Nickel Plater	4.50	"	"	"
Sheet Metal Worker	5.00	"	"	"

GRADE 2 (T M 2)

TITLES OF POSITIONS—

FOREMAN BLACKSMITH
FOREMAN BOILERMAKER
FOREMAN BRIDGE MECHANIC AND RIVETER

DUTIES—

The duties of incumbents of these positions are to supervise and be responsible for the work of a number of employes in Grade 1 and of helpers in their own or related trades, including the planning and estimating of the cost of work, the requisition of and accounting for materials used, and the care of machinery, tools and equipment, and to perform the work of journeymen when required.

QUALIFICATIONS—

1. The minimum qualifications prescribed for Grade 1.
2. If appointed by promotion, not less than three years of appropriate experience in Grade 1, or if appointed as the result of an open competitive examination, experience in work of the character and standard of Grade 1.
3. Such additional qualifications as may be required by the Municipal Civil Service Commission.

---

[1]Persons working under these titles may be paid the prevailing rate only when employed on the duties prescribed above.

COMPENSATION—

Foreman Blacksmith, Foreman Boilermaker:

Regular Service Every Day in the Year:

Annual compensation[1]—$1740.

Regular Service Exclusive of Sundays:

Annual compensation[1]—$1500.

Regular Service Exclusive of Sundays, Holidays and Saturday Afternoons:

Annual compensation[1]—$1320.

Temporary Service:

Per diem compensation[2]—$5.

Foreman Bridge Mechanic and Riveter:

Regular Service Every Day in the Year:

Annual compensation[1]—$2100.

Regular Service Exclusive of Sundays:

Annual compensation[1]—$1800.

Regular Service Exclusive of Sundays, Holidays and Saturday Afternoons:

Annual compensation[1]—$1620.

Temporary Service:

Per diem compensation[2]—$6.

MOTOR DRIVER GROUP

SYMBOL (T X)

The term Motor Driver Group is applied to those offices or employments of the Skilled Trades Service in which incumbents are required to operate and to make minor repairs to motor vehicles, to supervise the activities of a municipal garage, or to direct an entire garage system.

GRADE 1 (T X 1)

TITLES OF POSITIONS—

MOTOR DRIVER[3]
MOTOR DRIVER (AMBULANCE)
MOTOR DRIVER (LAWN MOWER)
MOTOR DRIVER (TRUCK)

DUTIES—

Motor Driver, Motor Driver (Ambulance), Motor Driver (Truck):

The duties of incumbents of these positions are to operate, to make minor repairs and adjustments on, to clean, oil and maintain in good running condition delivery motor trucks, motor ambulances or passenger carrying automobiles; to load, unload, check and make record of supplies received and delivered; to keep trip records of speedometer readings, places visited, time elapsed, oil and gasoline consumed and detailed expenses incurred in repairs; or when detailed to act as foreman of a small municipal garage.

---

[1]Where work will last continuously throughout the year, the annual rate shall be paid.

[2]Where work is temporary and will not last continuously throughout the year, the daily rate shall be paid.

[3]The title Motor Driver includes only drivers of passenger carrying automobiles.

Motor Driver (Lawn Mower):

The duties of Motor Drivers (Lawn Mower) are to operate, clean, oil and make minor repairs on motor lawn mowers.

QUALIFICATIONS—

1. A license issued by the Secretary of State of the State of New York to operate motor vehicles.
2. Experience in operating and repairing motor vehicles.
3. Such additional qualifications as may be required by the Municipal Civil Service Commission.

COMPENSATION—

Motor Driver:

Range of annual compensation—$1020 to $1320 inclusive.
Salary rates—$1020, $1080, $1140, $1200, $1260, $1320.
Temporary service—$3.50 per diem.

Motor Driver (Ambulance):[1]

Range of annual compensation with or without part maintenance—$1020 to $1320 inclusive.
Salary rates—$1020, $1080, $1140, $1200, $1260, $1320.
Range of annual compensation with full maintenance—$780 to $1080 inclusive.
Salary rates—$780, $840, $900, $960, $1020, $1080.
Temporary service—$3.50 per diem.

Motor Driver (Lawn Mower):

Compensation per diem—$3.50.

Motor Driver (Truck):

Range of annual compensation—$960 to $1200 inclusive.
Salary rates—$960, $1020, $1080, $1140, $1200.
Temporary service—$3.50 per diem.

SPECIAL CONDITION GOVERNING ADVANCEMENT—

The following table indicates the minimum number of years of meritorious service required at each rate before advancement to the next rate. See also page 30.

Motor Driver:

$1020	1 year
1080	1 "
1140	1 "
1200	2 years
1260	2 "

Motor Driver (Ambulance):

Rate	Rate (full maintenance)	Years
$1020	$780	1 year
1080	840	1 "
1140	900	1 "
1200	960	2 years
1260	1020	2 "

---

[1]Motor Ambulance Drivers may receive part maintenance without deductions in salary in institutions where the exigencies of the service require that meals be served to Drivers in order that they may be ready to answer calls throughout the day. In other institutions where full maintenance is given in order that Drivers may be on call at all times, a special salary range is established including maintenance.

Motor Driver (Truck):

$960	1 year
1020	1 "
1080	2 years
1140	2 "

GRADE 2 (T X 2)

TITLES OF POSITIONS[1]—

GARAGE SUPERVISOR

DUTIES—

The duties of incumbents of these positions, which involve supervision of the work of employes in Grade 1 and of mechanics and other subordinates, are to supervise the activities of a municipal sub-garage, or departmental garage, including the making of repairs, the ordering and care of supplies and accessories and when required the assignment of motor drivers.

QUALIFICATIONS—

1. The minimum qualifications prescribed for Grade 1.
2. If appointed by promotion, not less than two years of appropriate experience in Grade 1, or if appointed as the result of an open competitive examination, experience in work of the character and standard of Grade 1, or as a mechanic in general automobile work.
3. Such additional qualifications as may be required by the Municipal Civil Service Commission.

COMPENSATION—

Range of annual compensation—$1440 to $1560 inclusive.
Salary rates—$1440, $1560.

SPECIAL CONDITION GOVERNING ADVANCEMENT—

The following table indicates the minimum number of years of meritorious service required at each rate before advancement to the next rate. See also page 30.

$1440	2 years

GRADE 3 (T X 3)

TITLES OF POSITIONS—

SUPERINTENDENT OF GARAGES
SUPERINTENDENT OF GARAGES (POLICE)

DUTIES—

Superintendent of Garages:

The duties of the Superintendent of Garages, which involve supervision of employes in Grades 1 and 2, of mechanics and other subordinates, are to direct the central garage system, including responsibility for the purchase and repair of supplies and equipment, the assignment and conduct of employes and the keeping of necessary records.

Superintendent of Garages (Police):

The duties of the Superintendent of Garages (Police), which involve supervision of employes in Grade 1, of mechanics and other subordinates, are to be responsible for the maintenance and operation of the motor vehicles of the Police Department, including responsibility for the purchase and repair of supplies and equipment, the assignment and conduct of employes and the keeping of necessary records.

---

[1]The following positions are among those appraised by the Bureau of Personal Service in this grade on the basis of duties performed by present incumbents:
Garage Supervisor of Bellevue and Allied Hospitals.

QUALIFICATIONS—

Superintendent of Garages:

1. The minimum qualifications prescribed for Grade 2.

2. If appointed by promotion, not less than two years of appropriate experience in Grade 2, or if appointed as the result of an open competitive examination, experience in work of the character and standard of Grade 2.

3. Such additional qualifications as may be required by the Municipal Civil Service Commission.

Superintendent of Garages (Police):

1. The minimum qualifications prescribed for Grade 1.

2. Experience in a supervisory capacity in the operation of a garage.

3. Such additional qualifications as may be required by the Municipal Civil Service Commission.

COMPENSATION—

Range of annual compensation—$1680 to $2340 inclusive.
Salary rates—$1680, $1800, $1980, $2160, $2340.

SPECIAL CONDITION GOVERNING ADVANCEMENT—

The following table indicates the minimum number of years of meritorious service required at each rate before advancement to the next rate. See also page 36.

$1680	1 year
1800	2 years
1980	2 "
2160	2 "

PAINTER GROUP

SYMBOL (T A)

The term Painter Group is applied to those employments of the Skilled Trades Service in which incumbents are required to perform duties pertaining to the painter's trade and its allied specialties of decorating, graining, lettering, striping and varnishing.

GRADE 1 (T A 1)

TITLES OF POSITIONS—

PAINTER
DECORATOR
GRAINER
LETTERER
STRIPER
VARNISHER

DUTIES—

Painter:

The duties of Painters, which require familiarity with the quality and use of the different kinds of paints and varnishes and a knowledge of rigging, are to mix paints and colors in proper proportions and to do painting and varnishing.

Decorator:

The duties of Decorators, which require that they shall be competent painters, are to do stenciling, lining, glazing, gilding, bronzing or other decorative work.

Grainer:

The duties of Grainers, which require that they shall be competent painters, are to do graining on walls, panels, doors or other woodwork.

Letterer:

The duties of Letterers, which require that they shall be competent painters, are to paint signs and to do lettering of any description.

Striper:

The duties of Stripers, which require that they shall be competent painters, are to do striping on wood or iron ornamental work, automobiles, carriages, wagons, fire engines and other apparatus.

Varnisher:

The duties of Varnishers are to prepare varnish and apply it to wood and metal; to enamel and varnish wood-work; to do hardwood finishing; to lacquer copper, brass and other metals; to polish furniture and wood-work.

QUALIFICATIONS—

1. Service as apprentice during the length of time locally stipulated by the respective trade.
2. Such additional qualifications as may be required by the Municipal Civil Service Commission.

COMPENSATION—

The per diem compensation for work performed in this grade shall be the prevailing rate of wages for these occupations as provided by Section 3 of Article 2 of the New York State Labor Law. The following rates appear to be the prevailing rates at the present time:[1]

Painter	$5.00	per	day,	8 hours
Decorator	5.00	"	"	"
Grainer	5.00	"	"	"
Letterer	5.00	"	"	"
Striper	5.00	"	"	"
Varnisher	5.00	"	"	"

GRADE 2 (T A 2)

TITLES OF POSITIONS—

FOREMAN PAINTER

DUTIES—

The duties of incumbents of these positions are to supervise and be responsible for the work of employes in Grade 1 and of helpers in their own or related trades, including the planning and estimating of the cost of work, the requisition of and accounting for materials used, and the care of machinery, tools, and equipment, and to perform the work of journeymen when required.

QUALIFICATIONS—

1. The minimum qualifications prescribed for Grade 1.
2. If appointed by promotion, not less than three years of appropriate experience in Grade 1, or if appointed as the result of an open competitive examination, experience in work of the character and standard of Grade 1.
3. Such additional qualifications as may be required by the Municipal Civil Service Commission.

---

[1]Persons working under these titles may be paid the prevailing rate only when employed on the duties prescribed above.

COMPENSATION—

Regular Service Every Day in the Year:

Annual compensation[1]—$1920.

Regular Service Exclusive of Sundays:

Annual compensation[1]—$1680.

Regular Service Exclusive of Sundays, Holidays and Saturday Afternoons:

Annual compensation[1]—$1500.

Temporary Service:

Per diem compensation[2]—$5.50.

PHOTOGRAPHER GROUP

SYMBOL (T F)

The term Photographer Group is applied to those employments of the Skilled Trades Service in which incumbents are required to make photographic exposures, to develop, fix and make prints of photographic negatives, to make lantern slides and enlargements, to operate the photostat, to prepare from basic salts all chemical solutions used in photographic work, to select suitable apparatus and supplies, and to direct the work of assistants both in field and laboratory.

GRADE 1 (T F 1)

TITLES OF POSITIONS—

PHOTOGRAPHER
PHOTOGRAPHER (X-RAY)

DUTIES—

Photographer:

The duties of incumbents of these positions, which may or may not involve supervision over clerks or other assistants, are to make photographic exposures; to develop, fix, retouch and make prints from photographic negatives; to mount and affix titles to finished photographs for permanent department records; to file all negatives and prints; to make and color lantern slides; to make bromide enlargements and blue prints from tracings; to operate the photostat; to make black line prints; to prepare all solutions from commercial salts or other basic components; to superintend repairs to apparatus; to select suitable supplies and to assist in the selection of new apparatus.

Photographer (X-ray):

The duties of Photographers (X-ray) are to act as assistant to Physicians (Roentgenologist) in the taking and preparation of X-ray photographs.

QUALIFICATIONS—

Photographer:

1. Experience in the practice of photography.
2. Such additional qualifications as may be required by the Municipal Civil Service Commission.

Photographer (X-ray):

1. Experience in the use of X-ray machines.
2. Such additional qualifications as may be required by the Municipal Civil Service Commission.

---

[1]Where work will last continuously throughout the year, the annual rate shall be paid.

[2]Where work is temporary and will not last continuously throughout the year, the daily rate shall be paid.

COMPENSATION—

Photographer:

Range of annual compensation—$1200 to $1620 inclusive.
Salary rates—$1200, $1260, $1320, $1380, $1440, $1500, $1560, $1620.

Photographer (X-ray):

Range of annual compensation—$900 to $1320 inclusive.
Salary rates—$900, $960, $1020, $1080, $1140, $1200, $1260, $1320.

SPECIAL REGULATION GOVERNING COMPENSATION—

Beginning with the lowest rate, advancement within this grade is conditional upon appraisal under the rules of the Board of Estimate and Apportionment, indicating that the rate requested does not exceed the value of the work to be performed.

PLUMBER AND STEAMFITTER GROUP

SYMBOL (T P)

The term Plumber and Steamfitter Group is applied to those employments of the Skilled Trades Service in which incumbents are required to perform duties pertaining to the plumbing, steamfitting and thermostat repairing trades.

GRADE 1 (T P 1)

TITLES OF POSITIONS—

PLUMBER
STEAMFITTER
THERMOSTAT REPAIRER

DUTIES—

Plumber:

The dutes of Plumbers are to install piping for gas, water, waste, soil and vent lines, piping to and from water filters and water meters, piping for hot and cold water for domestic and culinary purposes, piping or tubing put together with solder, icebox and refrigerator waste pipes; to cut and fit pipes to and from ranges and boilers; to set all plumbing fixtures; to replace old pipes with new ones; to fit up toilet and bathroom auxiliaries and water, gas and waste pipes to and from laundry machines; to perform such other work as may properly be required of plumbers.

Steamfitter:

The duties of Steamfitters are to install steam, hydraulic, gasoline or oil power piping, vacuum heating and pneumatic tube systems, and piping utilized for machinery; to set fixtures, pumps, tanks, and heaters in connection with steam power apparatus, and steam and return connections of kitchen utensils; to cut, fit and install piping which conveys steam, hot water, air, brine, ammonia or oil; to repair steam traps, heating and ventilating plants, defective and corroded pipes, vacuum and electrical pumps, dampers, and stop and pressure reducing valves; to perform such other work as may properly be required of steamfitters.

Thermostat Repairer:

The duties of Thermostat Repairers, which require knowledge of the different systems of thermostatic heat regulation, are to examine, fit and repair thermostats and the pipes and accessories connected therewith.

QUALIFICATIONS—

Plumber, Thermostat Repairer:

1. License to act as plumber issued by the Examining Board of Plumbers.
2. Service as apprentice during the length of time locally stipulated by the trade.
3. Such additional qualifications as may be required by the Municipal Civil Service Commission.

Steamfitter:

1. Service as apprentice during the length of time locally stipulated by the trade.
2. Such additional qualifications as may be required by the Municipal Civil Service Commission.

COMPENSATION—

The per diem compensation for work performed in this grade shall be the prevailing rates of wages for these occupations as provided by Section 3 of Article 2 of the New York State Labor Law. The following rates appear to be the prevailing rates at the present time:[1]

Plumber	$5.50 per day, 8 hours
Steamfitter	5.50 " " "
Thermostat Repairer	5.50 " " "

PRINTER GROUP

SYMBOL (T I)

The term Printer Group is applied to those employments of the Skilled Trades Service in which incumbents are required to care for and feed presses, to set type, to read copy and to perform other duties peculiar to the printing trade.

GRADE 1 (T I 1)

TITLES OF POSITIONS—

COMPOSITOR
PRESS FEEDER
PRESSMAN
PRINTER (BRAILLE)

DUTIES—

Compositor:

The duties of Compositors are to set and distribute type by hand, to correct errors, to read copy and to prepare forms for the press.

Press Feeder:

The duties of Press Feeders are to handle paper used in printing, to feed sheets into the press in perfect register and to assist the Pressman generally in the care of the press.

Pressman:

The duties of Pressmen are to prepare the press for the reception of forms, and to regulate, clean, care for and make minor repairs to the press.

---

[1]Persons working under these titles may be paid the prevailing rate only when employed on the duties prescribed above.

Printer (Braille):

The duties of Printers (Braille) are to emboss in braille on metal plates, textbooks and other material for reading or study, to print from these plates, to correct copy, to collect and bind sheets and to perform such other work as may properly be required of braille printers.

QUALIFICATIONS—

1. Service as apprentice during the length of time locally stipulated by the respective trade.
2. Such additional qualifications as may be required by the Municipal Civil Service Commission.

COMPENSATION—

Compositor, Press Feeder, Pressman:

The compensation for work performed under these titles shall be the prevailing rate of wages for these occupations as provided by Section 3 of Article 2 of the New York State Labor Law. The following rates appear to be the prevailing rates at the present time:[1]

Compositor	$25.00 per week
Press Feeder	18.00 " "
Pressman	26.00 " "

Printer (Braille):

Range of annual compensation—$900 to $1200 inclusive.
Salary rates—$900, $960, $1020, $1080, $1140, $1200.

GRADE 2 (T I 2)

TITLES OF POSITIONS—

FOREMAN PRINTER

DUTIES—

The duties of Foremen Printers are to supervise and be responsible for the work of employes in Grade 1 and of helpers in their own or related trades, including the planning and estimating of the cost of work, the requisition of and accounting for materials used and the care of machinery, tools and equipment, and to perform the work of journeymen when required.

QUALIFICATIONS—

1. The minimum qualifications prescribed for Grade 1.
2. If appointed by promotion, not less than three years of appropriate experience in Grade 1, or if appointed as the result of an open competitive examination, experience in work of the character and standard of Grade 1.
3. Such additional qualifications as may be required by the Municipal Civil Service Commission.

COMPENSATION—

Regular Service Every Day in the Year:

Annual compensation—$1680.

Regular Service Exclusive of Sundays:

Annual compensation—$1440.

---

[1]Persons working under these titles may be paid the prevailing rate only when employed on the duties prescribed above.

ROCKWORKER GROUP

SYMBOL (T R)

The term Rockworker Group is applied to those employments of the Skilled Trades Service in which incumbents are required to perform duties involved in drilling, blasting and the handling of explosives.

GRADE 1 (T R 1)

TITLES OF POSITIONS—

BLASTER

DUTIES—

The duties of incumbents of these positions are to direct workmen in the covering of blasts, to handle and to take charge of the storing of dynamite and to explode dynamite.

QUALIFICATIONS—

1. A certificate of fitness granted by the Fire Commissioner in accordance with the Code of City Ordinances.
2. Such additional qualifications as may be required by the Municipal Civil Service Commission.

COMPENSATION—

The per diem compensation for work performed in this grade shall be the prevailing rate of wages for this occupation as provided by Section 3 of Article 2 of the New York State Labor Law. The following rate appears to be the prevailing rate at the present time:[1]

Blaster .... $5.00 per day, 8 hours

SHOP SUPERVISOR GROUP

SYMBOL (T S)

The term Shop Supervisor Group is applied to those offices or employments of the Skilled Trades Service in which incumbents are required to perform duties requiring general administrative ability in the supervision of workers in the skilled trades, or of unskilled laborers engaged in shop repair work.

GRADE 1 (T S 1)

TITLES OF POSITIONS[2]—

GENERAL FOREMAN (SHOPS)

DUTIES—

The duties of incumbents of these positions, which involve supervision of workers in the skilled trades and of unskilled laborers, are to direct and be responsible for a large repair shop or group of small repair shops, the equipment of which is simple and not highly specialized, and to make such reports as may be required.

---

[1]Persons working under this title may be paid the prevailing rate only when employed on the duties described above.

[2]The following positions are among those appraised by the Bureau of Personal Service in this grade on the basis of duties performed by present incumbents:

General Foreman (Shops) in the Department of Parks, Manhattan and Richmond.

QUALIFICATIONS—

1. Practical experience in the supervision of repair and maintenance work.
2. Such additional qualifications as may be required by the Municipal Civil Service Commission.

COMPENSATION—

Range of annual compensation—$1380 to $1920 inclusive.
Salary rates—$1380, $1500, $1620, $1740, $1920.

SPECIAL REGULATION GOVERNING COMPENSATION—

Persons entering this grade need not necessarily begin at the lowest rate. Fixation of the initial salary rate and advancement within this grade are conditional upon appraisal under the rules of the Board of Estimate and Apportionment, indicating that the rate requested does not exceed the value of the work to be performed.

SPECIAL CONDITION GOVERNING ADVANCEMENT—

The following table indicates the minimum number of years of meritorious service required at each rate before advancement to the next rate. See also page 30.

$1380	1 year
1500	1 "
1620	2 years
1740	2 "

GRADE 2 (T S 2)

TITLES OF POSITIONS[1]—

SUPERINTENDENT OF SHOPS

DUTIES—

The duties of incumbents of these positions, which involve supervision of large numbers of workers in the skilled trades and of unskilled laborers, are to direct and be responsible for a group of large repair shops other than those mentioned in Grade 3, the equipment of which is not highly complex and specialized, and to make such reports as may be required.

QUALIFICATIONS—

1. The minimum qualifications prescribed for Grade 1.
2. If appointed by promotion, not less than one year of appropriate experience in Grade 1, or if appointed as the result of an open competitive examination, experience in work of the character and standard of Grade 1.
3. Such additional qualifications as may be required by the Municipal Civil Service Commission.

COMPENSATION—

Range of annual compensation—$2100 to $2700 inclusive.
Salary rates—$2100, $2280, $2460, $2700.

SPECIAL REGULATION GOVERNING COMPENSATION—

Persons entering this grade need not necessarily begin at the lowest rate. Fixation of the initial salary rate and advancement within this grade are conditional upon appraisal under the rules of the Board of Estimate and Apportionment, indicating that the rate requested does not exceed the value of the work to be performed.

---

[1]The following positions are among those appraised by the Bureau of Personal Service in this grade on the basis of duties performed by present incumbents:

Superintendent of Shops, Department of Street Cleaning. (The present incumbent of this position in the Department of Street Cleaning is a member of the uniformed force under the title of Assistant General Superintendent.)

GRADE 3 (T S 3)

TITLES OF POSITIONS[1]—

GENERAL SUPERINTENDENT OF SHOPS

DUTIES—

The duties of incumbents of these positions, which involve supervision of large numbers of workers in the skilled trades and of unskilled laborers, are to direct and be responsible for the largest departmental repair shops, the equipment of which is highly complex and specialized, and to make such reports as may be required.

QUALIFICATIONS—

1. The minimum qualifications prescribed for Grade 2.
2. If appointed by promotion, not less than one year of appropriate experience in Grade 2, or if appointed as the result of an open competitive examination, experience in work of the character and standard of Grade 2.
3. Such additional qualifications as may be required by the Municipal Civil Service Commission.

COMPENSATION—

Range of annual compensation—$2940 to $3960 inclusive.
Salary rates $2940, $3180, $3420, $3660, $3960

SPECIAL REGULATION GOVERNING COMPENSATION—

Persons entering this grade need not necessarily begin at the lowest rate. Fixation of the initial salary rate and advancement within this grade are conditional upon appraisal under the rules of the Board of Estimate and Apportionment, indicating that the rate requested does not exceed the value of the work to be performed.

UPHOLSTERER GROUP

SYMBOL (T U)

The term Upholsterer Group is applied to those employments of the Skilled Trades Service in which incumbents are required to perform duties peculiar to the upholstering and shade-fitting trades.

GRADE 1 (T U 1)

TITLES OF POSITIONS—

UPHOLSTERER
SHADE FITTER

DUTIES—

Upholsterer:

The duties of Upholsterers are to make, mend and repair all kinds of cushion seats or backs, automobile tops, carriage tops or sheds and to do other making, mending or repairing work with materials used in the trade.

Shade Fitter:

The duties of Shade Fitters are to cut, fit and hang shades.

QUALIFICATIONS—

1. Service as apprentice during the length of time locally stipulated by the respective trade.
2. Such additional qualifications as may be required by the Municipal Civil Service Commission.

---

[1]The following positions are among those appraised by the Bureau of Personal Service in this grade on the basis of duties performed by present incumbents:

General Superintendent of Shops, Fire Department.

COMPENSATION—

The per diem compensation for work performed in this grade shall be the prevailing rate of wages for these occupations as provided by Section 3 of Article 2 of the New York State Labor Law. The following rates appear to be the prevailing rates at the present time:

Shade Fitter	$4.00 per day, 8 hours
Upholsterer	4.50 " " "

WOODWORKER GROUP

SYMBOL (T W)

The term Woodworker Group is applied to those employments of the Skilled Trades Service in which incumbents are required to perform duties pertaining to the carpentry, dock building, machine woodworking, pattern making, ship carpentry, wood sawing and wheelwright trades.

GRADE 1 (T W 1)

TITLES OF POSITIONS—

CARPENTER
DOCK BUILDER
MACHINE WOODWORKER
PATTERN MAKER
SHIP CARPENTER
WHEELWRIGHT
WOOD SAWYER

DUTIES—

Carpenter:

The duties of Carpenters are to construct and repair temporary buildings, shanties, sheds, stalls, flooring, partitions, window frame sashes, bridge roadways, tool houses, tool boxes, park rustic structures, bridges, bandstands, bins, signs, boardwalks, fences and screens; to repair office furniture, doors, institutional buildings, ferryboats, docks, road machines, sprinklers, park benches; to shingle roofs; to perform such other work as may properly be required of carpenters.

Dock Builder:

The duties of Dock Builders, which require skill in the use of the axe, adze, canthook, cross-cut saw and auger, used in framing piles and timber in bulkhead wall and pier construction, in rope knotting, rafting timber for towing and the handling of piles, are to man pile drivers for the purpose of driving piles for pier and bulkhead wall construction; to operate landways, batter-ways, and pile-sawing machinery used in connection with or upon floating pile drivers; to perform such other work as may properly be required of dock builders.

Machine Woodworker:

The duties of Machine Woodworkers are to operate and maintain in good working condition planers, circular, cross-cut and bandsaws, moulds, and all woodturning machinery; to make and repair ladders, rungs, and wooden parts of wagons and buggies; to make necessary repairs to machines and tools; to perform such other work as may properly be required of machine woodworkers.

Pattern Maker:

The duties of Pattern Makers are to make from plans and specifications patterns or models in wood, metal or plaster to be used to form moulds for metal castings and parts.

Ship Carpenter:

The duties of Ship Carpenters, which require skill in the use of axe, adze, auger and other tools used in rough timber construction, are to frame up and build float stages and scows; to repair pontoons, scows, pile drivers and other floating equipment; to construct and fit mouldboards for concrete blocks and mass concrete on wall construction and forms for concrete construction in connection with pier work; to perform such other work as may properly be required of ship carpenters.

Wheelwright:

The duties of Wheelwrights are to repair bodies, shafts, poles, wheels, spokes and running gears of wagons, trucks, carts, sprinklers, sweeping machines, fire apparatus and all parts of vehicles requiring wood as material; to construct new bodies and other parts for wagons, trucks and carts; to perform such other work as may properly be required of wheelwrights.

Wood Sawyer:

The duties of Wood Sawyers are to shape lumber and timber by cross-cut or other saws to specified measurements for use by carpenters or wheelwrights in construction work; to perform such other work as may properly be required of wood sawyers.

QUALIFICATIONS—

1. Service as apprentice during the length of time locally stipulated by the respective trade.
2. Such additional qualifications as may be required by the Municipal Civil Service Commission.

COMPENSATION—

The per diem compensation for work performed in this grade shall be the prevailing rate of wages for these occupations as provided by Section 3 of Article 2 of the New York State Labor Law. The following rates appear to be the prevailing rates at the present time:[1]

Carpenter—Manhattan	$5.50	per	day,	8	hours
" The Bronx	5.00	"	"		"
" Brooklyn	5.00	"	"		"
" Queens	5.00	"	"		"
" Richmond	4.50	"	"		"
Dock Builder	4.25	"	"		"
Machine Woodworker	5.00	"	"		"
Pattern Maker	5.00	"	"		"
Ship Carpenter	4.00	"	"		"
Wheelwright	4.00	"	"		"
Wood Sawyer	4.00	"	"		"

GRADE 2 (T W 2)

TITLES OF POSITIONS—

FOREMAN CARPENTER
FOREMAN DOCK BUILDER
FOREMAN SHIP CARPENTER

---

[1]Persons working under these titles may be paid the prevailing rate only when employed on the duties prescribed above.

DUTIES—

The duties of incumbents of these positions are to supervise and be responsible for the work of employes in Grade 1 and of helpers in their own or related trades, including the planning and estimating of the cost of work, the requisition of and accounting for materials used, and the care of machinery, tools and equipment, and to perform the work of journeymen when required.

QUALIFICATIONS—

1. The minimum qualifications prescribed for Grade 1.
2. If appointed by promotion, not less than three years af appropriate experience in Grade 1, or if appointed as the result of an open competitive examination, experience in work of the character and standard of Grade 1.
3. Such additional qualifications as may be required by the Municipal Civil Service Commission.

COMPENSATION—

Foreman Carpenter (Manhattan):

Regular Service Every Day in the Year:
Annual compensation[1]—$2100.

Regular Service Exclusive of Sundays:
Annual compensation[1]—$1800.

Regular Service Exclusive of Sundays, Holidays and Saturday Afternoons:
Annual compensation[1]—$1620.

Temporary Service:
Per diem compensation[2]—$6.

Foreman Carpenter (Brooklyn, The Bronx, Queens):

Regular Service Every Day in the Year:
Annual compensation[1]—$1920.

Regular Service Exclusive of Sundays:
Annual compensation[1]—$1680.

Regular Service Exclusive of Sundays, Holidays and Saturday Afternoons:
Annual compensation[1]—$1500.

Temporary Service:
Per diem compensation[2]—$5.50.

Foreman Carpenter (Richmond):

Regular Service Every Day in the Year:
Annual compensation[1]—$1740.

Regular Service Exclusive of Sundays:
Annual compensation[1]—$1500.

Regular Service Exclusive of Sundays, Holidays and Saturday Afternoons:
Annual compensation[1]—$1320.

Temporary Service:
Per diem compensation[2]—$5.

Foreman Dock Builder:

Regular Service Every Day in the Year:
Annual compensation[1]—$1620.

---

[1]Where work will last continuously throughout the year, the annual rate shall be paid.

[2]Where work is temporary and will not last continuously throughout the year, the daily rate shall be paid.

Regular Service Exclusive of Sundays:
Annual compensation[1]—$1440.

Regular Service Exclusive of Sundays, Holidays and Saturday Afternoons:
Annual compensation[1]—$1260.

Temporary Service:
Per diem compensation[2]—$4.75.

Foreman Ship Carpenter:

Regular Service Every Day in the Year:
Annual compensation[1]—$1560.

Regular Service Exclusive of Sundays:
Annual compensation[1]—$1320.

Regular Service Exclusive of Sundays, Holidays and Saturday Afternoons:
Annual compensation[1]—$1200.

Temporary Service:
Per diem compensation[2]—$4.50.

MISCELLANEOUS SKILLED WORKER GROUP

SYMBOL (T Z)

The term Miscellaneous Skilled Worker Group is applied to those offices or employments of the Skilled Trades Service in which incumbents are required to perform routine or specialized work in the skilled trades of an exceptional nature not included in the other groups of the Skilled Trades Service, or general work requiring knowledge of several trades.

GRADE 1 (T Z 1)

TITLES OF POSITIONS[3]—

GENERAL MECHANIC

DUTIES—

General Mechanic:

The duties of General Mechanics, which may or may not involve supervision of artisans, helpers or inmates in institutions, are to perform general mechanical repair work about buildings and grounds, involving knowledge of and experience in several trades.

Examples:

Making power plant, plumbing, steamfitting, painting, locksmithing, electrical and other repairs.

QUALIFICATIONS—

General Mechanic:

1. Experience in the skilled trades and in the upkeep of buildings and grounds.
2. Such additional qualifications as may be required by the Municipal Civil Service Commission.

---

[1]Where work will last continuously throughout the year, the annual rate shall be paid.

[2]Where work is temporary and will not last continuously throughout the year, the daily rate shall be paid.

[3]The following positions are among those appraised by the Bureau of Personal Service in this grade on the basis of duties performed by present incumbents:

General Mechanic in Kings County Hospital or in the hospitals of the Department of Health.

COMPENSATION—

General Mechanic:

Range of annual compensation without maintenance—$1200 to $1440 inclusive.
Salary rates—$1200, $1260, $1320, $1380, $1440.
Range of annual compensation with maintenance—$900 to $1140 inclusive.
Salary rates—$900, $960, $1020, $1080, $1140.

SPECIAL REGULATION GOVERNING COMPENSATION—

General Mechanic:

Beginning with the lowest rate, advancement within this grade is conditional upon appraisal under the rules of the Board of Estimate and Apportionment, indicating that the rate requested does not exceed the value of the work to be performed.

SPECIAL CONDITION GOVERNING ADVANCEMENT—

The following table indicates the minimum number of years of meritorious service required at each rate before advancement to the next rate. See also page 30.

General Mechanic:

$1200	$900	1 year
1260	960	1 "
1320	1020	2 years
1380	1080	2 "

GRADE 2 (T Z 2)

TITLES OF POSITIONS—

ASSISTANT SUPERINTENDENT OF POLICE SIGNAL SYSTEM

DUTIES—

Assistant Superintendent of Police Signal System:

The duties of the Assistant Superintendent of Police Signal System are to assist the Superintendent of the Police Signal System in the maintenance, repair, and operation of the entire police signal system.[1]

QUALIFICATIONS—

Assistant Superintendent of Police Signal System:

1. Practical experience in the maintenance and repair of an electrical signal system.
2. Such additional qualifications as may be required by the Municipal Civil Service Commission.

COMPENSATION—

Assistant Superintendent of Police Signal System:

Range of annual compensation—$1500 to $2100 inclusive.
Salary rates—$1500, $1620, $1740, $1920, $2100.

SPECIAL CONDITION GOVERNING ADVANCEMENT—

The following table indicates the minimum number of years of meritorious service required at each rate before advancement to the next rate. See also page 30.

Assistant Superintendent of Police Signal System:

$1500	1 year
1620	2 years
1740	2 "
1920	2 "

[1]When this position becomes vacant, it should be filled under the title of Junior Engineer (Electrical) in Grade 2 of the Engineer Group of the Professional Service.

GRADE 3 (T Z 3)

TITLES OF POSITIONS—

SUPERINTENDENT OF POLICE SIGNAL SYSTEM

DUTIES—

Superintendent of Police Signal System:

The duties of the Superintendent of Police Signal System, which involve supervision of workers in the skilled trades and of other employes, are to direct and be responsible for the maintenance, repair and operation of the police signal system.[1]

QUALIFICATIONS—

Superintendent of Police Signal System:

1. The minimum qualifications prescribed for Grade 2.
2. If appointed by promotion, not less than one year of appropriate experience in Grade 2, or if appointed as the result of an open competitive examination, experience in work of the character and standard of Grade 2.
3. Such additional qualifications as may be required by the Municipal Civil Service Commission.

COMPENSATION—

Superintendent of Police Signal System:

Range of annual compensation—$2280 to $3180 inclusive.
Salary rates—$2280, $2460, $2700, $2940, $3180.

[1]When this position becomes vacant, it should be filled under the title of Assistant Engineer (Electrical) in Grade 3 of the Engineer Group of the Professional Service.

UNSKILLED SERVICE

SYMBOL (U)

The term Unskilled Service is applied to those offices or employments the duties of whose incumbents are to perform manual work outside of institutions not requiring skill in a recognized trade, or to perform duties requiring general administrative ability in the supervision of unskilled and mechanical forces engaged in maintenance work.

CLEANER GROUP

SYMBOL (U C)

The term Cleaner Group is applied to those employments of the Unskilled Service in which incumbents are required to perform such services in the maintenance of cleanliness in public buildings as may be assigned by superiors.

GRADE 1 (U C 1)

TITLES OF POSITIONS[1]—

CLEANER
CLEANER (WINDOWS)

DUTIES—

Cleaner:

The duties of Cleaners are to clean, sweep, dust, scrub and polish and to perform such other services in the maintenance of cleanliness in public buildings as may be assigned by superiors.

Cleaner (Windows):

The duties of Cleaners (Windows) are to clean and polish windows and to perform such other incidental work as may be assigned by superiors.

QUALIFICATIONS—

1. Such qualifications as may be required by the Municipal Civil Service Commission.

COMPENSATION—

Cleaner:

Regular Service Exclusive of Sundays:

Men:

Range of annual compensation for full-time service averaging not less than 7 hours a day—$768 to $864 inclusive.

Salary rates—$768, $792, $816, $840, $864.

Women:

Range of annual compensation for full-time service averaging not less than 7 hours a day—$600 to $768 inclusive.

Salary rates—$600, $624, $648, $672, $696, $720, $744, $768.

Range of annual compensation for part-time service averaging not less than 3 hours a day—$300 to $420 inclusive.

Salary rates—$300, $324, $348, $372, $396, $420.

---

[1]The following positions are among those appraised by the Bureau of Personal Service in this grade on the basis of duties performed by present incumbents:

Cleaner in the Municipal Building.
Cleaner (Windows) in the Municipal Building.

Temporary Service:

Men:

30c. per hour.

Women:

25c. per hour.

Cleaner (Windows):

Regular Service Exclusive of Sundays:

Range of annual compensation—$792 to $888 inclusive.
Salary rates—$792, $816, $840, $864, $888.

HOSTLER AND DRIVER GROUP

SYMBOL (U H)

The term Hostler and Driver Group is applied to those employments of the Unskilled Service in which incumbents are required to perform duties incident to the care and driving of horses and the maintenance and repair of stables and equipment, to supervise the performance of this work, or to direct and be responsible for an entire horse-drawn transportation system.

GRADE 1 (U H 1)

TITLES OF POSITIONS—

DRIVER
HOSTLER
STABLEMAN

DUTIES—

Driver:

The duties of Drivers are to drive and care for horses while outside of the stable.

Hostler:

The duties of Hostlers are to care for, clean, feed and bed horses.

Stableman:

The duties of Stablemen are to clean stables and equipment and to perform such other unskilled manual work in stables as may be required.

QUALIFICATIONS—

1. Such qualifications as may be required by the Municipal Civil Service Commission.

COMPENSATION—

Driver:

Regular Service Exclusive of Sundays:

Range of annual compensation—$840 to $936 inclusive.
Salary rates—$840, $864, $888, $912, $936.

Temporary Service:

Range of per diem compensation[1]—$2.70 to $3 inclusive.
Wage rates—$2.70, $2.80, $2.90, $3.

---

[1]Advancement from rate to rate shall be granted only to Drivers, Hostlers and Stablemen having served a minimum of 150 days during the preceding year.

Driver in the Department of Correction Having Charge of Prisoners:

Regular Service Exclusive of Sundays:

Range of annual compensation—$864 to $960 inclusive.
Salary rates—$864, $888, $912, $936, $960.

Hostler:

Regular Service Exclusive of Sundays:

Range of annual compensation—$816 to $912 inclusive.
Salary rates—$816, $840, $864, $888, $912.

Temporary Service:

Range of per diem compensation[1]—$2.60 to $2.90 inclusive.
Wage rates—$2.60, $2.70, $2.80, $2.90.

Stableman:

Regular Service Exclusive of Sundays:

Range of annual compensation—$792 to $888 inclusive.
Salary rates—$792, $816, $840, $864, $888.

Temporary Service:

Range of per diem compensation[1]—$2.50 to $2.80 inclusive.
Wage rates—$2.50, $2,60, $2.70, $2.80.

SPECIAL CONDITION GOVERNING ADVANCEMENT—

The following table indicates the minimum number of years of meritorious service required at each rate before advancement to the next rate. See also page 30.

Driver:

Employed at an annual rate:		Employed at a per diem rate:	
$840	1 year	$2.70	2 years
864	1 "	2.80	2 "
888	2 years	2.90	2 "
912	2 "		

Driver in the Department of Correction Having Charge of Prisoners:

$864	1 year
888	1 "
912	2 years
936	2 "

Hostler:

Employed at an annual rate:		Employed at a per diem rate:	
$816	1 year	$2.60	2 years
840	1 "	2.70	2 "
864	2 years	2.80	2 "
888	2 "		

Stableman:

Employed at an annual rate:		Employed at a per diem rate:	
$792	1 year	$2.50	2 years
816	1 "	2.60	2 "
840	2 years	2.70	2 "
864	2 "		

[1]Advancement from rate to rate shall be granted only to Drivers, Hostlers and Stablemen having served a minimum of 150 days during the preceding year.

GRADE 2 (U H 2)

TITLES OF POSITIONS—

FOREMAN OF STABLES (CORRECTION)
STABLE FOREMAN

DUTIES—

Foreman of Stables (Correction):

The duties of the Foreman of Stables (Correction), which involve supervision of the work of employes in Grade 1, of laborers and other employes, are to direct and be responsible for the entire horse-drawn transportation system of the Department of Correction, involving responsibility for the maintenance and operation of stables, the care of horses, equipment and supplies, the keeping of necessary records and the safe transportation of prisoners in prison vans and of department supplies and materials.

Stable Foreman:

The duties of Stable Foremen, which involves supervision of the work of employes in Grade 1, of laborers and other employes, are to be responsible for the maintenance and operation of a large stable or a group of small stables, including the care of horses, equipment and supplies and the keeping of necessary records.

QUALIFICATIONS—

1. The minimum qualifications prescribed for Grade 1.
2. If appointed by promotion, not less than three years of appropriate experience in Grade 1, or if appointed as the result of an open competitive examination, experience in work of the character and standard of Grade 1.
3. Such additional qualifications as may be required by the Municipal Civil Service Commission.

COMPENSATION—

Foreman of Stables (Correction):

Range of annual compensation—$1500 to $1740 inclusive.
Salary rates—$1500, $1620, $1740.

Stable Foreman:

Range of annual compensation—$1080 to $1440 inclusive.
Salary rates—$1080, $1140, $1200, $1260, $1320, $1380, $1440.
Range of per diem compensation[1]—$3.40 to $4.25 inclusive.
Wage rates—$3.40, $3.60, $3.80, $4, $4.25.

SPECIAL REGULATION GOVERNING COMPENSATION—

Stable Foreman:

Persons entering this grade need not necessarily begin at the lowest rate. Fixation of the initial salary rate and advancement within this grade are conditional upon appraisal under the rules of the Board of Estimate and Apportionment, indicating that the rate requested does not exceed the value of the work to be performed.

SPECIAL CONDITION GOVERNING ADVANCEMENT—

The following table indicates the minimum number of years of meritorious service required at each rate before advancement to the next rate. See also page 30.

---

[1]Advancement from rate to rate shall be granted only to Stable Foremen having served a minimum of 150 days during the preceding year.

Foreman of Stables (Correction):

$1500	1 year
1620	2 years

Stable Foreman:

$1080	$3.40	1 year
1140	3.60	1 "
1200	3.80	1 "
1260	4.00	1 "
1320		1 "
1380		1 "

GRADE 3 (U H 3)

TITLES OF POSITIONS—

SUPERINTENDENT OF STABLES (POLICE)

DUTIES—

The duties of the incumbent of this position, which involve supervision of employes in Grades 1 and 2, and of mechanics, laborers and other employes, are to direct and be responsible for the activities of the horse-drawn equipment of the Police Department, including the maintenance and operation of stables, the purchasing and care of horses, equipment and supplies, the keeping of necessary records, the inspection of stables and investigation of complaints.

QUALIFICATIONS—

1. Experience in the supervision of stables.
2. Such additional qualifications as may be required by the Municipal Civil Service Commission.

COMPENSATION—

Range of annual compensation—$1920 to $2280 inclusive.
Salary rates—$1920, $2100, $2280.

SPECIAL CONDITION GOVERNING ADVANCEMENT—

The following table indicates the minimum number of years of meritorious service required at each rate before advancement to the next rate. See also page 30.

$1920	1 year
2100	2 years

LABORER GROUP

SYMBOL (U L)

The term Laborer Group is applied to those offices or employments of the Unskilled Service in which incumbents are required to perform manual work outside of institutions requiring little skill or training and for which physical strength is an essential qualification, or to perform duties requiring general administrative ability in the supervision of unskilled and mechanical forces engaged in maintenance work.

GRADE 1 (U L 1)

TITLES OF POSITIONS—

LABORER
LABORER (ASPHALT WORKER)
LABORER (COAL SAMPLER)[1]
LABORER (MARINE SOUNDER)

---

[1]For title and compensation of persons who make actual laboratory tests of coal and other supplies, see the Chemist and Physicist Group of the Professional Service and the Laboratory Assistant Group of the Sub-Professional Service.

DUTIES—

Laborer:

The duties of Laborers are to perform under supervision manual work in the construction or maintenance of public works or other work requiring little skill or training and for which physical strength is an essential qualification.

Laborer (Asphalt Worker):

The duties of Laborers (Asphalt Worker) are to cut, mix, rake and tamp asphalt in the construction and repair of pavements.

Laborer (Coal Sampler):

The duties of Laborers (Coal Sampler) are to obtain samples of coal and also of cement, stone, hose and other commodities for the purpose of laboratory tests, and to keep such records and make such reports as may be required.

Laborer (Marine Sounder):

The duties of Laborers (Marine Sounder) are to determine, by means of rods, chains, or discs, the nature of the river bottom and the position and depth under water of wrecks, derelicts, or other obstructions, and to perform such incidental related work as may be required.

QUALIFICATIONS—

1. Such qualifications as may be required by the Municipal Civil Service Commission.

COMPENSATION—

Laborers Employed on Ordinary Unskilled Manual Work:

Regular Service Exclusive of Sundays:

Range of annual compensation—$792 to $888 inclusive.
Salary rates—$792, $816, $840, $864, $888.

Temporary Service:

Range of per diem compensation[1]—$2.50 to $2.80 inclusive.
Wage rates—$2.50, $2.60, $2.70, $2.80.

Laborer (Asphalt Worker), Laborer (Coal Sampler), Laborer (Marine Sounder) and Other Laborers Employed on Difficult Manual Work Requiring Some Skill and Dependability, Such as Cleaning Spans of Bridges or Sewers, Sawing and Placing Timber for Shoring or Well-driving:

Regular Service Exclusive of Sundays:

Range of annual compensation—$888 to $936 inclusive.
Salary rates—$888, $912, $936.

Temporary Service:

Range of per diem compensation[1]—$2.80 to $3 inclusive.
Wage rates—$2.80, $2.90, $3.

Superannuated Laborers Assigned to Light Laboring or Watchman Work:[2]

Annual compensation—$720.

---

[1]Advancement from rate to rate shall be granted only to Laborers having served a minimum of 150 days during the preceding year.

[2]Superannuated Laborers who are unable to perform more arduous work and are assigned to light laboring work or watchman work of minor consequence, such as watching highway repair jobs or street openings or sewer and highway yards at night, may receive an annual compensation of $720.

SPECIAL REGULATION GOVERNING COMPENSATION—

Beginning with the lowest rate, advancement within this grade is conditional upon appraisal under the rules of the Board of Estimate and Apportionment, indicating that the rate requested does not exceed the value of the work to be performed.

SPECIAL CONDITION GOVERNING ADVANCEMENT—

The following table indicates the minimum number of years of meritorious service required at each rate before advancement to the next rate. See also page 30.

Laborers Employed on Ordinary Unskilled Manual Work:

Employed at an annual rate:		Employed at a per diem rate:	
$792	1 year	$2.50	2 years
816	1 "	2.60	2 "
840	2 years	2.70	2 "
864	2 "		

Laborer (Asphalt Worker), Laborer (Coal Sampler), Laborer (Marine Sounder) and Other Laborers Employed on Difficult Manual Work Requiring Some Skill and Dependability as Indicated Above:

Employed at an annual rate:		Employed at a per diem rate:	
$888	2 years	$2.80	2 years
912	2 "	2.90	2 "

GRADE 2 (U L 2)

TITLES OF POSITIONS[1]—

FOREMAN
FOREMAN ASPHALT WORKER

DUTIES—

Foreman:

The duties of Foremen are to supervise and be responsible for gangs of Laborers, including other employes in the lowest grades of the Unskilled Service, and to make such reports of location, time and quantity of and men and materials used on work as may be required.

Foreman Asphalt Worker:

The duties of Foremen Asphalt Workers are to take charge of street gangs including skilled asphalt workers in asphalt repair work.

QUALIFICATIONS—

1. The minimum qualifications prescribed for Grade 1.
2. If appointed by promotion, not less than three years of appropriate experience in Grade 1, or if appointed as the result of an open competitive examination, experience in work of the character and standard of Grade 1.
3. Such additional qualifications as may be required by the Municipal Civil Service Commission.

---

[1]The following positions are among those appraised by the Bureau of Personal Service in this grade on the basis of duties performed by present incumbents:

Foremen in charge of repair gangs in the Bureaus of Highways in the various boroughs.

Foremen in charge of mosquito prevention gangs in the Health Department.

COMPENSATION[1]—

Foreman in Charge of Ordinary Labor Gangs (Dirt Road, Cleaning or Sprinkler Gangs and Gangs Employed on Maintenance Work on Bridges):

Regular Service Every Day in the Year:

Range of annual compensation—$1080 to $1440 inclusive.
Salary rates—$1080, $1140, $1200, $1260, $1320, $1380, $1440.

Regular Service Exclusive of Sundays:

Range of annual compensation—$900 to $1200 inclusive.
Salary rates—$900, $960, $1020, $1080, $1140, $1200.

Temporary Service:

Range of per diem compensation[2]—$3 to $4 inclusive.
Wage rates—$3, $3.20, $3.40, $3.60, $3.80, $4.

Foreman Asphalt Worker and Foreman in Charge of Large Gangs Including Skilled Laborers (Stone and Wood Block Paving Gangs, Gangs Employed on Repairs to Flag and Curb, and Water Supply Repair Gangs):

Regular Service Every Day in the Year:

Range of annual compensation—$1440 to $1800 inclusive.
Salary rates—$1440, $1500, $1560, $1620, $1680, $1740, $1800.

Regular Service Exclusive of Sundays:

Range of annual compensation—$1200 to $1500 inclusive.
Salary rates—$1200, $1260, $1320, $1380, $1440, $1500.

Temporary Service:

Range of per diem compensation[2]—$4 to $5 inclusive.
Wage rates—$4, $4.25, $4.50, $4.75, $5.

SPECIAL REGULATION GOVERNING COMPENSATION—

Persons entering this grade need not necessarily begin at the lowest rate. Fixation of the initial salary rate and advancement within this grade are conditional upon appraisal under the rules of the Board of Estimate and Apportionment, indicating that the rate requested does not exceed the value of the work to be performed.

SPECIAL CONDITION GOVERNING ADVANCEMENT—

The following table indicates the minimum number of years of meritorious service required at each rate before advancement to the next rate. See also page 30.

Foreman in Charge of Ordinary Labor Gangs:

$900	$1080	$3.00	1 year
960	1140	3.20	1 "
1020	1200	3.40	1 "
1080	1260	3.60	1 "
1140	1320	3.80	1 "
	1380		1 "

[1]Appropriate deductions from salary will be made in the case of Foremen receiving part or full maintenance.

[2]Advancement from rate to rate shall be granted only to Foremen having served a minimum of 150 days during the preceding year.

Foreman Asphalt Worker and Foreman in Charge of Large Gangs, Including Skilled Laborers:

$1200	$1440	$4.00	1 year
1260	1500	4.25	1 "
1320	1560	4.50	1 "
1380	1620	4.75	1 "
1440	1680		2 years
	1740		2 "

GRADE 3 (U L 3)

TITLES OF POSITIONS[1]—

GENERAL FOREMAN

DUTIES—

The duties of incumbents of these positions are to direct and be responsible for the work of a number of gangs of Laborers under the supervision of Foremen, including other employes in the lowest grades of the Skilled Trades and Unskilled Services.

QUALIFICATIONS—

1. The minimum qualifications prescribed for Grade 2.
2. If appointed by promotion, not less than one year of appropriate experience in Grade 2, or if appointed as the result of an open competitive examination, experience in work of the character and standard of Grade 2.
3. Such additional qualifications as may be required by the Municipal Civil Service Commission.

COMPENSATION—

Range of annual compensation—$1500 to $1920 inclusive.
Salary rates—$1500, $1620, $1740, $1920.

SPECIAL REGULATION GOVERNING COMPENSATION—

Persons entering this grade need not necessarily begin at the lowest rate. Fixation of the initial salary rate and advancement within this grade are conditional upon appraisal under the rules of the Board of Estimate and Apportionment, indicating that the rate requested does not exceed the value of the work to be performed.

SPECIAL CONDITION GOVERNING ADVANCEMENT—

The following table indicates the minimum number of years of meritorious service required at each rate before advancement to the next rate. See also page 30.

$1500	1 year
1620	2 years
1740	2 "

---

[1]The following positions are among those appraised by the Bureau of Personal Service in this grade on the basis of duties performed by present incumbents:

General Foreman in charge of bridge tenders, enginemen, machinists, stokers, oilers and laborers comprising the operating and cleaning forces on movable bridges in the Department of Plant and Structures.

General Foreman in charge of gangs engaged in the repair work in a large district or ward in the Bureaus of Highways in the various boroughs.

General Foreman in charge of sewer and sewer basin cleaning gangs in the Bureaus of Sewers in the various boroughs.

GRADE 4 (U L 4)

TITLES OF POSITIONS[1]—

SUPERINTENDENT OF MAINTENANCE

DUTIES—

The duties of incumbents of these positions are to direct and be responsible for large gangs of Laborers and workers in the skilled trades under General Foremen and Foremen engaged in the maintenance and repair of an entire water distribution or electrical subway system or in other maintenance work of similar character and magnitude.

QUALIFICATIONS—

1. The minimum qualifications prescribed for Grade 3.
2. If appointed by promotion, not less than one year of appropriate experience in Grade 3, or if appointed as the result of an open competitive examination, experience in work of the character and standard of Grade 3.
3. Such additional qualifications as may be required by the Municipal Civil Service Commission.

COMPENSATION—

Range of annual compensation—$2100 to $2700 inclusive.
Salary rates—$2100, $2280, $2460, $2700.

SPECIAL REGULATION GOVERNING COMPENSATION—

Persons entering this grade need not necessarily begin at the lowest rate. Fixation of the initial salary rate and advancement within this grade are conditional upon appraisal under the rules of the Board of Estimate and Apportionment, indicating that the rate requested does not exceed the value of the work to be performed.

PARK WORKER GROUP

SYMBOL (U P)

The term Park Worker Group is applied to those offices or employments of the Unskilled Service in which incumbents are required to perform manual work incident to the maintenance of public parks or to supervise or direct such work.

GRADE 1 (U P 1)

TITLES OF POSITIONS—

CLIMBER AND PRUNER
GARDENER

DUTIES—

Climber and Pruner:

The duties of Climber and Pruners, which require ability to climb trees, are to perform under supervision simple manual work incident to the planting, spraying, pruning and trimming of trees or other related work.

Gardener:

The duties of Gardeners are to perform, under supervision, technical work relating to the planting, propagation, cultivation and care of flowers, plants and shrubs.

---

[1]The following positions are among those appraised by the Bureau of Personal Service in this grade on the basis of duties performed by present incumbents:

Superintendent of Maintenance in the boroughs of Manhattan and The Bronx in the Department of Water Supply, Gas and Electricity, responsible for the repair of all breaks in pipe lines.

QUALIFICATIONS—

1. Such qualifications as may be required by the Municipal Civil Service Commission.

COMPENSATION—

Range of per diem compensation[1]—$2.80 to $3 inclusive.
Wage rates—$2.80, $2.90, $3.

SPECIAL CONDITION GOVERNING ADVANCEMENT—

The following table indicates the minimum number of years of meritorious service required at each rate before advancement to the next rate. See also page 30.

$2.80	1 year
2.90	2 years

GRADE 2 (U P 2)

TITLES OF POSITIONS[2]—

FOREMAN GARDENER
INSPECTOR OF TREES
PARK FOREMAN

DUTIES—

Foreman Gardener:

The duties of Foremen Gardeners, which require a high degree of gardening skill, are to supervise and instruct employes in Grade 1 and other employes in the performance of technical work relating to the planting, propagation, cultivation and care of flowers, plants and shrubs.

Examples:

Assisting head gardener in greenhouse work.
Directing a gang of park laborers in the care of flower beds or shrubberies.

Inspector of Trees:

The duties of Inspectors of Trees are to receive and investigate complaints of citizens regarding the care and condition of trees in city streets, to make recommendations as to treatment, and to perform such work in the actual care of trees as may be required.[3]

Park Foreman:

The duties of Park Foremen are to plan and supervise the work of a group of employes in Grade 1 or of other laborers.

Examples:

Taking charge of a gang of climbers and pruners.
Taking charge of a gang repairing park roadways.

---

[1]Advancement from rate to rate shall be granted only to employes having served a minimum of 150 days during the preceding year.

[2]The following positions are among those appraised by the Bureau of Personal Service in this grade on the basis of duties performed by present incumbents:

Park Foreman in charge of a group of small parks or a section of a large park in the Department of Parks, Manhattan, Brooklyn, The Bronx or Queens.

[3]In future these positions, which exist only in the borough of Brooklyn, should be filled by Climbers and Pruners.

QUALIFICATIONS—

1. The minimum qualifications prescribed for Grade 1.

2. If appointed by promotion, not less than one year of appropriate experience in Grade 1, or if appointed as the result of an open competitive examination, experience in work of the character and standard of Grade 1.

3. Such additional qualifications as may be required by the Municipal Civil Service Commission.

COMPENSATION—

Regular Service Every Day in the Year:

Range of annual compensation—$1140 to $1320 inclusive.
Salary rates—$1140, $1200, $1260, $1320.

Regular Service Exclusive of Sundays:

Range of annual compensation—$960 to $1140 inclusive.
Salary rates—$960, $1020, $1080, $1140.

Temporary Service:

Range of per diem compensation[1]—$3.20 to $3.80 inclusive.
Wage rates—$3.20, $3.40, $3.60, $3.80.

SPECIAL REGULATION GOVERNING COMPENSATION—

Beginning with the lowest rate, advancement within this grade is conditional upon appraisal under the rules of the Board of Estimate and Apportionment, indicating that the rate requested does not exceed the value of the work to be performed.

SPECIAL CONDITION GOVERNING ADVANCEMENT—

The following table indicates the minimum number of years of meritorious service required at each rate before advancement to the next rate. See also page 30.

$1140	$960	$3.20	1 year
1200	1020	3.40	2 years
1260	1080	3.60	2 "

GRADE 3 (U P 3)

TITLES OF POSITIONS[2]—

ARBORICULTURIST
GENERAL PARK FOREMAN
HEAD GARDENER

---

[1]Advancement from rate to rate shall be granted only to employes having served a minimum of 150 days during the preceding year.

[2]The following positions are among those appraised by the Bureau of Personal Service in this grade on the basis of duties performed by present incumbents:

Arboriculturist in charge of a section, borough of Brooklyn.

Arboriculturist in charge of one large or a number of small gangs of laborers and other employes, borough of Manhattan.

General Park Foreman in charge of the park districts extending from the Battery to 59th Street, from 59th Street to 110th Street and from 110th Street north, in the Department of Parks, Manhattan and Richmond.

Head Gardener in charge of greenhouses in the Departments of Parks, Manhattan and Richmond, Brooklyn, The Bronx or Queens.

DUTIES—

Arboriculturist:

The duties of Arboriculturists are to supervise and inspect the work of groups of laborers and other employes engaged in the planting, cultivation and care of trees, shrubs and plants in public parks, streets and nurseries, or to take charge of and be responsible for the care of trees in an assigned section of a borough, to assist in making studies and preparing specifications relating to the conservation of trees, shrubs and plants, and to perform other related technical work.

General Park Foreman:

The duties of General Park Foremen, which include supervision of the work of employes in Grades 1 and 2, are to be responsible for the work of the largest park divisions or units.

Head Gardener:

The duties of Head Gardeners, which include supervision of Gardeners and Foremen Gardeners in Grades 1 and 2, are to take charge of greenhouses and to be responsible for the gardening work of one or more boroughs.

QUALIFICATIONS—

Arboriculturist:

1. Experience in planting, cultivating and caring for trees on large private estates or in public streets or parks, or other training or experience recognized by the Municipal Civil Service Commission as qualifying.
2. Such additional qualifications as may be required by the Municipal Civil Service Commission.

General Park Foreman, Head Gardener:

1. The minimum qualifications prescribed for Grade 2.
2. If appointed by promotion, not less than two years of appropriate experience in Grade 2, or if appointed as the result of an open competitive examination, experience in work of the character and standard of Grade 2.
3. Such additional qualifications as may be required by the Municipal Civil Service Commission.

COMPENSATION—

Regular Service Every Day in the Year:

Range of annual compensation—$1440 to $1800 inclusive.
Salary rates—$1440, $1560, $1680, $1800.

Temporary Service:

Range of per diem compensation[1]—$4 to $4.75 inclusive.
Wage rates—$4, $4.25, $4.50, $4.75.

SPECIAL REGULATION GOVERNING COMPENSATION—

Beginning with the lowest rate, advancement within this grade is conditional upon appraisal under the rules of the Board of Estimate and Apportionment, indicating that the rate requested does not exceed the value of the work to be performed.

SPECIAL CONDITION GOVERNING ADVANCEMENT—

The following table indicates the minimum number of years of meritorious service required at each rate before advancement to the next rate. See also page 30.

$1440	$4.00	1 year
1560	4.25	2 years
1680	4.50	2 "

[1]Advancement from rate to rate shall be granted only to persons having served a minimum of 150 days during the preceding year.

GRADE 4 (U P 4)

TITLES OF POSITIONS[1]—

SUPERINTENDENT OF PARKS

DUTIES—

The duties of incumbents of these positions are to direct, inspect and report on the work of employes in Grades 1, 2 and 3 and of other employes engaged in the care and maintenance of an entire system of parks and parkways, to advise with the Commissioner of Parks on questions involving the use of parks by the public, and to perform such other related work as may be assigned.

QUALIFICATIONS—

1. The minimum qualifications prescribed for General Park Foreman in Grade 3.
2. If appointed by promotion, not less than two years of appropriate experience as General Park Foreman in Grade 3, or if appointed as the result of an open competitive examination, experience in work of the character and standard of Grade 3.
3. Such additional qualifications as may be required by the Municipal Civil Service Commission.

COMPENSATION—

Range of annual compensation—$2700 to $3960 inclusive.
Salary rates—$2700, $2940, $3180, $3420, $3660, $3960.

SPECIAL REGULATION GOVERNING COMPENSATION—

Persons entering this grade need not necessarily begin at the lowest rate. Fixation of the initial salary rate and advancement within this grade are conditional upon appraisal under the rules of the Board of Estimate and Apportionment, indicating that the rate requested does not exceed the value of the work to be performed.

MISCELLANEOUS LABORER GROUP

SYMBOL (U Z)

The term Miscellaneous Laborer Group is applied to those offices or employments of the Unskilled Service in which incumbents are required to perform routine or specialized laboring work of an exceptional nature not included in the other groups of the Unskilled Service.

GRADE 1 (U Z 1)

TITLES OF POSITIONS—

GATE TENDER
LABORATORY HELPER
LABORER (STORES)
TICKET CHOPPER

---

[1]The position of Superintendent of Parks at present exists only in the boroughs of Brooklyn and The Bronx.

It is recommended that a position as Engineer and Superintendent be established in each borough. (See Grades 4 and 5 of the Engineer Group of the Professional Service.) Should consolidation of the various existing park units be effected under a single Commissioner, a position as Chief Engineer of Parks should be established combining the duties of Engineer and Superintendent over the whole park system of Greater New York, and the incumbent should supervise the work of four borough engineers of maintenance and operation.

DUTIES—

Gate Tender:

The duties of Gate Tenders, which involve cleaning and light laboring work about the gate-house, are to be on watch at gate-houses of the water supply system and to operate the gates either by hand or electrically in accordance with instructions.

Laboratory Helper:

The duties of Laboratory Helpers are to clean and sterilize glassware and utensils, to fill, cap and label bottles and to perform such other manual work about laboratories as may properly be performed by laboratory helpers.[1]

Laborer (Stores):

The duties of Laborers (Stores), which require ability to read, write and understand English and to perform simple arithmetical calculations, are to pack, unpack, receive, distribute and otherwise handle supplies, materials and equipment under the supervision of a Stores Foreman or a Storekeeper, to be responsible for the cleaning and orderliness of bins, floors, etc., and to perform under supervision such simple clerical work as may be required.

Ticket Chopper:

The duties of Ticket Choppers are to receive and chop tickets at entrances to municipal ferries or other means of transportation and to prevent persons not holding tickets from gaining access to such places.

QUALIFICATIONS—

1. Such qualifications as may be required by the Municipal Civil Service Commission.

COMPENSATION—

Gate Tender:

Regular Service Every Day in the Year:

Range of annual compensation—$876 to $984 inclusive.
Salary rates—$876, $912, $948, $984.

Laboratory Helper:

Range of annual compensation—$360 to $780 inclusive.
Salary rates—$360, $420, $480, $540, $600, $660, $720, $780.

Laborer (Stores):

Regular Service Exclusive of Sundays:

Range of annual compensation—$816 to $912 inclusive.
Salary rates—$816, $840, $864, $888, $912.

Temporary Service:

Range of per diem compensation—$2.60 to $2.90 inclusive.
Wage rates—$2.60, $2.70, $2.80, $2.90.

Ticket Chopper:

Regular Service Exclusive of Sundays:

Range of annual compensation—$792 to $888 inclusive.
Salary rates—$792, $816, $840, $864, $888.

Temporary Service:

Per diem compensation—$2.50.

---

[1]See grades 1 and 2 of the Laboratory Assistant Group.

SPECIAL REGULATION GOVERNING COMPENSATION—

Laboratory Helper:

Persons entering this grade need not necessarily begin at the lowest rate. Fixation of the initial salary rate and advancement within this grade are conditional upon appraisal under the rules of the Board of Estimate and Apportionment, indicating that the rate requested does not exceed the value of the work to be performed.

SPECIAL CONDITION GOVERNING ADVANCEMENT—

The following table indicates the minimum number of years of meritorious service required at each rate before advancement to the next rate. See also page 30.

Gate Tender:

$876	1 year
912	1 "
948	2 years

Laborer (Stores):

Employed at an annual rate:		Employed at a per diem rate:	
$816	1 year	$2.60	1 year
840	1 "	2.70	2 years
864	1 "	2.80	2 "
888	2 years		

Ticket Chopper:

$792	1 year
816	1 "
840	2 years
864	2 "

APPENDIX

RULE OF OCTOBER 3, 1916.

October 3, 1916.

To the Heads of Departments:

At an executive meeting of the Board of Estimate and Apportionment, held on September 27th, the question of regular periodic increases in salaries as recommended in the standard specifications was considered. The Board agreed to grant a substantial number of increases among the lower paid employees in order to put the recommendations of the proposed standard specifications into partial effect in the 1917 Budget.

As a basis for determining the final appropriation for this purpose the Budget Committee has decided to ask the heads of Departments to prepare lists of employees who would be eligible for increases under restrictive conditions as indicated below. The Budget Committee wishes to emphasize to the heads of Departments that the conditions are to be regarded as minimum requirements and that they are not under any obligation to recommend all employees who would be eligible.

Co-operation of Department Heads.

The plan for the coming Budget must be regarded as somewhat experimental in character. Its success this year and its future development will depend in large measure on the intelligent co-operation of administrative officers in preparing and reviewing the departmental service ratings.

Preparation of Departmental Eligible List.

The lists should be prepared by codes following the order of the original Budget requests. Opposite each name on the list it should be indicated whether or not the person has already been recommended for increase in the departmental estimate. It is suggested that the capital letters " R " and " N. R." be used for this purpose to indicate whether the persons have been " already recommended " or " not recommended."

It is also requested that a supplemental list be submitted carrying the names of employees who have been recommended for increases in the estimate, but would not be eligible under the proposed conditions.

Minimum Conditions Regarding Increases for Employees in the Lower Grades.

Clerical Service.

Employees in the following grades:

Clerk Group, Grade 1 ($300 to $540).
Grade 2a ($600 to $720).
Stenographer Group, Grade 1 ($720 to $900).
Telephone Operator Group, Grade 1 ($600 to $900).
Typist Group, Grade 1 ($600 to $780).

—who have served one year or more at their present salary rates and have received a departmental rating of "Average" in efficiency and punctuality for the four quarters of the year ending June 30, 1916.

Employees in the Clerical Service other than those mentioned above whose salary is less than $1,200, who have served two years or more at their present salary rates and have received a departmental rating of "Above average" in efficiency and punctuality for at least two quarters of the year ending June 30, 1916; or who have served one year or more at their present salary rate and have received a departmental rating of "Far above average" in efficiency and punctuality for at least two quarters of the year ending June 30, 1916.

Custodial Service.

Employees in the following grades:

- Animal Keeper Group, Grade 1 ($900 to $1,080).
- Bridge Tender Group, Grade 1 ($860 to $960).
- Carctakcr Group, Grade 1 ($780 to $960).
- Elevator Operator Group, Grade 1 ($780 to $960).
- Watchman Group, Grade 1 ($720 to $840).
- Ticket Chopper Group, Grade 1 ($744 to $864).

—who have served one year or more at their present salary rates and have received a departmental rating of "Average" in efficiency and punctuality for the four quarters of the year ending June 30, 1916.

Employees in the Custodial Service, other than those mentioned above, whose salary is less than $1,200, who have served two years or more at their present salary rates and have received a departmental rating of "Above average" in efficiency and punctuality for at least two quarters of the year ending June 30, 1916; or who have served one year or more at their present salary rates and have received a departmental rating of "Far above average" in efficiency and punctuality for at least two quarters of the year ending June 30, 1916.

Professional, Sub-Professional, Investigational and Educational Services.

Employees on full time whose salary is less than $1,200, who have served three years or more at their present salary rate and have received a departmental rating of "Average" in efficiency and punctuality for the four quarters of the year ending June 30, 1916, or who have served two years or more at their present salary rates and have received a departmental rating of "Above average" in efficiency and punctuality for at least two quarters of the year ending June 30, 1916, or who have served one year or more at their present salary rates and have received a departmental rating of "Far above average" in efficiency and punctuality for at least two quarters of the year ending June 30, 1916.

In the case of employees in the non-competitive or exempt class, such as Nurses in hospitals, for whom no departmental service records are prepared a special certificate of excellent service must be submitted by the department head to justify an increase for employees who have served less than three years at their present salary rates.

Inspectional Service.

First Grade Inspectors whose salary is less than $1,500, who have served for three years or more at their present salary rates and have received a departmental rating of "Average" in efficiency and punctuality for the four quarters of the year ending June 30, 1916, or who have served for two years or more at their present salary rates and have received a departmental rating of "Above average" in efficiency and punctuality for at least two quarters of the year ending June 30, 1916, or who have served at least one year at their present salary rates and have received a departmental rating of "Far above average" in efficiency and punctuality for at least two quarters of the year ending June 30, 1916.

Institutional Service.

Employees in this service whose salary is less than $660 with maintenance or $900 without maintenance and who have served at least one year or six months, according to the provisions of the standard specifications, and whose records are considered satisfactory by the head of the department.

Street Cleaning and Unskilled Service.

Employees in this service in the labor class (*i. e.*, employees below the competitive class in the Civil Service classification) who have served at least one year at their present salary rates and whose services are considered satisfactory by the head of the department.

Employees in these services, in the competitive class, whose salaries are less than $1,200, who have served three years or more at their present salary rates and have received a departmental rating of "Average" in efficiency and punctuality for the four quarters ending June 30, 1916, or who have served two years or more at their present salary rates and have received a departmental rating of "Above average" in efficiency and punctuality for at least two quarters of the year ending June 30, 1916, or who have served one year at their present salary rates and have received a departmental rating of "Far above average" in efficiency and punctuality for at least two quarters of the year ending June 30, 1916.

The increase of $12 in the salaries of Assistant Foremen in the Street Cleaning Department in the 1916 Budget, which was made in order to raise these employees to the minimum of the standard grade shall not be considered as an increase in making advancements in the 1917 Budget.

NOTE—The above rules shall not be construed so as to permit of an increase to a rate higher than the maximum appraised value of the work to be done, or so as to prevent an increase to the minimum of the grade in which the position is appraised.

WM. A. PRENDERGAST,
Comptroller, Chairman Tax Budget Committee.

PROPOSED RESOLUTION OF THE BOARD OF ESTIMATE AND APPORTIONMENT PROVIDING FOR APPROVAL OF TITLES BY THE MUNICIPAL CIVIL SERVICE COMMISSION.

Resolved, That the Board of Estimate and Apportionment hereby approves the following procedure pending amendments to Sections 56 and 226 of the Charter:

The Board of Estimate and Apportionment shall include in the budget schedules supporting appropriations for salaries, wages and other compensations, only those titles which shall have been approved by the Municipal Civil Service Commission, and shall have been certified to the Board of Estimate and Apportionment by said Commission as being properly descriptive of the duties to be performed and uniform for similar duties.

In recommending to the Board of Aldermen the fixing of salaries of officers or persons, the Board of Estimate and Apportionment shall certify that the titles of such officers or persons have been approved by the Municipal Civil Service Commission.

PROPOSED STANDARD FORM OF REPORT ON CHANGES IN THE STANDARD SPECIFICATIONS FOR PERSONAL SERVICE TO BE SUBMITTED BY THE COMMITTEE ON SALARIES AND GRADES TO THE BOARD OF ESTIMATE AND APPORTIONMENT.

Report of the Committee on Salaries and Grades on proposed changes in the Standard Specifications for Personal Service affecting the position(s) of ....in Grade(s)............of the............Group of the............... Service.

The Bureau of Personal Service reports to the Committee that the purpose is to[1]...
....
....

In view of this report the Committee recommends......................
....

....

....

....

Committee on Salaries and Grades.

The Municipal Civil Service Commission approves these changes so far as they affect the titles, duties and qualifications of positions and so far as they affect changes in salaries which involve changes in the civil service salary grades.

....

President, Municipal Civil Service Commission.

---

[1]The following is a list of the major changes one or more of which is to be inserted in the above space:

a. Add the new group of.................in the.................Service, the group definition being as follows:

b. Add the new position of...............involving new duties and qualifications and an appropriate range of compensation as follows:

c. Eliminate the position of...............

d. Change the qualifications for the position of...............as follows:

e. Change the compensation for the position of...............as follows:

f. Change the regulation governing compensation for the position of.........
..........as follows:

g. Change the condition governing advancement for the position of.........
..........as follows:

h. Change the notes on the position of...............as follows:

PROPOSED STANDARD FORM OF REPORT ON TEMPORARY SUSPENSION OF THE PROVISIONS GOVERNING INITIAL COMPENSATION IN THE STANDARD SPECIFICATIONS FOR PERSONAL SERVICE TO BE SUBMITTED BY THE COMMITTEE ON SALARIES AND GRADES TO THE BOARD OF ESTIMATE AND APPORTIONMENT.

Report of the Committee on Salaries and Grades on proposed temporary suspension of provisions of the Standard Specifications for Personal Service governing initial compensation affecting the position(s) of............in the Grade(s)............of the............Group of the............Service.

The Bureau of Personal Service reports to the Committee that the reason for this temporary suspension is..................

In view of this report the Committee recommends................

....

....

....

Committee on Salaries and Grades.

INCREASED COST OF LIVING FOR AN UNSKILLED LABORER'S FAMILY IN NEW YORK CITY.[1]

The following table shows a comparison of the results of studies made in February, 1915, and February, 1917, of the cost of living for an unskilled laborer's family in New York City. The increase in cost in those two years seems to be not less than $135, or approximately 16%. The family under consideration is assumed to consist of five members, a wage earner, his wife and three children of school age (boy of 13 years, girl of 10 years and boy of 6 years) who cannot be expected to contribute anything to the family support. Objects of expenditure have been classified in eight standard groups, among which the total has been apportioned as follows:

	February, 1915 Per Year	February, 1917 Per Year
I.—Housing	$168.00	$168.00
II.—Carfare	30.30	30.30
III.—Food	383.812	492.388
IV.—Clothing	104.20	127.10
V.—Fuel and Light	42.75	46.75
VI.—Health	20.00	20.00
VII.—Insurance	22.88	22.88
VIII.—Sundries	73.00	73.00
Total	$844.942	$980.418
Sundries Classified—		
Papers and other reading matter	$5.00	
Recreation	40.00	
Furniture, utensils, fixtures, moving expenses, etc.	18.00	
Church dues	5.00	
Incidentals—soap, washing material, stamps, etc.	5.00	
Total	$73.00	
		844.942
Amount of increase		$135.476

[1]For a detailed report of this study see Report on the Increased Cost of Living for an Unskilled Laborer's Family in New York City, Bureau of Personal Service, 1917.

DIGEST OF STANDARD SPECIFICATIONS

Executive Service

Group	Gr.	Title	Salary Range	Rates
Executive Council			No recommendations	
Commissioner	1	Assessor Commissioner	$3600–6000	$3600 4500 5100 6000
	2	Chamberlain Commissioner Corporation Counsel Executive Manager (Education)	7500–15000	7500 9000 10500 12000 13500 15000
Deputy Commissioner	1	Deputy Commissioner Deputy Comptroller	3600–7500	3600 3900 4200 4500 4800 5100 5400 6000 6600 7500
Executive Secretary	1	Executive Secretary	3000–5100	3000 3240 3480 3780 4080 4380 4680 5100
Executive County Officer		See note on page 34		

Professional Service

Group	Gr.	Title	Salary Range	Rates
Accountant	1	Junior Accountant	$1260–1920	$1260 1380 1500 1620 1740 1920
	2	Accountant Auditor	2100–3180	2100 2280 2460 2700 2940 3180

DIGEST OF STANDARD SPECIFICATIONS—Continued

Professional Service—Continued

Group	Gr.	Title	Salary Range	Rates
Accountant—Cont'd	3	Senior Accountant Senior Auditor	$3420–4560	$3420 3660 3960 4260 4560
	4	Chief Accountant Chief Auditor	4860 and up (No recommendation above $6120)	4860 5280 5700 6120
Architect	1	ArchitecturalAssistant	1020–1380	1020 1140 1260 1380
	2	Junior Architect Junior Architect (Landscape)	1500–2100	1500 1620 1740 1920 2100
	3	Assistant Architect Assistant Architect (Landscape)	2280–2940	2280 2460 2700 2940
	4	Architect Architect and Deputy Superintendent of School Buildings Architect (Landscape)	3180–4560 Per diem: $25 and up	3180 3420 3660 3960 4260 4560
	5	Senior Architect Senior Architect and Deputy Superintendent of School Buildings	See note on page 43	
	6	Chief Architect Chief Architect and Superintendent of School Buildings Consulting Architect	6120 and up (No recommendation above $10200)	6120 6600 7200 7800 8400 9000 9600 10200
Bacteriologist	1	Assistant Bacteriologist	1500–2100 (Full time)	1500 1620 1740 1920 2100
			1200–1800 (Not less than 28hrs. a week)	1200 1320 1440 1560 1680 1800

DIGEST OF STANDARD SPECIFICATIONS—Continued

Professional Service—Continued

Group	Gr.	Title	Salary Range	Rates
Bacteriologist—Cont'd	2	Bacteriologist	$2280–3180 (Full time)	$2280 2460 2700 2940 3180
			1980–2820 (Not less than 28hrs. a week)	1980 2160 2340 2580 2820
	3	Senior Bacteriologist	See note on page 46	
	4	Director of Health Laboratories	5100 and up (No recommendation above $5940)	5100 5520 5940
Chaplain	1	Chaplain	900 with or without maintenance (full time) 480 without maintenance (Not less than 1 day a week)	
		Assistant to Chaplain in institutions or group of institutions	600	
Chemist and Physicist	1	Junior Chemist Junior Physicist	1020–1380 Monthly rate: $100	1020 1140 1260 1380
	2	Assistant Chemist Assistant Chemist (Food and Drugs) Assistant Physicist	1500–2100 (Full time)	1500 1620 1740 1920 2100
			1020–1380 (Not less than 18 hours a week)	1020 1140 1260 1380
	3	Chemist Chemist (Microanalyst) Chemist (Pharmaceutical) Physicist	2280–3180	2280 2460 2700 2940 3180
	4	Senior Chemist Senior Physicist	See note on page 50	

DIGEST OF STANDARD SPECIFICATIONS—Continued

Professional Service—Continued

Group	Gr.	Title	Salary Range	Rates
Chemist and Physicist—Cont'd	5	Director (Central Testing Laboratory)	$5100 and up (No recommendation above $5940)	$5100 5520 5940
Dentist	1	Dental Interne	120–240 with maintenance	120 240
	2	Dentist	900–1380 with maintenance for full time service	900 1020 1140 1260 1380
			1020–1380 without maintenance (Not less than 18 hours a week)	1020 1140 1260 1380
			1140–1500 without maintenance (Not less than 24 hours a week)	1140 1260 1380 1500
	3	Supervising Dentist	1500–1740 with maintenance for full time service	1500 1620 1740
			1500–1740 without maintenance (Not less than 18 hours a week)	1500 1620 1740
Engineer	1	Engineering Assistant	1020–1380	1020 1140 1260 1380
	2	Junior Engineer Junior Engineer (Civil) Junior Engineer (Electrical) Junior Engineer (Mechanical) Junior Engineer (Sanitary)	1500–2100	1500 1620 1740 1920 2100

DIGEST OF STANDARD SPECIFICATIONS—Continued

Professional Service—Continued

Group	Gr.	Title	Salary Range	Rates
Engineer—Cont'd	3	Assistant Engineer Assistant Engineer (Civil) Assistant Engineer (Electrical) Assistant Engineer (Mechanical) Assistant Engineer (Power Plant Supervision) Assistant Engineer (Sanitary)	$2280–3180	$2280 2460 2700 2940 3180
	4	Senior Assistant Engineer Senior Assistant Engineer (Civil) Senior Assistant Engineer (Electrical) Senior Assistant Engineer (Mechanical) Senior Assistant Engineer (Sanitary)	3420–4560	3420 3660 3960 4260 4560
	5	Engineer Engineer (Civil) Engineer (Electrical) Engineer (Mechanical) Engineer (Sanitary)	4860–5700	4860 5280 5700
	6	Chief Engineer Consulting Engineer	6120 and up (No recommendation above $10200) Per diem: $25 and up	6120 6600 7200 7800 8400 9000 9600 10200
Forester	1	Forester	2100 and up (No recommendation above $2700)	2100 2280 2460 2700
Lawyer	1	Junior Law Assistant	1020–1380	1020 1140 1260 1380
	2	Junior Assistant Corporation Counsel Junior Legal Examiner	1500–2280	1500 1620 1740 1920 2100 2280

DIGEST OF STANDARD SPECIFICATIONS—Continued

Professional Service—Continued

Group	Gr.	Title	Salary Range	Rates
Lawyer—Cont'd	3	Deputy Assistant Corporation Counsel Legal Examiner	$2520–4680	$2520 2760 3000 3240 3480 3780 4080 4380 4680
	4	Assistant Corporation Counsel Chief Legal Examiner Senior Legal Examiner	5100 and up (No recommendation above $10200)	5100 5520 5940 6600 7200 7800 8400 9000 9600 10200
Nurse	1	Nurse[1]	600–720 with maintenance Per diem: $3.50	600 660 720
		Field Nurse	960–1140	960 1020 1080 1140
	2	Chief Nurse[2]	780–1200 with maintenance	780 840 900 960 1020 1080 1140 1200
		Senior Field Nurse	1200–1440	1200 1260 1320 1380 1440
	3	Assistant Superintendent of Nurses	1320–1560 with maintenance	1320 1440 1560

[1] A special range of $660 to $720, inclusive, may be paid for continuous service in tuberculosis, psychopathic or alcoholic hospitals or wards.

[2] Chief nurses engaged in instruction of pupil nurses or in charge of nurses in operating room may be paid $900 to $1200, inclusive.

A special range of $840 to $1200, inclusive, may be paid for continuous service in tuberculosis, psychopathic or alcoholic hospitals or wards, or in night supervision.

DIGEST OF STANDARD SPECIFICATIONS—Continued

Professional Service—Continued

Group	Gr.	Title	Salary Range	Rates
Nurse—Cont'd		Assistant Director of Field Nurses	$1560–1680	$1560 1680
	4	Superintendent of Nurses	1680–1980 with maintenance	1680 1800 1980
		Director of Field Nurses	1800–2160	1800 1980 2160
	5	General Superintendent of Nurses	2160–3060 with maintenance	2160 2340 2580 2820 3060
Pathologist	1	Assistant Pathologist	1740–2100	1740 1920 2100
	2	Pathologist	2280–3180 (Full time)	2280 2460 2700 2940 3180
			1500–1920 (Not less than 18 hours a week)	1500 1620 1740 1920
	3	Senior Pathologist	3420–4560	3420 3660 3960 4260 4560
	4	Director of Pathological Laboratories	5100 and up (No recommendation above $5940)	5100 5520 5940
Pharmacist	1	Assistant Pharmacist	600–840 with maintenance	600 720 840
			900–1140 without maintenance	900 1020 1140
	2	Pharmacist	960–1200 with maintenance	960 1080 1200

DIGEST OF STANDARD SPECIFICATIONS—Continued

Professional Service—Continued

Group	Gr.	Title	Salary Range	Rates
Pharmacist—Cont'd			$1260–1500 without maintenance	$1260 1380 1500
	3	Head Pharmacist	1620–2460	1620 1740 1920 2100 2280 2460
Physician	1	Medical Interne[1]	120–240	120 240
	2	Assistant Physician (Hospital)	900–1380 with maintenance	900 1020 1140 1260 1380
		Assistant Physician (Hospital) in exclusive tuberculosis or contagious disease work or in institutions of Dept. of Correction	1260–1380 with maintenance	1260 1380
		Assistant Physician (Medical Clerk)	1140–1500	1140 1260 1380 1500
	3	Physician (Anaesthetist) Physician (Field)[2] Physician (Hospital)[3] Physician (Laryngologist) Physician (Oculist)	1500–2280 with maintenance in hospital or institutional service (Full time)	1500 1620 1740 1920 2100 2280
		Physician (Roentgenologist)	2100–2760 without maintenance (Full time)	2100 2280 2520 2760
			1380–1500 (Not less than 24 hrs. a week)	1380 1500
			1140–1380 (Not less than 18 hrs. a week)	1140 1260 1380

[1] Additional compensation of $10 per month may be paid to Medical Internes engaged exclusively in tuberculosis work.

[2] For not less than 6 nor more than 12 hours a week in the Dept. of Education, a range of $480 to $720 may be paid.

[3] The first assistant to a resident physician in charge of a hospital in the Dept. of Health may be paid a range of $1740 to $2280.

DIGEST OF STANDARD SPECIFICATIONS—Continued

Professional Service—Continued

Group	Gr.	Title	Salary Range	Rates
Physician—Cont'd		Physician (Diagnostician) Physician (Supervising District)	$2280–2760 with maintenance (Full time)	$2280 2520 2760
			1260–1500 (Not less than 18 hrs. a week)	1260 1380 1500
		Physician (Clinic)	300–660 (Not less than 8 hrs. a week)	300 420 540 660
		Physician (Alienist)	1920–2280 with maintenance (Full time)	1920 2100 2280
			2520–2760 without maintenance (Full time)	2520 2760
	4	Senior Physician (Alienist) Senior Physician (Field) Senior Physician (Orthopedist) Assistant Medical Superintendent	2520–3480 with maintenance (Full time)	2520 2760 3000 3240 3480
			3000–3480 without maintenance (Full time)	3000 3240 3480
			1620–2100 (Not less than 18 hrs. a week)	1620 1740 1920 2100
		Senior Physician (Assistant Registrar)	2520–3000	2520 2760 3000
	5	Chief Physician (Alienist) Chief Physician (Diagnostician) Chief Physician (Field)	3780–4680 with maintenance in hospital or institutional service (Full time)	3780 4080 4380 4680
		Medical Consultant (Law Department) Medical Superintendent	2280-2700 (Not less than 18 hrs. a week)	2280 2460 2700

DIGEST OF STANDARD SPECIFICATIONS—Continued

Professional Service—Continued

Group	Gr.	Title	Salary Range	Rates
Physician—Cont'd	6	Chief Medical Examiner Director of Psychopathic Service General Medical Superintendent Health Director	$5100 and up with maintenance in hospital or institutional service (No recommendation above $5940)	$5100 5520 5940
Veterinarian	1	Veterinarian	1800–2340 (Full time)	1800 1980 2160 2340
			1500–1740 (Not less than 28 hrs. a week)	1500 1620 1740
			1200-1440 (Not less than 18 hrs. a week)	1200 1320 1440
	2	Supervising Veterinarian	2580–3300 (Full time)	2580 2820 3060 3300
			1800–2340 (Not less than 21 hrs. a week)	1800 1980 2160 2340

Sub-Professional Service

Group	Gr.	Title	Salary Range	Rates
Apprentice Pharmacist	1	Apprentice Pharmacist	$360–480 with maintenance	$360 420 480
			600–720 without maintenance	600 660 720
Dental Assistant	1	Dental Assistant	720-900	720 780 840 900

DIGEST OF STANDARD SPECIFICATIONS—Continued
Sub-Professional Service—Continued

Group	Gr.	Title	Salary Range	Rates
Draftsman	1	Junior Draftsman	$900-1200	$900 960 1020 1080 1140 1200
	2	Draftsman Plan Examiner	1320-1800	1320 1440 1560 1680 1800
Instrumentman	1	Junior Instrument-man	900-1200	900 960 1020 1080 1140 1200
	2	Instrumentman	1320-1800	1320 1440 1560 1680 1800
Laboratory Assistant	1	Laboratory Apprentice	360-600	360 480 600
	2	Laboratory Assistant (Bacteriology) Laboratory Assistant (Chemistry) Laboratory Assistant (Pathology) Laboratory Assistant (Physics)	720-1200	720 840 960 1080 1200
Law Clerk	1	Junior Law Clerk	900-1200	900 960 1020 1080 1140 1200
	2	Law Clerk	1320-1800	1320 1440 1560 1680 1800
	3	Senior Law Clerk	1980-2820	1980 2160 2340 2580 2820
	4	Assistant Chief Law Clerk Assistant Managing Clerk (Law Dept.)	3060-4140	3060 3300 3540 3840 4140

DIGEST OF STANDARD SPECIFICATIONS—Continued

Sub-Professional Service—Continued

Group	Gr.	Title	Salary Range	Rates
Law Clerk—Cont'd	5	Managing Clerk (Law Dept.)	$4440–5160	$4440 4740 5160
Pupil Nurse	1	Pupil Nurse: Bellevue & Allied Hospitals Dept. of Public Charities	96 with maintenance 120–180 with maintenance	96 120 144 180
Title Examiner	1	Junior Title Examiner	960–1320	960 1080 1200 1320
	2	Title Examiner	1440–1980	1440 1560 1680 1800 1980
	3	Senior Title Examiner	2160–3060	2160 2340 2580 2820 3060
Miscellaneous Sub-Professional Worker	1	Psychologist	1500–1920 (Full time)	1500 1620 1740 1920
			900–1260 (Not less than 21 hrs. a week)	900 1020 1140 1260

Investigational Service

Group	Gr.	Title	Salary Range	Rates
Attendance Officer	1	Attendance Officer	$1200–1560	$1200 1260 1320 1380 1440 1500 1560
	2	Senior Attendance Officer	1680–2160	1680 1800 1980 2160

DIGEST OF STANDARD SPECIFICATIONS—Continued

Investigational Service—Continued

Group	Gr.	Title	Salary Range	Rates
Attendance Officer—Cont'd	3	Assistant Chief Attendance Officer	$2340-2820	$2340 2580 2820
	4	Chief Attendance Officer	3060-3540	3060 3300 3540
	5	Assistant Director of School Attendance	3840-4140	3840 4140
	6	Director of School Attendance	4440-5160	4440 4740 5160
Civil Service Examiner	1	Physical Examiner (Civil Service)	1680-2160	1680 1800 1980 2160
		Civil Service Examiner	2100-2700 Per diem: $5 or $7	2100 2280 2460 2700
	2	Senior Civil Service Examiner Senior Civil Service Examiner (Engineering)	2940-3420 Per diem: $10	2940 3180 3420
		Senior Civil Service Examiner (Medical)	2940-3420 (Full time)	2940 3180 3420
			2100-2460 (Not less than 18 hrs. a week) Per diem: $10	2100 2280 2460
	3	Assistant Chief Civil Service Examiner	3660-4260	3660 3960 4260
		Supervising Civil Service Examiner (Medical)	3660-4260 (Full time)	3660 3960 4260
			2700-3180 (Not less than 18 hrs. a week)	2700 2940 3180
	4	Chief Civil Service Examiner	4560-4860	4560 4860

DIGEST OF STANDARD SPECIFICATIONS—Continued

Investigational Service—Continued

Group	Gr.	Title	Salary Range	Rates
Civil Service Investigator	1	Civil Service Investigator	$1500–1740	$1500 1560 1620 1680 1740
	2	Supervising Civil Service Investigator	2400–3120	2400 2640 2880 3120
Claim Investigator	1	Claim Investigator	1080–1500	1080 1140 1200 1260 1320 1380 1440 1500
	2	Senior Claim Investigator	1620–2280	1620 1740 1920 2100 2280
	3	Chief Claim Investigator	2520–3000	2520 2760 3000
Fire Marshal	1	Assistant Fire Marshal	1500–1740	1500 1560 1620 1680 1740
	2	Senior Assistant Fire Marshal	1920–2280	1920 2100 2280
	3	Fire Marshal	2520–3000	2520 2760 3000
	4	Chief Fire Marshal	3600–4800	3600 3900 4200 4500 4800
Municipal Examiner	1	Assistant Municipal Examiner Assistant Municipal Examiner (Special)	1200–1800	1200 1320 1440 1560 1680 1800
	2	Municipal Examiner Municipal Examiner (Special)	1980–2820	1980 2160 2340 2580 2820

DIGEST OF STANDARD SPECIFICATIONS—Continued

Investigational Service—Continued

Group	Gr.	Title	Salary Range	Rates
Municipal Examiner—Cont'd	3	Senior Municipal Examiner Senior Municipal Examiner (Special)	$3060–3840	$3060 3300 3540 3840
	4	Chief Municipal Examiner	4140–4740 (Full time)	4140 4440 4740
		Chief Municipal Examiner (Pensions) Chief Municipal Examiner (Personal Service) Chief Municipal Examiner (Special)	2400–2880 (Not less than 18 hrs. a week) Per diem: $15	2400 2640 2880
	5	Director (Bureau of Personal Service)	6000 and up[1] (Full time)	
		Director (Bureau of Contract Supervision) Supervising Statistician and Examiner	3000 and up (Not less than 18 hrs. a week) Per diem: $20 or $25	
Probation Officer	1	Probation Officer Parole Officer	1200–1560	1200 1260 1320 1380 1440 1500 1560
	2	Senior Probation Officer Senior Parole Officer	1680–2160	1680 1800 1980 2160
	3	Deputy Chief Probation Officer	2340–2820	2340 2580 2820
	4	Chief Probation Officer Chief Parole Officer	3060–4140	3060 3300 3540 3840 4140
Social Investigator	1	Charity Application Investigator	600–900	600 660 720 780 840 900

[1] See note on page 115.

DIGEST OF STANDARD SPECIFICATIONS—Continued

Investigational Service—Continued

Group	Gr.	Title	Salary Range	Rates
Social Investigator—Cont'd	2	Social Investigator	$1080–1380	$1080 1140 1200 1260 1320 1380
	3	Senior Social Investigator	In charge of district office: 1500–1740	1500 1620 1740
			In charge of a division of domestic relations: 1740–2100	1740 1920 2100
		Senior Social Investigator (Institutions)	1500–1920	1500 1620 1740 1920
	4	Chief Social Investigator	2280–2940	2280 2460 2700 2940
	5	Director of Social Investigation	3900–4500	3900 4200 4500
Statistician	1	Junior Statistician Junior Actuary	1200–1800	1200 1320 1440 1560 1680 1800
	2	Assistant Statistician Assistant Actuary	1980–2820	1980 2160 2340 2580 2820
	3	Statistician Actuary	3060–3840	3060 3300 3540 3840
	4	Chief Statistician Chief Actuary (Pensions)	4140–4740	4140 4440 4740
Tax Officer and Appraiser	1	Deputy Tax Commissioner	2400–3600	2400 2640 2880 3120 3360 3600

DIGEST OF STANDARD SPECIFICATIONS—Continued

Investigational Service—Continued

Group	Gr.	Title	Salary Range	Rates
Tax Officer and Appraiser—Cont'd	2	Senior Deputy Tax Commissioner (Borough Chief) Senior Deputy Tax Commissioner (Real Estate of Corporations) Senior Deputy Tax Commissioner (Personal Estate of Borough) Senior Deputy Tax Commissioner (Personal Estate of Corporations)	$3900-4200	$3900 4200
	3	Assistant Chief Deputy Tax Commissioner (Real Estate)	4200–4500	4200 4500
	4	Chief Deputy Tax Commissioner (Real Estate) Chief Appraiser (Real Estate)	4800–7200	4800 5220 5640 6060 6600 7200
Miscellaneous Investigator	1	Examiner of Plumbers	Per diem: $5	
	2	Superintendent (Public Employment Bureau)	3000–3480	3000 3240 3480
		Examiner (Fire Prevention)	Per diem: $10	

Educational Service

Group	Gr.	Title	Salary Range	Rates
Industrial Instructor	1	Assistant Industrial Instructor	$480–600 with maintenance	$480 540 600
			720–840 without maintenance	720 780 840

DIGEST OF STANDARD SPECIFICATIONS—Continued

Educational Service—Continued

Group	Gr.	Title	Salary Range	Rates
Industrial Instructor—Cont'd	2	Industrial Instructor (Farming) Industrial Instructor (Handicrafts) Industrial Instructor (Trades)	$900–1500 with or without maintenance	$900 960 1020 1080 1140 1200 1260 1320 1380 1440 1500
	3	Superintendent of Industries	2460–3660	2460 2700 2940 3180 3420 3660
Recreation Instructor	1	Farm Garden Instructor Recreation Instructor Recreation Instructor (Athletics) Recreation Instructor (Swimming)	900–1080 Per diem: $3	900 960 1020 1080
	2	Head Farm Garden Instructor Head Recreation Instructor	1200–1440 Per diem: $4	1200 1320 1440
	3	Assistant Supervisor of Recreation Supervisor of Farm Gardens Supervisor (Volunteer Life Saving Corps)	1560–1800	1560 1680 1800
	4	Supervisor of Recreation	Manhattan: 2340–3300 Brooklyn: 1980–2580	2340 2580 2820 3060 3300 1980 2160 2340 2580
Miscellaneous Instructor	1	Institutional Instructor (Band Music)	900–1200	900 960 1020 1080 1140 1200
	2	Supervisor of Training (Randall's Island)	1620–2100 with or without maintenance	1620 1740 1920 2100

DIGEST OF STANDARD SPECIFICATIONS—Continued

Clerical Service

Group	Gr.	Title	Salary Range	Rates
Bookkeeper	1	Junior Bookkeeper	$840–1200	$840 960 1080 1200
	2	Bookkeeper	1320–1800	1320 1440 1560 1680 1800
	3	Senior Bookkeeper	1980–2820	1980 2160 2340 2580 2820
Clerk	1	Junior Clerk	360–540	360 420 480 540
	2A	Assistant Clerk A	600–720	600 660 720
	2B	Assistant Clerk B	840–1200	840 960 1080 1200
		Assistant Clerk (Multigraph Operator) Assistant Clerk (Tabulating Machine Operator)	720–960	720 840 960
	3	Clerk Clerk (Bertillon) Clerk (Computer) Clerk (Finger Print)	1320–1800	1320 1440 1560 1680 1800
	4	Senior Clerk Senior Clerk (Finger Print)	1980–2580	1980 2160 2340 2580
		Senior Clerk (Computer)	1980–2340	1980 2160 2340
	5	Chief Clerk Executive Clerk	2820–3540	2820 3060 3300 3540

DIGEST OF STANDARD SPECIFICATIONS—Continued

Clerical Service—Continued

Group	Gr.	Title	Salary Range	Rates
Court Clerk	1	Assistant Court Clerk	$1800–2340	$1800 1980 2160 2340
	2	Court Clerk	2340–3300	2340 2580 2820 3060 3300
	3	Deputy Chief Court Clerk	In Magistrates' Court: 3540–4140 In Children's Court: 3540–3840	3540 3840 4140 3540 3840
	4	Chief Court Clerk	4140–5160	4140 4440 4740 5160
Librarian [1]	3	Departmental Librarian	1020–1260	1020 1080 1140 1200 1260
	5	Court Librarian Law Librarian	1980–2820	1980 2160 2340 2580 2820
Interpreter	1	Interpretor	1080–1260	1080 1140 1200 1260
		Court Interpreter	City Magistrates' Courts, Municipal Courts, or Court of Special Sessions: 1380–2100	1380 1500 1620 1740 1920 2100
			City Court: 1500–2280 Temporary service: $5 per diem	1500 1620 1740 1920 2100 2280

[1] See note on page 150.

DIGEST OF STANDARD SPECIFICATIONS—Continued

Clerical Service—Continued

Group	Gr.	Title	Salary Range	Rates
Messenger	1	Messenger[1] Process Server[2]	$840–1200	$840 900 960 1020 1080 1140 1200
Private Secretary	1	Private Secretary	1800–2160	1800 1980 2160
	2	Senior Private Secretary	2340–3540	2340 2580 2820 3060 3300 3540
	3	Executive Private Secretary	3840–6000	3480 4140 4440 4740 5160 5580 6000
Purchasing Agent	1	Purchasing Agent Purchasing Agent and Assistant Supervisor (City Record)	2100–2940	2100 2280 2460 2700 2940
		Purchasing Agent (Bookbinding Supplies)	1800–2160	1800 1980 2160
		Purchasing Agent (Printing Supplies) Purchasing Agent (Stationery Supplies)	2100–2700	2100 2280 2460 2700
	2	Assistant Director of Central Purchase	3660–4260	3660 3960 4260
		Purchasing Agent and Assistant Superintendent of School Supplies (Education)	3180–3960	3180 3420 3660 3960
	3	Chief Purchasing Agent and Supervisor (City Record)	4560–5280	4560 4860 5280

[1] $300 additional may be paid for service as Messenger to members of Board of Estimate and Apportionment.

[2] Process Servers temporarily employed shall be paid $1.15 for each paper actually served.

DIGEST OF STANDARD SPECIFICATIONS—Continued
Clerical Service—Continued

Group	Gr.	Title	Salary Range	Rates
Purchasing Agent—Cont'd		Chief Purchasing Agent and Superintendent of School Supplies (Education)	$6120–7200	$6120 6600 7200
		Director of Central Purchase	4860–5700	4860 5280 5700
		Superintendent of Purchase and Maintenance (Fire)	4560	4560
Revenue Officer	1	Ticket Seller	313 days: 960–1200 Per diem: $3.25	960 1020 1080 1140 1200
	2	Cashier	1320–1800	1320 1440 1560 1680 1800
	3	Deputy Superintendent of Markets Deputy Collector of City Revenue Senior Cashier	1980–2160	1980 2160
	4	Chief Stock and Bond Clerk City Paymaster Collector of City Revenue and Superintendent of Markets Deputy Collector of Assessments and Arrears Deputy Receiver of Taxes Pension Officer	2340–4140	2340 2580 2820 3060 3300 3540 3840 4140
	5	Collector of Assessments and Arrears Receiver of Taxes	4440–5160	4440 4740 5160
Stenographer	1	Junior Stenographer Junior Stenotypist	Men: 840–900 Women: 720–900	840 900 720 780 840 900
	2	Stenographer Stenotypist	960–1200	960 1020 1080 1140 1200

DIGEST OF STANDARD SPECIFICATIONS—Continued
Clerical Service—Continued

Group	Gr.	Title	Salary Range	Rates
Stenographer—Cont'd	3	Senior Stenographer Senior Stenotypist	$1320–1680	$1320 1440 1560 1680
		Senior Stenographer or Senior Stenotypist supervising stenographic bureau or doing important reporting work	1320–1980	1320 1440 1560 1680 1800 1980
	4	Court Stenographer	2160–3060	2160 2340 2580 2820 3060
Telephone Operator	1	Telephone Operator	Men: 660–1020	660 720 780 840 900 960 1020
			Women: 600–1020	600 660 720 780 840 900 960 1020
Typist	1	Junior Typist	Men: 720–780	720 780
			Women: 600–780	600 660 720 780
		Junior Typist (Dictaphone)	720–780	720 780
	2	Typist	840–1020	840 900 960 1020
		Typist (Dictaphone)	840–900	840 900
	3	Senior Typist Senior Typist (Computing)	1140–1380	1140 1260 1380
Miscellaneous Clerk	4	Editor (City Record)	2100–2940	2100 2280 2460 2700 2940

DIGEST OF STANDARD SPECIFICATIONS—Continued

Inspectional Service

Group	Gr.	Title	Salary Range	Rates
Inspector of Buildings	1	Building Inspector Building Inspector (Elevators) Building Inspector (Fire Prevention) Building Inspector (Heating) Building Inspector (Iron and Steel) Building Inspector (Piers) Building Inspector (Plastering) Building Inspector (Plumbing and Sanitation) Building Inspector (Tenements)	$1200–1500	$1200 1260 1320 1380 1440 1500
	2	Senior Building Inspector Senior Building Inspector (Elevators) Senior Building Inspector (Fire Prevention) Senior Building Inspector (Iron and Steel) Senior Building Inspector (Plumbing and Sanitation) Senior Building Inspector (Tenements)	1620–1920	1620 1740 1920
	3	Assistant Chief Building Inspector (Bureau of Buildings, The Bronx or Brooklyn) Assistant Superintendent (Bureau of Buildings, Queens or Richmond) Chief Building Inspector (Bureau of Buildings, Queens or Richmond) Chief Building Inspector (Tenements)	2100–2940	2100 2280 2460 2700 2940
		Chief Building Inspector (Fire Prevention)	Manhattan, The Bronx and Richmond: 2100–2700	2100 2280 2460 2700
			Brooklyn and Queens: 2100	2100

DIGEST OF STANDARD SPECIFICATIONS—Continued

Inspectional Service—Continued

Group	Gr.	Title	Salary Range	Rates
Inspector of Buildings—Cont'd	4	Assistant Superintendent (Bureau of Buildings; Manhattan; The Bronx or Brooklyn) Chief Building Inspector (Bureau of Buildings, Manhattan, The Bronx or Brooklyn) Superintendent (Bureau of Buildings, Queens or Richmond)	$3180–4260	$3180 3420 3660 3960 4260
		Assistant Chief (Bureau of Fire Prevention)	3180–3660	3180 3420 3660
	5	Superintendent (Bureau of Buildings, Manhattan, The Bronx or Brooklyn)	4560–6120	4560 4860 5280 5700 6120
		Chief (Bureau of Fire Prevention)	4560–5280	4560 4860 5280
	6	Chairman (Board of Standards and Appeals)	7200–8400	7200 7800 8400
		Member (Board of Standards and Appeals)	10 per service	
Inspector of Combustibles and Blasting	1	Inspector of Combustibles Inspector of Blasting	1200–1500	1200 1260 1320 1380 1440 1500
	2	Senior Inspector of Combustibles Senior Inspector of Blasting	1620–1920	1620 1740 1920
	3	Chief Inspector of Combustibles and Blasting	Manhattan, The Bronx and Richmond: 2460–3420	2460 2700 2940 3180 3420
			Brooklyn and Queens: 2100–2460	2100 2280 2460

DIGEST OF STANDARD SPECIFICATIONS—Continued

Inspectional Service—Continued

Group	Gr.	Title	Salary Range	Rates
Inspector of Electricity	1	Inspector of Electricity	$1200–1500 Outage work: 1200	$1200 1260 1320 1380 1440 1500
	2	Senior Inspector of Electricity	1620–1920	1620 1740 1920
	3	Chief Inspector of Electricity	2100–2940	2100 2280 2460 2700 2940
Health Inspector	1	Health Inspector Health Inspector (Drugs) Health Inspector (Food) Health Inspector (Milk) Health Inspector (Sanitation)	1200–1500	1200 1260 1320 1380 1440 1500
	2	Senior Health Inspector Senior Health Inspector (Food) Senior Health Inspector (Milk) Senior Health Inspector (Sanitation)	1620–1920	1620 1740 1920
	3	Chief Health Inspector (Food) Chief Health Inspector (Sanitation)	2100–2700	2100 2280 2460 2700
	4	Assistant Health Director (Bureau of Food Inspection) Assistant Health Director (Bureau of Sanitary Inspection)	2940–3420	2940 3180 3420
	5	Health Director (Food Inspection)	5100–5940	5100 5520 5940
Inspector of Licenses	1	Inspector of Licenses Inspector of Licensed Vehicles	1200–1500	1200 1260 1320 1380 1440 1500

DIGEST OF STANDARD SPECIFICATIONS—Continued

Inspectional Service—Continued

Group	Gr.	Title	Salary Range	Rates
Inspector of Licenses—Cont'd	2	Senior Inspector of Licenses	$1620–1920	$1620 1740 1920
	3	Chief Inspector of Licenses	2100–2700	2100 2280 2460 2700
		Chief Inspector of Licensed Vehicles	2280–3180	2280 2460 2700 2940 3180
Inspector of Meters	1	Inspector of Meters	1020–1200	1020 1080 1140 1200
	2	Senior Inspector of Meters	1320–1560	1320 1440 1560
	3	Chief Inspector of Meters	1680–2340	1680 1800 1980 2160 2340
Inspector of Public Works	1	Inspector of Public Works Inspector of Public Works (Dredging) Inspector of Public Works (Highways) Inspector of Public Works (Sewers) Inspector of Public Works(WaterMains)	1200–1500 (on construction work) Per diem: $4.50 Per month: $100	1200 1260 1320 1380 1440 1500
			1200–1380 (On routine or patrol work)	1200 1260 1320 1380
	2	Senior Inspector of Public Works Senior Inspector of Public Works (Highways) Senior Inspector of Public Works (Sewers) Senior Inspector of Public Works (Shop and Foundry) Senior Inspector of Public Works (Water Mains)	1620–1920	1620 1740 1920

DIGEST OF STANDARD SPECIFICATIONS—Continued

Inspectional Service—Continued

Group	Gr.	Title	Salary Range	Rates
Inspector of Public Works —Cont'd	3	Superintendent of Public Works Superintendent of Public Works (Asphalt Plant)	$2100–3180	$2100 2280 2460 2700 2940 3180
Inspector of Supplies	1	Inspector of Supplies Inspector of Supplies (Egg Candler)	1200–1500	1200 1260 1320 1380 1440 1500
	2	Senior Inspector of Supplies	1620–1920	1620 1740 1920
	3	Chief Inspector of Repairs and Supplies	2100–3660	2100 2280 2460 2700 2940 3180 3420 3660
Watershed Inspector	1	Watershed Inspector	900–1020	900 960 1020
	2	Senior Watershed Inspector	1140–1500	1140 1260 1380 1500
Inspector of Weights and Measures	1	Inspector of Weights and Measures	1200–1500	1200 1260 1320 1380 1440 1500
	2	Senior Inspector of Weights and Measures	1620–1920	1620 1740 1920
		Senior Inspector of Weights and Measures (Mechanical)	1920–2460	1920 2100 2280 2460
Miscellaneous Inspector	1	Inspector of Boiler and Pipe Covering[1] Inspector of Boilers	1200–1500	1200 1260 1320 1380 1440 1500
		Inspector of Gas	1200–1260	1200 1260

[1] See note on page 203.

DIGEST OF STANDARD SPECIFICATIONS—Continued

Custodial Service

Group	Gr.	Title	Salary Range	Rates
Animal Keeper	1	Animal Keeper Aquarium Attendant	$900–1080	$900 960 1020 1080
	2	Head Animal Keeper Head Aquarium Attendant	1140–1380	1140 1200 1260 1320 1380
	3	Menagerie Superintendent Aquarist	1800–2580	1800 1980 2160 2340 2580
Bridgetender	1	Bridgetender	313 days: 876–984 Per diem: $2.75	876 912 948 984
	2	Head Bridgetender	1020–1200	1020 1080 1140 1200
Caretaker	1	Caretaker Assistant Custodian	Men: (313 days) 840–984 Per diem: $2.75 Women: (313 days) 660–840 Per diem: $2.25	840 876 912 948 984 660 696 732 768 804 840
	2	Head Caretaker Custodian	1020–1200	1020 1080 1140 1200
	3	Janitor Supervisor of Caretakers	1320–1800	1320 1440 1560 1680 1800
		Janitor-Engineman	No recommendation[1]	
	4	Assistant Chief Supervisor of Janitors Senior Janitor-Engineman	No recommendation[1]	

[1] See note on page 211.

DIGEST OF STANDARD SPECIFICATIONS—Continued

Custodial Service—Continued

Group	Gr.	Title	Salary Range	Rates
Caretaker—Cont'd	5	Assistant Superintendent of Public Buildings and Offices (Manhattan) Chief Supervisor of Janitors Superintendent of Public Buildings and Offices (Queens or Richmond)	$2820–3540	$2820 3060 3300 3540
	6	Superintendent of Public Buildings and Offices (Manhattan, Brooklyn, or The Bronx)	3840–5160	3840 4140 4440 4740 5160
Court and Legislative Attendant	1	Court Attendant	1080–1380	1080 1140 1200 1260 1320 1380
		Assistant Sergeant-at-Arms	1020–1200	1020 1080 1140 1200
	2	Sergeant-at-Arms	1320–1440	1320 1440
Dockmaster	1	Dockmaster	1800–2160	1800 1980 2160
	2	Superintendent of Docks	3000–3780	3000 3240 3480 3780
Elevator Operator	1	Elevator Operator	313 days: 840–984 Per diem: $2.75	840 876 912 948 984
	2	Elevator Starter	1020–1080	1020 1080
	3	Elevator Despatcher	1140–1200	1140 1200
Storekeeper	1	Stores Foreman	960–1200	960 1020 1080 1140 1200

DIGEST OF STANDARD SPECIFICATIONS—Continued
Custodial Service—Continued

Group	Gr.	Title	Salary Range	Rates
Storekeeper—Cont'd	2	Storekeeper	$1320–1800	$1320 1440 1560 1680 1800
	3	Senior Storekeeper	1980–2580	1980 2160 2340 2580
Watchman	1	Watchman	313 days: 792–888 Per diem: $2.50	792 816 840 864 888
Miscellaneous Custodian	1	Guard	900–1200	900 960 1020 1080 1140 1200
		Life Guard	Per diem: $3	
		Monitor	Per diem: $4	

Institutional Service

Group	Gr.	Title	Salary Range	Rates
Correction Officer	1	Correction Officer	$960–1320	$960 1020 1080 1140 1200 1260 1320
		Correction Matron Police Matron	720–960	720 780 840 900 960
	2	Head Correction Officer	1440–1800	1440 1560 1680 1800
		Head Correction Matron	1080–1440	1080 1200 1320 1440

DIGEST OF STANDARD SPECIFICATIONS—Continued

Institutional Service—Continued

Group	Gr.	Title	Salary Range	Rates
Correction Officer—Cont'd	3	Assistant Superintendent of Reformatory Assistant Superintendent of Women (Correction) Deputy Warden	$1920–2280	$1920 2100 2280
	4	Superintendent of Reformatory Superintendent of Women's Farm Warden	2520–3480	2520 2760 3000 3240 3480
Culinary Worker	1	Cook A	360–420 with maintenance	360 390 420
			Monthly compensation with maintenance 30–35	30.00 32.50 35.00
		Cook B	480–660 with maintenance	480 510 540 570 600 630 660
			Monthly compensation with maintenance 40–55	40.00 42.50 45.00 47.50 50.00 52.50 55.00
		Cook C	600–720 with maintenance	600 630 660 690 720
			Monthly compensation with maintenance 50–60	50.00 52.50 55.00 57.50 60.00
		Butcher	660–840 without maintenance	660 690 720 750 780 810 840

DIGEST OF STANDARD SPECIFICATIONS—Continued

Institutional Service—Continued

Group	Gr.	Title	Salary Range	Rates
Culinary Worker—Cont'd			$420–600 with maintenance	$420 450 480 510 540 570 600
			Monthly compensation without maintenance 55–70	55.00 57.50 60.00 62.50 65.00 67.50 70.00
			Monthly compensation with maintenance 35–50	35.00 37.50 40.00 42.50 45.00 47.50 50.00
		Baker	1080–1200 without maintenance	1080 1140 1200
			840–960 with maintenance	840 900 960
			Monthly compensation without maintenance 90–100	90 95 100
			Monthly compensation with maintenance 70–80	70 75 80
	2	Head Cook	1020–1140 without maintenance	1020 1050 1080 1110 1140
			780–900 with maintenance	780 810 840 870 900

DIGEST OF STANDARD SPECIFICATIONS—Continued

Institutional Service—Continued

Group	Gr.	Title	Salary Range	Rates
Culinary Worker—Cont'd			Monthly compensation without maintenance $85–95	$85.00 87.50 90.00 92.50 95.00
			Monthly compensation with maintenance 65–75	65.00 67.50 70.00 72.50 75.00
		Head Baker	1260–1380 without maintenance	1260 1320 1380
			Monthly compensation without maintenance 105–115	105 110 115
		Head Butcher	900–1140 without maintenance	900 930 960 990 1020 1050 1080 1110 1140
			660–900 with maintenance	660 690 720 750 780 810 840 870 900
			Monthly compensation without maintenance 75–95	75.00 77.50 80.00 82.50 85.00 87.50 90.00 92.50 95.00
			Monthly compensation with maintenance 55–75	55.00 57.50 60.00 62.50 65.00 67.50 70.00 72.50 75.00

DIGEST OF STANDARD SPECIFICATIONS—Continued

Institutional Service—Continued

Group	Gr.	Title	Salary Range	Rates
Dietitian	1	Pupil Dietitian	$120 with maintenance	$120
	2	Dietitian	720–900 with maintenance	720 780 840 900
	3	Head Dietitian	1020–1380 with maintenance	1020 1140 1260 1380
	4	Departmental Dietitian	1800–2820 with or without maintenance	1800 1980 2160 2340 2580 2820
Helper	1	Junior Hospital Helper	120–150 with maintenance	120 150
			Monthly compensation with maintenance 10–12.50	10.00 12.50
	2	Hospital Helper A[1] Prison Helper A[1]	528–600 without maintenance	528 552 576 600
			288–360 with maintenance	288 312 336 360
			Monthly compensation without maintenance 44–50	44 46 48 50
			Monthly compensation with maintenance 24–30	24 26 28 30
		Hospital Helper B[1] Prison Helper B[1] Seamstress	504–576 without maintenance	504 528 552 576

[1] See specifications for Helper Group.

DIGEST OF STANDARD SPECIFICATIONS—Continued

Institutional Service—Continued

Group	Gr.	Title	Salary Range	Rates
Helper—Cont'd			$264–336 with maintenance	$264 288 312 336
			Monthly compensation without maintenance 42–48	42 44 46 48
			Monthly compensation with maintenance 22–28	22 24 26 28
		Hospital Helper C[1]	480–552 without maintenance	480 504 528 552
			240–312 with maintenance	240 264 288 312
			Monthly compensation without maintenance 40–46	40 42 44 46
			Monthly compensation with maintenance 20–26	20 22 24 26
	3	Senior Hospital Helper A[1] Senior Prison Helper A[1]	630–780 without maintenance	630 660 690 720 750 780
			390–540 with maintenance	390 420 450 480 510 540

[1] See specifications for Helper Group.

DIGEST OF STANDARD SPECIFICATIONS—Continued

Institutional Service—Continued

Group	Gr.	Title	Salary Range	Rates
Helper—Cont'd			Monthly compensation without maintenance $52.50–65	$52.50 55.00 57.50 60.00 62.50 65.00
			Monthly compensation with maintenance 32.50–45	32.50 35.00 37.50 40.00 42.50 45.00
		Head Seamstress Senior Hospital Helper B[1] Senior Prison Helper B[1]	600–690 without maintenance	600 630 660 690
			360–450 with maintenance	360 390 420 450
			Monthly compensation without maintenance 50–57.50	50.00 52.50 55.00 57.50
			Monthly compensation with maintenance 30–37.50	30.00 32.50 35.00 37.50
Hospital Attendant	1	Pupil Hospital Attendant	180 with maintenance	180
	2	Hospital Attendant A[2]	600–780 without maintenance	600 630 660 690 720 750 780
			360–540 with maintenance	360 390 420 450 480 510 540

[1] See specifications for Helper Group.
[2] See specifications for Hospital Attendant Group.

DIGEST OF STANDARD SPECIFICATIONS—Continued
Institutional Service—Continued

Group	Gr.	Title	Salary Range	Rates
Hospital Attendant—Cont'd			Monthly compensation without maintenance $50–65	$50.00 52.50 55.00 57.50 60.00 62.50 65.00
			Monthly compensation with maintenance 30–45	30.00 32.50 35.00 37.50 40.00 42.50 45.00
		Hospital Attendant B[1]	720–900 without maintenance	720 750 780 810 840 870 900
			480–660 with maintenance	480 510 540 570 600 630 660
			Monthly compensation without maintenance 60–75	60.00 62.50 65.00 67.50 70.00 72.50 75.00
			Monthly compensation with maintenance 40–55	40.00 42.50 45.00 47.50 50.00 52.50 55.00
		Hospital Attendant C[1]	540–720 without maintenance	540 570 600 630 660 690 720
			300–480 with maintenance	300 330 360 390 420 450 480

[1] See specifications for Hospital Attendant Group.

DIGEST OF STANDARD SPECIFICATIONS—Continued

Institutional Service—Continued

Group	Gr.	Title	Salary Range	Rates
Hospital Attendant—Cont'd			Monthly compensation without maintenance $45–60	$45.00 47.50 50.00 52.50 55.00 57.50 60.00
			Monthly compensation with maintenance 25–40	25.00 27.50 30.00 32.50 35.00 37.50 40.00
		Nurse's Assistant	420–540 (Not less than 28 hours per week)	420 450 480 510 540
Institutional Clerk	1A	Assistant Institutional Clerk A	600–720 without maintenance	600 660 720
			360–540 with maintenance	360 420 480 540
	1B	Assistant Institutional Clerk B	840–1200 without maintenance	840 960 1080 1200
			600–960 with maintenance	600 720 840 960
Institutional Supervisor	1	Matron Overseer	600–780[1] with maintenance	600 660 720 780
			Monthly compensation with maintenance 50–65	50 55 60 65
	2	Employment Agent Head Matron Head Overseer Assistant Steward	840–1020[2] with maintenance	840 900 960 1020

[1] A special range of $660 to $780 may be paid to Matrons acting also as working Dietitians.

[2] A special range of $900 to $1020 may be paid to Head Matrons acting also as working Dietitians.

DIGEST OF STANDARD SPECIFICATIONS—Continued

Institutional Service—Continued

Group	Gr.	Title	Salary Range	Rates
Institutional Supervisor—Cont'd	3	Deputy Lay Superintendent	$1080–1800 with maintenance	$1080 1200 1320 1440 1560 1680 1800
		Steward	1080–1560 with maintenance	1080 1200 1320 1440 1560
	4	Lay Superintendent	2100–2940 with maintenance	2100 2280 2460 2700 2940
		Departmental Steward	1920–2940[1] with or without maintenance	1920 2100 2280 2460 2700 2940
	5	General Lay Superintendent	3180 and up with maintenance (No recommendation above $4260)	3180 3420 3660 3960 4260
Laundryman	1	Laundry Helper A	480–552 without maintenance	480 504 528 552
			240–312 with maintenance	240 264 288 312
			Monthly compensa- without maintenance 40–46	40 42 44 46
			Monthly compensation with maintenance 20–26	20 22 24 26

[1] In the case of Departmental Stewards receiving maintenance, alary rate shall not exceed $1920.

DIGEST OF STANDARD SPECIFICATIONS—Continued

Institutional Service—Continued

Group	Gr.	Title	Salary Range	Rates
Laundryman—Cont'd		Laundry Helper B	$504–576 without maintenance	$504 528 552 576
			264–336 with maintenance	264 288 312 336
			Monthly compensation without maintenance 42–48	42 44 46 48
			Monthly compensation with-maintenance 22–28	22 24 26 28
		Laundry Helper C	528–600 without maintenance	528 552 576 600
			288–360 with maintenance	288 312 336 360
			Monthly compensation without maintenance 44–50	44 46 48 50
			Monthly compensation with maintenance 24–30	24 26 28 30
	2	Senior Laundry Helper A	630–780 without maintenance	630 660 690 720 750 780
			390–540 with maintenance	390 420 450 480 510 540

DIGEST OF STANDARD SPECIFICATIONS—Continued

Institutional Service—Continued

Group	Gr.	Title	Salary Range	Rates
Laundryman—Cont'd			Monthly compensation without maintenance $52.50–65	$52.50 55.00 57.50 60.00 62.50 65.00
			Monthly compensation with maintenance 32.50–45	32.50 35.00 37.50 40.00 42.50 45.00
		Senior Laundry Helper B	690–840 without maintenance	690 720 750 780 810 840
			450–600 with maintenance	450 480 510 540 570 600
			Monthly compensation without maintenance 57.50–70	57.50 60.00 62.50 65.00 67.50 70.00
			Monthly compensation with maintenance 37.50–50	37.50 40.00 42.50 45.00 47.50 50.00
	3	Laundryman	840–900 without maintenance	840 870 900
			600–660 with maintenance	600 630 660
	4	Head Laundryman	960–1440 without maintenance	960 1020 1080 1140 1200 1260 1320 1380 1440

DIGEST OF STANDARD SPECIFICATIONS—Continued

Institutional Service—Continued

Group	Gr.	Title	Salary Range	Rates
Laundryman—Cont'd			$720–1200 with maintenance	$720 780 840 900 960 1020 1080 1140 1200
	5	Superintendent of Laundries	1800–2580	1800 1980 2160 2340 2580
Masseur	1	Masseur	960–1140 (Full time)	960 1020 1080 1140
			600–720 (Not less than 18 hours a week)	600 660 720
	2	Chief Masseur	1200–1440 (Full time)	1200 1260 1320 1380 1440
			900–1080 (Not less than 18 hours a week)	900 960 1020 1080
Mortuary Keeper	1	Mortuary Helper	792–888 without maintenance[1]	792 816 840 864 888
			Monthly compensation without maintenance 66–74	66 68 70 72 74
	2	Mortuary Keeper	900–1020 without maintenance	900 960 1020
			660–780 with maintenance	660 720 780

[1] For rates with maintenance, see Senior Hospital Helper A in Grade 3 of Helper Group.

DIGEST OF STANDARD SPECIFICATIONS—Continued

Institutional Service—Continued

Group	Gr.	Title	Salary Range	Rates
Mortuary Keeper—Cont'd	3	Head Mortuary Keeper	$1080–1200 without maintenance	$1080 1140 1200
			840–960 with maintenance	840 900 960
	4	Superintendent of Mortuary	1980–2160	1980 2160
Tailor	1	Tailor	720–1020 without maintenance	720 780 840 900 960 1020
			480–780 with maintenance	480 540 600 660 720 780
	2	Head Tailor	1140–1260	1140 1200 1260
Miscellaneous Institutional Worker	1	Coffee Roaster	900–1080	900 960 1020 1080
		Farmer	720–900 with maintenance	720 780 840 900
		Fire Officer	840–960 with maintenance	840 900 960

Street Cleaning Service

Group	Gr	Title	Salary Range	Rates
Motor Refuse Collector	1	Loader (Dept. of Street Cleaning)	$864–936[1]	$864 888 912 936
		Extra Loader	1-313 per diem of min. annual rate for Loader	

[1] Additional compensation of $24 may be paid to Loader who is leader of gang. Loaders assigned in charge of section stations or yards shall receive a flat rate of $840.

DIGEST OF STANDARD SPECIFICATIONS—Continued

Street Cleaning Service—Continued

Group	Gr.	Title	Salary Range	Rates
Motor Refuse Collector—Cont'd	2	Recruit Motor Truck Driver (Dept. of Street Cleaning)	Rate paid in position from which employe is assigned	
		Motor Truck Driver (Dept. of Street Cleaning) Motor Truck Driver (Bur. of Street Cleaning, Richmond)	$960-996	$960 996
		Extra Motor Truck Driver	1-313 per diem of min. annual rate for Motor Truck Driver	
Recruit	1	Recruit (Dept. of Street Cleaning)	1-313 per diem of min. annual rate for appropriate position	
Refuse Collector	1	Driver (Dept. of Street Cleaning) Driver (Bur. of Street Cleaning, Queens) Driver (Bur. of Street Cleaning, Richmond)	840-936 [1]	840 864 888 912 936
		Hostler (Dept. of Street Cleaning) Hostler (Bur. of Street Cleaning, Queens) Hostler (Bur. of Street Cleaning, Richmond)	816-912 [1]	816 840 864 888 912
		Stableman (Dept. of Street Cleaning) Stableman (Bur. of Street Cleaning, Queens) Stableman (Bur. of Street Cleaning, Richmond)	792-888 [1]	792 816 840 864 888
		Extra Driver Extra Hostler Extra Stableman	1-313 per diem of min. annual rate prescribed for the position in question	

[1] Drivers, Hostlers and Stablemen assigned in charge of section stations or yards shall receive a flat rate of $840.

DIGEST OF STANDARD SPECIFICATIONS—Continued

Street Cleaning Service—Continued

Group	Gr.	Title	Salary Range	Rates
Refuse Collector—Cont'd	2	Assistant Stable Foreman (Dept. of Street Cleaning)	$1020–1140	$1020 1080 1140
		Assistant Stable Foreman (Bur. of Street Cleaning, Queens)	1020–1080	1020 1080
	3	Stable Foreman (Dept. of Street Cleaning)	1200–1620	1200 1260 1320 1380 1440 1500 1560 1620
			Assigned as Assistant District Superintendent: 1620–1740	1620 1740
		Stable Foreman (Bur. of Street Cleaning, Richmond) Stable Foreman (Bur. of Street Cleaning, Queens)	1140–1440	1140 1200 1260 1320 1380 1440
Refuse Disposer	1	Boardman (Dept. of Street Cleaning) Boardman (Bur. of Street Cleaning, Queens)	840–936*	840 864 888 912 936
		Extra Boardman	1-313 per diem of min. annual rate for Boardman	
	2	Assistant Dump Inspector (Dept. of Street Cleaning)	1020–1140	1020 1080 1140
		Assistant Dump Inspector (Bur. of Street Cleaning, Queens)	1020–1080	1020 1080
	3	Dump Inspector (Dept. of Street Cleaning)	1200–1500	1200 1260 1320 1380 1440 1500

* Boardmen assigned in charge of section stations or yards shall receive a flat rate of $840.

DIGEST OF STANDARD SPECIFICATIONS—Continued

Street Cleaning Service—Continued

Group	Gr.	Title	Salary Range	Rates
Refuse Disposer —Cont'd			Assigned as Assistant District Superintendent: $1620–1740	$1620 1740
		Dump Inspector (Bur. of Street Cleaning, Queens)	1140–1440	1140 1200 1260 1320 1380 1440
Street Cleaner	1	Sweeper (Dept. of Street Cleaning) Sweeper (Bur. of Street Cleaning, Queens) Sweeper (Bur. of Street Cleaning, Richmond)	792–888[1]	792 816 840 864 888
		Extra Sweeper	1-313 per diem of min. annual rate for Sweeper	
	2	Assistant Section Foreman (Dept. of Street Cleaning)	1020–1140	1020 1080 1140
		Assistant Section Foreman (Bur. of Street Cleaning, Queens)	1020–1080	1020 1080
	3	Section Foreman (Dept. of Street Cleaning)	1200–1500	1200 1260 1320 1380 1440 1500
			Assigned as Assistant District Superintendent: 1620–1740	1620 1740
		Section Foreman (Bur. of Street Cleaning, Queens) Section Foreman (Bur. of Street Cleaning, Richmond)	1140–1440	1140 1200 1260 1320 1380 1440
Supervisor	1	District Superintendent (Bur. of Street Cleaning, Richmond)	1500–1740	1500 1620 1740

[1] Additional compensation of 15c. per diem may be paid to Sweepers employed on flushing work.

DIGEST OF STANDARD SPECIFICATIONS—Continued

Street Cleaning Service—Continued

Group	Gr.	Title	Salary Range	Rates
Supervisor—Cont'd		District Superintendent (Bur. of Street Cleaning, Queens)	$1620–1920	$1620 1740 1920
	2	District Superintendent (Dept. of Street Cleaning) AssistantSuperintendent of Final Disposition (Dept. of Street Cleaning) AssistantSuperintendent of Snow Removal (Dept. of Street Cleaning) AssistantSuperintendent (Bur. of Street Cleaning,Richmond)	1920–2460 [1]	1920 2100 2280 2460
	3	Assistant General Superintendent (Dept. of Street Cleaning) Borough Superintendent (Dept. of Street Cleaning, Brooklyn) Superintendent of Final Disposition (Dept. of Street Cleaning)	2700–2940	2700 2940
		Superintendent (Bur. of Street Cleaning, Queens) Superintendent (Bur. of Street Cleaning, Richmond)	2940–3180	2940 3180
	4	General Superintendent (Dept. of Street Cleaning)	3180-3660	3180 3420 3660

[1] A special rate of $2580 shall be paid to the District Superintendent who is assigned as Borough Superintendent of The Bronx, and to the District Superintendent who is assigned as Superintendent of Inspection and Instruction.

DIGEST OF STANDARD SPECIFICATIONS—Continued

Skilled Trades Service

Group	Gr.	Title	Salary Range for Service Every Day in Year	Rates	Salary Range for Service Exclusive of Sundays	Rates	Salary Range for Service Exclusive of Sundays, Holidays & Saturday Afternoons	Rates	Per Diem Rate 8 Hours	No Time Limit Specified	R
Bookbinder	1	Bookbinder								$1140–1320	$1 1 1 1
Builder	1	Bricklayer Cement-mason Flagger Glazier Marble-setter Paver Plasterer Rammerman Stone-cutter Stone-mason							$6.00 5.30 4.50 4.00 5.50 5.00 5.50 4.00 5.00 5.00		
Diver	1	Assistant Diver							3.50		
	2	Diver							1.25 hourly		
	3	Chief Diver								1620–1920	1 1 1
Electrical Worker	1	Batteryman Lineman Wireman			$960–1140	$960 1020 1080 1140			3.00 3.00 3.00		
		Craneman			900–1080	900 960 1020 1080			3.00		
	2	Electrician Battery Constructor							5.20 5.00		
		Cable Splicer Foreman Lineman			1260–1440	1260 1320 1380 1440	$1140–1320	$1140 1200 1260 1320	5.00		
	3	Foreman Cable Splicer	$1920		1680		1500				
		Foreman Electrician							5.50		
Engineman	1	Fireman							3.00		
		Fireman employed on pile-driving							3.50		
		Oiler							3.00		

DIGEST OF STANDARD SPECIFICATIONS—Continued

Skilled Trades Service—Continued

Group	Gr.	Title	Salary Range for Service Every Day in Year	Rates	Salary Range for Service Exclusive of Sundays	Rates	Salary Range for Service Exclusive of Sundays, Holidays & Saturday Afternoons	Rates	Per Diem Rate 8 Hours	No Time Limit Specified	Rates
gineman Cont'd	2	Engineman							$4.50		
		Engineman (Pile Driving and Hoisting)							5.50		
		Engineman (Steam Roller)							5.50		
	3	Supervising Engineman								In charge of large plants or institutions not covering shift: $1740–2100 without maintenance	$1740 1920 2100
										1320–1560 with maintenance	1320 1440 1560
										Covering one shift in smaller buildings and institutions: 1620–1920 without maintenance	1620 1740 1920
										1200–1440 with maintenance	1200 1320 1440
										In charge of large pumping station or small group of pumping stations: 1620–2100 without maintenance	1620 1740 1920 2100
	4	Chief Engineman								2280–2460	2280 2460

DIGEST OF STANDARD SPECIFICATIONS—Continued

Skilled Trades Service—Continued

Group	Gr.	Title	Salary Range for Service Every Day in Year	Rates	Salary Range for Service Exclusive of Sundays	Rates	Salary Range for Service Exclusive of Sundays, Holidays & Saturday Afternoons	Rates	Per Diem Rate 8 Hours	No Time Limit Specified	Rate
Fire Telegraph Despatcher	1	Fire Telegraph Despatcher								Manhattan, Brooklyn: $1200–1500	$1200 1260 1320 1380 1440 1500
										The Bronx, Queens, Richmond: 1200–1440	1200 1260 1320 1380 1440
	2	Senior Fire Telegraph Despatcher								In charge of tour, Manhattan, Brooklyn: 1620–1920	162 174 192
										In charge of tour, The Bronx, Queens, Richmond: 1560–1680	156 168
										In charge of entire borough, The Bronx, Queens and Richmond: 1800–1980	180 198
	3	Chief Fire Telegraph Despatcher								2100–2280	210 228
Journeyman's Helper	1	Blacksmith's Helper Bookbinder's Helper Electrician's Helper Elevator Mechanic's Helper Horseshoer's Helper Machinist's Helper Marble-setter's Helper							$2.80–3.00		2.8 2.9 3.0

DIGEST OF STANDARD SPECIFICATIONS—Continued

Skilled Trades Service—Continued

Group	Gr.	Title	Salary Range for Service Every Day in Year	Rates	Salary Range for Service Exclusive of Sundays	Rates	Salary Range for Service Exclusive of Sundays, Holidays & Saturday Afternoons	Rates	Per Diem Rate 8 Hours	No Time Limit Specified	Rates
rney-an's Helper—Cont'd		Mason's Helper Mechanic's Helper Plumber's Helper Steamfitter's Helper									
ther orker	1	Harnessmaker Shoemaker							$4.00 3.50		
ine gineman	1	Marine Oiler Marine Stoker Marine Water Tender							3.20 3.00 3.20		
	2	Marine Engineman	$1440–1680	$1440 1560 1680	$1260–1500	$1260 1380 1500					
	3	Chief Marine Engineman	1800		1560						
ine ficer	1	Deckhand			792–888	792 816 840 864 888			2 50		
	2	Mate							3.00	$936–1032	$936 984 1032
		Mates acting as Quartermasters on passenger steamboats or ferryboats of over 1,000 gross tons								984–1080	984 1032 1080
	3	Captain									
		On steamboats other than largest ferries and boats of corresponding tonnage:	1500–1740	1500 1620 1740	1320–1560	1320 1440 1560					
		On largest ferries and boats of corresponding tonnage:	1920		1620						

DIGEST OF STANDARD SPECIFICATIONS—Continued

Skilled Trades Service—Continued

Group	Gr.	Title	Salary Range for Service Every Day in Year	Rates	Salary Range for Service Exclusive of Sundays	Rates	Salary Range for Service Exclusive of Sundays, Holidays & Saturday Afternoons	Rates	Per Diem Rate 8 Hours	No Time Limit Specified	Rat
Marine Officer—Cont'd		Fire Pilot								$1500–1620	$150 156 162
	4	Superintendent of Ferries								3600–4500	360 390 420 450
Mechanic	1	Caulker							$4.50		
		Clock Repairer							4.00		
		Hose and Tire Repairer							4.00		
		Machinist							5.00		
		Machinist (Automobile)							5.00		
		Mechanic (Adding Machine)							.50 per hour		
		Mechanic (Elevator)							5.28		
		Orthopedic Mechanic							4.50		
		Rigger							4.00		
		Saw Filer							4.00		
		Ship Caulker							4.00		
		Tapper							4.50		
		Welder							4.50		
		Instrument Maker Mechanic (Laboratory)								1200–1320	120 126 132
	2	Foreman Machinist	$1920		$1680		$1500		5.50		
		Foreman Machinist (Automobile)	1920		1680		1500		5.50		
		Foreman Mechanic	1920		1680		1500		5.50		
		Foreman Rigger	1560		1320		1200		4.50		
Metal Worker	1	Blacksmith							4.50		
		Boilermaker							4.50		
		Brass Finisher							4.00		
		Bridge Mechanic and Riveter							5.50		
		Coremaker							4.25		
		Horseshoer							4.50		
		Housesmith							5.50		
		Moulder							4.25		
		Nickel Plater							4.50		
		Sheet Metal Worker							5.00		

DIGEST OF STANDARD SPECIFICATIONS—Continued
Skilled Trades Service—Continued

;roup	Gr.	Title	Salary Range for Service Every Day in Year	Rates	Salary Range for Service Exclusive of Sundays	Rates	Salary Range for Service Exclusive of Sundays, Holidays & Saturday Afternoons	Rates	Per Diem Rate 8 Hours	No Time Limit Specified	Rates
al 'orker— Cont'd	2	Foreman Blacksmith	$1740		$1500		$1320		$5.00		
		Foreman Boilermaker	1740		1500		1320		5.00		
		Foreman Bridge Mechanic and Riveter	2100		1800		1620		6.00		
or iver	1	Motor Driver							3.50	$1020–1320	$1020 1080 1140 1200 1260 1320
		Motor Driver (Ambulance)							3.50	1020-1320 with or without part maintenance	1020 1080 1140 1200 1260 1320
										780–1080 with full maintenance	780 840 900 960 1020 1080
		Motor Driver (Lawn Mower)							3.50		
		Motor Driver (Truck)							3.50	960–1200	960 1020 1080 1140 1200
	2	Garage Supervisor								1440–1560	1440 1560
	3	Superintendent of Garages								1680–2340	1680 1800 1980 2160 2340
		Superintendent of Garages (Police)									
ter	1	Decorator							5.00		
		Grainer							5.00		
		Letterer							5.00		
		Painter							5.00		
		Striper							5.00		
		Varnisher							5.00		
	2	Foreman Painter	1920		1680		1500		5.50		

DIGEST OF STANDARD SPECIFICATIONS—Continued
Skilled Trades Service—Continued

Group	Gr.	Title	Salary Range for Service Every Day in Year	Rates	Salary Range for Service Exclusive of Sundays	Rates	Salary Range for Service Exclusive of Sundays, Holidays & Saturday Afternoons	Rates	Per Diem Rate 8 Hours	No Time Limit Specified	Ra
Photo-grapher	1	Photographer								$1200–1620	$12 12 13 13 14 15 15 16
		Photographer (X-ray)								900–1320	9 9 10 10 11 12 12 13
Plumber and Steamfitter	1	Plumber Steamfitter Thermostat Repairer							$5.50 5.50 5.50		
Printer	1	Compositor								25 per week	
		Press Feeder								18 per week	
		Pressman								26 per week	
		Printer (Braille)								900–1200	9 9 10 10 11 12
	2	Foreman Printer	$1680		$1440						
Rockworker	1	Blaster							5.00		
Shop Supervisor	1	General Foreman (Shops)								1380–1920	13 15 16 17 19
	2	Superintendent of Shops								2100–2700	21 22 24 27
	3	General Superintendent of Shops								2940–3960	29 31 34 36 39

DIGEST OF STANDARD SPECIFICATIONS—Continued

Skilled Trades Service—Continued

Group	Gr.	Title	Salary Range for Service Every Day in Year	Rates	Salary Range for Service Exclusive of Sundays	Rates	Salary Range for Service Exclusive of Sundays, Holidays & Saturday Afternoons	Rates	Per Diem Rate 8 Hours	No Time Limit Specified	Rates
holsterer	1	Upholsterer							$4.50		
		Shade Fitter							4.00		
odworker	1	Carpenter (Manhattan)							5.50		
		Carpenter (The Bronx, Brooklyn, Queens)							5.00		
		Carpenter (Richmond)							4.50		
		Dockbuilder							4.25		
		Machine Woodworker							5.00		
		Patternmaker							5.00		
		Ship Carpenter							4.00		
		Wheelwright							4.00		
		Wood Sawyer							4.00		
	2	Foreman Carpenter (Manhattan)	$2100		$1800		$1620		6.00		
		Foreman Carpenter (The Bronx, Brooklyn, Queens)	1920		1680		1500		5.50		
		Foreman Carpenter (Richmond)	1740		1500		1320		5.00		
		Foreman Dockbuilder	1620		1440		1260		4.75		
		Foreman Ship Carpenter	1560		1320		1200		4.50		
scellaneus Skilled Vorker	1	General Mechanic								$1200–1400 without maintenance	$1200 1260 1320 1380 1440
										900–1140 with maintenance	900 960 1020 1080 1140
	2	Assistant Superintendent of Police Signal System								1500–2100	1500 1620 1740 1920 2100
	3	Superintendent of Police Signal System								2280–3180	2280 2460 2700 2940 3180

DIGEST OF STANDARD SPECIFICATIONS—Continued

Unskilled Service

Group	Gr.	Title	Salary Range	Rates
Cleaner	1	Cleaner	Men: $768–864 (Full time) 30c per hour	 $768 792 816 840 864
			Women: 600–768 (Full time)	 600 624 648 672 696 720 744 768
			300 420 (Not less than 3 hours a day) 25c per hour	300 324 348 372 396 420
		Cleaner (Windows)	792–888	792 816 840 864 888
Hostler and Driver	1	Driver	840–936	840 864 888 912 936
			Per diem: 2.70–3.00	 2.70 2.80 2.90 3.00
		Hostler	816–912	816 840 864 888 912
			Per diem: 2.60–2.90	 2.60 2.70 2.80 2.90
		Stableman	792–888	792 816 840 864 888
			Per diem: 2.50–2.80	 2.50 2.60 2.70 2.80

DIGEST OF STANDARD SPECIFICATIONS—Continued

Unskilled Service—Continued

Group	Gr.	Title	Salary Range	Rates
Hostler and Driver—Cont'd		Driver having charge of prisoners in Dept. of Correction	$864–960	$864 888 912 936 960
	2	Stable Foreman	1080–1440	1080 1140 1200 1260 1320 1380 1440
			Per diem: 3.40–4.25	3.40 3.60 3.80 4.00 4.25
		Foreman of Stables (Correction)	1500–1740	1500 1620 1740
	3	Superintendent of Stables (Police)	1920–2280	1920 2100 2280
Laborer	1	Laborers employed on ordinary unskilled manual labor	792–888	792 816 840 864 888
			Per diem: 2.50–2.80	2.50 2.60 2.70 2.80
		Laborer (Asphalt Worker) Laborer (Marine Sounder) Laborer (Coal Sampler) and other Laborers employed on difficult manual work requiring some skill and dependability	888–936	888 912 936
			Per diem: 2.80–3.00	2.80 2.90 3.00
		Superannuated Laborer assigned to light laboring or watchman work	720	720

DIGEST OF STANDARD SPECIFICATIONS—Continued

Unskilled Service—Continued

Group	Gr.	Title	Salary Range	Rates
Laborer—Cont'd	2	Foreman in charge of ordinary labor gangs [1]	365 days: $1080–1440	$1080
				1140
				1200
				1260
				1320
				1380
				1440
			313 days: 900–1200	900
				960
				1020
				1080
				1140
				1200
			Per diem: 3.00–4.00	3.00
				3.20
				3.40
				3.60
				3.80
				4.00
		Foreman Asphalt Worker Forman in charge of large gangs	365 days: 1440–1800	1440
				1500
				1560
				1620
				1680
				1740
				1800
			313 days: 1200–1500	1200
				1260
				1320
				1380
				1440
				1500
			Per diem: 4.00–5.00	4.00
				4.25
				4.50
				4.75
				5.00
	3	General Foreman	1500–1920	1500
				1620
				1740
				1920
	4	Superintendent of Maintenance	2100–2700	2100
				2280
				2460
				2700
Park Worker	1	Climber and Pruner Gardener	Per diem: 2.80–3.00	2.80
				2.90
				3 00

[1] Appropriate deduction from salary will be made in the case of Foremen receiving part or full maintenance.

DIGEST OF STANDARD SPECIFICATIONS—Continued

Unskilled Service—Continued

Group	Gr.	Title	Salary Range	Rates
Park Worker—Cont'd	2	Foreman Gardner Park Foreman Inspector of Trees	365 days: $1140-1320	$1140 1200 1260 1320
			313 days: 960-1140	960 1020 1080 1140
			Per diem: 3.20-3.80	3.20 3.40 3.60 3.80
	3	Arboriculturist General Park Fore-man Head Gardener	365 days: 1440-1800	1440 1560 1680 1800
			Per diem: 4.00-4.75	4.00 4.25 4.50 4.75
	4	Superintendent of Parks	2700-3960	2700 2940 3180 3420 3660 3960
Miscellaneous Laborer	1	Gate Tender	365 days: 876-984	876 912 948 984
		Laboratory Helper	360-780	360 420 480 540 600 660 720 780
		Laborer (Stores)	816-912	816 840 864 888 912
			Per diem: 2.60-2.90	2.60 2.70 2.80 2.90
		Ticket Chopper	792-888 Per diem: 2.50	792 816 840 864 888

INDEX TO TITLES AND SYMBOLS

www.ingramcontent.com/pod-product-compliance
Lightning Source LLC
LaVergne TN
LVHW011149110826
845150LV00006B/1194

* 9 7 8 1 4 2 5 5 4 7 4 6 2 *